To Violet and Chris

With much gratitude
for your friendship

Michio and Walter

Japanese Americans

FROM RELOCATION TO REDRESS

Japanese Americans

FROM RELOCATION TO REDRESS

Edited by

Roger Daniels, Sandra C. Taylor, and Harry H. L. Kitano

Contributions by
Leonard J. Arrington, Howard Ball, Jane Beckwith,
Shirley Castelnuovo, F. Alan Coombs, John J. Culley,
David Drummond, Evarts C. Fox, Jr., C. Harvey Gardiner,
Asael T. Hansen, Gordon K. Hirabayashi, Lane Ryo Hirabayashi,
William Hohri, Bill Hosokawa, Tetsuden Kashima,
Toyo Suyemoto Kawakami, Amy Iwasaki Mass, Dale Minami, Dennis M. Ogawa,
Gary Y. Okihiro, Barry Saiki, Floyd Schmoe, Eleanor Gerard Sekerak,
Robert C. Sims, Geoffrey S. Smith, John Tateishi,
and Take Uchida

University of Utah Press
Salt Lake City, Utah

Library of Congress Cataloging-in-Publication Data

Japanese Americans, from relocation to redress.

Based on the International Conference on Relocation
and Redress held in Salt Lake City in March 1983.
Includes bibliographies.
1. Japanese-Americans—Evacuation and relocation,
1942–1945—Congresses.   2. World War, 1939–1945—
Reparations—Congresses.   I. Daniels, Roger.
II. Taylor, Sandra C.   III. Kitano, Harry H. L.
IV. Arrington, Leonard J.   V. International Conference
on Relocation and Redress (1983 : Salt Lake City, Utah)
D769.8.A6J364   1986   940.53'14   85-29583
ISBN 0-87480-258-X (alk. paper)

The University of Utah Press acknowledges the
Japanese American Research Project of the
Japanese American Citizens League
for its generous assistance in funding this volume.

Contents

Preface

The idea for a conference in Salt Lake City on the relocation of Japanese Americans and the current movement for redress was born in the spring of 1981, when Professor Roger Daniels suggested to me that Salt Lake City would be a natural site for such a gathering. It was an important crossroads in the history of relocation: the wartime home of the Japanese American Citizens League, the site of a small community of Japanese Americans, and a point of transition for many who were held at the concentration camps at Topaz, Minidoka, and Heart Mountain.

The Center for Historical Population Studies at the University of Utah, ably directed by Professor Dean L. May, undertook the organization of the conference. He and his staff, Margaret Mower and Joy Cella, applied for grants and funding from many agencies and then undertook all the necessary and time-consuming details of correspondence and local arrangements. May suggested the idea of a field trip to Topaz which became one of the highlights of the conference. Ms. Jane Beckwith, whose students at Delta High School were working on a project concerning nearby Topaz, provided a program for those who journeyed there. May also gathered people from Salt Lake City to participate in the project. Members of the local chapter of the Japanese American Citizens League, Judge Raymond Uno and his wife, Yoshiko, and Mrs. Alice Kasai were particularly helpful in involving the JACL and the local Japanese American community.

The organizers are grateful for the major financial support received from the National Endowment for the Humanities and the Utah Endowment for the Humanities. In addition, numerous departments at the University of Utah contributed to support the conference, as did the Utah State Historical Society. The Olive Castle Foundation provided seed money for the conference. The College of Humanities of the University of Utah and Myrla Bauman generously assisted with the preparation of the final manuscript for publication. To all these people and to these funding agencies, the editors of this book are deeply indebted.

The conference program and the articles in this book are not identical. As program chair of the conference, I was anxious to obtain participation from local scholars, experts in the field, and people whose lives had been affected by the relocation. Many who spoke at the conference did so extemporaneously, and their reminiscences moved all who heard them. Especially impressive were Minoru Yasui, Toaru Ishiyama, James Tsujimura, Judge Raymond Uno, Judge William Marutani, David Nakayama, Ron Wakabayashi, and Masayuki Sato.

This book is a collaborative editorial venture by Roger Daniels, Sandra C. Taylor, and Harry H. L. Kitano. Although their inspiration was the International Conference on Relocation and Redress held in Salt Lake City in March 1983, their goal was to do more than simply publish conference proceedings. The intent was to present a look at less well known aspects of relocation, to emphasize its impact on the Intermountain West, and to give a preliminary assessment of the movement for redress. In order to accomplish this, they selected papers presented at the conference and, with the help of editorial assistant Ruth Henson, edited those papers, asked the authors for revisions, and solicited additional papers from people who had not attended the conference but who could add material that would round out the volume by providing historical perspective and insight into the ongoing struggle for redress.

Sandra C. Taylor

Salt Lake City
August 12, 1985

A Note on the Editors and Authors

Roger Daniels was born in New York City in 1927. After serving in the armed forces in World War II and the Korean War, he was educated at the University of Houston and the University of California, Los Angeles, where he received his Ph.D. in 1961. He has published widely, but is especially known for his works on Japanese Americans. These publications include *The Politics of Prejudice* (Berkeley and Los Angeles: University of California Press, 1962; 2nd ed., 1978); *American Racism* (with Harry H. L. Kitano) (Englewood Cliffs, N.J.: Prentice-Hall, 1970); *Concentration Camps, USA* (New York: Holt, Rinehart and Winston, 1971); *The Decision to Relocate the Japanese Americans* (Philadelphia: Lippincott, 1975); and *Concentration Camps, North America* (Melbourne, Fla.: Krieger, 1981). *Asian America: Chinese and Japanese in the United States since 1850* is scheduled to be published soon by the University of Washington Press. He served as a consultant to the Commission on Wartime Relocation and Internment of Civilians (CWRIC) and has participated in making a number of historically oriented films for television, including *Refugee Road* (1982), *Nisei Soldier* (1984), and *Unfinished Business* (1985). He is a professor of history at the University of Cincinnati.

Harry H. L. Kitano was born in San Francisco in 1926 and, as he puts it, "grew up in the relocation center at Topaz," where he was senior class president of Topaz High School and co-captain of its football team. After the war he returned to California and received his B.A., M.S.W., and Ph.D. degrees from the University of California, Berkeley. He is currently a professor of social welfare and sociology at the University of California, Los Angeles, where he also served as academic assistant to the chancellor and co-director of the Alcohol Research Center. He has also been a visiting professor at the International Christian University in Tokyo, the University of Bristol in England, and the University of Hawaii. His books include *Race Relations* (Englewood Cliffs, N.J.: Prentice-Hall, 3rd ed., 1984); *Japanese Americans: Evolution of a Sub-Culture* (Englewood Cliffs, N.J.: Prentice-Hall, 1969); and *American Racism* (with Roger Daniels) (Englewood Cliffs, N.J.: Prentice-Hall, 1970).

Sandra C. Taylor was born in Sacramento, California, and educated at Stanford University and the University of Colorado, receiving her Ph.D. in 1966. She has published many articles in American diplomatic history, where her special interests lie in American-East Asian relations and the history of Japanese Americans. She has recently published *Advocate of Understanding: Sidney Gulick and the Search for Peace with Japan* (Kent, Ohio: Kent State University Press, 1984); "The

Federal Reserve Bank and the Relocation of the Japanese in 1942," *The Public Historian* 5 (Winter 1983); and is working on an article, "Japanese Americans and Keetley Farms: Utah's Relocation Colony" to be published by the *Utah Historical Quarterly* in 1986. She is a professor of history at the University of Utah.

The editors have also authored one or more contributions to this volume and have contributed the introductory pieces and bibliographic notes. Others who have contributed to this volume come from a wide variety of backgrounds—some are academics, others are people whose lives were affected in some way by the relocation experience. They are listed here alphabetically.

Leonard Arrington, a native of Twin Falls, Idaho, was educated at the University of Idaho and received his Ph.D. from the University of North Carolina. After serving in World War II, he went to Utah State University, where he was on the faculty for twenty-six years. A distinguished historian of Utah and the West, Arrington is the author of many publications, including *Great Basin Kingdom: An Economic History of the Latter-day Saints, 1830–1900* (Lincoln: University of Nebraska Press, 1958). An important publication about Japanese Americans was his 1962 Faculty Honor Lecture, *The Price of Prejudice: The Japanese-American Relocation Center in Utah During World War II* (Logan: Utah State University Press, 1962), which has been widely reproduced. In 1972 he was appointed Lemuel Redd Professor of Western History at Brigham Young University, a post he still holds.

Howard Ball, a native of New York City, was educated at Hunter College and the City University of New York, and received his Ph.D. from Rutgers University. A political scientist, his primary scholarly interest is constitutional and administrative law/judicial process. The author of numerous articles and books, Professor Ball has just published *Downwind Justice* (New York: Oxford University Press, 1984), which focuses on the politics and law of the atomic testing litigation. He is presently a professor of political science and dean of the College of Social and Behavioral Science at the University of Utah.

Jane Beckwith, a native of Delta, Utah, graduated from Brigham Young University in 1969. She has taught English and worked as a librarian in Utah and Arizona, presently teaches English and journalism at Delta High School in Delta, Utah, and is a correspondent for the *Salt Lake Tribune*. She is a member of the board of the Utah Endowment for the Humanities and received an award from the Board of State History for a project on the camp at Topaz which her high school class carried out in 1983.

Shirley Castelnuovo was born in Jersey City, New Jersey, in 1930. She was educated at Rutgers University, New York University, and the University of California, Los Angeles, where she received her Ph.D. in 1969. A professor of political science at Northeastern Illinois University in Chicago, Castelnuovo teaches political and legal theory. Her publications and papers focus on social justice issues from the perspective of legal, political, and human rights.

F. Alan Coombs was born in Belleville, Kansas, in 1938. He was educated at the University of Kansas and the University of Illinois, where he received a Ph.D. in history. He has published on twentieth-century western politics and is currently working on a biography of Senator Joseph C. O'Mahoney of Wyoming. Professor Coombs is an associate professor of history at the University of Utah.

John C. Culley was born in 1938 and is a native of New Mexico, reared in Albuquerque. He was educated at the University of New Mexico and the University of Virginia, where he received his Ph.D. His article, "World War II and a Western Town: The Internment of the Japanese Railroad Workers of Clovis, New

Mexico," *Western Historical Quarterly* (January 1982) won the Oscar O. Winther Award given by the Western History Association for the best article of the year appearing in its journal. He is a professor of history at West Texas State University.

Evarts C. Fox, Jr., was born in Pueblo, Colorado, in 1933. He is a retired naval officer and Ph.D. candidate in the American Studies Department at the University of Hawaii, Manoa. He writes and publishes in the area of historic preservation, especially buildings important to the Japanese community in Hawaii. He also assists Dennis Ogawa in courses on Japanese Americans and teaches a course on historic preservation.

C. Harvey Gardiner, who received his Ph.D. from the University of Michigan, is a retired research professor of Latin American history. He has authored, edited, or contributed to more than thirty volumes and numerous professional journals in Mexico, Spain, Colombia, Peru, Japan, and the United States. He has published two books concerning Japanese Peruvians: *The Japanese and Peru, 1873–1973* (Albuquerque: University of New Mexico Press, 1975) and *Pawns in a Triangle of Hate: The Peruvian Japanese and the United States* (Seattle: University of Washington Press, 1981).

Asael T. Hansen was educated at Utah State University and received his Ph.D. from the University of Wisconsin in 1931. He has taught at three universities and, in the course of fifty years, conducted anthropological work in three extended projects in Yucatan, for which he was honored in May 1981 by the state of Yucatan. His work as an applied anthropologist at Heart Mountain, Wyoming, stands out in his mind as his most difficult assignment.

Gordon K. Hirabayashi was born in Seattle in 1918. He deliberately violated the curfew imposed on Japanese Americans in March 1942 to test its legality and, as a result, spent most of the war in prison. First he was in King County Jail in Seattle and then in a federal prison in Tucson. He spent the last year of the war in the federal penitentiary at McNeil Island, where he served a sentence of twelve months, less time off for good behavior. He was the principal in *Hirabayashi v. United States* (1943), the leading Supreme Court case during World War II on the curfew order's legality. After the war he resumed his education at the University of Washington, where he received B.A., M.A., and Ph.D. degrees. In 1984 he received honorary degrees from Hamline University and Haverford College. He is now a professor emeritus of sociology at the University of Alberta in Edmonton. Hirabayashi's research interests are twofold: social change among peasants in the Third World and visible minorities in North America. His many publications include *Visible Minorities and Multiculturalism: Asians in Canada*, edited with K. Victor Ujimoto with the assistance of P. A. Saram (Toronto and Boston: Butterworth's, 1980.)

Lane Ryo Hirabayashi was born after the war in Seattle. He was educated at Sonoma State College, received his doctorate in sociocultural anthropology at the University of California, Berkeley, and held a post-doctoral fellowship at the Asian American Studies Center, University of California, Los Angeles. He is presently a member of the Asian American Studies Department at San Francisco State University. He is also a member of the Center for Japanese American Studies and the Japanese Community Youth Council in San Francisco. He has recently published, with James A. Hirabayashi, "A Reconsideration of the United States Military's Role in the Violation of Japanese-American Citizenship Rights," in Winston A. Van Horne, ed., *Ethnicity and War*, (Milwaukee: University of Wisconsin System, 1984).

William Hohri was born in San Francisco in 1927. The Manzanar Relocation Camp was the location of his high school education, and he graduated from the University of Chicago after the war. A computer programmer and writer, he is the chairperson of the National Council for Japanese American Redress.

Bill Hosokawa was born in Seattle and is a graduate of the University of Washington. He and his family were evacuated to the assembly center at Puyallup and then to Heart Mountain. He was released from the center, moved to Iowa, and worked on the *Des Moines Register*. After the war he worked on the *Denver Post* where his last position prior to retirement was as editor of the editorial page. Hosokawa has written a general comment column continuously since 1942 for the *Pacific Citizen*, the weekly publication of the Japanese American Citizens League, and is the author of five books on the Japanese American experience including *Nisei: The Quiet Americans* (New York: William Morrow, 1969). His most recent book is *JACL: In Quest of Justice* (New York: William Morrow, 1982).

Tetsuden Kashima, born less than a year before the outbreak of war between the United States and Japan, spent his early years in the Tanforan Assembly Center and the Topaz Relocation Center. His father, a Buddhist priest, served the Ogden sangha after the war and then assisted at the San Diego Buddhist temple. Kashima received his education at the University of California, Berkeley, and a doctorate from the University of California, San Diego. His major publication is *Buddhism in America* (Westport, Conn.: Greenwood Press, 1977). He is currently the director of Asian American studies at the University of Washington.

Toyo Suyemoto Kawakami, born and raised in California and relocated to Topaz, is a graduate of the University of California, Berkeley, and has a master's degree from the University of Michigan. Before retiring she was head of the Social Work Library and assistant head of the Education/Psychology Library at Ohio State University.

Amy Iwasaki Mass, born in Los Angeles and relocated to the Pomona Assembly Center and Heart Mountain, was educated at the University of California, Berkeley, and the University of Southern California, and has completed a doctorate in social work at the School of Social Welfare, University of California, Los Angeles. She is currently an instructor at Whittier College and has a part-time clinical practice in Whittier.

Dale Minami was born in San Francisco in 1946 and educated at the University of Southern California and the University of California's School of Law (Boalt Hall). He is a practicing attorney and has taught in Asian American studies at Mills College and the University of California, Berkeley. He is an active spokesman on civil rights and Asian Americans and, among his many association ties, is chairperson of the Asian American Law Caucus.

Dennis Ogawa was born in the relocation center at Manzanar, California, in 1943. After receiving his doctorate at the University of California, Los Angeles, he joined the faculty at the University of Hawaii, where he is a professor of American studies. His works on Japanese Americans include two anthologies: *Jan Ken Po: The World of Hawaii's Japanese* (Honolulu: University of Hawaii Press, 1973) and *Kodomo No Tame Ni: For the Sake of the Children: The Japanese American Experience in Hawaii* (Honolulu: University of Hawaii Press, 1978).

Gary Y. Okihiro was born in Aiea, Hawaii, in 1945. His graduate education was at the University of California, Los Angeles, where he received his Ph.D. He is the director of the ethnic studies program at the University of Santa Clara and a member of the history department. He has published articles on Japanese Americans and the relocation camps in such journals as *Amerasia, Phylon,* and *The Journal of Ethnic Studies.* His book, *Gardens Amidst Orchards: Japanese Americans and the San Jose Political Economy, c. 1890–1950,* will be published soon. He is presently at work on a book comparing the wartime experiences of Japanese Americans in Hawaii and on the West Coast. David Drummond, a history major at the University of Santa Clara, assisted Okihiro with *Gardens Amidst Orchards* and with the article in the present volume.

Barry Saiki was born in Stockton, California, in 1919. He was educated at Stockton Junior College and the University of California, Berkeley, where he graduated in May, 1942. Saiki was relocated to the Stockton Assembly Center and the Rohwer Relocation Center, from which he was furloughed to Chicago. He joined the army in November 1944 and served until November 1966, twenty-one of those years as an intelligence officer. His last position, with the rank of lieutenant colonel, was as a general staff officer with the Sixth Army Headquarters, Presidio of San Francisco. Ironically, this was a position equivalent to that held by Colonel Karl Bendetsen in 1941. He notes that his replacement was also a Nisei, which, he comments, was a complete vindication by the army of the Nisei, who were then and still are loyal Americans. Since his retirement from the army Saiki has been employed in Tokyo. He is working on a book about his wartime experiences.

Floyd Schmoe, a Quaker biologist, was born in Kansas in 1895. He has worked as a national park ranger and naturalist, has taught at two universities, and was a relief worker during three wars. He is the author of a dozen books and a recipient of Japan's Order of the Sacred Treasure and an honorary degree of Doctor of Humane Letters from Tufts University. He now lives in Kirkland, Washington.

Eleanor Gerard Sekerak, a native Californian still living in the Bay Area, graduated from the University of California, Berkeley, prior to taking up a teaching assignment at Topaz. Now retired after thirty years as a social studies teacher and counselor at Hayward High School, she works in historic preservation.

Robert C. Sims was born in Fort Gibson, Oklahoma, and was educated at Northeastern Oklahoma State College and the University of Oklahoma, receiving his doctorate from the University of Colorado. He held a fellowship awarded by the National Endowment for the Humanities on race and ethnicity in America at Columbia University. As a professor of history at Boise State University, Sims has written about relocation especially as it affected Idaho, most notably " 'A Fearless Patriotic, Clean-Cut Stand': Idaho's Governor Clark and Japanese-American Relocation in World War II," *Pacific Northwest Quarterly* (1979). He also prepared an audio cassette on Japanese Americans in the West for Richard Etulain, ed., *The New Frontier: The Twentieth Century West* (Delano, Fla.: Everett/Edwards, Inc., 1978). Sims is currently working on a book about the Minidoka relocation camp.

Geoffrey S. Smith was born in San Francisco and educated at the University of California, Berkeley. He received his Ph.D. from the University of California, Santa Barbara. He is interested in the domestic context of twentieth-century American foreign relations and has published "Doing Justice: Relocation and Equity in Public Policy," *The Public Historian* (Fall, 1984). His book, *To Save a Nation: American Countersubversives, The New Deal and the Coming of World War II* (New York: Basic Books, 1973), was nominated for a Pulitzer Prize. He is a professor of history at Queen's University, Kingston, Ontario, Canada.

John Y. Tateishi was born in Los Angeles and relocated to Manzanar as a small child. After serving in the army, he was educated at the University of California, Berkeley, and the University of California, Davis, where he received a master's degree in English literature. He has taught at Barking College of the University of London and at City College of San Francisco. He is the national redress director for the Japanese American Citizens League and has represented the JACL before congressional committees and the Commission on Wartime Relocation and Internment of Civilians. He has recently published *And Justice For All: An Oral History of the Japanese American Detention Camps* (New York: Random House, 1984).

Take Uchida, whose life story is recounted in "An Issei Internee's Experiences," was in 1985 still living in Utah. As one of the oldest Isseis in Utah, she has been the subject of much interest here and in Japan.

Chronology of
Japanese American History

The following selected chronology was prepared to give the reader a better general picture of the events that led to evacuation and of the evacuation/incarceration itself.

1868 — First "colony" of Japanese immigrants in California (Alameda County).

1890 — Census finds 2,039 Japanese in United States.

1900 — Census finds 24,326 Japanese in United States.

1906 — San Francisco "School Board Crisis" over segregation of Japanese and Japanese American schoolchildren.

1907– Gentlemen's Agreement between the United States and Japan
1908 — limits immigration of male laborers.

1910 — Census finds 72,157 Japanese in United States.

1913 — California Alien Land Act forbids ownership of land by aliens "ineligible to citizenship." Quickly followed by similar statutes in most far-western states.

1920 — Census finds 110,010 Japanese in United States.

1920 — Second California Alien Land Act adopted by initiative forbids leasing of land to aliens "ineligible to citizenship."

1922 — In *Ozawa v. U.S.*, Supreme Court confirms that Japanese and other Asians are ineligible for naturalization by reason of race.

1924 — Immigration Act of 1924, the National Origins Act, abrogates Gentlemen's Agreement, and forbids immigration by aliens "ineligible to citizenship." Had Japanese been given a quota, as European nations were, immigration of 100 Japanese per year would have been allowed.

1940 — Census finds 126,947 Japanese in United States; 79,642 (62.7%) were native-born citizens.

1941
December 7 Japan attacks Pearl Harbor
Authorized by a blanket presidential warrant, United States Attorney General Francis Biddle directs the Federal Bureau of Investigation to arrest a predetermined number of "enemy aliens" classified

as "dangerous." This list includes Japanese, German, and Italian nationals. By the end of the day 737 Japanese are in federal custody.

December 8   The United States declares war on Japan.

December 11   1,370 Japanese classified as "dangerous enemy aliens" are detained by the FBI.

December 22   The Agriculture Committee of the Los Angeles Chamber of Commerce recommends that all Japanese nationals in the United States be placed "under absolute Federal control."

December 29   All enemy aliens in California, Oregon, Washington, Montana, Idaho, Utah, and Nevada are ordered to surrender all "contraband." "Contraband" includes: radios with short wave bands, cameras, binoculars, and a variety of weapons.

1942

January 5   All Japanese American selective service registrants placed in Class IV-C along with enemy aliens. Many Japanese Americans already in military service were discharged or put on "kitchen police" or other menial tasks.

January 6   Los Angeles Congressman Leland Ford sends a telegram to Secretary of State Cordell Hull urging the removal of all Japanese from the West Coast. "I do not believe that we could be any too strict in our consideration of the Japanese in the face of the treacherous way in which they do things," Ford wrote.

January 28   California State Personnel Board votes to bar all "descendants of natives with whom the United States [is] at war" from all civil service positions. This rule is enforced only against persons of Japanese ancestry.

January 29   Attorney General Biddle issues the first of a series of orders establishing prohibited zones which must be cleared of all enemy aliens. German, Japanese, and Italian aliens are instructed to evacuate areas on the San Francisco waterfront.

January 30   California Attorney General Earl Warren calls the Japanese situation in California the "Achilles heel of the entire civilian defense effort." He further states that "unless something is done it may bring about a repetition of Pearl Harbor."

February 4   The U.S. Army defines twelve "restricted areas." Enemy aliens in these designated areas must observe a curfew (9 p.m. to 6 a.m.), and are allowed to travel only to and from their place of employment. In addition, they are forbidden to travel any further than five miles from their place of residence.

February 6   A Portland post of the American Legion circulates a resolution urging the removal of all "enemy aliens, especially from critical Coast areas." The cover letter attached to the resolution indicates that the post is urging the removal of all Japanese regardless of citizenship.

February 13   In a letter to the President, the West Coast congressional delegation urges the removal of "all persons of Japanese lineage . . . aliens and citizens alike, from the strategic areas of California, Oregon and Washington."

February 14   Native Sons of the Golden West urges the evacuation of all Japanese, regardless of citizenship status.

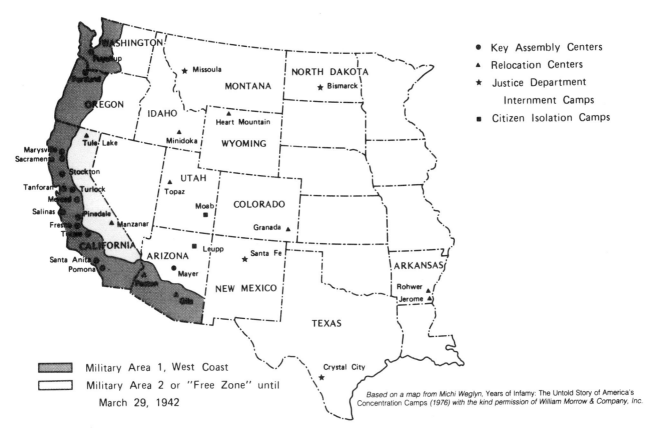

Key Assembly Centers
▲ Relocation Centers
★ Justice Department
   Internment Camps
■ Citizen Isolation Camps

Military Area 1, West Coast
Military Area 2 or "Free Zone" until
March 29, 1942

Based on a map from Michi Weglyn, Years of Infamy: The Untold Story of America's
Concentration Camps (1976) with the kind permission of William Morrow & Company, Inc.

1942

February 16   California Joint Immigration Committee urges that all Japanese be
               removed from the Pacific Coast and any other areas designated vital
               by the U.S. government. FBI arrests and detention of Japanese
               aliens reported to be 2,192.

February 19   President Roosevelt signs Executive Order 9066. This order gives
               the secretary of war the authorization to establish military areas
               "from which any or all persons may be excluded as deemed neces-
               sary or desirable."

February 20   Secretary of War Henry L. Stimson appoints Lieutenant General
               John L. DeWitt as the military commander responsible for execut-
               ing Executive Order 9066.

February 21   Hearings by the House Select Committee Investigating National
               Defense Migration (Tolan Committee) begin on the West Coast to
               investigate problems of enemy aliens and others living along the
               Pacific shore.

February 23   A Japanese submarine fires several shells at a Santa Barbara oil field
               causing neither damage nor injury.

February 25   An unidentified aircraft flies over Los Angeles. It is believed at the
               time to be an enemy and is fired upon by local antiaircraft batteries.
               The only resulting damage was from the antiaircraft shell fragments
               falling on residential areas of the city.

February 26   All Japanese on Terminal Island, San Pedro, California, are given
               forty-eight hours to evacuate homes and businesses by naval order.
               They are allowed to resettle where they can.

1942

February 28	House Committee on Un-American Activities makes public its Yellow Book. The 300-page document contains almost every possible charge against the Japanese in America.
March 2	General DeWitt issues Public Proclamation No. 1 designating military areas in the states of Washington, Oregon, California, and portions of Arizona. It further states that certain persons or classes of persons might be excluded from these areas should the situation require it. The restrictions apply to Japanese, German, and Italian aliens, or any person of "Japanese Ancestry" living in Military Areas No. 1 and 2.
March 6	The Federal Reserve Bank is designated as a cooperating agency to help persons being evacuated to dispose of their property or help persons in making arrangements to administer property left behind. Later the Farm Security Administration is authorized to offer similar help involving agricultural property.
March 16	General DeWitt issues Public Proclamation No. 2 making Idaho, Montana, Nevada, and Utah Military Areas No. 3 through 6 respectively.
March 18	President Roosevelt issues Executive Order 9102 creating the War Relocation Authority (WRA). Milton S. Eisenhower is named the first director and charged with the task of implementing a program of orderly evacuation of designated persons from the restricted military areas.
March 21	Congress enacts a law providing penalties for persons who violate orders to enter or leave the designated military areas.
March 23	Civilian Exclusion Order No. 1 is issued by General DeWitt. It directs that all persons of Japanese ancestry, both alien and non-alien (American citizens) evacuate Bainbridge Island near Seattle, Washington, on or before March 30, 1942.
March 24	Public Proclamation No. 3 extends travel restrictions, curfew, and contraband regulations to Japanese Americans, regardless of citizenship.
March 27	Public Proclamation No. 4 issued by General DeWitt. It prohibits the voluntary evacuation from Military Area No. 1 by Japanese aliens.
April 7	WRA Director Eisenhower meets with the governors or representatives of ten states at Salt Lake City. States represented are Nevada, Idaho, Oregon, Utah, Montana, Colorado, New Mexico, Wyoming, Washington, and Arizona. The meeting is to ascertain the views of these states on accepting Japanese evacuees. Only Governor Ralph Carr of Colorado offers to cooperate.
May 7	National Japanese American Student Relocation Council is organized through the efforts of the American Friends Service Committee. The council is designed to assist evacuee college students to continue their education outside the proscribed military areas.
May 8	Evacuation of all Japanese living within the Arizona Military Area is reported complete.
May 16	The Atlantic Coast is declared a military area by the Eastern Defense Command.

May 21	Initial group of incarcerated Japanese Americans leave the Portland Assembly Center to do agricultural work in Eastern Oregon.
June 7	General DeWitt announces that the removal of 100,000 persons of Japanese ancestry from Military Area No. 1 is completed.
June 12	Action filed in U.S. District Court for Northern California charging Fred T. Korematsu with a violation of Exclusion Order No. 34.
June 17	Milton Eisenhower resigns as the Director of the War Relocation Authority. Dillon S. Myer is appointed as his successor.
June 26	Suit brought by the Native Sons of the Golden West starts in San Francisco. Its purpose is to strip Japanese Americans of their citizenship.
June 29	1,600 evacuees released from assembly centers and relocation centers to relieve a labor shortage in the sugar beet producing areas of Oregon, Utah, Idaho, and Montana.
July 9	Relocation of all Japanese and persons of Japanese descent living in Military Area No. 2 begins.
July 13	Writ of Habeas Corpus filed in the name of Mitsuye Endo, asking that she be released from the relocation center or show just cause why she should continue to be kept in custody.
August 7	General DeWitt announces that the evacuation of all persons of Japanese ancestry from Military Areas No. 1 and 2 is completed. He further reports that this move involved over 110,000 persons.
August 18	The War Department issues a proclamation designating the four relocation centers outside the Western Defense Command as military areas.
September 10	Lieutenant General Hugh A. Drum announces an "individual exclusion program" for the Eastern Military Area. He authorizes the removal of any person "deemed dangerous to the national defense."
September 15	The Western Defense Command allows agricultural workers from Poston to return to designated portions of Military Area No. 1 to help harvest cotton.
September 30	The national convention of the American Legion meeting at Kansas City passes a resolution asking that the control of the relocation centers "be returned to military authorities and that . . . evacuees be denied the privilege of leaving these camps under any pretext for the duration of the war."
October 1	War Relocation Authority regulations allowing evacuees to seek temporary or permanent residence outside the relocation centers if certain conditions are met go into effect.
October 20	Trial of Gordon K. Hirabayashi starts in Seattle with Judge Lloyd L. Black presiding.
October 24	Over 8,000 evacuees involved in agricultural harvests in the western states to save the crops and relieve a farm labor shortage.
October 30	War Relocation Authority announces that the last assembly center is deactivated with the transfer of evacuees from the Fresno Assembly Center to the Jerome Relocation Center.
November 3	Final group of evacuees from Fresno reaches Jerome, Arkansas. This marks the end of direct army jurisdiction over evacuees. All

1942

such have been transferred to the control of the War Relocation Authority, except for those remaining in West Coast institutions.

November 18 Poston Relocation Center demonstration over the arrest of two evacuees accused of beating a third who was thought to be a camp "informer."

November 23 A general strike called at Poston.

December 6 Following the arrest of evacuees at Manzanar charged with beating another evacuee, violence breaks out. Military police are called out and fire into the crowd killing two evacuees and wounding at least ten others.

1943

January 5 Ninth Circuit Court of Appeals upholds the conviction of Gordon K. Hirabayashi for curfew violation.

January 28 The privilege of volunteering for military service is restored to the Nisei. As a result over 2,500 men volunteer for military service.

February 3 The War Relocation Authority begins administering a loyalty questionnaire to all evacuees over seventeen years of age.
The 442nd Regimental Combat Team is officially activated by the U.S. Army. The unit is initially made up of the 100th Battalion from Hawaii and Japanese American volunteers from the mainland.

February 20 Ninth Circuit Court of Appeals dismisses suit brought by Native Sons of the Golden West to strip American-born Japanese of U.S. citizenship.

April 22 Ninth Circuit Court of Appeals forwards by certification the petition of Mitsuye Endo to the Supreme Court.

June 9 Earl Warren, now governor of California signs an anti-Japanese fishing bill prohibiting the issuance of commercial fishing licenses to alien Japanese.

June 23 The Supreme Court upholds the conviction of Gordon K. Hirabayashi.

July 31 Tule Lake Relocation Center is designated as a "segregation camp" for "disloyal" evacuees by the War Relocation Authority.

November 1 U.S. Army assumes control of Tule Lake Relocation Center with resulting mass demonstrations by evacuees.

1944

January 14 Army control of Tule Lake terminated.

January 20 Secretary of War Stimson announces that Japanese Americans are again eligible for the draft.

1944 June 30 Jerome Relocation Center in Arkansas becomes the first of the relocation centers to close. The 5,000 remaining evacuees are transferred to other camps.

July 18 Sixty-three men from Heart Mountain convicted of draft resistance in federal district court, Cheyenne, Wyoming. Sentenced to three years in federal penitentiary.

December 17 Major General Henry C. Pratt, acting commander, Western Defense Command, issues Public Proclamation No. 21 which restores the rights of evacuees to return to their former homes. In addition all contraband regulations are lifted. The proclamation is to become effective January 2, 1945.

December 18   The Supreme Court hands down its decision on the *Korematsu* and *Endo* cases. In the *Korematsu* case, a six to three decision of the Court upholds Executive Order 9066, and the army's subsequent evacuation of Japanese and Japanese Americans. Justice Frank Murphy's dissent condemns the ruling as "a legalization of racism." In the *Endo* case the Supreme Court rules unanimously that the War Relocation Authority cannot detain "loyal" citizens nor prevent them from going to the West Coast.

December 30   The War Relocation Authority announces the opening of relocation offices in Seattle, San Francisco, and Los Angeles. These offices are to assist returnees to the Pacific Coast.

1945   Hood River, Oregon, American Legion Post removes the names of seventeen Nisei from the town's honor roll.

January
through
October   Evacuees returning home are faced with a number of hostile attacks. These include: defacing of Japanese American homes in Seattle; an attempt to dynamite a Japanese American packing shed in Placer County, California; countless attacks on the person and property of newly released evacuees; and, by the state of California, escheat actions against Japanese American property.

May 14   Secretary of the Interior Harold L. Ickes denounces the continuing acts of terror directed against Japanese Americans returning to the West Coast.

August 11   Japan agrees to unconditional surrender terms of the Allies.

September 4   The Western Defense Command revokes all restrictions against Japanese and Japanese Americans.

1946
March 20   Tule Lake Relocation Center closed. All the relocation centers are now empty.

June 30   The War Relocation Authority officially goes out of business.

TEN WORLD WAR II WRA CAMPS	Opened	Closed	Maximum population
Gila River, Arizona	7-20-42	11-10-45	13,348
Granada, Colorado	8-24-42	10-15-45	7,318
Heart Mountain, Wyoming	8-12-42	11-10-45	10,767
Jerome, Arkanas	10-6-42	6-30-44	8,497
Manzanar, California	6-1-42	11-21-45	10,046
Minidoka, Idaho	8-10-42	10-28-45	9,397
Poston, Arizona	5-8-42	11-28-45	17,814
Rohwer, Arkansas	9-18-42	11-30-45	8,475
Topaz, Utah	9-11-42	10-31-45	8,130
Tule Lake, Calfornia	5-27-42	3-20-46	18,789

PART I

Relocation, Redress, and the Report

The Conference Keynote Address:
Relocation, Redress, and the Report
A Historical Appraisal

Roger Daniels
March 10, 1983
Salt Lake City, Utah

Although I have spoken about the relocation and its ongoing aftermath many times, it was very difficult for me to decide what to say to this audience. I knew that many here would be individuals who had gone through the whole evacuation-incarceration process and that there would be others present who had studied it at length and in depth. What could I say that would have meaning for these members of the audience and yet still communicate something to those who are less aware of what happened, when it happened, and how it evolved? It occurred to me that in one sense at least this talk was different from all the others that I had given. For the first time I was speaking after the publication of the long-awaited report of the Commission on the Wartime Relocation and Internment of Civilians, *Personal Justice Denied*. Once I had realized this, I decided to try to show how perceptions of the evacuation and the relocation have changed over time and are still changing.

While it is true that what happened, happened, it is also true that at different distances in time our perspective of a given event or a complex of events will change.

I am going to discuss, therefore, the relocation as it has appeared at three specific times in the past: in 1967, as it appears in 1983, and during the Second World War. Then, abandoning the role of historian, I will speculate about the possible course of redress.

Certainly 1967 is the most artificial of my three snapshots in time. It was exactly twenty-five years after the evacuation; but I choose it because that spring Harry Kitano and I, with the help of Robert Conhaim and the staff of UCLA Extension, organized what we believe was the first academic conference devoted to an analysis of the evacuation and some of its conse-

quences. Among the speakers was Leonard Arrington, who was visiting UCLA that year; and we were fortunate in having one repentant wartime sinner—the always genial and entertaining Judge Robert W. Kenny, who had succeeded Earl Warren as attorney general of California in January 1943—who confessed that he had been wrong about some things and remiss about others. We could not find anyone in southern California who was willing, in 1967, to stand up and say that the evacuation was justified, that relocation had been the proper course for the country to pursue.

The atmosphere at and preceding that conference sixteen years ago was quite different from the atmosphere here in Salt Lake City in March 1983. There had been a good deal of genteel pressure from some of the leadership of the Japanese community in Los Angeles not to have the conference at all. Things were going well, some thought; why stir up old bad feelings. None of us thought that we were saying the last word about the relocation; but no one, I think, dreamed that less than two decades later there would be a mass movement for redress, a mass movement that may get significant support from an organ of the federal government. Our chief concern was the awful question "Can it happen again?" and our major suggestions for remedial legislation concerned the desirability of keeping the Japanese American Claims Act open and the possibility of having the preventive detention section of the Internal Security Act of 1950 repealed, since that legislation sanctioned procedures modeled directly on those used to incarcerate Japanese Americans in 1942.

It is not surprising, in retrospect, that our horizons were so limited. Great progress had been made by many if not most of the victims of Executive Order 9066. Sociologist William Petersen was already hailing

Japanese Americans as "our model minority," as much, I suggest, a way of putting down groups he regarded as disruptive as a way of hailing the undoubted achievements of the Nikkei in recovering from the disasters of World War II. And the progress was real. There had been a Japanese American Claims Act in 1948, although with utterly inadequate funding, and in 1952 racial and ethnic bars were removed from the naturalization statutes—no longer were Issei "aliens ineligible to citizenship"—and a token immigration quota had been awarded to Japan. In 1959 Hawaii had been belatedly admitted to the Union, so from that point on, there were Asian American legislators in Washington. A people who had owned no political "clout" in 1942 were now, in a technical sense, overrepresented, an overrepresentation that would be increased when California began to send Asian Americans, one of them a naturalized citizen, to Washington.

By the 1960s the socioeconomic gains of the bulk of the Nisei and the Sansei were beginning to push many of them into the middle and upper-middle classes. Figures compiled by the state of California in 1965 showed that persons of Japanese ancestry had, on average, more education than whites, but, somewhat paradoxically, earned significantly less money: Japanese American males over fourteen had a median income of $4,388 as opposed to $5,109 for whites. If we look only at the well-to-do, the gap is even greater. Only 7.7 percent of Japanese American men twenty-five years of age and older earned as much as $10,000, while 12.1 percent of the similar white group did. There are many explanations for this discrepancy, including, of course, a reluctance by some employers to put Asian Americans in positions in which they supervised, hired, and fired whites. A major reason surely stemmed from the fact that the war years were, for most Americans, years of relative prosperity, years in which old debts were paid and savings and investments increased. But many Japanese Americans were simply financially wiped out, and they and their families would always suffer from being a step or two behind where they would have been if the government had only let them continue to live industrious, productive, law-abiding lives. A quarter of a century after the evacuation and twenty-one years after the last camp had closed, the effects of the wartime incarceration were still present. It was quite clear then, as it is today, that the relocation was and is the central event in Japanese American history, the event from which all other events are dated and compared. "Before the war" and "after camp" are the phrases that provide the essential periodization of Japanese American life.

Now, sixteen years later, some of us are again at a conference, but a conference with a different mood, in a different time, and with a different purpose. Perhaps the greatest single difference is the difference in community attitudes, a difference that was becoming apparent even before the traumatic Commission hearings began. No one has articulated that change better than the Nisei writer, Yoshiko Uchida, in her moving memoir, *Desert Exile*.[1]

Today some of the Nisei, having overcome the traumatizing effects of their incarceration and participated in a wide spectrum of American life with no little success, are approaching retirement. Their Sansei children, who experienced the Vietnam War, with its violent confrontations and protest marches, have asked questions about those early World War II years.

Why did you let it happen? they ask of the evacuation. Why didn't you fight for your civil rights? Why did you go without protest to the concentration camps? They were right to ask these questions, for they made us search for some obscured truths and come to a better understanding of ourselves and of those times. They are the generation who taught us to celebrate our ethnicity and discover our ethnic pride.

It is my generation, however, who lived through the evacuation of 1942. We are their link to the past and we must provide them all we can remember, so they can better understand the history of their own people. As they listen to our voices from the past, however, I ask that they remember they are listening in a totally different time; in a totally changed world.

This generational difference is one of the hallmarks of American immigrant life. Almost half a century ago, the Norwegian American historian, Marcus Lee Hansen, considered the father of immigration history, wrote that the second generation in its eagerness to become as fully Americanized as possible tends to reject the heritage of its fathers and mothers; while the third generation, to a degree, tends to reject the values and experience of their own parents, to embrace some of the cultural values of their grandparents' generation, and begins to try to recapture at least some of the ethnic past. Hansen, in the 1930s, did not have Issei, Nisei, and Sansei in mind; he was generalizing from his own Norwegian American experience. That his generalizations seem to have some relevance to the Japanese American experience testifies both to the relative universality of Hansen's insights and to the essential Americanness of the experience of the Nikkei here.

To anyone at all concerned or connected with the Japanese American community once the drive for redress had begun in the late 1970s, it was clear that the winds of change were blowing. Some of the change was not pretty: animosities and resentments, arising out of intracommunity conflicts in the months after Pearl Harbor, came to the surface after more than three decades of repression. The word "inu," literally "dog," but in this context "informer" or, colloquially, "rat fink," began again to be applied to persons, living and dead, for what they allegedly had done or not done in late 1941 and early 1942. Even more common were displays of emotion: Time and time again, at meetings in various communities—Seattle, Cleveland, Philadelphia, Chicago—I saw grown men and women of my own age break down and cry in public as they spoke, or tried to speak, of those events during the war that affected them the most. The instance that sticks most in my mind is the man in Cleveland who couldn't quite finish his story about his military leave just prior to going overseas to fight with the 442nd Regimental Combat Team. His folks were still in camp at Minidoka, Idaho, so he went there. What he remembered most was his mother apologizing profusely because she simply was not able to prepare his favorite foods to give him the kind of meal appropriate for a soldier going off to battle. These, and other experiences, convinced me, even before the Commission was created, that the therapeutic effects of the struggle for redress were important events in the history of the community and would be so even if no Commission were established, even if its report papered over the truth.

That, happily, is not the case. On February 24th we got the Commission report, and it was a good one. At other sessions of this conference the report will be examined and discussed at length. I merely want here to read and applaud its major conclusion:[2]

> The promulgation of Executive Order 9066 was not justified by military necessity, and the decisions which followed from it . . . were not driven by analysis of military conditions. The broad historical causes which shaped these decisions were race prejudice, war hysteria, and a failure of political leadership. Widespread ignorance of Japanese Americans contributed to a policy conceived in haste and executed in an atmosphere of fear and anger at Japan. A grave injustice was done to American citizens and resident aliens of Japanese ancestry who, without individual review or any probative evidence against them, were excluded, removed and detained by the United States during World War II.

These uncompromising conclusions—"not justified by military necessity" and shaped by "race prejudice, war hysteria, and a failure of political leadership"—were not new. At the UCLA conference in 1967, all of these points were made; and they have been made by many historians and other writers. What was important about the Commission report, was that it was a report of an official body created by the United States Congress, and that, when coupled with President Gerald R. Ford's 1976 proclamation—"We know now what we should have known then: not only was

[the] evacuation wrong, but Japanese-Americans were and are loyal Americans"—two of the three branches of the federal government have disavowed the evacuation. And without in any way denigrating what President Ford did, it is quite clear that the Commission's affirmation is much the more important of the two. It made the front page of the *New York Times* and of most newspapers in the United States and Japan and was highlighted by television networks in both countries. Ford's proclamation, except in the western states, was largely ignored; it was not considered "fit to print" by the editors of the *New York Times*, which published nothing about it until the editors ran a letter from me chiding its lapse. And perhaps, even more tellingly, the Commission's report drew an angry reply from the chief living architect of the relocation, John J. McCloy. McCloy, about whom more later, finds the report an "outrage." He could ignore the work of historians—he has never answered letters of inquiry I have sent him—and he ignored President Ford's proclamation. The Commission's report simply could not be ignored.

That report, most of us here tonight hope, will merely be another step on the road to redress, but even if no more steps are taken the journey will have been worthwhile. In 1983 the relocation is out of the closet. That is not to say that the pain is gone, that the controversies are over; almost certainly they are not. And, when the commissioners make their recommendations about redress more bitterness will surely emerge and a new struggle commence. But, never again, I suspect, will the community be able to return to the collective social amnesia that has marked so many of the years since 1942. This is not said as a form of rebuke, and, it seems to me, there has been more than enough pointing of fingers about who did what to whom within the Japanese American community in 1941–42. This kind of internal examination is not just a Japanese American trait: the American Jewish community, for example, still numbed by the dimensions of the Holocaust, is at this very moment involved in an angry dispute about what American Jewish leaders did and did not do, during the Hitler era, to help rescue Jews of Europe. Listening to some of the polemics, one could get the impression that American Jewish leaders, like Rabbi Stephen S. Wise, were actually operating the gas chambers. Some Japanese Americans, in like fashion, talk as if the JACL promulgated Executive Order 9066. In each instance, it seems to me, the criticism is out of balance. We must remember, as Ms. Uchida reminds us, the critics are talking about "a totally different time . . . a totally changed world." The real enemy of the Japanese Americans was their own government: we know the names of the leaders, from

FDR down, who failed us all, then. To be sure, the Japanese American leadership did not always act wisely, and, even more seriously, I think, has tried very hard to "manage" Japanese American history ever since. No historian, least of all me, would ever suggest that the wartime and postwar actions of community leaders should go unprobed. But those probes should be conducted with balance and should avoid both saccharine self-congratulation and paranoid-style fantasy.

Clearly then, there are both advantages and disadvantages in looking at the events of the relocation from more than four decades away. But we must concentrate on the events of 1941 to 1945. And it is important that we call things by their proper names. George Orwell has taught us that twentieth-century political speech is largely "the defense of the indefensible" and that political language consists "largely of euphemism." This certainly has been true of language used to describe the relocation. From Karl R. Bendetsen's memos, which habitually describe Japanese American citizens as "non aliens," to the congressional statute that created the Commission and beyond, euphemisms have prevailed. Rather than the "Commission on Wartime Relocation and Internment of Civilians," it should have been "incarceration" of civilians. "Internment" is a well-defined legal process by which enemy nationals are placed in confinement in time of war. The roughly 2,000 male Issei leaders who were rounded up in the days immediately after Pearl Harbor were interned. They were, although separated from their families, given better treatment than were most incarcerated Japanese Americans; and, above all, once they were locked up, there was a kind of due process as each internee was entitled to an individual hearing. In short, however unjust, the internment of these enemy aliens did follow the forms of law and did conform, generally, to the terms of the Geneva Convention.

What happened to the rest of the West Coast Japanese was lawless. Citizen and alien, male and female, old and young, all were simply swept up, placed in the holding pens from Santa Anita to Puyallup, and then shipped out to ten desolate camps. The Commission report—and this is the one serious difference I have with it—argues, in a footnote, that "to use the phrase 'concentration camps' summons up images and ideas which are inaccurate and unfair" and goes on to argue that the term "concentration camp" is synonymous with "death camp." In wanting to avoid the use of the term "concentration camp," the Commission and John J. McCloy are in agreement. As early as March 16, 1942, before the first group of Bainbridge Islanders had been sent to Manzanar, McCloy is on

record as wanting to avoid the use of the term "concentration camp." At that same meeting, Dr. Calvert Dedrick, a specialist from the Census Bureau who was loaned to the army to help in the roundup, suggested that the relocation be called a "residence control program."[3] At the other extreme, Raymond Okamura has recently charged me and other scholars with being part of a "cover-up": "although many authors have used titles like . . . Concentration Camps, USA . . . none has systematically replaced euphemistic terminology in their text."[4]

Both of these positions are extreme. It is necessary to differentiate between at least three main types of camps in which Japanese Americans were kept during the war: the assembly centers, such as Tanforan or Portland; the relocation centers, such as Topaz and Heart Mountain; and the internment camps, such as Bismarck and Missoula. The first were run by the army, the second by the War Relocation Authority, and the third, eventually, by the Immigration and Naturalization Service. To ignore completely the names used in contemporary documents would be as shortsighted as the Commission's refusal to call the camps what they really were: places to which persons were sent, not for crimes or legal status, but because of race or ethnicity. Such places have been known, since the end of the nineteenth century, as concentration camps. They were first established by the British to pen up Boer civilians in South Africa; and the term "concentration camps" was used by Franklin D. Roosevelt himself, on at least three separate public occasions, to describe the camps run by the War Relocation Authority. These camps were not, thank God, death camps or extermination camps. More people were born in the American concentration camps than died in them. At Topaz, for example, there were 384 births and 139 deaths. Most of those who died in camp did so from disease or just simply old age, although some did commit suicide and a few were actually killed by the government.

One of those latter victims was James Hatsuki Wakasa who had come to the United States in 1903.[5] He had been graduated from Keio College in Tokyo and had studied for two years at the University of Wisconsin. A chef by trade, he had been a civilian instructor of cooking at Camp Dodge, Iowa, during World War I. In World War II he had been rounded up with the other Bay Area Japanese and sent to Topaz. There, half an hour before sunset on Sunday, April 11, 1943, this sixty-three-year-old bachelor was shot to death by one of the soldiers who guarded the camp. According to the story released to the press by the army, Mr. Wakasa was killed "while attempting to crawl through the fence." It is now clear that the story was fabricated and, based on an internal WRA report of the following month, this seems to be what really happened: The shooting took place in a relatively isolated corner of the camp, and apparently no one inside knew about it until about forty-five minutes later when 1st Lt. Henry H. Miller, commander of the Military Police company, informed a WRA staff member that "a Japanese resident had been shot and killed . . . and that his body had been removed."

Evidence developed later by the WRA indicated that the victim had been inside the fence when shot—the center of a large bloodstain was five feet inside the fence—and a postmortem examination of the body found that there was "a perforating wound point of entry made probably by a bullet which entered the thoracic cage [anterior to posterior at the] 3rd rib 2½ cm left of mid-thoracic line. No powder burn. There is an exit wound measuring 1 cm by 3 cm jagged posteriorly at 6th thoracic vertebra 3 cm right of mid thoracic line." In other words, Wakasa was facing the soldier who shot him, which is, of course, incompatible with the story that the army put out. In the meantime the M.P. commander armed his troops with riot weapons, high-powered rifles, and tear gas. An idea of the overreaction by the military police detachment may be gleaned from the following statement made by Eiichi Sato, a social worker for Block 36, who, with four other inmates went to inspect the scene of the crime about 10 o'clock the following morning. As he told it later that day:

We approached the west-south fence, approximately 35 feet away, when an army "jeep" came speeding from the north on the road beyond the fence and, upon seeing us, came to an abrupt halt. The driver stood up from his seat, turned to his companion, and grabbed the submachine gun from the latter's hand. He jumped off jeep and came dashing to the fence pointing his gun at us [and saying] "Scatter or you'll get the same thing as the other guy got."

That was Monday morning. By 4 p.m. on Tuesday, Lieutenant Miller, perhaps so ordered by higher authority, lifted his "alert," withdrew what he called "emergency armament," and promised that "the Military Police will not molest, injure or exercise any unusual surveillance upon the evacuees at Topaz Center" and that "orders have been issued that members of the Military Police are not to enter the Project Center except on official business approved by the Commanding Officer who will clear with the Acting Project Director in advance." Two weeks later, on April 28, at Fort Douglas, Utah, the sentry who shot Wakasa stood a general court-martial and was found "not guilty."

Thus ended what Russell Bankston, the WRA reports officer on whose account I have drawn, called "the Wakasa Incident."

The death of James Wakasa was but an incident in a global war that destroyed millions of other human beings. Unlike the deaths at Dachau or Auschwitz, it was not a crime planned by higher authority, not part of a final solution. It was, nevertheless, a crime—a war crime if you wish. And the chain of responsibility for that crime goes all the way up the ladder—from the sentry who pulled the trigger; to Lieutenant Miller, who helped to cover it up; on up to those soldiers, bureaucrats, and politicians who planned and executed the relocation and who arranged it so that over a hundred thousand persons were deprived of their liberty and much of their property, if not their lives—ending, finally, in the Oval Office, where Franklin D. Roosevelt okayed it, and on Capitol Hill, where the Congress, without a dissenting vote, ratified the decisions of the executive branch.

Of those still alive today, the most important architect of the relocation is John J. McCloy (b. 1895), who, as Secretary of War Henry L. Stimson's deputy, was the ranking member of the government who dealt with the Japanese Americans on a day-to-day basis. McCloy was also one of the chief architects of the 442nd Regimental Combat Team, whose magnificent fighting record did so much to rehabilitate and improve the image of the Nisei. But he was also the man who, in the crucial days of February 1942, threw his weight behind mass evacuation, telling his co-conspirators that: "You are putting a Wall Street lawyer in a helluva box, but if it is a question of the safety of the country [and] Constitution . . . why the Constitution is just a scrap of paper to me."[6]

McCloy, who called the Commission's Report an "outrage," had testified earlier that he hoped that the Commission would "conclude . . . that under the circumstances . . . and with the exigencies of wartime security, the action of the President of the United States and the United States Government in regard to our then Japanese population was reasonably undertaken and thoughtfully and humanely conducted."[7] Was James Wakasa treated humanely? Was it thoughtful to brand Japanese Americans as security risks, as not to be trusted by their own country? And for the Wall Street lawyer to insist, forty-one years later, that what was done was in the national interest is merely to compound the felonies he helped to commit then.

"Military necessity." "The safety of the country." "The exigencies of wartime security." For over four decades these have been the reasoned excuses for the relocation, for depriving almost 70,000 American citizens of their constitutional rights, for treating Japanese Americans differently from German Americans and Italian Americans. Is it just civil libertarian hindsight, mere historical Monday morning quarterbacking, that finds the relocation unnecessary? I think not. The best possible judge of military necessity during World War II was Gen. George C. Marshall, chief of staff of the U.S. Army throughout the war and perhaps our greatest soldier. Marshall and his colleagues at army GHQ had already determined that relocating the Japanese Americans was *not* a rational military precaution when the political leaders of the army, Stimson and McCloy, without consulting him, opted for mass evacuation and got the concurrence of the Commander in Chief. Marshall, the good soldier, obeyed the orders of his lawful superiors. Later, however, he and his protege, Gen. Delos E. Emmons, did forestall the mass evacuation of the Hawaiian Japanese, which some highly placed politicians wanted. The incongruity of the decisions about the West Coast Japanese and the Hawaiian Japanese—why evacuate the one and not the other?—can be explained rather simply. The first was a political decision, the second a military one.

* * * * *

What, then, of the future? What are the chances for some kind of meaningful redress? When Congress, at the end of 1980, established the Commission, it charged it with two tasks. First, to inquire whether any wrong was done to Japanese Americans (and later to Aleuts) under the provisions of Executive Order 9066, and second, if it did so find, to make specific recommendations to the Congress as to how redress could be provided for any such wrong. The Commission has, with its February report, *Personal Justice Denied*, fulfilled its first obligation. The report and its conclusions unambiguously establish that wrong was done to both the Japanese American people and the Aleuts. Some have been disappointed that no recommendations for redress were contained in the report and have been critical of this omission. The omission, of course, was deliberate, and I think that the Commission's strategy was both logical and effective. Had the report contained recommendations—especially recommendations involving monetary redress—public attention would have been diverted from the report's historical conclusions and focused on the proposed remedies. It was important that the Commission's conclusions—that the evacuation was not "justified by military necessity," that its root historical causes were "race prejudice, war hysteria, and a failure of political leadership"—be disseminated as widely as possible. With

that accomplished, a predicate has been established for the Commission to perform its second task, to make its recommendations to the Congress by June 30, 1983, at which time it is slated to go out of existence.

What will the Commission recommend? Frankly, I do not know. It is always tempting to try to foretell the future, and, perhaps unwisely, it is a temptation that I will yield to tonight. I ought first to establish my bias in the matter. I spoke before the Commission almost two years ago in favor of monetary redress to individuals. This has been a traditional and long-standing method of providing redress for damages since time out of mind. Since the Commission has established, unambiguously, that grievous wrongs were done to both the Aleut and Japanese American peoples, I cannot believe that it will not follow through. I am convinced that some kind of payment to individuals will be recommended to the Congress. This opinion is not based on hard evidence; it is, rather, an act of faith, although I have, over the past two years, spoken personally to all but one of the commissioners and have some notion of how some of them feel. I will not, here, speculate about amounts and methods of payment. I would hope that the method is made simple and that legal proceedings be avoided whenever possible.

Records exist of who was incarcerated: A flat payment to every such person still alive should be step one in any meaningful redress procedure. Over and above that, it ought to be possible to reopen the whole question of Japanese American and Aleut property claims, and it has often been suggested that, in addition, some kind of foundation for research into race relations should be established.

Some have suggested that real redress will come only in the courts and some ingenious suits have been initiated recently. Without in any way denigrating the merit or the integrity of any such suits, all have what seems to me a fatal weakness: they depend for their success on a creative, liberal approach by the federal judiciary; and, while there are those on the federal bench who are susceptible to innovation, the last word is held by the nine in Washington whose views, as a group, are anything but innovative. To imagine that a court appointed largely by Richard Nixon and Ronald Reagan will rule favorably on such suits is to ignore fourteen years of largely unhappy judicial history.

The Commission's recommendations, then, will have to be enacted by Congress, and will be political. In a sense, this is appropriate. The relocation, as has been shown, was a political decision: it is entirely appropriate that redress from it be political as well. That a recommendation for monetary redress will face certain difficulties in these recessionary times is axiomatic. Any meaningful redress bill will aggregate at least a billion dollars. I will not, here, attempt to rehearse the arguments against such redress. They are not, I think, compelling. Yet we should not be surprised if redress, once recommended, is not immediately enacted into law. But, despite the recession, despite the political problems involved, positive congressional action on redress is possible. When Congress, in late 1980, created the Commission, its financial implications were clear, and both houses overwhelmingly passed the bill, appropriated money for the Commission to do its work, and, in December 1982, voted it additional funds. Redress is politically possible although it might take more than one Congress.

The arguments for redress are, it seems to me, implicit in the Commission's report. In addition, redress has, I think, great symbolic value, and, we must remember, as Oliver Wendell Holmes, Jr., liked to point out, "we live by symbols." It is one of our most vaunted boasts that an important argument for our system of government is that "democracy corrects its own mistakes." I am not convinced, as a historian, of the universal validity of that adage, but there are times when we can at least try to rebalance the skewed scales of justice. For many of the victims of Executive Order 9066, like James Wakasa, no redress is possible. For the survivors it has been long delayed, and even if Congress acts expeditiously, many more will die before the first payments are made. No redress can wipe out the wrongs of 1942, wrongs exacerbated by more than four decades of neglect. But redress is important, and not just for the survivors. Meaningful monetary redress, more than anything else now possible, will show that the government now realizes that what the late Morton Grodzins once called "the betrayal of all Americans" can no longer be condoned.

NOTES

1. Yoshiko Uchida, *Desert Exile: The Uprooting of a Japanese American Family*, (Seattle: University of Washington Press, 1982), 147.

2. Commission on Wartime Relocation and Internment of Civilians, *Personal Justice Denied* (Washington: Government Printing Office, 1982), p. 18.

3. Report of the Special Meeting of the Federal Advisory Council, San Francisco, March 16, 1942, Record Group 210, National Archives. For Dedrick's role, see Roger Daniels, "The Bureau of the Census and the Relocation of the Japanese Americans: A Note and a Document," *Amerasia Journal* 9 (1982): 101–5.

4. Raymond Y. Okamura, "The American Concentration Camps: A Cover-Up Through Euphemistic Terminology," *Journal of Ethnic Studies* 10 (1982) 3: 95–109.

5. My account is based on a report, "The Wakasa Incident" done contemporaneously by Russell A. Bankston, who was reports officer for WRA at Topaz at the time. It includes copies of a number of documents. It may be found in a collection called "U.S. War Relocation Authority" in the University of Washington Archives, Seattle.

6. McCloy quoted in Transcript of Telephone Conversation, Allen W. Gullion and Mark W. Clark, February 4, 1942, Record Group 389, National Archives.

7. McCloy's testimony, November 3, 1981, quoted in *Personal Justice Denied*, 383–84. McCloy's reaction in *New York Times*, February 25, 1983, and John J. McCloy, "Repay U.S. Japanese," *New York Times*, "Op Ed" page, April 10, 1983.

PART II
Prewar Japanese America

On the eve of Pearl Harbor, the census showed just over 125,000 persons of Japanese birth or ancestry in the continental United States, while another 150,000 lived in the Territory of Hawaii. The mainland Nikkei, the focus of this volume, were concentrated heavily in California, Washington, and Oregon, where almost nine out of ten of them lived. Significant numbers of Japanese had begun to migrate to the United States in the 1890s, many using Hawaii as an intermediate way station. Governmental actions twice inhibited the "natural" flow of this immigration: the Gentlemen's Agreement of 1907–1908 by the American and Japanese governments and the Immigration Act of 1924, through which Congress barred further Japanese immigration by the transparent device of forbidding entrance to any "aliens ineligible to citizenship."

Like many other ethnic groups in the United States, Japanese immigrants, the Issei, and their native-born citizen children, the Nisei, made a successful adaptation to American life, although, because of discrimination, adaptation was distinctly a success with limitations. By the 1940s few were truly integrated into the larger community: instead, they lived largely within ethnic enclaves in certain West Coast cities and rural areas. In the cities the Nihonmachis, literally Japan towns, were not only residential areas, but also commercial centers. They were utilized not only by the urban Japanese Americans, but also by those who lived in the surrounding rural hinterlands. For historical reasons, San Francisco was the cultural capital of Japanese America—the Japanese consul general had his headquarters there, as did the major organizations of each generation: the Japanese associations of the Issei and the Japanese American Citizens League of the Nisei. But, insofar as population was concerned, Los Angeles had become, by 1910, the metropolis of Japanese America, while Seattle was, in every census, its second city.

That Japanese America was, at best, a transitory stage in the acculturative process, few can doubt. There were already signs of intracommunal and intergenerational stress, stress whose major fracture lines involved attitudes toward Japan and Japanese culture. The Issei, like most immigrant generations, had tried to recapitulate the world they had left, the world of Meiji Japan. Their children, nurtured by American institutions, largely innocent of either Japanese culture or language, were clearly Americans, but Americans whose race and ethnicity first made them, like other Asian or Afro-Americans, second-class citizens, and then, after the onset of the great Pacific War, American citizens with enemy faces. That, in the normal course of events, there would have been a serious cultural clash between first- and second-generation Japanese Americans, a clash that the peculiar demographic history of Japanese America would have heightened, is quite clear. That clash would surely have changed and might well have shattered

Children being evacuated from the Oakland railroad terminal. Photo by Dorothea Lange. Courtesy Bernard K. Johnpoll.

Japanese America, at least as it had existed. But, in any event, the U.S. government simply destroyed Japanese America in the spring and summer of 1942, sweeping up the entire ethnic population of California and western Washington and Oregon and transporting it first to the assembly centers of the War Relocation Authority.

In the essays that follow, two survivors, both adults in 1942, reflect on the great crisis of Japanese American history. Barry Saiki, a Nisei whose business career has taken him to booming Japan, notes his experiences as a college student in cosmopolitan Berkeley and as a son of a Stockton Nihonmachi at the time of the great crisis in the history of Japanese America. Bill Hosokawa, who achieved great success after relocation as a Denver journalist and author, reflects on the tragic events in his hometown of Seattle. Although the focus on Topaz largely precluded participation by Nikkei from Los Angeles (people from Southern California were sent elsewhere) that omission is not the most serious one. Whatever their differences may be, Saiki and Hosokawa share at least one nonethnic characteristic: both survived and not just in a physical sense. Both were able, after the war, to resume their lives and build careers for themselves. What must be missing from these first-person accounts is any real notion of those who did not survive, whose lives were broken or hopelessly warped by the abuse they suffered at the hands of the American government. Mute as those witnesses must be, their suffering should not be forgotten.

Because the wartime removal and incarceration is the central event of Japanese American history, a serious historiographical imbalance has developed in its literature. The focus has been upon the events that followed Pearl Harbor, and the crucial decades that preceded the war have been slighted. We are beginning to get useful works about the first or Issei generation—books such as Akemi Kikumura's *Through Harsh Winters* (Novato, Calif.: Chandler & Sharp, 1981) and a string of articles by the finest historian of the Issei, Yuji Ichioka. Major scholarly work about the emergence of the Nisei generation in the pre-Pearl Harbor years is still quite scanty, although we do have a number of books that survey the entire Japanese American experience. The best of these are: Harry H. L. Kitano, *Japanese Americans: The Evolution of a Sub-culture* (Englewood Cliffs, N.J.: Prentice-Hall, 1969; 2nd ed., 1976); Bill Hosokawa, *Nisei: The Quiet Americans* (New York: William Morrow, 1969); William Petersen, *Japanese Americans: Oppression and Success* (New York: Random House, 1971); and Robert A. Wilson and Bill Hosokawa, *East to America* (New York: William Morrow, 1980). There are only two good studies of urban life in Japanese America: S. Frank Miyamoto, *Social Solidarity Among the Japanese in Seattle* (Seattle: University of Washington Press, 1939; 2nd ed., 1981; revised edition, 1984) and John Modell, *The Economics and Politics of Racial Accommodation: The Japanese of Los Angeles, 1900–1942* (Urbana, Ill.: University of Illinois Press, 1977). San Francisco, the cultural capital of Japanese America, remains largely unstudied and we know very little about agricultural communities. The best work on Japanese American agriculture is still Masakasu Iwata, "The Japanese Immigrants in California Agriculture," *Agricultural History* 36 (1962):25–37; however, Iwata is finishing a book tentatively entitled "Planted in Good Soil: Issei Agriculture in the Pacific Coast States." While a number of the personal memoirs that focus on the evacuation have preliminary sections depicting family and community life "before the war," these are usually written by persons who were children or adolescents when the war began. Among the most useful of these for the light that they throw on the prewar community are Monica Sone, *Nisei Daughter* (Boston: Little, Brown, 1953; 2nd ed., Seattle: University of Washington Press, 1979) and Yoshiko Uchida, *Desert Exile: The Uprooting of a Japanese American Family* (Seattle: University of Washington Press, 1982), each of which depicts an urban childhood, in Seattle and Berkeley respectively. For a discussion of the notion of a "Japanese America," see Roger Daniels, *Asian America: Chinese and Japanese in the United States since 1850*, soon to be published by the University of Washington Press.

Roger Daniels

The Uprooting of My Two Communities

Barry Saiki

THE UPROOTING OF A UNIVERSITY GROUP

Approximately 500 Nisei students attended the University of California in Berkeley. Perhaps half were commuters from Bay Area cities who usually entered as freshmen. The other half, who lived on or near campus, were from the rest of the state and tended to be junior college transfers.

Although the Nisei mixed with their Caucasian classmates in and around campus, they tended to keep together in their housing and social activities. Cognizant of the California law banning intermarriage, they focused their off-campus lives around the Japanese Students' Club, the Buddhist churches, the Japanese Christian churches, and fellowship groups.

As undergraduates, we were all imbued with hopes for the future—being the young of heart who had not yet felt the full impact of the real world. All male upperclassmen were registered with the Selective Service and either had high draft numbers or had been deferred.

Pearl Harbor jolted us just a week before final exams. Nisei reactions ranged from stunned silence to uncertainty and frustration. We were Americans imbued with American concepts and ideals, yet we were also deeply conscious of and grateful to our alien parents. The attack had suddenly changed our parents into enemy aliens. During the following week, the reactions of the other students were tolerant and many were openly kind. With finals coming, no obvious or overt actions against us occurred.

Overnight, we found that we could not cash checks, as our parents' accounts were frozen under government orders. The university administration was sympathetic and announced that small loans would be advanced to Nisei so that we could return home. The

president also encouraged students to return for the spring semester. Yet even as final exams were concluded, many Nisei said good-bye to their friends, convinced they would not return.

Returning home after finals on borrowed money, I found the Nihonmachi of Stockton, my hometown, tense with uncertainty. The FBI had already questioned most prominent Issei leaders and arrested some of them. Stores normally open until 9 or 10 p.m. closed early. A resident had been shot down on a street in Nihonmachi, and a Japanese farmer had reported his farmhouse had been hit by a shotgun blast one night. With their bank accounts frozen, stores were forced to curtail their business.

Despite parental remonstrances, I returned to Berkeley in early January 1942 for the new semester, determined to graduate in May. However, fewer than half of the Nisei returned.

As the weeks passed, more and more anti-Japanese sentiments began to appear in the newspapers. Disturbed, I found myself prompted to write several protest letters, but only two were printed, buried under an avalanche of anti-Japanese letters.

Increasingly, the chief concern of the Nisei undergraduates became whether we could finish the term. In late January, the Western Defense Command announced the list of Category A areas, areas from which Japanese residents would be moved. Concurrently, the exodus of students whose families lived in these areas began. Others left as they received letters from home indicating that their fathers had been apprehended. A message from my home told me that my father had been questioned twice but had not been detained because of his poor health. My younger brother sent me a clipping from our hometown newspaper, showing two of my brothers turning in the family pistol, radios, and cameras to the local police department.

February brought other signs of heightened emotions as several classmates decided to marry, fearful they would be separated when evacuated. Learning that the Tolan Committee hearings were being held in San Francisco—hearings reportedly investigating the need for evacuation—several of us from Berkeley attended them on February 21. We sat, listening with complete disillusionment as a steady stream of anti-Japanese witnesses testified, their opinions hardly balanced by those speaking on behalf of Japanese Americans. Even worse, unknown to us, the decision on evacuation had already been made. Years later, we learned that Executive Order 9066 had been signed two days previously.

On March 2, Lieutenant General John L. DeWitt issued a proclamation delineating Military Areas No. 1 and No. 2. Area No. 1, including the western halves of the three West Coast states, was to be cleared of all those of Japanese descent. Since it covered nearly all the families of Nisei students at U.C., the Nisei exodus from Berkeley quickened and by mid-March fewer than one-third of the fall enrollment remained. As March ended, the university announced that Nisei would be given credit for their terms if they could meet the requirements of their courses; they urged continued attendance if possible. In early April, only Nisei students within commuting distance remained. By complying with the requirements of the course instructors, I eventually received my diploma through the mail as a member of the Class of 1942, shortly after I had been incarcerated at Stockton. Many seniors received their degrees this way.

But what happened to the 500 Nisei enrolled at U.C. before Pearl Harbor? Most of my closest friends continued their education elsewhere. Several earned Ph.D.s and became professors, including Tamotsu Shibutani of U.C., Santa Barbara; James Sakoda, Kenny Murase, Charles Kikuchi, Warren Tsuneishi, and Harvey Itano. Others gained prominence in medicine, dentistry, law, engineering, and architecture. Many served in the military forces, while others took up fruitful careers in civil service.

THE UPROOTING OF A COMMUNITY

In 1940, Stockton had a population of 55,000. Located a few miles below the confluence of the Stanislaus and San Joaquin rivers, it grew as a river town, collecting agricultural products from the surrounding farms for shipment to San Francisco Bay. In the early 1900s, its importance grew as the tule lands along the San Joaquin delta reclaimed by George Shima, the Issei potato king, and others, increased the amount of produce for shipment. By 1910, a small Nihonmachi had formed in the southern part of Stockton.

In 1941, Stockton had 1,500 persons of Japanese ancestry, while another 2,500 were engaged in agriculture within San Joaquin County. Nihonmachi covered about eight city blocks within five minutes of city hall. While most businesses depended primarily on Japanese American clientele, my family operated a rooming house and coffee shop close by the riverfront. Our customers were dock workers, farm laborers, and pensioners, and were primarily of European stock. Cheap, bare, but clean rooms and inexpensive meals were the drawing cards of a business that had begun in 1916.

One of the earliest residents, my father moved to Stockton in 1909 and was active in the Buddhist church, the Japanese Association, and the Japanese Fencing Association. Over sixty-five and weakened by a recent siege of pneumonia, he was semiretired and waiting hopefully for the day when one of his six sons would volunteer to return to Japan with him. Since he was the only child and heir to the family farm and house, he secretly felt it his duty to maintain the family line. His eldest son was now operating the rooming house. Two married daughters were also in the hotel business, his second son operated a small business, and the four younger boys were still attending school.

Shortly after Pearl Harbor, the FBI questioned him about his connection with the Japanese Association, but he was not confined because of his doctor's certificate. When I returned to Stockton for the winter recess, he was apprehensive about my returning to school. My mother suggested I remain in Stockton, but I was determined to finish my final term.

When I returned to Stockton in early April, the familiar Nihonmachi had only a small fraction of its former vitality. Daily reports revealed new areas to be evacuated. By late April, orders for the evacuation of Stockton and San Joaquin County were announced. We were given less than four weeks to prepare for the move.

Rumors were rampant and confusion widespread. A registration of all persons of Japanese descent was conducted at the local armory. Since all of our businesses were under lease contracts, we could find no buyers for our small enterprises willing to pay anything approximating their true worth. We stored some of our personal possessions in the basement of a hotel owned by my uncle. Then we began to dispose of our furniture and equipment at fire-sale discounts. Our 1939 Dodge, with five brand-new tires, fetched $400 and our restaurant chinaware, cutlery, and refrigerators netted several hundred dollars. The two weeks before May 20 were chaotic as the family sorted the accumulation of the preceding decades into the two suitcases allowed each person. Some families owning homes boarded them up, hoping that they would not be vandalized during their absence.

On May 20, our family group, assisted by a sundry assortment of our former customers (including two Irishmen, an Indian, and a Mexican), carried our baggage to the plaza facing the San Joaquin County Courthouse, about three hundred yards from home. Labeled with identification tags, just like the baggage, we boarded busses for the San Joaquin Fairgrounds two miles away. Our family unit consisted of my father, my mother, two younger brothers, and myself, with my married brothers and sisters entering as separate family units.

By the time our health had been checked at the clinic and our baggage was cleared, it was late afternoon. We were told that my father required a more detailed physical examination, and we eventually found our way to our newly assigned living quarters, No. 8-141-E—meaning Block 8, Barracks No. 141, Apartment E—an end unit.

The barracks consisted of hastily erected wooden frame buildings, built with two-by-four struts and rafters and covered with three-quarter-inch pinewood boards. Our unit was better than most, for, being an end unit, it had windows on three sides. The fourth side was a partition separating it from the next unit, a seven foot, half-inch plasterboard, with several feet of open space to the roof. Thus, normal conversation from neighboring units could be heard.

No. 8-141-E was approximately eighteen by twenty feet and contained five army cots, five straw-filled mattresses, ten blankets, five pillows. A single light bulb hung limply from the rafters. We had been told to bring our own sheets and pillowcases as well as durable clothes.

More than an hour had passed since we moved in, but there was still no sign of my father. Then as sunset approached, a black sedan drove up and parked near our barracks. Two men approached our apartment and asked, "Is this the Saiki family?"

As I nodded, one of the strangers said, "We came to pick up your father's baggage. He can only take one suitcase, so he can repack."

The other man brought my father in as I pointed out his bags. Sensing these were FBI men, I groped for something to say. "I don't understand. Where is my dad going?"

After a short silence, one replied, "The health exam showed that your father is physically well, so he's being sent to another camp. We brought him here to pick up his baggage and not for long farewells."

Upon finishing his repacking, my father turned over a thin envelope to my mother, saying, "Keep this. Maybe the family will need it sometime." In it were U.S. war bonds.

In ten minutes they were gone. It was to be almost a year before we learned of his whereabouts—the Lordsburg Internment Camp in New Mexico. I have often wondered why it was necessary to intern him separately when our family already had been moved into an assembly center. He eventually rejoined the family at the Rohwer Relocation Center in Arkansas in July 1944. He died in 1948, after returning to Stockton, from a recurring illness that had kept him in the hospital for a year. I remember him as a strict man, quick to reprove and slow in praise, with a pride in family honor.

The Uprooting of Seattle

Bill Hosokawa

I was born in Seattle, spent the first twenty-three years of my life there, and was an interested if not a trained observer of the local scene before leaving in 1938.

Let me set the background: Seattle in my boyhood was a city of some 300,000 and home for some 7,000 persons of Japanese origin, perhaps a few more. In the entire state of Washington, there were about 14,000. Seattle's Japanese American community was centered around Jackson, Main, and Washington streets, a few blocks east of Union Station, which was just a few blocks east of the waterfront. City Hall and police headquarters were only a few blocks north of Japantown, but it had very little contact with either.

Shortly after the turn of the century, Seattle became an important port of entry for a growing number of Japanese immigrants, virtually all young and unmarried. Almost as soon as they landed, many were sent by labor contractors to railroad section gangs in eastern Washington, Idaho, Montana, and as far east as the Dakotas and Minnesota. Others found work in sawmill camps and nearby farms.

So, for a time, Seattle was a sort of service center for Japanese immigrants who passed through on their way to work assignments and then came back between jobs to stay at Japanese-operated hotels, to eat at Japanese restaurants, to shop at Japanese-run stores, perhaps to gamble at Chinese-operated gambling dens, and to enjoy each others' company. After a number of years some of the men returned to Japan and came back with brides. Others had friends, relatives, or marriage brokers line up picture brides—the two principals exchanged photographs and went through a proxy marriage if they liked what they saw. The picture brides saw their husbands for the first time when they came ashore in Seattle.

As families were established and children born, the community became more stable. Small shops were opened to meet the needs of other Japanese—shoe and grocery stores, furniture and dry-goods stores, fish stores, hotels and rooming houses, tailor shops, restaurants, beer parlors, and pool halls. Truck farmers from nearby areas brought their produce to local markets and stopped in Japantown to shop. It was a close-knit community concentrated in a limited area just off skid row and largely unnoticed by the rest of the city. With only minor differences, this is pretty much the story of other Japantowns on the West Coast.

Most Nisei children made their first acquaintance with the world outside Japantown when they enrolled in school. In Seattle it was Bailey Gatzert School, at first in the heart of Japantown but soon moved to a new building some distance away. In time the enrollment at Bailey Gatzert was somewhere close to 95 percent Nisei, with a few Chinese Americans and whites providing the balance.

Before it was time for me to go to school my parents moved a few blocks farther east and I attended Washington Grade School, which had an international student body, mostly Jewish, but they were German Jews, Polish Jews, Russian Jews, and Spanish Jews. During Jewish holidays there would be only five or six of us in each class. We were Japanese, Russian, Irish, Italian, and almost all of us were the offspring of immigrants.

By the time the Nisei were ready for high school, they were divided almost equally among three of the nine high schools in the city: Broadway, Franklin, and Garfield, which I attended together with a rather cosmopolitan mix of Jews, blacks, middle-class and blue-collar whites, and a small number of Asians. During the school day these diverse ethnic groups got along reasonably well, although after school all of us were inclined to disappear into our own neighborhoods.

But to get back to the Japanese American community: We continued to be a fairly compact, self-sufficient entity. We had our ethnic churches—the Buddhist church was the largest, followed by the Japanese Methodist Church, the Japanese Baptist Church, the Japanese Congregational Church, and the Japanese St. Peter's Episcopal Church. The Issei had their prefectural associations, the Kenjin Kai, and the Japanese Association, the Nihonjin Kai, which were a combination of social and mutual welfare associations. Much of the Nisei activity centered around athletics; because most of them were too slight physically to compete on equal terms for positions on high school varsity teams, they played in their own baseball, basketball, and football leagues.

In the mid-1930s, the Japanese American Citizens League, made up of earnest and civic-minded Nisei, began to assert itself. JACL's basic platform was Americanism and it sought to help Nisei find a place in the economic, social, and political life of the nation. Early on, some Issei leaders perceived JACL as an unwelcome rival for community influence. But other Issei, acutely aware of the limitations imposed by America's refusal to grant them naturalization, looked to citizen Nisei and their agency JACL to help them gain legal and social equality and justice.

Their hopes and faith rested on a slender reed: JACL in the 1930s reflected the youth and inexperience of its members, who were a small minority in the community. Hardly a JACL meeting was convened without a discussion about what could be done to increase membership. Issei still controlled the purse strings and were the dominant force in community affairs. That was the situation in Seattle when, late in 1938, I left to take a job in the Far East.

I returned to Seattle late in the fall of 1941, just a few weeks before the outbreak of war. The Issei were still dominant in Japanese American community affairs. The Buddhists had just built a handsome new temple, primarily with Issei money. The Nisei were, of course, three years older and had made considerable economic progress, but it was obvious the Issei were still in charge.

The attack on Pearl Harbor changed the situation abruptly. Within a few hours, FBI agents arrested several hundred Issei, some of them men of influence but others harmless individuals who simply had the misfortune of having paid dues to equally harmless—but, to federal authorities, potentially dangerous—organizations. Left leaderless, frightened, and confused, the community turned to the only organization even remotely able to fill the leadership gap—the JACL.

JACL at the local and community level performed yeoman service in the frantic months before evacuation. It served as a buffer between the community and the authorities, conducted public relations campaigns, and provided food and services to families in need. Somehow, members of the community saw in JACL assurance and confidence; JACL became a symbol of loyalty and many Nisei rushed to become members. But to no avail. Nothing could halt the evacuation, and area by area Seattle's Japanese Americans were placed aboard buses and sent off to the crude, temporary camp at the Puyallup Fairgrounds, ironically called Camp Harmony.

The overall story of camp life need not be recounted here. I think it is sufficient to say that the appalling experience of confinement behind barbed wire in a concentration camp both strengthened and damaged the sense of community that had existed in Seattle. On the one hand, there was festering resentment that was directed at any authority figure, including other Japanese Americans; on the other hand,

there was a sense of circling the wagons and offering comfort and support to each other in a time of mutual distress. What kept the community going, I think, was the anticipation of moving out of the rude, crowded, uncomfortable, demeaning chicken coops that passed for residential quarters. The mood of the camp rose when it was announced Idaho would be the ultimate destination of most of the Seattle group.

Yet I didn't go to Idaho. I was one of four or five persons shipped out of Puyallup on short notice, without explanation. My destination was Heart Mountain, Wyoming. Under the circumstances, I had to conclude that for some reason the authorities wanted to separate me from my Seattle friends and associates and drop me among strangers. In other words, since they could not put me into an isolation cell, they did the next best thing. I was never told why I was exiled and at this point in life I am not sure I want to know.

I was in the Heart Mountain WRA camp for fourteen months before relocating to Des Moines, Iowa. The evacuees at Heart Mountain were mainly from Los Angeles, San Jose, and San Francisco. Since I knew few of them, I was isolated from community politics. By the same token, I was in the dark about what was happening among the Seattleites in their camp at Minidoka, Idaho. My next physical contact with any number of them was in 1946, after the war, when I visited my parents who had returned to Seattle.

The people I had known were picking up the broken strings of their lives, but much had happened during the four years they had been barred from the West Coast. Many of the prewar Nisei community leaders were no longer on the scene. Jimmie Sakamoto, the blind publisher of the weekly community newspaper, had decided not to revive his paper. He had been a real leader, but, perhaps disillusioned by the criticism he had had to endure in the camp, he had dropped out of the spotlight. Eventually he went to work as director of telephone solicitations for the St. Vincent de Paul thrift shop program. Clarence Arai, attorney and another former JACL leader, was in ill health. Takeo Nogaki was living in New Jersey, commuting to a good job in New York, and had no intention of returning to Seattle. The extent of his transplantation can be measured in the fact that he had been a Buddhist stalwart but in his new surroundings had joined a Christian church and was devoting his enthusiasm and organizational talents to its programs. Attorney Tom Masuda was building an impressive clientele in Chicago and wasn't planning to come back to Seattle. George Ishihara was doing well as a produce shipper in Idaho and saw no reason to abandon his business.

An uncertain parting at the Oakland railroad terminal during evacuation. Photo by Dorothea Lange. Courtesy Bernard K. Johnpoll.

Of course, many Nisei and Issei had returned to Seattle by 1946, and many more continued to drift back, for the Pacific Northwest is a delightful place to live. For most, the first priority was to make up the economic loss suffered during the evacuation years. Shops and businesses had to be reestablished. Doors to jobs which had been closed to Nisei on a racial basis prior to the war were, oddly enough, flung open, and they were diligently making up for lost time. They were buying homes and cars, upgrading their belongings, and finding little time to bother with community affairs. They left that mostly to the Issei, some of whom had returned and were pleased to have something to do.

But time continued to take its toll and, in the natural course of events, the Issei dropped away and Nisei took over leadership roles, such as they were. While my parents lived, I went back to Seattle occa-

sionally and was pleased to see the economic and civic progress achieved by some of my friends. But at the same time I was saddened to see how little the appearance and, more importantly, the outlook had changed in Japantown. In that area, it was as though the evacuation had never taken place.

That, of course, is not the whole story. Today Nisei and an ever-increasing number of Sansei and Yonsei have achieved positions of respect, influence, and importance in the greater Seattle community, as discriminatory barriers fell and individuals were able to demonstrate their abilities. This progress would have come about in time, but the trauma of the evacuation for both the evacuees and for society at large helped speed the process. It can be said that there was a silver lining to the ghastly mistake of the evacuation. But what a price was paid in individual suffering and humiliation, and in loss of national esteem and honor.

PART III
Life in the Camps

There are a number of ways of describing camp life. The term "homogeneity" is one. Residents were all of Japanese ancestry, of similar height and weight, with features darkened by constant exposure to the wind and sun. Clothing had a uniformly drab look reflecting army surplus and leftover Sears and Roebuck; housing consisted of row after row of tar-paper barracks, and inside were identical potbelly stoves, army cots, and fine Topaz dust.

Standing in line is another: mess hall lines, entertainment lines, co-op canteen lines, toilet and shower lines, lines for coal, and lines for washing clothes. Camp vocabulary took on a distinctive flavor—"waste time," "bootchie," "slop suey," "inu," and the "yes-yes's" and the "no-no's." And perhaps the most important, the standard administrative setup of the camps: "white on the top" and "yellow on the bottom."

But surface similarities are deceptive, for the evacuees behaved in a wide variety of ways. Some rebelled, some conformed; some followed old norms while others developed newer patterns of behavior. Many resigned themselves to their powerless positions (*shikataganai*), while a few turned on their fellow evacuees. Most swallowed their feelings and carried on their lives one day at a time.

"Good" adaptations to camp life depended a great deal on the position of the observer. Camp administrators defined the good evacuee as a person who cooperated peacefully and followed all rules and regulations. Residents held less doctrinaire positions. For them good evacuees might include those who agreed with the administration or those who rebelled against it, those who professed loyalty to the United States or those who were sympathetic to Japan, volunteers for the U.S. Army or the draft resisters. Some residents considered evacuees who left camp at the earliest opportunity good, while for others good evacuees were those who remained with their families to the bitter end. Diverse definitions of a good evacuee lay at the root of many of the schisms and tensions which occasionally erupted in violence.

The camps were modeled on a colonial pattern; bureaucrats in Washington made policy, programs, and major decisions and delegated authority to appointed white camp officials. Lower level outsiders supervised the programs, while the actual enforcement and the effects were left up to the evacuees. In sum, decisions made at the top by outsiders went through white administrators in the middle and eventually filtered down to the Japanese Americans at the bottom.

The camps were segregated, closed systems with very few alternatives. It was a classless system with occupation and wages bringing little distinction ($16 to $19 per month) and housing and neighborhood carrying no prestige. There were no automobiles or other conspicuous consumption items such as fashionable clothes and innovative appliances. There were no prestige stores or good restaurants.

What meager entertainment there was came from resident amateurs. Rich, middle class, and poor alike lined up for the movies (I believe they cost ten cents); former bosses and employees found themselves sharing the same space and similar life-styles. Within this framework, we present the articles reflecting life in the camps.

The article "Camp Memories: Rough and Broken Shards" by Toyo Kawakami describes the camps, their barracks and their rooms. Kawakami attempted to bring a degree of normalcy to her life by working in the camp library. The tie to the outside world for many residents of Topaz remained the Bay Area, as evidenced by the popularity of the *San Francisco Chronicle* and the *Oakland Tribune*. The Hearst Press, probably the most virulent of the anti-Japanese newspapers, was not popular.

Take Uchida, born in 1890, is the sole Issei voice, and her experience is far from representative. She lived in the Intermountain West, a region with a very small Nikkei population; she was interned as an enemy alien rather than relocated as a Japanese American. And, unlike the overwhelming majority of Issei women, she had a professional career. But, in the final analysis, her story, "An Issei Internee's Experiences," is worth hearing, and, in its essentially positive orientation, resonates to the bamboo-like resiliency that so typified her generation.

Asael T. Hansen, in "My Two Years at Heart Mountain: The Difficult Role of an Applied Anthropologist," raises questions with universal significance. What is the role of an outsider preparing reports on a captive population, who knows that these reports, if they are to be useful, will be used in dealing with that population? Hansen presents a sensitive account of the difficulties of such a role, as it appears that under the administrative structure of the camps, an analyst, no matter how sympathetic he or she may have been to the evacuated population, has to deal with a government employer that put the people into camps in the first place.

Comments to Hansen by several of the evacuees anticipated the criticism of social scientists by minority communities several decades later. Japanese Americans raised questions about being used as guinea pigs and about scientists writing reports to please their superiors in Washington in order to get a raise in salary.

Questions of objectivity can also be raised. Is it possible to be objective without resorting to judgements of good and bad? Under the camp colonial system, it is probable that analysts saw disrupters as the bad guys and cooperators and informers as the good guys.

Eleanor Sekerak, a former high school teacher, shares her experiences in "A Teacher at Topaz." She describes the steps leading to her decision to accept a teaching post at Topaz. She portrays the excitement of the residents about the hiring of a "fully credentialed" California teacher, and the desire of most parents to have a college preparatory curriculum. The author was one of the most respected teachers at Topaz High School; she maintained discipline and expected high standards of performance, perspectives which were not totally appreciated by many of her students. Mrs. Sekerak was one of my high school teachers and I remember her as a good, tough, fair teacher. Understanding of our plight, she did not let us feel sorry for ourselves.

Lane Hirabayashi's article, "The Impact of Incarceration on the Education of Nisei Schoolchildren," provides another perspective on the camp schools. He points out the many inadequacies, ranging from educational philosophy to curriculum, personnel, physical setting, and lack of materials. One criticism, the lack of ethnic teachers, may be valid from today's perspective. There was evidence of a colonial mentality; many residents felt that Caucasian teachers were "better" so that other things being equal, white teachers were treated with more deference.

Poor white teachers could and did leave while poor ethnic teachers did not. Hirabayashi assesses the role of the school as acculturative and assimilationist and questions its purpose. His question remains a timely one, given the current debates over pluralistic, bicultural, and assimilationist models of the American society.

Tetsuden Kashima's article, "American Mistreatment of Internees During World War II: Enemy Alien Japanese" and John J. Culley's "The Santa Fe Internment Camp and the Justice Department Program for Enemy Aliens" provide information about a number of relatively unknown camps. These were special camps for enemy aliens, presumed to be more dangerous than the other evacuees, although in reality most of them had found their way to special camps through leadership and prominence in Japanese community organizations and because of monetary contributions to their home country. Culley points out the extreme vulnerability of enemy aliens in time of war (U.S. citizenship was of little protection to the Japanese Americans); the irony for the Japanese was the Catch 22 policy forcing an alien status on Japanese immigrants by categorizing them as aliens ineligible for citizenship.

Kashima and Culley discuss some minor advantages to life in alien camps. Alien status was akin to being a prisoner of war and meant coverage by the Geneva Convention. Outside sources, such as the Spanish government, could be contacted for complaints. The quality of food in the alien camps was better than in the relocation camps. The late Edison Uno, who grew up in one of the alien camps, used to delight in telling me how their diet was better than the one I grew up with in Topaz; however, it would be difficult to find a camp where the food was worse than at Topaz.

But Culley summarizes the reality of the camps: people placed involuntarily in authoritarian settings, deprived of normal stimulation for psychological, emotional, and occupational growth, a loss of liberty, limited access to goods and services, and restrictions on movement and autonomy. In Santa Fe, an all-male camp, they were also deprived of heterosexual relationships.

Harry H. L. Kitano

BIBLIOGRAPHIC NOTE

Although the topic is far from exhausted, no aspect of Japanese American life and history has been so well documented as the years of wartime incarceration. Beginning with two volumes produced almost contemporaneously by the University of California Japanese American Evacuation and Resettlement Study (JERS), headquartered on the Berkeley campus between February 1942 and July 1948, social science studies, memoirs, and histories have explored many facets of camp life. In addition, but not included in this bibliography, the traumas of camp life have been portrayed in short stories, novels, plays, and in theatrical and television films. The listing here is selective, not comprehensive.

The two JERS volumes, Dorothy S. Thomas and Richard S. Nishimoto, *The Spoilage* (Berkeley and Los Angeles: University of California Press, 1946) and Dorothy S. Thomas with the assistance of Charles Kikuchi and James Sadoka, *The Salvage* (Berkeley and Los Angeles: University of California Press, 1952), were pioneering examples of social science research whose methodological and ethical standards have been questioned. Two volumes by JERS field-workers, John Modell, ed., *The Kikuchi Diary: Chronicle From An American Concentration Camp: The Tanforan Journals of Charles Kikuchi* (Urbana, Ill.: University of Illinois Press,

1973) and Rosalie H. Wax, *Doing Fieldwork: Warnings and Advice* (Chicago: University of Chicago Press, 1971), help point up some of the strengths and weaknesses of the wartime study. Two other important, nearly contemporary social science studies are Leonard Broom (ne Bloom) and Ruth Riemer, *Removal and Return: The Socio-Economic Effects of War on Japanese Americans* (Berkeley and Los Angeles: University of California Press, 1949) and Leonard Broom and John I. Kituse, *The Managed Casualty: The Japanese American Family in World War II* (Berkeley and Los Angeles: University of California Press, 1965).

The most important books written about the relocation by former War Relocation Authority staffers are the sensitive reflections of the psychiatrist Alexander H. Leighton, whose *The Governing of Men: General Principles and Recommendations Based on Experience at a Japanese Relocation Camp* (Princeton, N.J.: Princeton University Press, 1945) is about Poston, and the often obtuse apologia by the WRA's second director, Dillon H. Myer, *Uprooted Americans: The Japanese Americans and the War Relocation Authority During World War II* (Tucson: University of Arizona Press, 1971). In addition, the WRA produced dozens of books and pamphlets and many of its social scientists published essays about their work. The most comprehensive bibliography of this kind of material appears in Appendices I and II of Edward H. Spicer, Asael T. Hansen, Katherine Luomala, and Marvin K. Opler, *Impounded People: Japanese-Americans in the Relocation Centers* (Tucson: University of Arizona Press, 1969).

Life in the camps has been recounted by many former inmates. Among the most insightful are Mine Okubo, *Citizen 13660* (New York: Columbia University Press, 1946; 2nd ed., New York: Arno Press, 1978; 3rd ed., Seattle: University of Washington Press, 1983); Monica Sone, *Nisei Daughter* (Boston: Little, Brown, 1953; 2nd ed., Seattle: University of Washington Press, 1979); Daisuke Kitagawa, *Issei and Nisei: The Internment Years* (New York: The Seabury Press, 1967); Jeanne Wakatsuki Houston and James D. Houston, *Farewell to Manzanar* (Boston: Houghton Mifflin, 1973); and Yoshiko Uchida, *Desert Exile: The Uprooting of a Japanese American Family* (Seattle: University of Washington Press, 1982). Karl G. Yoneda, *Ganbatte: Sixty-year Struggle of a Kibei Worker* (Los Angeles: UCLA Asian American Studies Center, 1983), is from the point of view of a dedicated Stalinist. The diversity of reactions over time may be seen in the oral histories published in Arthur A. Hansen and Betty E. Mitson, eds., *Voices Long Silent: An Oral Inquiry into the Japanese American Evacuation* (Fullerton, Calif.: California State University, 1974), and John Tateishi, *And Justice For All: An Oral History of the Japanese American Detention Camps* (New York: Random House, 1984). In a class by themselves are Allen H. Eaton, *Beauty Behind Barbed Wire: The Arts of the Japanese in Our Relocation Camps* (New York: Harper, 1952) and a collection by one of America's greatest photographers, Ansel Adams, *Born Free and Equal: The Story of Loyal Japanese Americans* (New York: U.S. Camera, 1944).

A number of volumes survey the whole camp experience. Among the most important are Carey McWilliams, *Prejudice: Japanese-Americans: Symbol of Racial Intolerance* (Boston: Little, Brown, 1944); Morton Grodzins, *Americans Betrayed: Politics and the Japanese Evacuation* (Chicago: University of Chicago Press, 1949); Jacobus tenBroek, Edward N. Barnhart, and Floyd W. Matson, *Prejudice, War, and the Constitution* (Berkeley and Los Angeles: University of California Press, 1958); Allan R. Bosworth, *America's Concentration Camps* (New York: W. W. Norton, 1967); Audrey Girdner and Anne Loftis, *The Great Betrayal: The Evacuation of the Japanese-Americans During World War II* (New York: Macmillan, 1969); Roger

Daniels, *Concentration Camps, USA: Japanese Americans and World War II* (New York: Holt, Rinehart and Winston, 1971); and Michi Weglyn, *Years of Infamy: The Untold Story of America's Concentration Camps* (New York: William Morrow, 1976). Of volumes devoted to individual camps, the best are the very brief treatment of Topaz by Leonard J. Arrington, *The Price of Prejudice: The Japanese-American Relocation Center in Utah During World War II* (Logan: Utah State University Press, 1962) and Douglas W. Nelson, *Heart Mountain: The Story of an American Concentration Camp* (Madison: State Historical Society of Wisconsin, 1976). A brilliant doctoral dissertation by Thomas James, "Exile Within: The Schooling of Japanese Americans, 1942–1945" completed at Stanford in 1984 will surely see print soon. For an account of interrelationships between a relocation center and the community around it, see Jessie A. Garrett and Ronald C. Larson, eds., *Camp and Community: Manzanar and the Owens Valley* (Fullerton, Calif.: California State University, 1977).

Despite this rich literature much remains to be done. Perhaps our greatest lack is a good study of Tule Lake; more comprehensive studies of the kind pioneered in this volume by Professors Culley and Kashima are needed, as is a study of the quasi-internment camp at Seabrook Farms, New Jersey.

Roger Daniels

Camp Memories: Rough and Broken Shards

Toyo Suyemoto Kawakami

In his book *The Immense Journey*, anthropologist Loren Eiseley wrote: "It is a funny thing what the brain will do with memories and how it will treasure them, and finally bring them into odd juxtapositions with other things, as though it wanted to make a design, or get some meaning out of them, whether you want it or not, or even see it." So it is that I have retained memories of the evacuation and internment that my people on the West Coast were subjected to in 1942. And so it was in September 1981 when I testified at the Chicago hearings before the Commission on Wartime Relocation and Internment of Civilians; I was made keenly aware that the burden of memories, many sad and heavy, remains in the minds of many.

My family—my parents, sisters, brothers, and not-quite-year-old son—and I arrived on October 3, 1942, at the Central Utah Relocation Project, known more familiarly as Topaz and dubbed "The Jewel of the Desert." We were among the last to leave the Tanforan Assembly Center, a former racetrack in San Bruno, California. We had traveled for three days on an old, rickety train to Delta, a farming town about seventeen miles from the camp and then by bus to Topaz.

As we stepped down from the bus, we were at the entry gate and I could see the earlier arrivals, among them my brother Bill, waiting to greet us. Bill had come in the advance work group of 214 volunteers who had reached Topaz on September 11. He was a bacteriologist, so he was included in the sanitary engineering crew. A small band of uniformed Boy Scouts stood in the hot sun and played on their brass instruments.

When I heard them blare out the strains of "Hail to California," the song of my alma mater, I was suddenly homesick for Berkeley.

Although we had grown accustomed to the barracks in Tanforan, this permanent camp was a strangely desolate scene of low, black, tar-paper buildings, row on row, through each block. The camp was only two-thirds finished, construction continuing even after people were moved into the unroofed barracks. The camp contained forty-two blocks, thirty-five of which were residential. All the blocks looked alike, so that later, weeks after we had settled in, camp residents would occasionally lose their sense of direction at night and wander into a barracks not their own, much to their embarrassment and that of the occupants.

With eleven members, our family was larger than most, so we were assigned to the two middle rooms of a barracks in Block 4. To go from one room to the other, we had to go outside. My brothers quickly opted to occupy one of these. Mother soon became tired of going out whenever she needed to see one of them, so one day Father cut a door-sized opening between them.

The first sight of our rooms was dismal—no furniture, unfinished walls and ceiling, a two-inch layer of fine dust on the floor and windowsills. We had to sweep out the dust and mop before we could bring our suitcases in. Army cots were delivered that night, giving us something to sit on. Eventually Father made a table and stools of varying heights from scrap lumber. Long afterwards I captured the initial impression of that moment in a sonnet.

Monument at Topaz, 1983. Courtesy Sandra C. Taylor.

Worker irrigating in the bleak landscape of Topaz. Photo by Francis Stewart, March 15, 1943. Courtesy National Archives, Washington, D.C.

Barracks Home
This is our barracks, squatting on the ground,
Tar-papered shack, partitioned into rooms
By sheetrock walls, transmitting every sound
Of neighbors' gossip or the sweep of brooms
The open door welcomes the refugees,
And now at last there is no need to roam
Afar: here space enlarges memories
Beyond the bounds of camp and this new home.

The floor is carpeted with dust, wind-borne
Dry alkali, patterned by insect feet.
What peace can such a place as this impart?
We can but sense, bewildered and forlorn,
That time, disrupted by the war from neat
Routines, must now adjust within the heart.

As at Tanforan, we adjusted to restricted living and made the best of going to the mess hall at specified times for our meals; walking half a block to the latrine building in any weather; applying for the available jobs; opening schools, churches, and libraries; and trying to lead as normal an existence as possible. Several of my sisters and brothers applied for work at the hospital and I for teaching in the camp high school and in the adult education division. Since education is traditionally respected among the Japanese, two nursery schools were established for preschool children and elementary and high schools for the older children.

I taught high school English and Latin during the day and basic English to Issei and Kibei students in the evening. The high school students were Americanized in their speech, manners, and attitudes, whereas the adults were almost deferential towards me as their teacher, although I was as young as some of their children.

I found teaching adult education rewarding. The classes in basic English were on three levels: the beginning group, whose comprehension of English was about that of the second grade; the intermediate, whose reading skill approximated that of the fourth grade; and the advanced, about the seventh grade. Among the advanced were some Kibei, who had been born in the United States, but were sent to Japan to live with relatives during their childhood. For one semester I taught an evening extension course in creative writing and had college-level Nisei students, several from Hawaii, and one Englishwoman from Yorkshire in camp because of her half-Japanese son.

The beginning adult students were mainly the Issei, a few of them the parents of my high school pupils. I truly enjoyed their presence in my classes, and my fellow teachers in the adult education division felt the same about their groups. The Issei's reason for learning English, so they stated, was to better adapt to the "outside" when war was over and to understand their children, whose values sometimes conflicted with theirs. These adult students often had difficulty with pronunciation, providing hilarious moments for all of us. They would even pun on some words. By saying "So Utah!" and prolonging the vowels, they could imply in Japanese, "So it is said!" The l and r, the v and b, and th were difficult for them, yet they did practice earnestly. I would hear suppressed giggling among the women when *salary* and *celery* came out sounding the same as *sa-ra-ri* or when *very* was enunciated as *berry*. Then they would apologize for their mistakes. Many a time as

I faced them in the classroom, I felt humbled that here I was teaching them when I myself should have been their pupil learning from them of their enduring patience, reticent affection, and wise sense of humor.

After teaching for almost two years, I was transferred to work in the public library. The Topaz Public Library originated when 5,000 books, gifts from personal friends and from California schools, colleges, and public libraries had been assembled and shipped to Utah. Topaz residents donated additional books and magazines until the library's holdings numbered almost 7,000 books and several thousand issues of periodicals. The public library was dependent upon minimal fines and donations to purchase needed supplies and books. From this meager income we started a rental collection of current best-sellers. A five cents per week rental charge and a quick turnover enabled us to order more new titles.

There were delays in getting the roof of the library tarred, the cast-iron stoves installed for heating, and the walls and ceilings sheetrocked for insulation. The climate in Utah sometimes necessitated closing the library in the afternoon because of the bitter cold.

The library opened on December 1, 1942, and the next day presented a concert of classical recordings. Audience response was so enthusiastic that concerts were given every Wednesday. Program notes, with information about the selections, composers, and the following week's program, were mimeographed for those attending the concerts. Library notes and book reviews appeared in the *Topaz Times*, the camp newspaper, which was also mimeographed. The library was later moved to another barracks in Block 16. Half the building space, totaling 20 by 100 feet, contained adult fiction and nonfiction and the other half, the children's section and periodicals. One small end room was used for bookbinding and mending, the other end for an office and cataloging; mess-hall tables, with attached benches, filled the reading room.

A rotating collection of selected titles was borrowed from the Salt Lake County Library at Midvale and shelved in a special section, adding variety to the overall collection. In January 1943, college libraries of Utah and the University of California at Berkeley granted interlibrary loan services, extending the scope of the public library considerably.

Towards the end of February 1943, gravel was laid for a pathway from the unpaved road to the library so people could come to the building without slipping in mud or slush. When attendance reached about 450 persons each day, the library was kept open in the evenings. To brief the residents on world news, the reports division of the camp administration sent weekly news-maps for posting on the library bulletin

The high school library at Topaz. Courtesy National Archives, Washington, D.C.

board. Outside newspapers were received on subscription, among them the *Oakland Tribune* and the *San Francisco Chronicle* for the many Bay Area residents in camp.

In time, Relocation Authority funding increased the number of magazine subscriptions from fourteen to fifty-two. The rental collection also grew, and bright covers from new books decorated the library walls. Since the rental books had been made possible from fees paid by the camp people, they were sold just before the library closed, at greatly reduced prices, to benefit the Topaz Scholarship Fund and help high school students to relocate.

As 1945 turned towards autumn, the relocation camps began to close and people left to start life over on the outside. In Topaz, as more residents left and the blocks emptied, I thought wonderingly of this place, a community created by government order and now dispersed. Conjecture and wonderment remained long after my family had moved to Cincinnati, and still more time had to pass before I could write farewell to our internment camp.

Topaz, Utah
The desert must have claimed its own
Now that the wayfarers are gone,
And silence has replaced voices
Except for intermittent noises,
Like windy footsteps through the dust,
Or gliding of a snake that must
Escape the sun, or sage rustling.
Or soft brush of a quickened wing
Against the air.—Stillness is change
For this abandoned place, where strange

Toyo Suyemoto Kawakami at the monument at Topaz, March, 1983. Courtesy Sandra C. Taylor.

And foreign tongues had routed peace
Until the refugees' release
Restored calm to the wilderness,
And prairie dogs no longer fear
When shadows shift and disappear.
The crows fly straight through settling dusk,
The desert like an empty husk,
Holding the small swift sounds that run
To cover when the day is done.

Thus it was, as I wrote my friend Mine Okubo, the Nisei artist, now of New York, who recorded our stay at Tanforan and Topaz with her sketches in her book *Citizen 13660*; I have shared with you some camp memories:

Camp Memories
I have dredged up
Hard fragments lost
I thought, in years
Of whirlwind dust.

Exposed to light,
Silently rough
And broken shards
Confront belief.

An Issei Internee's Experiences

Take Uchida

I was born in Kyoto, Japan, on January 2, 1890. In 1914, I came to Pasadena, California. I was already engaged to Setsuzo Uchida and married him in Los Angeles. We were well acquainted in Japan; he was a graduate from the Imperial University of Tokyo and I from a Methodist-affiliated college, Aoyama Jo-Gakuin. He came to America in 1912. We both taught Japanese in Los Angeles, San Pedro, and Salt Lake City, and then spent ten years in Idaho Falls, Idaho. We have two sons, Kenichi and Ryo.

My husband, Setsuzo, and I were picked up by the FBI early in the morning of December 8, 1941, in Idaho Falls because we were Japanese-language teachers and my husband was the secretary of the Japanese Association, an organization assisting Issei needing help in interpreting business and legal problems. We were taken to the Seattle Immigration office immediately. We were not given a chance to store our belongings or furniture—just enough time to finish breakfast. From Seattle, my husband was immediately sent to Bismarck, North Dakota. I remained interned in Seattle until April 1942, when I was sent to the Federal Women's Penitentiary in Seagoville, Texas, where many Japanese ladies and their children from Peru and the Panama Canal Zone were already interned. A little later, a group of ladies from Hawaii joined us. Most of the ladies were schoolteachers and the educated wives of influential businessmen engaged in business with Japan. I was interned in Seagoville for about two years, but in May 1944 transferred to a family internment camp in Crystal City, Texas. About a month before our transfer to Crystal City, I was joined by my husband, who had been interned at Fort Sill, Oklahoma, and Camp Livingston, Louisiana. In Seagoville and Crystal City, I helped with camp affairs as an interpreter and counselor because most of the internees from Panama and Peru spoke only Japanese and Spanish.

At this time, men interned in Lordsburg, New Mexico; Camp Livingston, Louisiana; and Bismarck, North Dakota, were allowed to join their families in Crystal City. Some families left the relocation centers to join husbands and fathers who were sent to the family camp.

One person I remember very well was a Mr. O'Rourke, who was the superintendent of the camp. He was a most compassionate gentleman and an acquaintance of Ambassador Kichisaburo Nomura of

Japan. We were all very well treated, with kindness and respect. We remained in Crystal City until July 1945, when we were paroled to go to Ogden, Utah, where we stayed with friends on a big farm.

We were discriminated against, especially when we knew that the United States was at war with Germany and Italy as well as with Japan. Especially wronged were our sons and daughters, born and raised in this country, who were American citizens but suffered because they had Japanese faces and parents born in Japan, who were denied citizenship even though they had been residents for many, many years. My son, Kenichi, joined the Utah National Guard in July 1940, right after graduating from Utah State Agricultural College. The National Guard was federalized for active duty in March 1941. Ken served on active duty during World War II until December 1945. Our second son, Ryo, was accepted by Brigham Young University, the only college in Utah that accepted Japanese students during wartime. Ryo joined the army in 1944 after graduating from BYU and served in Italy and France with the 442nd Regimental Combat Team.

We lost almost all our material possessions when we were so suddenly uprooted and shipped out of Idaho. Because we are Christians, we were not bitter about being singled out and discriminated against during the war years. I felt it was my duty to help and love all the frustrated, displaced people and especially to help the children and youths who couldn't understand why they were in camp. Since there were no Christian ministers with us in Seagoville or Crystal City while I was there, many believers gathered on Sundays and sang hymns, read the scriptures, and prayed together.

I did not notice any terribly depressed or angry internees. We were all trying to make the best of the situation and helping each other keep spirits up. I was always so busy working in the camp office or helping the families with their children's problems that I had little time to think about my impressions of the internment. We Isseis were not even granted the right to apply for citizenship although we had lived here some thirty years. We were like the "man without a country."

Upon arriving in Ogden, Utah, we had to start our lives all over again. We were not farmers and the hard work was quite a change for us. In December 1945, Ken was discharged from the army and he and his wife, Susan, and son, Don, joined us on the 540-acre farm. In the meantime, my husband had contracted Hodgkin's disease; he passed away in 1948 at age sixty-seven. Ryo remained in the army and his wife, Ruth, and daughter, Chiyo, were with him in Europe and in Japan. They are now living in San Francisco.

I decided to go back to teaching Japanese after I moved with Ken and his family to a new home in the city. Ken commuted to the farm each day. I taught on Saturdays at Clearfield Junior High and taught private classes in our home to Mormon missionaries and air force members who were going to be stationed in Japan. I became the first Japanese language teacher at Weber State College in Ogden in 1955. Another language teacher and I taught English to a class of 160 Issei so they could pass the examination for their citizenship papers, which they all received.

In June 1969, I received the Sixth Order of the Sacred Treasure from the Emperor of Japan at a ceremony in San Francisco, an award for contributing to the furtherance of cultural relations between the United States and Japan. As small as my contributions were, I felt highly honored in receiving this award.

In 1981, I still live in Ogden with Ken and Susan. I have enjoyed retirement doing oil paintings, attending the senior citizens' classes at the Golden Hour Center, and still trying to do my share of church work. I still write as a correspondent for the newspaper *Utah Nippo* and try to keep healthy by faithfully doing physical exercises. These exercises were taught to me at Seagoville by a lady from Hawaii at the time of our internment. I met this lady on my last trip to Hawaii and she looked so well—she is eighty-nine years old. I am trying to keep healthy not only in body but in mind and soul. I am very grateful to God for all the rich blessings and for allowing me to live this long. My motto has always been: "To serve my fellowmen to the best of my ability" by the help and grace of God.

My Two Years at Heart Mountain:
The Difficult Role of an Applied Anthropologist

Asael T. Hansen

EDITOR'S NOTE

The role of the community analyst in the WRA camps, an example of social science in the service of the government, was, is, and will probably remain a controversial one. It has been charged, foolishly, that anthropologists planned the whole evacuation so that they would have subjects to study. Other quite serious charges have been made by Professor Peter T. Suzuki in "Anthropologists in the Wartime Camps for Japanese Americans: A Documentary Study," *Dialectical Anthropology* 6(1981):23–60.

This memoir by a community analyst is thus an important element in an ongoing debate. The editors note that the perceptions of the analyst and his circle of informants are not universally shared. The considerable group that supported the principled draft resistance do not share Hansen's notion that "the trial stirred very little interest in the camp." The draft resisters were men who answered "yes-yes" to the crucial questions in the loyalty questionnaire: the government did not try to draft those who said "no-no." For an account of the Heart Mountain draft resisters from a generally sympathetic point of view see Douglas W. Nelson, *Heart Mountain: The History of an American Concentration Camp*, Madison, Wis., University of Wisconsin Press, 1976.

Roger Daniels

My role, and that of other community analysts, was to establish rapport with the evacuees confined in Heart Mountain Relocation Center, Wyoming, and to provide realistic information on evacuees to WRA administrators. If rapport could be established, I hoped to inquire into the thinking, feeling, and behavior of the camp residents. Then, assuming sufficient skill in organizing basic data, my reports would present some of the realities of evacuee life.

The reason for setting up the Community Analysis Section within the War Relocation Authority several months after its creation was the belief, or hope, that trained social scientists with no other duties would learn enough about the internees to improve their situation. If the formula was to work, the administrators, as well as the residents, would need to accept my competence as an observer and reporter.

A few words should be said about official rules governing my duties as a community analyst. In no way was I to be involved in security or police matters. In written reports, my sources were to be anonymous; no one could demand a name. And I was to be assigned no administrative responsibility, even temporarily.

Did evacuees respond readily to my efforts to establish rapport? Of course not, except for a very few. The government that had uprooted them and sent them into exile paid my salary. This identified me with their keepers. The whole experience had been bruising and hurtful for them. Besides, there was a widespread view that no *hakujin* (white person) could ever empathize with Japanese Americans. Their lives for decades tended to justify this conviction. I had to rely on those who, for one reason or another, were willing to share their experiences with me. My early weeks in the camp were a bit lonely.

Did WRA administrators actually believe that the information I gathered and transmitted would contribute to better administration? Actually, many administrators, both in the camps and in Washington, had opposed the creation of the Community Analysis Section, and some remained skeptical. This should astonish no one. Even as my appointment was being processed, the Heart Mountain project director made it clear that he would prefer not to have a community analyst on his staff.

From the outset three men well up in the Washington WRA bureaucracy wished me well and viewed me as one seriously interested in the Japanese Americans and seeking to improve the reputation of the social sciences. The chief analyst had said in an extended Washington briefing, "What we really want are detailed, day-by-day, eyewitness accounts of what goes on in the camps." He suggested that trend reports be done weekly; these became my primary mission. From time to time, special reports done upon request dealt with crises and topics of particular interest.

Material transmitted to Washington went first to Heart Mountain's chief of community services, my immediate superior in the camp hierarchy. He kept a copy, handed one to the project director, and gave four others to the reports office for dispatch to Community Analysis Headquarters in Washington.

From the start at Heart Mountain, the community-service chief did all he could to encourage me. His university training had been in social science, and in his career with the Department of Agriculture he had

Heart Mountain towers at the end of F Street, the main thorough-
fare of the Heart Mountain Relocation Center. Photo by Tom
Parker, August 28, 1942. Courtesy National Archives, Washington, D.C.

Bill Hosokawa, editor of the *Heart Mountain Sentinel*, camp newspaper, a University of Washington graduate and former West Coast
newspaperman and foreign correspondent, conducts a biweekly
class in journalism for the reporters of his *Sentinel* staff. Photo by
Tom Parker, January 8, 1943. Courtesy National Archives,
Washington, D.C.

dealt mainly with people rather than things. The project director welcomed me politely, of course; some of
my early reports evoked his favorable comment.

This essay is based upon a much longer memoir of
my experiences at Heart Mountain, part of an oral
history archive compiled by Lawrence C. Kelly, Department of History, North Texas State University in
Denton, Texas. Let me begin with the impact the
camp first had on me.

I arrived at Heart Mountain on a cold Monday morning in late January [1942]. . . . [I]t was still dark. . . .
There were introductions and . . . I was sworn in and put
on the payroll. After it was full daylight, . . . someone
[said] that it might be a good idea for me to get an overall
look at the Camp, . . . that it would be all right to crawl
through the barbed-wire fence; it had long since become
just a symbol of confinement. . . . Passage through the
front gate required a pass, authorized by someone in the
administration and issued and collected by a soldier at the
gate. Anywhere else, the evacuees who had terrified
Californians in January of 1942 could crawl through the
fence and walk at will over the Wyoming hills.

The camp sat on a partially developed reclamation
project . . . surrounded by plenty of unoccupied territory.
I carefully avoided the barbs as I crawled through . . . and
climbed the next higher ancient river terrace above the
one on which the Camp was situated. A feeble sun shone
through a light haze and revealed the scene clearly. It
spread below me, row after row of black barracks, spaced
with rigid army regularity. The barracks were clumped
into blocks to provide a system of fire breaks—a proper
precaution in arid Wyoming with its brisk winds. Wisps
of smoke arose from hundreds of chimneys, generated by
hundreds of army-issue coal-burning stoves (space heat-
ers). There was a thin layer of snow on the ground. . . . Its
whiteness set off the utter blackness of the barracks. At

that date, this was the temporary and involuntary residence of a few more than 10,000 persons. As I gazed, the
scene really shook me: My God, I thought, evacuation
really did happen; this thing I see actually does exist.
Other shocks and tremors disturbed me over the months
ahead.

Inside the barracks, the scene became less stark.
The builders had been accustomed to putting up army
installations with rooms of uniform size. Somehow,
word had reached them that this arrangement hardly fit
a civilian population composed of individuals and
families. The rooms, euphemistically called apartments, were of three sizes. The smallest apartments
were at the ends of each barracks and came to be
known as honeymoon apartments, as newly married
couples greatly preferred them.

While it is obvious that my work at Heart Mountain could not begin until I got there, some evacuees
had investigated me before my arrival. The federal
forms I had completed in applying for employment had
been submitted to Washington and then forwarded to
the camp where they were available for inspection
several weeks before I showed up. Interested officials
looked at them; so did interested evacuees, mostly
Nisei with college backgrounds. Perhaps as many as
thirty evacuees knew that I was born in Utah, that my
bachelor's degree was from Utah State and my Ph.D.
from Wisconsin, that I had done research for three
years in Mexico, and that I was on leave from Miami
University in Ohio.

Who were these evacuee investigators? One had
been the assistant of the previous community analyst

and was to be my assistant. Others were friends of his, and together they constituted a loosely knit cluster of persons with university backgrounds. Once on the job, my assistant proved to be extremely competent. After some thirty hours of intense conversation, we were colleagues and friends. When he went into the army four months later, I missed him, for he had helped me greatly in getting started and in moving into the camp community.

Soon his friends were my friends or comfortable acquaintances. They told me a great deal about Japanese Americans, evacuation, and camp life. I sensed they wanted me to accept their interpretation of the Japanese American minority. But my assistant was also a good social scientist and strove for objectivity. He recognized that there were various interpretations of the Japanese Americans and their world. Probably most Issei and many Nisei considered the college people "too assimilated." It was necessary that I establish communication with these more conservative elements, for the Issei made the major decisions for the camp community.

Before turning to the Issei, let me give a brief example of the problems of assimilation and the generation gap: Two Nisei girls in their early twenties worked for me as clerk-typists. Each had grown up in a situation where she associated with as many non-Japanese as Japanese. Then the evacuation plunged them into an environment that was totally Japanese American. Soon they discovered they lacked an awareness of many of the details of their culture that other Nisei had. This deficiency caused occasional awkwardnesses. Both were striving to fit in with the flow of camp life. In addition, each was in love with a Nisei boy whose parents were more "japanesy" than her own parents. One girl reported that her boyfriend had told her seriously that her Japanese speech would have to improve greatly and that she would have to acquire the behavior his parents expected of a bride-to-be or they might disapprove of the marriage—maybe not block it, but there would be strains. These relationships intensified their desire to reabsorb the culture they had gotten away from.

I realized that, in a sense, they were striving to do what I was striving to do: Their objective was to learn to live in a Japanese American context, and mine to learn enough about that context to function acceptably as an ethnographer and applied anthropologist.

Very soon after I reached camp, an Issei sought me out to offer his help. He came recommended by the administrators who had always found him cooperative. He had reason to be cooperative, for he was a lonely Issei, outside the mainstream. Little by little, I got his story:

His birthplace was Okinawa; his parents had had enough resources to send him to Tokyo to finish his schooling, but he experienced many unpleasantries because of his Okinawan background. He emigrated to California with a working command of English and a little capital. Californians, he discovered, generally held similar attitudes toward all persons from Japan, and Okinawans were no different. His import business prospered and he became active in the Los Angeles Chamber of Commerce. Many Issei considered him too pro-American. It was my opinion that he just felt that America had been good to him, that is, until the war and evacuation. Anyway, he was definitely a fringe Issei and did help me, though not as an Issei. He was intelligent and possessed a lot of information.

Five months after my arrival at Heart Mountain I established rapport with a mainstream Issei who had served continuously as the representative of his block in the camp's council, an indication of his acceptance. He was more assimilated to American ways than the average Issei, but he was Honshu-born and generally acceptable in spite of his partial conversion to Christianity in Japan, his bachelor's degree in economics from Columbia University, his marriage to the daughter of a Japanese Methodist minister, and his half-American half-Japanese life-style.

Almost everything conspired to bring us together as friends. He was an intellectual and enjoyed talking with me on many topics. He had gone into the seed and fertilizer business in order to support his wife and three children. His wife's sister, her husband, and two daughters relocated to Oxford, Ohio, just after I went to Heart Mountain. My wife had the family in for tea while they were very new newcomers, a gesture they appreciated. The very next day an airmail letter was on the way to Heart Mountain from the wife in Oxford to the wife in the camp. They *must* do something for the Miami University professor serving as the project's community analyst. A few evenings later, I had a pleasant meal in a barracks room, the wartime home of a family of five.

Why then did it require five months for me to establish full rapport with this amiable Issei gentleman? One night, after we had been drinking coffee and conversing for quite a while, he explained in his beautiful and eloquent broken English something that had been on his mind for some time. My rendering loses much of the flavor of his speech:

> I liked you from the very first. I felt certain that you were a professor on leave and not a spy of some kind that many people in the camp think you are. And I thought you were a good man. But it was not clear to me what you really intended to do here. Were you here only to collect information on the Japanese to report to your WRA

bosses in Washington? You explained that the idea was that, if Washington had good information on us, they would understand us better and administer us better. But I couldn't be sure. And then I wondered if you intended, as a professor of anthropology, to study the Japanese as if they were guinea pigs and to write some articles and maybe to get a raise in salary.

I really wanted to help you. Still, I hesitated. You may have noticed that I sometimes changed the subject when you raised questions that I preferred not to talk about. . . .

What I had to settle in my mind and heart was that you really *cared* about the Japanese, that you were sincerely and deeply concerned with their future. I had to feel that the welfare of the Japanese was more important to you than your professional career. And that, when you wrote to Washington about us evacuees, your purpose *was not* to please your Washington bosses or to make their job easier but to bring them to a better understanding of us and our problems.

A few weeks ago I . . . made up my mind that you really did care. So tonight I assure you that, from now on, you can ask me any questions; I will tell you what I know. If I believe that there are better informed persons in this camp, I will seek their counsel.

This Issei had placed a heavy burden on me. I had to accept it willingly if not gladly. The better the quality of the information I received, the better I might be able to do my job for the WRA—and for the administration and the evacuees.

A year later (July 1945), I had acquired about as many Issei friends as I could communicate with regularly enough to keep the relationship warm and relaxed. One of these was the councilman of the block where my office was located. (In January 1944, the administration building was overcrowded, so I had been assigned a room in a barracks. My presence worried my evacuee neighbors for many months.) As our friendship finally ripened, he confessed that for a long time he had carefully avoided my office and me. To be seen with me might alienate his constituents, the residents of his block. Eventually, he invited me to his barracks room for coffee and conversation. He called his barracks room his "abode" to make it seem more homelike. His mastery of English was impressive. He complained jocosely, "A problem I have faced living in this country is buying Japanese-English dictionaries. I've been here for forty years. See that dictionary? It's about number thirty-nine and needs replacing soon."

I listened with fascination to his reminiscences of his childhood on the beautiful island of Shikoku in the Inland Sea and of a period when he was a successful fish merchant in British Columbia. It was the rich detail that evoked my fascination; and he was extremely well informed on the conditions of the world.

One day in July 1945 as we walked toward his abode and my office, he indicated some things had disturbed him that he had decided to share with me. His words are reproduced almost as they came from his lips.

Before the defeat of Germany, there was a war in the East and a war in the West. Now, there is only a war in the Pacific. Before, I thought that the conflict would exhaust both nations and end in a stalemate and a negotiated peace. Now, I fear for Japan.

On Seasonal Leave I worked for many months in Spokane's railroad yards. It was clear what was happening. An endless stream of freight trains went through the yards. Those going East were almost empty, to be reloaded for another trip West. It seems that Japan will finally be overcome.

WRA cancelled my Seasonal Leave and forced me to return to the camp. I don't know why. I was just building up a reserve to take care of my family. And I thought I was helping this country, too.

When I re-entered the camp, I was shocked. Many Issei still believed that Japan would be victorious. They pay no attention to real news, just to Japanese propaganda. When I tell them about the many freight trains going West through Spokane, they don't believe me. Sometimes they say that I just made it up and become angry at me. They don't know what is going on and they don't want to know.

I follow the real war news. When Saipan and Guam fell, it worried me profoundly. Japan could be bombed from the air. When American forces invaded Okinawa and could not be repelled, I realized that the Empire was wounded, that it might bleed to death and suffer utter destruction.

But I do not think that will happen. At some point the Emperor will say, *cease*. He will want to save the seed of the Japanese people.

During the summer of 1945, a request came from the Washington office of WRA, instructing analysts to find out how the Issei felt towards the United States and Japan. What were their long-term plans? The request, it seemed to me, verged on asking me to engage in espionage, and it was my understanding that espionage lay outside my duties. I hoped that by sufficient indirection anything approaching interrogation could be avoided and began with an intelligent Issei friend, a successful landscaper from Los Angeles and a man respected among Issei. We talked about his sons, both of whom were doing well in schools of higher education outside of the camp, and about other topics. Eventually, I wondered what he expected to do after the war. He replied that he would go back to Los Angeles and seek to reestablish his business. "And when you are old enough to retire?" I asked.

His answer really told me. "I'll retire in Los Angeles. And when I die, I'll be buried there. I own a cemetery lot large enough for me and my family. I do not know what to think about the United States. This country excludes me from citizenship. But I feel that I am a Californian. Even more strongly, I feel that Los Angeles is my home city."

In a different context, another Issei mentioned with some pride that he was one of the founders of the Japanese Cemetery Association of San Jose. Can there be any question about which country he expected to be his home and that of his descendents? Did prewar army intelligence experts gather information on this point?

An event that occurred during the winter of 1944–45 gives an indication of the degree of acceptance I achieved that first year.

My first mainstream Issei friend recommended that I become a sponsor of a Kabuki play; this would involve a contribution of $10 or so. The rewards: a privileged seat and a 10″ × 10″ cardboard notice (in Japanese) giving my name and my contribution for the admiration of the audience. There were dozens of such notices about Issei who, even in camp, could still afford to be patrons of the arts. And there I was among them—which had been my friend's intent. He pointed to mine, read it in English, and commented that the calligraphy was excellent.

An account of my experiences at Heart Mountain should include information about two crises that took place while I was there. I noted earlier that WRA regulations defined my job in a way that exempted me from anything involving security or the police; however, this did not prevent my participation in the following incidents:

A federal judge and a federal prosecutor paid no attention to the regulations of WRA. I (along with several others of the Project staff) was subpoenaed to testify at the trial of seven evacuees charged with conspiracy to interfere with the operation of Selective Service at Heart Mountain. (Selective Service, closed to Nisei even before the evacuation decision in early 1942, was reopened to them in January 1944.) Heart Mountain had experienced considerable disturbance during February, March, and April, 1944—tapering off thereafter. And about 88 draftees from our camp refused to accept induction and were sentenced to prison. I had submitted a substantial report near the end of March, covering the peak of the crisis. It was written with difficulty, increased by my having been on the job for such a short time. . . . As soon as the document was turned in and scanned by certain Project officials, a telephone call told Washington that a report by the community analyst was on its way by air. Probably nothing I have ever written has been read more avidly and more carefully; . . . readers included FBI investigators.

The trial of the seven accused conspirators was finally held in October 1944. By then, the draft crisis had subsided. Still, when the subpoena came, I felt heartsick. To me it seemed entirely possible that my presence at the trial might end my usefulness as a community analyst. . . . My Project Director did all in his power to have me exempted. He appealed to the Judge and Prosecutor and asked the Washington office to intervene in my behalf, . . . to no avail. I went with the other . . . witnesses from our Camp and spent a week or so in Cheyenne. As it developed, I was in the courtroom only one or two days; only during the process of jury selection. . . .

Back in the Camp, I sought out my closest evacuee friends and inquired about my reputation among evacuees. Their reports encouraged me greatly: (1) The acute draft crisis was months in the past and those called had been accepting induction, perhaps with misgivings but without protest. (2) The Cheyenne trial (June 1944) stirred little interest in the Camp—tension was greatest in March. (3) Very few persons even knew that I had gone to Cheyenne as a potential witness. (4) Those who did know blamed me not at all. They told me what I'd been told before—that, generally, Japanese and Japanese Americans held that subjects/citizens should obey the orders of their Government, and that was what I had done. The months that followed indicated that the Cheyenne episode had had no influence on my subsequent effectiveness (or ineffectiveness) as a community analyst.

In retrospect, I have told friends that I lived for about two years behind barbed-wire fence at Heart Mountain with 10,000 other Japanese. It took many months before I felt that way. And, as the closing of the camp approached, I felt a strong urge to be a part of the exodus. I wanted to go among the resettled (or unsettled) evacuees to observe how they were faring and then go back to Washington to help prepare the final report. I mentioned this to my project director, who thought it a bit crazy, but forwarded my request to Washington. It was turned down.

The last trainload of evacuees left Heart Mountain on the evening of Saturday, November 10, 1945, and the final trend report was written in an empty camp on November 19. The two paragraphs that follow completed that report:

Heart Mountain was never a lovely place. But when it was full of people and one knew many of the people, even the barracks did not look so black and bleak. On Sunday and Monday, November 11 and 12, it was truly unlovely. It was cold, quiet, and empty. Trash heaps lined the streets. The atmosphere of desertion and desolation was made more marked by lonesome, hungry cats crawling over the trash heaps.

The community was obviously and totally dead. Since then, the project staff, acting now in the role of morticians, have been preparing the physical remains for such disposition as awaits a dead community.

A Teacher at Topaz

Eleanor Gerard Sekerak

I was teaching a criminology class at San Francisco City College when a field trip took us to observe a camp set up at Sharps Park by the Immigration and Naturalization Service after Pearl Harbor. This was my first contact with internment. Other contacts quickly followed: I volunteered time as an interviewer for those Oakland residents of Japanese ancestry who wished to move east before the "freeze" date set for evacuation. A hastily assembled crew worked all day and late into the night, checking destination addresses and writing travel passes. By midnight, March 29, 1942, long lines of Japanese Americans were still standing outside waiting to be processed. Dramatically, an army officer strode in, climbed up to a huge wall clock, set the hands at 11:55 p.m. and announced, "Ladies and gentlemen, it will remain this time until you are finished— please proceed." By 4 a.m., all those who planned to relocate voluntarily had been processed and the army gallantly escorted the weary interviewers home. For me, the evacuation had become real.

The next event, a few days later, made it even more personal. In a graduate class on the Berkeley campus, the professor unexpectedly informed us that one of our colleagues would be giving his final oral presentation early. Hiro Katayama bade us farewell and left the classroom—his destination Tanforan. He had stayed in class until the last possible moment on Friday, April 3.

A number of Nisei students attended Technical High School in Oakland, the location of my second supervised teaching assignment. Faculty members worried aloud about their Nisei students. What would happen, especially to the seniors removed from classes before the end of the semester? What about their plans for college? I had no Nisei in my class, but during hall duty I had occasion to admonish, almost daily, a youngster who always dashed by as though on roller skates. Once while reminding him not to run in the halls, I asked his name. "Bill Oshima," he told me.

The halls seemed very quiet after evacuation. From neither the teachers nor the students did I hear any anti-Nisei sentiment; no one identified the "enemy" with our students.

At last, the semester ended and evaluation and interviews occupied my days. One of California's most prestigious districts accepted my application for a teaching position and told me that a contract would be mailed later in the summer. That settled, I happily departed for the summer as a counselor at Camp Sunset in Bartlett, Illinois, near Chicago.

However, the teaching contract did not arrive and, finally, I wrote my dean asking him to inquire. Back came his regrets, informing me that the district had decided to hire a man. This was long before the days when one could rush into court claiming discrimination!

As I wondered what to do next, a telegram arrived from Lorne Bell, formerly a YMCA executive in the Los Angeles area and then a regional supervisor for the National Youth Administration. During the early summer of 1942, he had left the NYA to work for the War Relocation Authority. His wire read, "If you have not yet signed a contract, will you consider a position at Topaz, Utah. We are in desperate need of teachers." When Camp Sunset closed, I took a crowded wartime train home, was processed for civil service employment in the San Francisco Western Regional Office of the WRA, packed, and caught a train for Utah, arriving there October 1.

It was my good fortune to have supportive, liberal-minded parents not overly concerned with public opinion. They not only encouraged me but later sent to Topaz cartons of pencils, paper, chalk, crayons, tacks, and other things necessary for a classroom but in short supply in our early days. Occasionally, a package would be stamped "Contents examined or acceptability verified under Order No. 19008 at Station B, Oakland, Calif."

I never did learn what the postal inspectors were actually looking for, but evidently FBI "clearances" were run on all WRA employees, for reports of these came trickling to us from the hometowns of staff members. My father, an electrician, was working on the Manhattan Project at UC, Berkeley, all unknowing of what that was to mean! My brother, a machinist and engineer, was a civilian employee at the Mare Island Navy Yard. Both of them had security clearances, clearances that involved the FBI talking to our neighbors. When yet a third FBI check was circulated concerning the Gerard family, Mother lost her sweet disposition and gave the agent who called on her a frank opinion of such a waste of taxpayers' money. Two FBI men who were in almost full-time residence at Topaz during our first year reported my mother's interview to me with much amusement.

I had no illusions about what I would find at

Topaz High School, 1945. Courtesy E. Sekerak (Miss Gerard).

Topaz; Lorne Bell had warned, "This is an internment camp with barbed wire and military police." The advice at the San Francisco office of the WRA had been, "Take warm clothes; Utah winters are cold at 4,700 feet." And further, "Don't expect gourmet meals—you'll eat mass cooking in a staff dining hall." The preceding three months as a camp counselor proved good preparation for dorm life.

Mr. and Mrs. Bell met my train at Delta, Utah, a small, Mormon town with wide streets surrounded by alfalfa fields. Delta was an oasis in the midst of the alkali Pahvant Desert, part of prehistoric Lake Bonneville. On the seventeen-mile drive from Delta to Topaz, the Bells alerted me to two conditions I never did become accustomed to: dust storms and the sticky, slippery mud that followed rain. With a sudden crack of wind, the dust storms seemed to whirl up and around in blinding fury, leaving a talcumlike film on everything—clothes, hair—even sifting into clenched mouths and gritting between teeth! One simply learned to endure dust and mud. However, other aspects of the high desert country made up for the unpleasant ones—the wonderful silhouette of Mt. Swazey on the horizon, the enticing sparkle of Topaz Mountain, the clarity of the stars at night, and the scent of sage after rain.

Despite our location in the middle of an alkali desert, we did enjoy one great advantage—we didn't displace any local residents. We were made to feel as welcome as was possible under the distressing conditions. We experienced none of the really nasty epi-

sodes that plagued some of the other centers, and I personally credit the basic goodness of our neighboring Mormon residents.

Within hours of arriving at the staff women's dorm, my trunk was delivered by a crew of young men, one of whom shrieked upon seeing me and dropped the trunk on his toes. It was my hall-runner from Technical High. He dashed away shouting, "Guess who's here? That strict teacher from Tech!" By noon, the whole of Topaz knew that a California teacher had arrived.

Charles Ernst, an experienced settlement-house director from Boston, dignified and imposing but warm and considerate, was our first project director. He was an excellent administrator, undaunted by the bureaucratic paperwork from Washington. With a deep concern for human values, Mr. Ernst kept representatives of the community in touch with developments.

Evening meetings to introduce new staff were one procedure. Never was an ordinary teacher made to feel more welcome. People crowded around to ask questions, shake hands, bow, and thank me for being there. When questioners learned that I was from Oakland and from UC, out of the crowd emerged classmates from University High and a smiling Hiro Katayama who had told us "good-bye" only six months before. Thus on my first day there were three meshings with past experiences.

The next day those teachers who had aready arrived met with the administrators and other faculty. For some months I was the only California-credentialed teacher, giving me enormous prestige with the resident families. This standing also gave me an "instant" tool for discipline: I had only to remark to a reluctant student, "Homework not done? I think I'll stop to talk with your folks on the way home," to see an immediate transformation to eager scholar.

Most of our first-year teachers were trained in Utah; at that time a fifth year of college for secondary credentials was not required in Utah. For this reason, the Topaz residents felt shortchanged and worried about their children's academic preparation. However, our superintendent, a Utah native, had a Ph.D. from the University of California, Berkeley, and this mollified the parents. "Appointed," i.e., U.S. Civil Service, faculty were augmented by the resident staff, many of whom had excellent backgrounds but were without formal teacher-training credits. Hiro Katayama joined us in this capacity, having been recruited by Henry Tani. Henry, himself a graduate of Stanford University in business administration, became our administrative assistant. He had organized the high school at the Tanforan Assembly Center and would later become a national staff member with the United Church of Christ.

The first Sunday at Topaz arrived and, at breakfast, the appointed staff idly talked about their plans for the day. I was the only one at my table planning to go to church. I was told, "The only church is the one the residents have." "I know," I said, "but since I went to the Rev. Tsukamoto's church in San Francisco, why not here?" As an active Episcopalian in Berkeley and in Oakland, I had met many Bay Area clergymen. So, seated on a makeshift bench in the first row of a tarpaper "rec hall," I listened to Rev. Tsukamoto's sermon and to Goro Suzuki (who later became television's Jack Soo) sing "The Lord's Prayer." During the three years at Topaz, only a few of the appointed staff attended the evacuee church.

This common commitment brought the rich rewards of deep and lasting friendships with the Nisei whom we came to love and admire. There is a special quality to these friendships, both among staff and evacuee—whenever we meet, we pick up where we left off the last time we visited. (In 1946 I married the man I went to church with that first day, one of the staff who came from Ohio to work in the consumer co-ops.)

The school buildings were far from complete when I arrived. A half-block of barracks at each end of the project was to house the two elementary schools, called "Mountain View" and "Desert View." Block 32, midway in the camp, constituted the six-year high school with a total anticipated enrollment of 1,720. Residents were arriving from Tanforan as fast as barracks could be built. Priority for the available carpenter time was to go to the elementary schools; volunteer labor sped up high school construction—the students and teachers all fell to. Alumni still laugh at the memory of Miss Gerard, teetering precariously on a wobbly table, holding a sheetrock slab with both arms while hammer-wielding students banged nails on each edge—and presto, a ceiling!

As soon as the barracks were winterized, huge "pot belly" stoves were moved into the middle of a room, tables and benches brought in to accommodate thirty-six students, and we were in business—it was October 26, 1942. The lack of supplies was desperate, so a phone call to my mother (and we waited hours to place a wartime call) resulted in her calling my former teachers at University High. Thanks to their efforts, outdated "surplus" texts began to arrive. "History is history, government is government," I sternly told my juniors and seniors, "you don't need a brand-new book!" Thus were we launched on an idealistic curriculum designed for us by a summer-session graduate class in curriculum development at Stanford University.

The curriculum began with the concept of the "community school," that is, the school is looked upon as an extended home, the community furnishing observations and opinion. This approach proved most valuable for students in the vocational area, and some of our students (those over sixteen years) were soon spending half their time in apprentice training or work experience. The schools in all relocation centers were to be affiliated with, and to meet the standards of, the states in which they were located. Utah had long been active in the vocational education field, so advisory committees were organized and planning help generously given. Consultants from the state board of education and even the board itself visited us.

The curriculum designed for us was based on a "core" of general education in agriculture, commercial, or college preparatory, and, in addition, a guidance program in which every teacher was expected to have a role. Our sequential theme for the entire school system was to be "Adaptation of Our Socioeconomic Arrangements to the Control and Direction of Technological Development." We were provided with illustrations of how to adapt this theme to the various grades, e.g., in grade one, "How can the yard at school be made more useful and beautiful?" In reality, the yard was dust (or mud) with huge piles of coal, and not a leaf could be coaxed from that alkali soil. In grade eleven, it was suggested, "How may the community take advantage of improved transportation and communication to make better living conditions for its people?" Our transportation consisted of walking the gravel roads of a one-mile square; no one went to Delta unless by special pass and by riding in an army truck.

Classroom lecture by Miss Gerard, Topaz. Courtesy E. Sekerak.

Bulletin board quiz in Miss Gerard's classroom, Topaz. Courtesy E. Sekerak.

In the beginning, faculty meetings were an exercise in how to tolerate frustration, as we wrestled with the "how to" of a core curriculum in a community school with few supplies and practically no library. Then we ran into opposition from the community itself—the parents did not want an experimental curriculum. They wanted their children to be prepared for college and to lose no academic ground because of the evacuation. So, with apologies to Stanford's Professor Paul Hanna, we modified the curriculum procedures by combining social studies and English as the "core" for the 1942–43 school year.

The first semester we covered federal, state, county, and city government, and administration. An update on the creation and administration of wartime agencies was included. Then an intensive study of the WRA calling our project a "federally created municipality" followed. Staff members came to class to discuss the various phases of the administration of Topaz, and students took field trips and participated in an actual week of work experience in one phase of the community.

In May 1942 our community participation took a very active form when all seniors and their teachers went into the fields to plant onions and celery in areas of tillable ground scattered beyond the alkali deposits. Thereafter, whenever crooked celery stalks appeared on mess hall tables, much merriment ensued concerning whose responsibility it was to have produced such a deformity.

The second semester each student decided on the town in which he wished to resettle, and we set up a community survey of this locality and state. Using a Russell Sage publication, *Your Community* by Joanna Colcord, they sent for materials (writing model letters), did primary and secondary research, and wrote a term paper in college manuscript form summing up their results. At a recent reunion, there was amuse-ment as alumni recounted that they had arrived at their chosen resettlement destinations knowing more than the natives.

Underlying all this was my personal determination that standards of behavior and of learning and performance were in no way to be lessened. As I faced my first day I wondered how I could teach American government and democratic principles while we sat in classrooms behind barbed wire! I never ceased to have a lump in my throat when classes recited the Pledge of Allegiance, especially the phrase, "liberty and justice for all."

In our opening discussion, the students and I agreed that the whole evacuation process had been traumatic but could not last forever—and we could not permit academic achievement to be interrupted. So they arrived at class on time, with homework completed, worked diligently, took their exams, and otherwise observed normal classroom standards. (We had one exception: the day the first snow fell, the California Bay Area students and their teacher rushed to the window to watch.) All the normal life of a typical high school was set up: school chorus, student newspaper, yearbook, student government, drama, athletics, dances, and the usual senior week activities. Borrowing caps and gowns graciously loaned by the University of Utah, 218 seniors marched across the dusty wind-swept plaza to outdoor graduation exercises on June 25, services complete with an invocation and a begowned faculty.

Just as we thought we were settling down to a stable community, there was an uproar in the news media outside the camps over student resettlement, Nisei registration for the draft, and the anti-administration incidents at the Manzanar, Poston, and Tule Lake centers. As a consequence, "applications for leave clearance" to permit evacuees to go farther east

"Buzz session" in Miss Gerard's classroom, Topaz. Courtesy E. Sekerak.

Recitation in Miss Gerard's classroom, Topaz. Courtesy E. Sekerak.

were combined with registration of every man of military age into a single questionnaire. The controversial questions were worded for simple "yes" and "no" answers. Question 27 concerned a person's willingness to serve in the armed forces and 28 asked for unqualified allegiance to the U.S. and the foreswearing of allegiance to Japan. All activities were suspended for a week while staff members interviewed the adult residents to complete the questionnaires. To the Issei, question 28 was impossible to answer because they were not allowed to become American citizens; for them the wording was later changed. "No" answers to either or both questions were given by Issei desiring repatriation or by Issei and Nisei desiring to verbalize a protest against evacuation.

More interviews followed, and anxiety flourished as family loyalty and faith in and hope for the future were all called into doubt. It was a very unsettling experience for staff and residents alike. There were many meetings, many committees, and much speech-making. I thought at the time that my students and the whole Topaz community remained amazingly calm. Months later reports surfaced that there had been scattered threats against the staff; I was deeply touched to learn that two of my most stalwart students had spent several nights on guard outside my room in the Block 2 barracks.

September and October 1943 found us facing the actual transfer (called "segregation") of a small minority classified as a result of the questionnaire. They were either repatriates or voluntary segregants who were accompanying their families. After tearful farewells, the buses bound for the Tule Lake Center pulled out and I waved off several of my best students.

On one occasion, I chaperoned the first experimental group of senior girls and young women to work for the summer in a tomato cannery near Ogden.

We started with light-hearted attitudes, anticipating hard work but making money. The grim realities of migratory agricultural life met us when we found utterly unacceptable, unsanitary, and crowded housing conditions plus an employer who couldn't or wouldn't consider any improvements. I had to appeal to nearby military to place me in phone contact with our project director. Upon hearing of the conditions, he ordered us back to Topaz, explaining to grateful parents that their daughters were not to be exploited.

To thank me for heading off a potentially embarrassing incident for the WRA administration, the director assigned my roommate and me an apartment in the new staff housing. Until that time we had lived in barracks rooms just as the evacuees did. Unlike some centers, at no time were there barriers between staff and evacuee housing. From then on, our apartment became a center for visitor and student meetings and parties.

My first roommate, Emily Minton, community activities director, was married at Topaz in December 1942. Her husband, Norman Center, arrived from San Francisco carrying Reverend Tsukamoto's altar candlesticks, and Goro Suzuki sang "I'm Dreaming of a White Christmas" at the reception. Mary MacMillan, my second roommate, taught at the high school until she left for graduate work in Nashville, Tennessee. "Mary Mack," much beloved by the students, would later go to postwar Hiroshima to teach. Third to move in was Muriel Matzkin, a biology teacher from New York. Muriel and I later went to Washington, D.C., to help close out the WRA. Later Muriel married Milton Shapp and became "first lady" of Pennsylvania.

Good-byes to those actually relocating to jobs out of the evacuation zone were far happier than parting with those destined for Tule Lake. When the first large group of families left for resettlement in the East, and not just on seasonal leave, staff and friends crowded around the gate to say their farewells. Voices raised in song—"God be with you till we meet again"—as tears ran unashamedly down dusty cheeks.

Happiest of all leave-takings were those when students left for college. Many educators, such as my faculty colleagues at Technical High, had worried about the evacuee students who were then in college or planning to enter in the spring of 1942, and about those who would be graduating during the war years. During the early summer of 1942, some thirty deans and registrars met to consider the problem. With the eventual cooperation of over 300 colleges and universities, they established five requirements: (1) The student had to be accepted academically by the college while still in camp; (2) students could attend any school approved or "cleared" by the War and Navy departments; (3) students had to be able to provide for themselves financially for one year; (4) they had to be assured of a welcome in the college community; and (5) all students had to provide an autobiography.

The fourth stipulation created problems, as many of the large universities had war-related projects on their campuses; as a consequence, the need for an agency to handle a multitude of details became obvious. John J. McCloy, assistant secretary of war, and Milton Eisenhower, the first director of the WRA, requested that the American Friends Service Committee coordinate the activities of all interested groups, such as the churches, the YMCA, the YWCA, and the Fair Play Committee. The result was the National Japanese American Student Relocation Council funded by church boards and two philanthropic foundations. Thomas R. Bodine was appointed to the position of field director, and thereby hangs a tale of true dedication and commitment. Tom Bodine was a member of the Society of Friends and brought to the position the personal resources of extraordinary patience, understanding, and tremendous good cheer. He had charm, compassion, integrity, and aplomb with which to cajole, console, and counsel evacuee students and their parents, relocation center high school faculty, foundation boards of directors, and college presidents.

When we finally built a school auditorium at Topaz, had an adequate library, fielded uniformed athletic teams, and had "settled in," Tom made us realize the stagnation of the human spirit that was occurring behind barbed wire. Spurred by him, we set up a student relocation office; our first was run very efficiently by the gracious Louise Watson. It later became a part of the high school, and I was called the "student relocation advisor" so as not to offend the high school "guidance counselor." We organized our own scholarship fund to which both residents and outsiders contributed. (Once, when a dental problem forced me to make a quick train trip home, my only other engagement during that one-day visit was to talk with a group of teachers. Asking me to please wait, they withdrew and returned with a check for a thousand dollars. "If Hayward students are awarded scholarships, tell them Hayward High teachers gave the money, otherwise we are to be anonymous," they said.)

The scholarships awarded, plus a $25 leave grant made when an evacuee departed camp, helped establish the student's financial ability. However, jobs, housing, and community acceptance were the concern and responsibility of the National Japanese American Student Relocation Council. By summer 1945, at least 3,000 students had been placed in various kinds of post-secondary education, having been relocated from all ten centers.

Topaz's closure was official on October 31, 1945, and I left immediately for Washington, D.C. My responsibility there was to handle correspondence concerning student records, especially transcripts, as the relocated students had entered schools all over the nation. Several months later, when all seemed quiet on the school front, Dr. John Provinse and I went to lunch with an official from the National Archives. We turned over the educational records from all the centers, everything in good order and all students accounted for.

Now, when at class reunions (the Topaz Class of 1945 has five-year reunions and the '43–'44 classes recently held a forty-year affair attended by 400 persons) I happily acknowledge the gratitude and applause of "my" alumni; and I am deeply aware of all those upon whom I leaned. Tom Bodine and his "support system" picked up and guided the alumni so that today our reunions are attended by a host of distinguished professionals and a multitude of wonderful, decent people from all over the United States.

Also supporting my efforts were fine colleagues, such as my principals Drayton Nuttall and Golden Woolf, superintendents John Carlisle and LeGrand Noble, project directors and assistants Lorne Bell, Roscoe Bell, Charles Ernst, and Luther Hoffman. Behind them stand my parents, my own instructors from high school and college, my faculty peers and dear friends. I was a link in that great chain. Henry Brooks Adams said "A teacher affects eternity; he can never tell where his influence stops." It was my privilege, my joy to have been a teacher at Topaz.

The Impact of Incarceration on the Education of Nisei Schoolchildren

Lane Ryo Hirabayashi

The effects of the wartime incarceration experience on the education of the Nisei can be viewed from three basic perspectives:[1] The first praises the enlightened philosophy behind the educational program of the camps. Jerome T. Light maintains that the War Relocation Authority program for teaching democracy, Americanism, and assimilation in schools that were planned to be "community schools" was successfully implemented in the camps.[2] Similarly, both Robert George and William D. Zeller applaud the philosophical premises of the educational program, but fault the actual implementation.[3] Other authors have reasoned that assimilation was taking place anyway, and the camp schools (and the National Japanese American Council program) nurtured this trend along its natural course.[4]

A second perspective has been to focus upon the outcome—that is, the outstanding scholastic achievements of the Nisei. While doing this, authors have largely ignored the episode of the camps; instead, they have tried to account for the Nisei's accomplishments in education by examining such variables as value orientations and the degree of assimilation to the dominant society.[5]

My own interpretation, the third perspective, controverts these analyses, as well as their evaluation of the ultimate implications and long-term effects. My thesis is that the educational process for the Nisei was drastically altered during the incarceration period and resulted in irreparable social and psychological consequences that have never been fully acknowledged or accounted for.

This hypothesis is based on the following assumptions: first, since the beginning of this century, a major shift has taken place in the U.S. that has been manifested in the increasingly critical role schools play in the intellectual, social, and personal formation of youth.[6] Correspondingly, the formal educational system has been and is the principal means used for socializing future citizens.[7] However, socialization and educational processes also take place within the context of close, primary relationships, such as the family, the church, and the community.[8] Second, for racial-ethnic minorities, the whole (formal and informal) educational process must be understood within the historical context of the racism inherent in U.S. soci-

ety; it is also necessary to understand how racism has affected each minority group.[9]

These assumptions place this study within a third perspective, which criticizes the philosophy and the practices of the educational program within the camps and raises questions about the implications and the impact the camp schools had on the Nisei schoolchildren. By drawing on contemporary accounts by the incarcerated, by other researchers, by teachers, and by the Nisei students, an "insider's" perspective on the education in the camp schools will be presented. Finally, an analysis of the contradictions Nisei students faced will account for the patterns derived from the data.

Little information and analysis exist concerning many aspects of the educational experiences of Nisei in the camps. We do know that the war interrupted Nisei educational careers and, in some cases, terminated them forever.[10] In addition, it is a matter of record that between 1942 and 1945 over 30,000 children attended segregated schools in the ten WRA-run camps.[11]

An immediate reality was the difficulty of obtaining the buildings and the staff necessary to run the schools. Estelle Ishigo comments on conditions at the Heart Mountain camp:

> On the 30th of September drab barracks with drafty windows and doors began to fill with children ready for school. . . . There were as many as 60 children in a classroom 16 by 20 feet and there were very few books. Even though there were highly qualified college graduates among the evacuees teachers from neighboring towns were employed. One person of Japanese ancestry was permitted on the faculty with 12 apprentices.
>
> At first there were no desks; some sat on benches, some on the floor and some stood leaning against the walls to write their lessons.[12]

Although conditions improved after these first trying months, research indicates that persistent problems plagued camp schools such as obtaining books, tools and materials, equipment and supplies, and even heating at many of the camps.[13] One teacher at Poston even complained that in the winter, "the weather was so cold it was often difficult to talk to the class. The students found it hard to take notes because their hands would get numb. . . . Before class most of the students gathered around a bonfire and teachers had to use all their powers of persuasion to start their classes on time."[14]

Beyond these rather obvious physical and material deprivations, however, camp classes left a negative impact on the lives and the self-images of many of the Nisei students. Working largely with the comments of those who experienced or observed the situation firsthand, one finds a variety of evidence.

One observer of the camp schools was internee Reverend Daisuke Kitagawa, a Japanese-born Christian, who was the resident minister of St. Paul's Church in the White River Valley, Washington, at the outbreak of war. Incarcerated with the members of that community, Reverend Kitagawa was in a unique position to observe the catastrophe. In regard to the educational program at Tule Lake, he noted:

> The schools came to reflect this low community morale. Children did not show enthusiasm for, or interest in, school work. Parents did not seem to care about it, either. The place . . . was not conducive to study . . . and the fact that they had to be there simply because they were of Japanese descent made the children question whether there would be any use for their education in America at all.[15]

Accounts by former internees provide additional insights. In *Camp II, Block 211*, artist Jack Matsuoka commented on three types of students, some very eager to write and learn, some uninterested but sports-crazy, and "a third group (that) was discouraged and disillusioned. To them the future was dim, and education had no value. They were the ones who didn't give a damn."[16] He recounted how the Pledge of Allegiance "somehow sounded hollow. Even the teacher's voice trailed off to a murmur at the part about liberty and justice for all."[17]

Ishigo provides a poignant anecdote, further illustrating the psychological dilemmas of the situation: "Once in awhile a child would confide timidly about not wanting to go to school—ashamed of being a Japanese in front of his teacher who read every morning from a newspaper about the horrible Japanese soldiers and how the fine American soldiers were fighting and winning."[18] Others confirmed these observations on a more general level. Henry Tani, writing as an internee in the Topaz camp publication, *All Aboard*, despaired of student attitudes. "This . . . attitude is characterized by a general disrespect for the faculty, a lack of proper concern for school property, and a general lowering of moral values," which he attributed to "economic losses, the creation of bitterness and the instability that these produce in family life."[19]

An attitude and values inventory in the Miles Carey High School at the Poston camp in Arizona

A young Japanese American preparing to leave the Oakland railroad terminal for evacuation. Photo by Dorothea Lange. Courtesy Bernard K. Johnpoll.

made in May 1945 provides additional information about the effect the camps had on Nisei.[20] Although it is not clear if Edith Derrick, the principal researcher, was trained in social science research methods, and she was tentative about the representativeness of the findings, she made several important points. "A large percentage of the pupils declined in common courtesies, increased in their use of slang, discontinued attendance at church, and decreased interest in school life."[21] Derrick, commenting in more detail on the educational situation in Poston, stated that "Waning . . . interest in school life developed as a result of the continued discouragements experienced throughout the three years. . . . The rapid turnover of teacher personnel did not facilitate the problems of education nor contribute to favorable behavior situations."[22] Derrick's general evaluation was that "the most alarming findings concerning attitudes are found in the large number of respondents who indicate that indifference towards many of the items which influence character development."[23]

Official reports about student morale at the WRA camps at Jerome, Minidoka, and Colorado River

(Poston) all correspond to Derrick's findings at Poston.[24] Yet another observer, who based his comments on visits to the camps, reported that "the whole atmosphere of the centers is so abnormal that it is debatable whether, given the best in personnel and equipment, much could be done in creating an adequate educational program."[25]

The teachers themselves made statements, observers uniquely positioned to document the impact of the educational system in the camps. One teacher who visited his former students in camp reflected that "a sort of apathy has settled over them. They eat, they sleep, they look well, but something like... 'prison stupor' seems to have affected their minds."[26] Zeller noted that the students were distrustful of the Caucasian teachers and either indifferent or resentful of their teachers' initiatives. He quoted one teacher, a Mr. Slate, to the effect that

> I cannot remember any student, who although he followed the class organization to the very letter, ... did so with spirit or enthusiasm.... The bitterness, the fear, and his lack of understanding of the tragedy which had just occurred to him was not to be easily overcome by a teacher's enthusiasm or understanding or by however good an organization we were able to set up.[27]

Arthur Ramey, another camp educator, recounted the teachers' attempts to involve students in extracurricular activities and groups: "A questionnaire was issued to all students containing a long list of clubs, with instructions to check the ones they would like to join.... On the basis of these results, a list of proposed clubs was issued. Then a club sign-up period was held the last period of the day. Most of the students went home."[28]

Similarly, Bob Sakai reported extensively on student attitudes and "disciplinary" problems he faced as a teacher in Poston. Noting the effect of the high rates of teacher "turnover" on his students, Sakai stated: "By this time the students were thoroughly disgusted and disillusioned. Two of the favorite expressions of the 'Peacock Gang,' a clique of five boys in the morning class, were 'no use' and 'waste time' expressed with a Postonese drawl. One girl said to me, 'Gee, there's no future in going to school here.' "[29]

It is critical that the responses of the Nisei students also be examined. No quantitative figures prove how many Nisei actually felt embittered or alienated, but such feelings must have been common.

An important source of data comes from student essays of the period. Charles Kikuchi collected one sample for the University of California Japanese American Evacuation and Resettlement Study.[30] These essays reveal that many Nisei schoolchildren had fond remembrances of their former schools, classmates, and teachers.[31] However, there were many negative comments on the camp schools.

Some of the complaints were general. One student wrote: "The school is another dry place of life. Although learning a little is better than nothing at all. I hope as many hope that the new school building will be erected by next semester."[32] Another stated: "After the war I would like to go back to California because I don't like the weather, school, and houses [here]. If I was in California the weather would be fine and the schools 100 times better."[33] Other students compared their experiences to a bad dream from which they hoped they would awaken:

> Although we here are in such bad conditions, we must study hard and realize that if we don't, the future will look cloudier, darker and more uncertain. (This applies to me also) I sometimes pinch myself, am I really in Utah or is this California, do I live in a barrack with other people and have only 2 rooms, not 7 or 8 I used to live in, are we going to school learning a new system, which seems odd to me, and do we have teachers of our own race, do we go to school in barracks and then I pinch myself once, twice and then I am out of my daze.[34]

More specifically, a number of essays were critical of the behavior of their fellow students and of the lack of respect shown for teachers. One example illustrates this: "The boys in our group are the silliest, noisiest and rowdiest of the whole Junior High School.... Every time we go to music Mr. I. takes the whole period to take the roll call because the boys are so noisy."[35]

According to one authority, many of the early student papers, written in the camps, "reflected... hopelessness and despair."[36] One student even ended his theme, "Before I was going to be an engineer, but now I decided to be a farmer because of the *lack of educational facilities*."[37]

As another example, Zeller cites a WRA study to the effect that one of the causes of the Manzanar riots was related to a delayed school-building program. The school setting reflected tensions in the form of discipline problems, intimidation, gangs, and hysterical outbursts by the pupils. During this period in Manzanar, an official report even noted that a child in the fourth grade had burst into tears, screaming, "I hate you, I hate all Caucasians!"[38]

Robert Mossman, who made an extensive effort to read and analyze student essays, quotes passages that reflect similar "feelings of despair and of wasted effort."[39] "I am an American, although for the last three years I have been so in name only. I am writing these words behind the shadows of barbed wire. I've done no wrong. My only crime is that my hair is black, my skin yellow, my eyes slant; because I am of Japanese ancestry. This is my account of prejudice and human blindness."[40]

Although underplaying the significance and meaning of such materials, Mossman argues that the covert functions of the WRA schools were to provide "removal activities," that is, activities designed to occupy and distract the youth, and "institutional ceremonies."[41]

In summary, an examination of school essays and papers in the University of California Japanese American Evacuation and Resettlement Study shows that some students accepted and repeated the ideas and values of their teachers. For example, in writing a term paper about Butte High School at Gila River, Arizona, one student dutifully recorded the educational philosophy of the superintendent of schools that "our educational program will . . . teach the beauties of a Democracy."[42] Similarly, two high school students, writing about the "self-governance" system of the internees at Hunt, commented: "The people are trying to make Hunt as much as possible like a model of the United States. . . . Of course we are not far along, but this is due to not having been here very long."[43]

At the same time there is clear evidence that Nisei students were disturbed, and that some knew that what had transpired was terribly wrong. Bob Sakai—a sensitive and perceptive teacher at Poston—wrote of his students:

> They relished mimicking for me the idiosyncrasies of the various teachers, how one would twitch her eyes, how another would squeakingly exclaim in her high pitched voice "how sorry she was for the Japanese," or how she would bore them stiff by relating her experiences in Japan. "My goodness," they said, "we know that things aren't perfect for us, but we don't want anyone to make us feel sorry for ourselves." But they were even more disgusted with the other teacher who assured them, "Oh, but you do have freedom and self-government here. They're guaranteed to you in the Constitution."[44]

ANALYSIS

Ethnic communities are not mere replicas of the cultures and societies from whence the migrants came. They are unique, the results of the creative adaptations of migrants in a new setting.[45] In the case of the Japanese Americans, despite the positive aspects of this adaptation, negative conditions seriously affected the Issei's attempts to integrate their children into the total society.

Racism was a fact of life for Japanese Americans. In part, racism against the Japanese can be seen as a continuation of the racist attitudes perpetrated against the Chinese since the middle of the eighteenth

century.[46] The history of racism against the Issei has been extensively documented[47] and is well illustrated by discrimination in all phases of the adjustment of Japanese immigrants to North American society, including the areas of jobs and economics,[48] politics,[49] social and cultural life,[50] education,[51] and the legal aspects of their adaptation.[52] As Yuji Ichioka suggests, racism against Japanese Americans is a complex phenomenon with both economic and ideological dimensions.[53]

In spite of racism and its negative effects, a unique life-style developed, one based on the intimate ties between the individual, the family, and the Japanese American community.[54] Thus, the Japanese American community had evolved over a fifty-year period into a functional entity with an integrity that has adjusted to the conditions and constraints of the dominant society. Into this community the Nisei were born and socialized. It was this setting that gave the Nisei their social and psychological identity, specifically, a sense of self and of the relationship of the self to the total social environment. In this sense, even in areas where Japanese Americans were more dispersed, the Issei regulated parts of the socialization of the Nisei.

At the same time, the Issei retained their traditional Japanese values regarding education. Despite instances of overt racism in the U.S. educational system, including segregation and the "tracking" of Japanese American students within the public schools,[55] the Issei often made great sacrifices to educate their children.[56] Thus, with their emphasis on education, the Issei left to the schools the task of training their Nisei children to adapt to the larger society.[57] But since one of the principal functions of the educational system in the United States is to effect the enculturation of the population to the values and norms of the dominant society,[58] the discrepancies between the ideals stated and the actual realities created problems of adjustment for the Nisei. In particular, the Nisei were formally socialized in an educational system that promoted the ideals of a democratic society for all citizens. The actual experience of Japanese Americans, though, was marked by hostility, prejudice, and discrimination.

Given a historical pattern of racism, what special problems were posed in terms of the camp schools? As we have seen, there was an initial lack of buildings, staff, and supplies. Beyond the material deprivations, it is apparent that the educational system in the camps embodied a series of contradictions making the educational process there inherently disturbing.

One contradiction was the natural product of the forced Americanization process that required Japanese

Americans to put a negative value on everything related to the Japanese culture and tradition, even the many positive elements. In its place, things American received positive emphasis, even those things that had little relevance to the daily lives and experiences of Japanese Americans. To confirm this, one need only examine the underlying assumptions of the camp planners and officials (initially, anyway) that the Japanese language and culture inhibited the Americanization process and, therefore, needed to be prohibited.[59]

The second, central contradiction was between the ideals of American democracy and the Bill of Rights and the actuality of what was done to Japanese Americans. It is relevant at this point to discuss the premises of the educational program in the WRA-run camps.

The first indication of an educational philosophy and program for the WRA camps is contained in a letter by JACL national secretary and field executive, Mike M. Masaoka, to Milton S. Eisenhower, then director of the WRA. Dated April 6, 1942, the letter contains over a page of ideas about how education should be handled in the "resettlement project."[60] Speaking for the JACL, Masaoka made a series of recommendations, including one which said "all classes should be so integrated that every student will be inculcated with the spirit of Americanism and democratic process."[61] There is evidence to suggest that Eisenhower took this letter very seriously and implemented many of its recommendations, although no one as yet has traced its effect on the evolution of the educational policies described below.[62]

In addition, it is often claimed that the formal educational philosophy behind the camp school program—under the administration of the new director of the WRA, Dillon S. Myer—was the product of a summer graduate class in curriculum development at Stanford University that met in 1942 under the direction of Professor Paul Hanna.[63]

To study the process of assimilation, seminar members did library research, met with WRA staff for consultation and evaluation about the educational problems that would be faced, and went on a two-day field visit to the Tule Lake camp. As a result of these activities, the seminar decided it was imperative that a philosophical framework be developed to provide the rationale for curriculum development.[64] The core philosophical element was that, if camp schools were to be of value, "they would have to teach the democratic way of life."[65] In addition, because of the unusual conditions faced by the internees, the class developed a "community school" approach, which they believed would maximize participation as well as the school's usefulness to the students and the camp alike.[66]

But what neither the Stanford summer seminar, nor the WRA, nor most of the educational specialists fully emphasized was the true nature of the schools in the camps: they constituted a racially segregated educational system controlled by the U.S. government.[67] Despite the WRA vision of democratic principles and procedures as the cornerstones of camp policy and administration, it was impossible for the camps—or the schools for that matter—to be run as a participatory democracy.[68] Since the educational system was based upon and oriented towards teaching democratic principles, it was caught in a classic "double-bind." As Charles Wollenberg points out, "The inconsistency between these 'typical' American schools with their 'progressive' ideals and the reality of camp life surrounded by barbed wire and armed guards was not lost on Nisei students. When school opened at the camp in Rohrer, Arkansas, in September 1942, a student chalked the words 'Jap Prison' on the tar paper wall."[69]

As a result of these contradictions, many Nisei responded to the traumas of the war and the forced internment by trying to become 110 percent American. Surrounded by a hostile society doubting Japanese American affiliations and loyalties, many Nisei responded with a strategy of aggressive assimilation to dominant society norms. There are larger implications in this. What can be seen as assimilation and integration from one point of view (that is, the WRA's point of view), can also be seen as cultural destruction from another; although there were cases of protest and rebellion,[70] many Japanese Americans decided, consciously or unconsciously, to reject any association with the Japanese American culture and community. These decisions were made for reasons of survival, given the war and the realities of racism in the larger society.

Racism has always been found in U.S. society, and the history of the education of the Nisei is a specific example of this phenomenon. Racism against Japanese Americans in the educational system has been well documented for the prewar period,[71] and to some extent for the postwar period.[72] Nevertheless, given the conditions in the larger occupational structure, mobility through advanced education may have been more promising (albeit, risky) than the pursuit of other skills or careers completely closed to Asians.[73]

Although conditions did vary according to the particular location, racism in education for the Japanese Americans reached its zenith during the concentration camp period. As a result, many Nisei experienced a serious curtailment of their scholastic and personal development within totally segregated circumstances. This was especially true for the Nisei who were in the late elementary grades and in high school, as well as for the college-age Nisei. On one hand, internment terminated the education or the chosen careers, or both, of many; on the other hand, for those who continued their education, the schools in the camps were set in such a context that racist attitudes and policies obliterated the very ideals the curriculum was contrived to instill. Obviously, it would be wrong to portray the Nisei as always being victims, to argue that all teachers and administrators had bad intentions, or to argue that all Nisei had negative experiences in the camp schools. The point remains that the identities and self-images of the Nisei schoolchildren were frequently devastated because of the situation into which they were forcibly placed. The evidence supporting this interpretation is clear, once it is sought.

Concomitantly, from an alternative perspective, the scholarly studies reviewed earlier were written from an outsider's analytic perspective. The studies fail (1) to acknowledge openly their assimilationist orientation, (2) to perceive the extensive colonial implications of the incarceration, and (3) to show the link between this condition (that is, point 2) and the structure and content of the educational program and institutions in the camps. These biases affect even the liberal educationalists; for example, both George and Light emphasize the progressive and experimental nature of the camp pedagogy, and this focus appears to blind them to the injustices and constraints of the incarceration as the framework within which the educational program took place.

Similarly, we see that historians,[74] sociologists,[75] and anthropologists[76] have all focused on the outstanding achievements of the Nisei in the field of education. What has been overlooked is the full extent of racism that the Nisei had to face in pursuing their educational careers. Many were unable to overcome these barriers. Regarding those who did, one must agree with Wollenberg's assessment that "Excellence in educational achievement was often gained at great psychological and cultural cost."[77]

Important parallels exist between the education of the Nisei during World War II and the larger Japanese American educational experience[78] as well as the experience of other racial-ethnic minorities—most notably a striking parallel with American Indian "education" under the supervision of the Bureau of Indian Affairs.[79] Education, from this point of view, is an actual instrument of assimilationist policy rather than an objective process designed to produce a populace that can think clearly and act upon its ideas and values.[80]

More generally, this case suggests that the traditional focus on Japanese Americans and their academic achievements must take into account the following question: What is the trade-off between educational success and the psychological and cultural costs of assimilation in a society that still continues to discriminate systematically against its racial-ethnic minorities?[81]

NOTES

1. This paper is a revised and expanded section of the written testimony, originally written with James A. Hirabayashi, presented to the Commission on Wartime Relocation and Internment of Civilians in 1981. Thus I would like to acknowledge my father's many contributions to this work; I dedicate it to him and the other Nisei schoolchildren. I would also like to thank Dr. Jere Takahashi (U.C., Berkeley) and Dr. Leonore Stiffarm (UCLA) for suggestions about bibliographic references, as well as Professors Nelson H. H. Graburn (U.C., Berkeley), Lloyd Inui (California State University, Long Beach), and Elizabeth Parent (San Francisco State University) for their comments.

2. Jerome T. Light, "The Development of a Junior-Senior High School Program in a Relocation Center for People of Japanese Ancestry During the War with Japan" (Ph.D. diss., Stanford University, 1947).

3. Robert Chipman Lee George, "The Granada (Colorado) Relocation Center Secondary School" (M.A. thesis, University of Colorado, 1944); William D. Zeller, "The Educational Program Provided the Japanese Americans During the Relocation Period, 1942–1945" (Ph.D. diss., Michigan State University, 1963); and William D. Zeller, An Educational Drama: The Educational Program Provided the Japanese Americans During the Relocation Period, 1942–1945 (New York: The American Press, 1969).

4. Robert W. O'Brien, The College Nisei (New York: Arno Press, 1978; originally published in 1949); Charles Wollenberg, All Deliberate Speed (Berkeley: University of California Press, 1976).

5. See Darrell Montero and Ronald Tsukashima, "Assimilation and Educational Achievement: The Case of Second Generation Japanese Americans," The Sociological Quarterly 18 (1977): 490–503.

6. Kenneth Keniston and the Carnegie Council on Children, All Our Children: The American Family Under Pressure (New York: Harcourt Brace Jovanovich, 1977).

7. Keniston 1977; Bob H. Suzuki, "Education and the Socialization of Asian Americans: A Revisionist Analysis of the 'Model Minority' Thesis," Amerasia Journal 4 (1977): 23–51.

8. John Singleton, "Schooling: Coping with Education in a Modern Society," in To See Ourselves: Anthropology and Modern Social Issues, ed. Thomas Weaver, (Glenview, Ill.: Scott, Foresman and Co., 1973).

9. Robert Blauner, Racial Oppression in America (New York: Harper and Row, 1972), 51–84; Pierre Van den Berghe, Race and Racism: A Comparative Perspective (New York: John Wiley, 1967), 11.

10. Commission on Wartime Relocation and Internment of Civilians, Personal Justice Denied (Washington, D.C.: Government Printing Office, 1982), 180.

11. Wollenberg, 1976.

12. Estelle Ishigo, Lone Heart Mountain (Los Angeles: Anderson, Richie and Simon, 1972), 21–22.

13. Henry Tani, "Year's End," All Aboard (produced by internees in the camp in Topaz, Utah), Spring 1944, 19–20; Light, 588;

Zeller, "The Educational Program," 125–31; Wollenberg, 75–79. See also *Personal Justice Denied*, 170.

14. Bob Sakai, "Education Report," Japanese American Evacuation and Resettlement Study, Bancroft Library, U.C., Berkeley, Folder J 7.10. (Hereafter cited as JERS.)

15. Daisuke Kitagawa, *Issei and Nisei: The Internment Years* (New York: Seabury Press, 1967), 92.

16. Jack Matsuoka, *Camp II, Block 211: Daily Life in an Internment Camp* (Tokyo: Japan Publications, 1974), 144.

17. Matsuoka, 151.

18. Ishigo, 21–22.

19. Tani, 22.

20. Edith W. Derrick, "Effects of Evacuation on Japanese-American Youth," *School Review* 55 (1947): 356–62.

21. Ibid., 358.

22. Ibid., 360–62.

23. Ibid., 362.

24. Robert Alan Mossman, "Japanese American War Relocation Centers as Total Institutions with Emphasis on the Educational Program" (Ph.D. diss., Rutgers University, 1978), 101–3; *Topaz Times* Vol. 6, No. 31, p. 7; Vol. 9, No. 19, p. 2; Sakai, JERS, folder J 7.10; Zeller, *Educational Drama*, 151–54.

25. Carey McWilliams, *Prejudice: Japanese-Americans: Symbol of Racial Intolerance* (Boston: Little, Brown, 1945), 160.

26. Zeller, "The Educational Program," 133.

27. Ibid., 136–37.

28. Ibid., 135.

29. Sakai, JERS, folder J 7.10.

30. Charles Kikuchi, ed., Student compositions from 8th grade classes at Topaz, 1942–1943, JERS, folder H 2.88.

31. Kikuchi, JERS, folder H 2.88.

32. Ibid., Essay by H. M., December 8, 1942, JERS, folder H 2.88.

33. Ibid., Essay by K. H., February 3, 1943, JERS, folder H 2.88.

34. Ibid., Essay by L. S., November 30, 1942, JERS, folder H 2.88.

35. Ibid., Essay by Y. F., December 8, 1943, JERS, folder H 2.88.

36. Zeller, "The Educational Program," 137.

37. Ibid., 137.

38. Ibid., 138.

39. Mossman, 99–111.

40. Ibid., 99–100.

41. Ibid., 113–26.

42. Kimiko Kodani, "Butte High School" (chapter 5 of an untitled term project, Gila River, 1943), 1. JERS, folder K 4.27.

43. Chiyeko Ishida and Kana Kawase, "Hunt Government" (as a paper in the "Government Committee" project, Hunt High School, Minidoka, n.d.). JERS, folder P 3.04 B.

44. Sakai, JERS, folder J 7.10.

45. James A. Hirabayashi, "Ethnic Education: Its Purposes and Prospects," *On Common Ground: A Journal of Ethnic Thought* (San Francisco State University) 1 (1979): 1–3.

46. Alexander Saxton, *The Indispensible Enemy: Labor and the Anti-Chinese Movement in California* (Berkeley: University of California Press, 1971); Stanford M. Lyman, *Chinese Americans* (New York: Random House, 1974), 54–85.

47. McWilliams, 1945; Roger Daniels, *The Politics of Prejudice: The Anti-Japanese Movement in California and the Struggle for Japanese Exclusion* (Berkeley and Los Angeles: University of California Press, 1962).

48. Masakazu Iwata, "The Japanese Immigrants in California Agriculture," *Agricultural History* 36 (1962): 25–37; John Modell, *The Economics and Politics of Racial Accommodation: The Japanese of Los Angeles, 1900–1942* (Urbana, Ill.: University of Illinois Press, 1977).

49. Jerrold Haruo Takahashi, "Changing Responses to Racial Subordination: An Exploratory Study of Japanese American Political Styles" (Ph.D. diss., University of California, Berkeley, 1980).

50. Yamato Ichihashi, *Japanese in the United States* (New York: Arno Press and the *New York Times*, 1969; originally published in 1932), 215–17.

51. Wollenberg, 1976.

52. Daniels; Frank Chuman, *The Bamboo People: The Law and Japanese Americans* (Del Mar, Calif.: Publisher's, 1976).

53. Yuji Ichioka, "The 1921 Turlock Incident: Forceful Expulsion of Japanese Laborers," in *Counterpoint: Perspectives on Asian America*, Emma Gee, ed. (Los Angeles: Asian American Studies Center, UCLA, 1976).

54. S. Frank Miyamoto, "Social Solidarity Among the Japanese in Seattle," *University of Washington Publications in Social Sciences* 11 (1939): 57–130.

55. Edward K. Strong, *The Second Generation Japanese Problem* (Stanford: Stanford University Press, 1970; originally published in 1934), 198–201; Ichihashi, 354–63.

56. Isao Horinouchi, *Educational Values and Preadaptation in the Acculturation of Japanese Americans* (Sacramento: Sacramento Anthropological Society; Sacramento Anthropological Association, Paper #7), 12, 40, 55–58; Edward H. Spicer, Asael T. Hansen, Katherine Luomala, and Marvin K. Opler, *Impounded People: Japanese Americans in the Relocation Centers* (Tucson: University of Arizona Press, 1969), 203; Wollenberg, 51–52.

57. Toshio Yatsushiro, *Politics and Cultural Values: The World War II Japanese Relocation Centers and the United States Government* (New York: Arno Press, 1978), 193–98.

58. Singleton, 1973; Keniston, 15.

59. *Personal Justice Denied*, 145–46.

60. Paul R. Spickard, "The Nisei Assume Power: The Japanese American Citizens League, 1941–1942," *Pacific Historical Review* 52 (1983) 2: 165–74. Letter, Mike Masaoka to Milton S. Eisenhower, April 6, 1942, JERS, folder T 6.10.

61. Ibid.

62. Spickard, 147–74.

63. Zeller, *An Educational Drama*, 57–67.

64. Zeller, "The Educational Program," 81.

65. Ibid., 81.

66. Light, 51–59.

67. Wollenberg, 1976.

68. William Foote Whyte, "Models for Building Changing Organizations," *Human Organization* 26 (1976): 22–31.

69. Wollenberg, 78.

70. Russell C. Leong, ed., 1981 Commission on Wartime Relocation and Internment of Civilians. Selected Testimonies from Los Angeles and San Francisco Hearings, *Amerasia Journal* 8 (1981): 55–105.

71. Ichihashi, 354–63; Strong, 1970; Wollenberg, 1976; Modell, 1977.

72. Russell Endo, "Japanese Americans: The 'Model Minority' in Perspective," 189–213 in *The Social Reality of Ethnic America*, ed. Rudolph Gomez, Clement Cottingham, Jr., Russell Endo, and Kathleen Jackson (Lexington, Mass.: D. C. Heath, 1974); Suzuki, 1977; and Ki-Taek Chun, "The Myth of Asian American Success and its Educational Ramifications," *I.R.D.C. Bulletin* 15 (1980): 1–12.

73. Horinouchi, 41; Suzuki, 1977; Takahashi, 1980.

74. Wollenberg, 1976.

75. Melvin S. Brooks and Ken Kunihiro, "Education and Assimilation of Japanese: A Study of the Houston Area of Texas," *Sociology and Social Research* 27 (1952): 16–22; Audrey James Schwartz, "The Culturally Advantaged: A Study of Japanese American Pupils," *Sociology and Social Research* 55 (1971): 341–53; Montero and Tsukashima, 490–503.

76. Horinouchi, 1967.

77. Wollenberg, 81.

78. Reed Ueda, "The Americanization and Education of Japanese Americans," in *Cultural Pluralism*, ed. Edgar G. Epps (Berkeley: McCutchan, 1974); Suzuki, 1977.

79. U.S. Senate: Committee on Labor and Public Welfare; Special Subcommittee on Indian Education, *Indian Education: A National Tragedy—A National Challenge* (Washington, D.C.: Government Printing Office, 1969).

80. Keniston, 15; John Higham, *Strangers in the Land: Patterns of American Nativism, 1860–1925* (New Brunswick, N.J.: Rutgers University Press, 1955); Suzuki, 1977.

81. United States Commission on Civil Rights, *Success of Asian Americans: Fact or Fiction?* (Washington, D.C.: U.S. Commission on Civil Rights; Clearinghouse Publication 64; September 1980); Stephen R. Graubard, ed., *American Indians, Blacks, Chicanos, and Puerto Ricans, Daedalus* 110 (1981): 1–299.

American Mistreatment of Internees During World War II: Enemy Alien Japanese

Tetsuden Kashima

This paper will cover the incarceration and internment of the Japanese enemy aliens, focusing on some abuses, threats of physical harm, physical beatings, shootings, and actual killings that occurred in some of the thirty-four detention stations and camps created by the Justice Department and military to house Japanese "enemy aliens." Certainly, not all Japanese internee prisoners suffered physical harm. However, the fact that some did, that others died as a result of this treatment, and that *most* suffered in some way from the experience has not been adequately discussed. Most incidents of mistreatment took place in the early years of internment. Later, according to internee reports, there were fewer such incidents. What contributed to the decrease? Two specific reasons for the decrease can be given. First was the concern among U.S. officials that adverse publicity regarding any mistreatment of enemy aliens might result in reciprocal abuses against Americans in the Asian lands occupied by the Japanese, especially China.[1] Such information could be transmitted through the Spanish government, a neutral country representing Japanese interests in America, as the Swiss government did for the United States in Japan. Second, the Japanese enemy alien internees were able to use the articles of the Geneva Convention, once it was recognized by the camp authorities, to dispute regulations, rules, conduct, and orders that the aliens perceived to be unjust.

The 1798 Alien Enemies Act states that in a declared war between the United States and a foreign nation, "natives, citizens, denizens, or subjects of the hostile nation," fourteen years or older, may be "apprehended, restrained, secured, and removed as alien enemies."[2] After the attack on Pearl Harbor, by the evening of December 7, 1941, the FBI had arrested and detained 736 mainland Japanese aliens; by December 11, the number was 1,370, and by February 16, 1942, 2,192 had been apprehended. In addition, by early 1942, 879 Japanese were under arrest in Hawaii.

By 1945, the Immigration and Naturalization Service (INS), after it was given jurisdiction over alien enemy proceedings, inherited the responsibility for a total of 24,886 "alien enemy" persons, including Japanese and Germans as the largest groups, some Italians, and a few other nationalities. This group included all those arrested under presidential warrants, as well as those voluntarily interned dependent family members, persons arrested from Hawaii and Alaska, the German and Italian merchant-seamen arrested on enemy ships, the civilians captured by the military in the various war theaters, the enemy aliens brought up from Central and South American countries, and the diplomatic personnel from enemy nations.

The majority of the Japanese aliens and Japanese Americans removed and confined after the promulgation of Executive Order 9066 came under the jurisdiction of the War Department's Wartime Civilian Control Administration and the civilian War Relocation Authority.[3] However, for another group, almost all of whom were Japanese aliens, a separate and still relatively unknown process began, one of identification, categorization, apprehension, detention, interrogation, and confinement was started before the internment of most Japanese Americans and alien Japanese.

As early as 1939, various governmental departments and, in particular, the special intelligence agencies of the Justice Department, the Federal Bureau of Investigation (FBI), the Office of Naval Intelligence and the army's Military Intelligence Division, were compiling lists of persons considered to be "dangerous" enemy aliens and citizens.[4] Most Japanese aliens apprehended on or after December 7, as a result of their names being included on such lists, were held in nearby county and city jails or Immigration and Naturalization Service stations. Some were questioned and then released, others were questioned and kept for days and weeks until they were either let go or, as in most cases, shipped to an alien detention station and later to a permanent internment camp in the hinterlands of the continental United States.

The exact number of Japanese involved in these "other" camps is difficult to specify because the statistics changed on any given day as individuals were arrested, detained, interned, paroled, repatriated, expatriated, released with few restrictions, released with the status of "internment at large," or died. However, in August 1945, records show there were 5,264 Japanese in actual custody (3,116 male adults, 589 female adults, and 1,559 children), with 153 Japanese diplomats and 1,573 other Japanese having been repatriated and five having been returned to South America—a total of 6,995 people.[5]

Earl G. Harrison, then Commissioner of the Immigration and Naturalization Service, wrote glowingly about the enemy alien internment program in a 1944 publicity piece:

Some day when the full story can be written, it will become known that in the United States that program [for alien enemy internment] has been carried out with all the strictness required to protect the country and at the same time with a spirit and understanding that have made new friends for the democratic way. After these years of bitterness and fighting have passed, no American need have any regret over the manner in which his government's representatives treated "alien enemies" during their days of internment.[6]

Harrison appeared to have conveniently forgotten or did not wish to acknowledge the shootings, killings, mistreatment, and beatings of the alien Japanese in these internment camps. At least three internees died by gunfire.

On July 27, 1942, around 2:30 a.m., two Issei internees, Toshio Kobata, a farmer from Brawley, California, and Hirota Isomura, a fisherman from San Pedro, California, were shot to death by the Lordsburg, New Mexico, camp guards. These two men were among the 147 or 148[7] internees transferred from the Fort Lincoln Internment Camp in Bismarck, North Dakota, to Lordsburg. All except these two men, who were too ill to walk, were forced to march the mile from the train station to the front gate of the camp. One account reports that these two men were driven by car to the front gate. While they waited for the other Japanese to arrive, the guards suddenly opened fire and killed the two men. Later, the internees were told that Kobata and Isomura had tried to escape and were shot in the attempt.[8] Another account does not specify where the actual shooting occurred.[9] When the internees asked about the condition of their two ill comrades, they were told by the camp physician that they had been taken to the camp hospital and were receiving medical care.[10] However, the next morning, some internees again asked the military doctor about the two prisoners, and were told that they had been shot trying to escape on the way to the camp.[11] Other inmates learned about their deaths through other means: Two Japanese inmates were forced to dig two holes, each approximating the dimensions of a human grave. Since the New Mexico earth is hard and difficult to shovel, the two workers asked for rest time. They were told, in effect, that "these graves are for the Japanese who died;

if you don't do your work quickly, I will make you dig two more graves."[12]

It was difficult for the internees to obtain sufficient accurate information about the incident. One internee, Aizo Miyahara from San Francisco, apparently talked to an American mess sergeant who corroborated the alleged murder stories.[13] The internees then demanded that the camp administration conduct an investigation and have an autopsy performed. But the bodies were already buried, and the military commander refused their request. Another report indicates that the commander ordered a funeral to be held at 4:00 p.m., July 18; the internees refused the order to attend and instead held individual moments of silence for the deceased. A telegram was given to the camp commander to be sent to the Spanish ambassador in New Orleans, since the Spanish government represented the interests of the Japanese in this country.

Eventually, perhaps to forestall an international incident, a hearing was held on September 2. The Japanese internees submitted their own report and some were allowed to present testimony.[14] The soldier on guard duty, who pulled the trigger, was Private First Class Clarence A. Burleson. Although the internees were unable to obtain the official results of the inquiry, they believed that Burleson was found innocent of all charges.

The other death by gunfire occurred at the Fort Sill (Oklahoma) Temporary Enemy Alien Internment Camp. Mr. Ichiro Shimoda, age forty-five, a gardener living with his family in Los Angeles, was arrested by the FBI on December 7, 1941. He was apparently apprehended and detained because the FBI had information about his status as a veteran of the Japanese armed forces. Once incarcerated and placed on a train to the Missoula, Montana, Detention Station, he suddenly became irrational, as one internee reported; he was concerned about his wife and family who were left behind.[15] He tried to commit suicide by biting off his tongue, but the other internees restrained him and placed a piece of wood between his jaws; he was kept under constant internee watch until they arrived in Missoula. Initially he appeared to get better there, but then he later tried to asphyxiate himself. When he was transferred to Fort Sill in mid-March 1942, he again became irrational, tried to climb the inner fence surrounding the camp and was shot to death by the guards. The internees reported that both the guards and the commander knew about Shimoda's psychological condition.

The government's file on this particular incident is particularly instructive. The FBI report, dated May 18, 1942 states that

One Jap became mildly insane and was placed in the Fort Sill Army Hospital. [He] . . . attempted an escape on May 13, 1942 at 7:30 a.m. He climbed the first fence, ran down the runway between the fencing, one hundred feet and started to climb the second, when he was shot and killed by two shots, one entering the back of his head. The guard had given him several verbal warnings. The name and address of the Japanese Enemy Alien was noted by the Agent after discussing the incident with Major Eckel and Major Eckel was now making a report to the Federal Bureau of Investigation. Major Eckel stated that the position of some of the light poles, electric wires, gates and guard towers were not most advantageously located, but explained that the camp was erected in twenty-four hours and without much planning. He indicated that he was presently erecting additional lighting to help compensate for these shortcomings.[16]

This FBI report implies that the guards feared an internee escape from this prison. However, it was then six months after the attack on Pearl Harbor, and the military, having had such extensive experience with the Japanese aliens, should have realized that these prisoners had not attempted to nor were they likely to escape or to use violent behavior. Moreover, the mental condition of this particular inmate was known; still, the internee was shot and killed.

The records include many other incidents of mistreatment of the Japanese enemy aliens. Internees reported cases of individual beatings while under restraint or in their detention cells, of guards threatening internees with unsheathed bayonets, of being ordered to cooperate with questionable rules and regulations made by camp commanders, of camp physicians giving questionable and unrequested injections to internee patients, of the continual use of handcuffs to restrain internees, and of the use of solitary confinement, all to "maintain" the Japanese internee population.

Initially, the Japanese internees believed that they had no basis on which to protest or effect changes in their treatment. Then, in mid-1942, an important document came to their attention—the Geneva Convention of July 27, 1929, Relative to the Treatment of Prisoners of War, more commonly known as the 1929 Geneva Convention.[17]

Although the Geneva Convention does not cover the treatment of interned enemy aliens, on December 18, 1941, in an effort to obtain fair treatment for the many prisoners of war captured by the Japanese military in Southeast Asia, U.S. government officers, through the Swiss government, informed the Japanese government that the United States

. . . intended to abide by the Geneva Prisoner of War Convention and the Geneva Red Cross Convention . . . that it further intended to extend and apply the provisions of the Geneva Prisoner of War Conven-

tion to any civilian aliens that it might intern, that it hoped that the Japanese Government would apply the provisions of these conventions reciprocally. . . .[18]

By the beginning of World War II, Japan had not ratified the convention; however, on January 29, 1942, Foreign Minister Tojo answered the American inquiry:

Japan strictly observes the Geneva Convention of July 27, 1929, relative to the Red Cross, as a signatory of that Convention. The Imperial Government has not yet ratified the Convention relating to treatment of prisoners of war of 27 July 1929. It is therefore not bound by the said Convention. Nevertheless it will apply "mutatis mutandis" the provisions of that Convention to American Prisoners of War in its power.[19]

A comprehensive examination of all relevant portions of the Geneva Convention is beyond the scope of this presentation, but to mention just a few: Article 2 states in part that prisoners of war must always be humanely treated and protected, particularly against acts of violence, insults, and public curiosity. Article 42 stipulates that prisoners of war have the right to inform their captors of their requests with regard to the conditions of captivity and to address to the representatives of the protecting powers any complaints about the conditions of their captivity. These complaints and requests are to be transmitted immediately, and there shall be no punishment even if these requests and complaints are unfounded. Article 46 forbids any corporal punishment, any imprisonment in quarters without daylight, and, in general, any form of cruelty. Article 47 deals with escapes and attempted escapes, which may be subject to preventive imprisonment and special surveillance. However, Article 54 stipulates that arrests are not to exceed thirty days, and are to be considered the most severe disciplinary punishment that may be imposed on a prisoner of war for such deeds as attempted escapes.[20] Yet, by the end of January 1942, although both parties had agreed to observe the Geneva Convention, and the United States government had specifically mentioned that civilian internees were to be included, violations would continue to take place within American camps housing the Japanese aliens.[21]

When the Japanese alien internees were first apprehended they had encountered various slights and mistreatments from their captors. Some forms appear to be more or less of a harassing nature; for example, in one reported case, their jail food was over-salted or so peppered as to render it unpalatable.[22] In other cases, the mistreatment was much more severe. One internee was reportedly kept in solitary confinement for weeks,[23] and another was periodically beaten until his front teeth were knocked in.[24]

From mid-December on, Japanese aliens discussed these stories of cruel and abusive behavior in the Missoula Detention Station where many of them were initially taken to obtain a hearing. Not until at least April 1942 did information about the Geneva Convention enter the camp. Its effects on the subsequent treatment of the inmates must be pieced together from various sources.[25]

From December 1941 to January 1942, any Japanese who was perceived by camp authorities as threatening or unacceptable was dealt with in a forceful manner. For example, when the chosen Japanese representative of the Missoula Camp protested to the INS officials that certain inmates were harshly treated in the initial holding areas, he was told that his objection was a form of interference and, if it continued, that he too would be placed in solitary confinement.[26] Moreover, the internees were ordered, without right of refusal, to work in sub-zero degree weather and to work without pay or compensation on labor projects outside of the Missoula Station. In early 1942, these complaints were made known to the Japanese ambassador, Kichisaburo Nomura, who was then confined in a State Department camp in West Virginia awaiting return to Japan. Nomura apparently protested to the State Department, and agents of the Justice and State departments flew to Missoula sometime after April 1942 to investigate. By June 1942, three Missoula immigration officials had been dismissed or transferred, and the internees' representatives had obtained copies of the 1929 Geneva Convention from the INS representatives[27] or from the Spanish consul.[28]

From June on, the internee-administration relationship at Missoula became calmer, not only as a result of the convention, but also because groups of internees, after their hearings, were able to leave the camp. Some went to join their families in the WRA relocation camps while others were sent to other detention stations or internment camps for permanent incarceration.

Many of the Missoula internees were thus transferred to the Lordsburg Internment Camp in New Mexico, especially after May 1942.[29] There, from June 19, 1942, the internees met further instances of harassment and abuse, this time from military authorities rather than the INS. They were ordered, for example, to work without pay while assisting in the construction of military airports, to clean the army's horse stables, to move ammunition, and to work outside the internment campgrounds.[30] The internees protested these apparent violations of the Geneva Convention, basing their objections on a copy of the convention brought from Missoula to the Lordsburg camp in June 1942. The Lordsburg military commander was appar-

ently unaware of, or chose to ignore, the applicability of the convention to the treatment of civilian alien internees. Their protests resulted in their representatives being threatened with physical harm and they were placed under barracks arrest; the internees demanded their right to telegraph the Spanish consul. The next day, the military commander informed the internees that he would abide by the Geneva Convention and would release their representatives.[31] Conflicts in the camp did not end here; until August 10, 1942, the military commander continued to issue orders that were often resisted by the internees based on their reading of the convention.[32]

It was during this time that the July 27 shooting and subsequent internee turmoil took place. There is some doubt about whether the Spanish consul actually received the telegram about the deaths of the two men since it was not until August 10 that he and a Mr. Young, of the State Department, came to Lordsburg to investigate the earlier protests of the internees about the violations of various articles of the Geneva Convention.[33]

The internees were promised that the State Department, through the Spanish Embassy, would report back to them on the interpretations of the various articles in the convention. They received this report on December 5, 1942; in it, the State Department acceded to many of their points, especially on the crucial issues concerning the proper employment of their labor. This particular issue then ceased to be a major point for conflict.

Thus, although the process took nearly a year, the internees found that they had a powerful document with which to prevent the many abuses and physical mistreatment they had experienced. The internees were eventually given permission to translate into Japanese the Geneva Convention and they distributed it to the internees at Lordsburg. The convention and its articles were discussed in the barracks and the level of inhumane treatment lessened.

However, life in these camps remained difficult. These were strong, active men who, before their internment, were leaders in their Japanese communities; now they were separated from their families and loved ones, wasting their days and nights, uncertain what the future held for them and for their wives and children who were interned in the relocation centers.

Emphasis has been placed on only one aspect of the Japanese alien internees' experience within the detention and internment camps during World War II. Attempts to gain information about this issue from the perspective of the United States government, especially that of the FBI or the INS, have been less than successful, even with the assistance of the Freedom of

Information Act, because certain files had pages missing while others have been "sanitized" with passages obliterated by large black marks. Certainly there are wartime experiences of the Japanese aliens and Japanese Americans yet to be uncovered. This paper should aid in correcting part of this historical void.

Also, our collective image of an America that represented the highest virtues in its conduct towards civilian internees should be reassessed in light of the data previously buried, often beyond public reach. Clearly, more work is needed before the entire story of these "forgotten concentration camps" is unearthed. Much of this "newer" story is unpleasant to tell and difficult to read. However, the one rationale that legitimates uncovering this sad chapter of American history is that it will help ensure that this will never happen again.[34]

NOTES

1. Michi Weglyn, *Years of Infamy: The Untold Story of America's Concentration Camps* (New York: William Morrow, 1976), 202.

2. Weglyn, 288.

3. Jacobus tenBroek, Edward N. Barnhart, and Floyd W. Matson, *Prejudice, War and the Constitution* (Berkeley: University of California Press, 1954), passim.

4. Ken Ringle, "What Did You Do Before the War, Dad?" *The Washington Post Magazine* (December 6, 1981), passim.

5. U.S. Department of Justice, Immigration and Naturalization Service, "Memo," 85-56125 (August 24, 1945).

6. Earl G. Harrison, "Civilian Internment—American Way" *Survey Graphics* 33 (May 1944): 270.

7. Miryo Fukuda, *Koryu Seikatsu Rokunen* (San Francisco: Konkokyo Kyokai, 1957), 66; and Daisho Tana, *Santa Fe, Lordsburg, Senji Tekikokujin Koryujo-nikki, Dai-Ikkan* (Tokyo: T. Tana, Y. Asaji, Yamaki Bo Futsu Shorin, 1976), report 148; Kazuo Ito, *America Shunju Hachijunen* (Tokyo: PMC Publishers, 1982), 109, states that it was 147.

8. Fukuda, 67; Tana, 290.

9. Tana, 290.

10. Ibid.

11. Ibid., 290–91.

12. Fukuda, 67.

13. Ibid.

14. Ibid., 68–69. Ito, 109, reports the soldier's name as Poston (undoubtedly a phonetic spelling); Provost Marshall General's files, 389-414-383.715 (August 10, 1942).

15. Fukuda, 58.

16. FBI memo, 62-63892, May 18, 1942.

17. Charles I. Bevans, comp., *Treaties and Other International Agreements of the United States of America, 1776–1949* (Washington D.C.: Department of State, 1969), 931–64.

18. Howard S. Levie, ed., *Documents on Prisoners of War*, International Law Studies, vol. 5, (Newport, R. I.: U.S. Naval War College, 1979), 462.

19. Levie, 463.

20. Ibid., 178–200.

21. Discussion on the Japanese military's mistreatment of their prisoners of war can be found in numerous sources. See for example, Courtney Browne, *Tojo: The Last Banzai* (New York: Holt, Rinehart and Winston, 1967), 141–51; Saburo Ienaga, *The Pacific War: 1931–1945* (New York: Pantheon Books, 1978), 181–202.

22. Ito, 99.

23. Ibid., 80.

24. Fukuda, 60.

25. Ibid.; Ito; Tana; and Shinichi Kato, ed., *Beikoku Nikkeijin Hyakunenshi* (America's Persons of Japanese Ancestry: 100 Year History) (Los Angeles: Shinnichibei Shimbunsha, 1961).

26. Fukuda, *Koryu*, 62.

27. Ibid.

28. Tana, 256.

29. Fukuda, passim.

30. Fukuda, 62.

31. Tana, 256.

32. Ibid., 288.

33. Kato, 339.

34. The author gratefully acknowledges the kind support and advice of Dr. Shin Roy Hasegawa; thanks go also to Kanako Kashima, Yasuko Iwai, Takika Susanne Lee, Sam Solberg, and Masato Uyeda for their assistance.

The Santa Fe Internment Camp and the Justice Department Program for Enemy Aliens

John J. Culley

The first duty is to win the war. The second duty, that goes hand in hand with it, is to win it greatly and worthily, showing the real quality of our power not only, but the real quality of our purpose and of ourselves.

Woodrow Wilson, May 18, 1918[1]

On May 3, 1943, using this quotation with unintended irony, Attorney General Francis Biddle concluded a series of lectures at the Law School of the University of Virginia entitled "Democratic Thinking and the War." Although he spoke within sight of Thomas Jefferson's Monticello, "where so much of the democratic hope was born, [and] where so much of its creed was written," and notwithstanding the title of his own lecture series, Biddle did not mention the preeminent civil liberties issue of the day, the internment of people of Japanese ancestry and the role of the Justice Department in that tragedy.[2] In the forty years since Biddle's lecture, scholars writing on the Japanese American experience have concentrated on the role of the War Relocation Authority and its relocation centers, to the neglect of Justice Department activities.[3] This paper examines one aspect of wartime civil liberties, the enemy alien control program of the Justice Department. Specifically, it is a study of the origins and operations of one enemy alien internment camp that the Justice Department maintained at Santa Fe, New Mexico.

The terminology applied to the various government camps has been inconsistent and confused. The government formally used the euphemistic term *relocation center* to describe the WRA camps, although informally officials often called them concentration camps, as do many scholars today. However, the term *internment camp*, which the government applied to the Justice Department camps, has a more precise meaning, having been identified historically with the process of detaining aliens. In this sense, the term is not a euphemism, and for purposes of clarity this study uses the terms *internment* and *internee* in reference to the Justice Department program.

In a nation at war, no group has a more tenuous hold on civil liberty than the resident alien who is a citizen of an enemy country. The discriminatory wording of the 1790 Naturalization Act, reinforced by a Supreme Court decision in 1922, denied naturalized citizenship to the Issei and subordinated them to alien, noncitizen status regardless of their length of residence. Since Japan was the only nation to offer them citizenship, after Pearl Harbor the government viewed them not simply as aliens but as enemy aliens.[4] Even before the West Coast evacuation of February and March 1942 swept both citizen and noncitizen, Nisei and Issei, into War Relocation Authority camps, some Issei followed another road to other less familiar camps. Immediately after Pearl Harbor the Justice Department activitated its prewar contingency plan for enemy alien control, leading to the arrest of thousands and to their confinement in Justice Department internment camps.

Over a year earlier the government had taken steps to deal with the potential problem of subversion and disruption by enemy aliens in the event of war. A presidential directive of September 1939 designated the FBI as the primary agency to handle matters relating to espionage, sabotage, and violations of neutrality regulations. With regard to aliens, the FBI investigated those whose backgrounds, activities, or associations aroused suspicions of possible disloyalty. The bureau also drew up its ABC list of individuals, classified into three categories according to the degree of potential danger, who would be taken into custody in wartime. The Justice Department filed this information for future use.[5] On June 28, 1940, Congress passed the Alien Registration Act, known as the Smith Act, a sweeping law with a misleading title, for it dealt with sedition as much as with the registration of aliens. Title III of the act required every alien over fourteen years old to be registered and fingerprinted. By December 1940, the Justice Department had supervised the registration and fingerprinting of almost five million aliens, assigned them numbers, and put this information on punch cards for tabulation.[6] In June 1940, the department acquired another instrument of control when it inherited the Immigration and Naturalization Service from the Labor Department. Thus, when the war began, the Justice Department had a plan and the means at hand to deal with the question of enemy aliens.[7]

The government's authority over enemy aliens came from Section 21, Title 50, United States Code.

After a public proclamation by the president that a state of war or a threat of invasion or predatory incursion existed, all natives, citizens, or subjects of a hostile government residing in the United States as unnaturalized aliens who were fourteen years of age or older were "liable to be apprehended, restrained, secured, and removed as alien enemies."[8] The courts had previously held that such arrests were not subject to the due-process clause of the fourteenth amendment or to review by habeas corpus. Nor did the presidential warrant on which each arrest was made have to disclose the specific grounds for the arrest.[9] On December 7 and 8, 1941, President Roosevelt issued three proclamations (2525, 2526, and 2527) which noted the existence of war and the threat of invasion and which made Japanese, German, and Italian aliens subject to summary arrest and detention.[10]

On December 7, 1941, the FBI began arresting the aliens on its preselected lists and turning them over to the INS for temporary detention. Within twenty-four hours the government had 1,771 enemy aliens in custody; 1,212 were Japanese.[11] The Justice Department repeatedly assured the nation that the program for dealing with enemy aliens was orderly, fair, and sufficient to meet the threat. Attorney General Francis Biddle declared on December 11 that "no alien was apprehended, and none will be, on the score of nationality alone. . . . Everyone of those taken into Federal custody had been under observation for more than a year." In all of his public statements Biddle continued to reject a policy of collective guilt and wholesale internment and asserted that the department's policy considered the merits of each individual case.[12] The arrests continued and by March 9 the INS held over 4,000 people in custody, primarily at Fort Missoula, Montana, and Fort Lincoln, North Dakota. Ultimately, the Justice Department had nine permanent and eighteen temporary internment camps.[13] By spring, a bureaucratic apparatus to manage this growing program was in place.

The Justice Department established a bilevel organization consisting of the Alien Enemy Control Unit (AECU) in Washington and an Alien Enemy Hearing Board in each of the more than one hundred federal judicial districts of the nation. Administration of the internment process flowed back and forth between national and local levels. The AECU coordinated all activities concerning enemy aliens both within the Justice Department and between the other departments, such as state, war, and navy.[14] Each Alien Enemy Hearing Board had three civilian members drawn from the local community, one of whom was an attorney. Their hearings were attended by representatives of the U.S. attorney for that district, the FBI, and the INS.

The process began when an FBI field office submitted its dossier on an individual to a U.S. attorney, who considered the evidence and, if he found cause, forwarded a request to the AECU for the attorney general to issue a presidential warrant of apprehension. After review, the AECU issued a warrant which the FBI executed, and the case moved on to the Alien Enemy Hearing Board.[15]

Edward J. Ennis, the head of the AECU, described the next step as giving the individual a "summary informal hearing," in which "every effort has been made to get away from costly time consuming judicial procedures." The alien appeared in person before the board and could present affidavits, but he could not be represented by an attorney nor could he object to the government's evidence. Ennis noted that "if there is substantial reason to sustain the charge against the alien, every doubt at this time must be resolved against him and in favor of the Government. The man cannot be given anything like a jury trial on these issues." The U.S. attorney presented the evidence the FBI had developed against the individual; the board then reached a decision and forwarded its recommendation, whether for release, parole, or internment, to the AECU in Washington, D.C., which reviewed the evidence and drew an order for the attorney general's signature. If the order called for internment, the alien entered into indefinite custody for the duration of the war.[16] Thus did individuals arrive at an internment camp such as the one at Santa Fe.

In the spring of 1942, the internment of enemy aliens created an urgent need for detention facilities and, by March 1, the Justice Department had selected Santa Fe as the site for a new detention camp. In 1940, New Mexico had a population of 531,818, and Santa Fe had only 20,325.[17] Located high in the western foothills of the Sangre de Cristo Mountains, Santa Fe was definitely off the beaten path. The nearest highway junction of importance, with U.S. 66, was seventy miles away over narrow, two-lane roads. Although there was a railroad spur and a depot in town, passengers ordinarily arrived at Lamy, sixteen miles away on the main line of the Santa Fe Railway. The surrounding mountains and the 7,000-foot elevation of the town also shaped the climate, featuring mild days and cool evenings in the summer, and cold days, colder nights, and snow in the winter. Although the stark beauty of the countryside, the crisp air, and the brilliant sunlight enchanted many visitors, some saw only a severe and inhospitable land.

In February, the INS acquired from the New Mexico State Penitentiary an eighty-acre tract some two and one-half miles from the center of town, containing an abandoned CCC camp built in 1933 to house 450 men. All utility lines were still intact, as were numerous semipermanent buildings and, by the end of March, construction workers had converted the CCC camp into a detention center to house 1,400 people.[18] The INS initially viewed the camp as a temporary facility to house West Coast detainees until hearing boards could determine their fate; this remained the operative assumption throughout 1942.

The first group of 425 detainees arrived on March 14, and two other arrivals in March and April brought the camp population to a maximum for 1942 of 826 people, all males and all from California. During April, May, and June, five separate Alien Enemy Hearing Boards from California sat at Santa Fe and, as a result, the camp population steadily declined. Of the original 826 detainees, hearing boards released or paroled 523, and ordered 302 interned in army custody. One man died of disease. On September 24, 1942, the last internee departed and by November the camp was deactivated and left in the hands of a caretaker staff.[19]

The second phase of the camp's existence began in February 1943 with the army's decision to transfer to the INS all civilian internees in its custody. The Santa Fe camp was reactivated and expanded to hold 2,000. As before, the camp was not a family camp; all of the inmates were males. On March 23, the first group of 357 men arrived and the population rapidly expanded, reaching 1,257 by June and 1,783 by August. The maximum number of internees at one time was 2,100 in June 1945. During the entire period of the camp's existence, a total of 4,555 individuals passed through its gates.[20]

It has long been recognized that men held in captivity constitute a distinct form of society. Any examination of a captive society should first establish the purpose, goals, or objectives of those in power, in this case, the government and the INS, and then examine the means administrators use to attain their goals. The characteristics of the captive population are also critical to the analysis, as is their response to captivity. At the same time, one must recognize certain truisms about custodial institutions. They are authoritarian societies with the characteristics of a totalitarian regime in which the threat of force is always present. They impose deprivation and frustration upon the inmates, either as the result of deliberate punishment or as the unplanned and even unavoidable concomitant of incarceration. These deprivations may be physical, or psychological, or both, for the two are often interrelated. Most aspects of physical and psychological deprivation fall into the following categories: the loss of liberty, the denial of heterosexual relationships, the reduction of goods and services, and the loss of autonomy. Thus, by viewing the Santa Fe camp in terms of its societal function, one may place the camp experience in a broader perspective and simultaneously acquire a more useful framework for analysis.[21]

The traditional reasons for a government to incarcerate an individual are to reform, punish, or deter undesirable behavior. While the Justice Department did not view the Issei as criminals, it did argue that as enemy aliens they were a potential threat to national security. This argument, however specious, establishes that the government's stated objective was to prevent this by confining the Issei in internment camps. Within these camps, the administrative policies used closely resembled the policies used in prisoner-of-war camps.

The treatment of all enemy alien internees held by the INS in its various camps was determined by the relevant provisions of the Geneva Convention of 1929. The United States had proposed to Japan that the Geneva provisions regarding the treatment of prisoners of war should apply to civilian enemy alien internees. Japan had not ratified the Geneva Convention, but promised de facto compliance regarding prisoners of war and also agreed to apply the convention to noncombatant enemy aliens, mutatis mutandis, subject to reciprocity, and on the condition that the belligerent nations did not subject Japanese noncombatant internees to manual labor against their will. Consequently, the Justice Department instructed the INS that the Geneva Convention would establish the minimum standards of treatment. To implement these instructions at the Santa Fe camp, the INS promulgated a list of over seventy detailed rules for the camp authorities to follow and enforce.[22] These rules determined the quality of the internees' lives.

The question of the internee's standard of living falls into the category of the deprivation of goods and services and includes the availability of the essentials of life—food, clothing, and shelter. Inadequacy in this area can be life threatening and may produce unrest and disruption among the internees. But at Santa Fe conditions were neither life threatening nor did they produce disruptive protest. The clothing furnished by the government, new and surplus U.S. Army issue, satisfied basic needs.[23]

The housing was adequate if not comfortable. The INS renovated the original wood and tar-paper CCC barracks and erected 100 smaller prefabricated Victory Huts. The local climate rendered these buildings inadequate and, by the fall of 1942, all but four-teen were replaced with standard barracks. The most common complaint about housing arose over the proper square footage allotted each person. Internees contended that the Geneva Convention entitled them to the same square footage as garrison troops of the U.S. Army—sixty square feet per man. Although the administration argued that for new construction the army standard was only forty square feet, it considered this inadequate.[24]

In fact, the housing space for each internee varied with the size of the camp population, and at the max-imum population of 2,000, it was forty-four square feet. The administration concluded that the frequent com-plaints of overcrowding were partly motivated by re-sentment when new arrivals entered the barracks and disturbed the social arrangements of the old residents.[25]

The question of food provides a better illustration of the role of the Geneva Convention and the degree to which the INS met the internees' basic physical needs. Justice Department instructions required that the food furnished the internees equal in quantity and quality that of U.S. troops at base camps and that it meet the standards of the Standard Ration Allowance of the Geneva Convention, 5.2980 pounds of food per man per day, consisting of specified amounts from the various food groups. Food preferences of the internee's national diet could be accommodated, provided that a balanced diet was preserved. In 1942, the camp pur-chased food on the open market from local suppliers, a practice that drained the already strained civilian sources and caused considerable public resentment. In addition, specialty foods peculiar to the Japanese diet were often unattainable or available only at premium prices. When the camp reopened in 1943, the army quartermaster general became the principal food sup-plier, supplemented by the production of an irrigated nineteen-acre farm the internees established adjacent to the camp. The farm supplied the fresh vegetables that were popular with the internees but not readily available elsewhere. Internees also ran a poultry farm that provided fresh chickens and eggs. The canteen, under internee management, stocked specialty foods for private purchase, and specialty foods also arrived from Japan via the International Red Cross. Although there were slight modifications to accommodate the internees' preferences, such as more fish and rice and less red meat and potatoes, the diet adhered to the Standard Ration Allowance with one exception. To eliminate excessive waste, camp authorities reduced the weight to slightly less than five pounds per man per day, after a study of the garbage convinced them that the average internee did not consume the Standard

Ration Allowance. The Geneva Convention also allowed the Standard Ration Allowance to be reduced in conformity with the rationing of food for civilians and, in April 1945, it was reduced to 4.83141 pounds to comply with the national food conservation program.[26] Like most institutional food, that served at the camp was no doubt tasteless, dull, and monoto-nous, but it provided balanced nutrition.

There are obvious difficulties in evaluating the standard of living of internees under custody. The physical facilities of the camp, with the renovation and new buildings, marked an improvement over the orig-inal structures. Living conditions at Santa Fe were probably superior to the conditions at some of the other camps, a fact the internees seemed to recognize. In June 1942, the internee spokesman, on behalf of over 100 men who had just been ordered interned for the duration of the war, appealed to the attorney general to let them remain at Santa Fe in preference to transfer to an army camp. Spokesman Atsuzi Okado stated that Ivan Williams, the officer-in-charge, and his staff had "made this station comfortable both mentally and phy-sically." Okado stated that among the camps, Santa Fe was "outstanding," and he praised the system of inter-nee self-government, the cooperation of the internees, and the unselfish efforts of the administration to aid the internees while still performing their duties.[27] The fact that Okado wanted to prevent the transfer of these men to army custody does not entirely invalidate his praise of Santa Fe.

A confidential survey of the camp made by State Department officials in May 1942 concluded that the camp and its commander made a most favorable im-pression and that the detainees appeared well satisfied with their treatment and place of detention. They noted that the camp had sufficient grounds for exercise and recreation, comfortable buildings, a healthful cli-mate, competent administration, and offered all that could be expected of an internment camp. In June, a representative of the International Red Cross reached a similar conclusion. In strictly physical terms, life in the camp was spartan, but not arduous or oppressive.[28]

The satisfaction of basic physical needs, however, is not the entire story. No matter how adequate these provisions, the goods and services available to inter-nees do not compare to those available in the free community. The captive individual wants and needs not just the necessities of life, but also the amenities, and inmates of custodial institutions view their forced material impoverishment as a painful loss. While the Issei, in the tradition of an Eastern culture, may not have been as materialistic as individuals reared in a Western culture, they no doubt felt their material deprivation deeply.

Another of the painful deprivations internment imposed was the loss of liberty. In a physical sense, the internees lost their freedom of movement and lived within a shrunken world whose boundaries were defined by a barbed-wire fence. The individual lost physical contact with family, friends, and colleagues and suffered a painful rupture of emotional relationships, resulting in loneliness and boredom.

Camp authorities recognized that the internees faced a difficult psychological adjustment and that the monotony and uncertainty of an internment sentence of indefinite duration could foster neurotic behavior. To prevent this in the interest of order and tranquility, the administration developed an elaborate program of recreation, entertainment, education, work, and visits, which also served as a means of controlling internee behavior.

The camp's physical plant offered varied facilities for these activities. It initially consisted of twenty-eight acres enclosed within a ten-foot-high wire fence, with a two-foot barbed-wire overhang, and with guard towers and searchlights at frequent intervals. In time, the physical plant expanded to include additional kitchens and mess halls, a bakery, canteen, visiting room, recreation hall, laundry, and library. Other facilities included gardens, a nineteen-acre farm, two softball diamonds, two tennis courts, a miniature nine-hole golf course, and a fenced forty-acre hiking area. The internees participated in volleyball, ping pong, medicineball, and wrestling. They also organized educational classes in calligraphy, Chinese and Japanese poetry, religion, American history, music, art, horticulture, poultry raising, foreign languages, math, science, and other subjects. Additional entertainment came from movies, which the administration selected, and from a very active internee theatrical group.[29]

Providing for medical care and easing the internees' concerns for their health not only met humanitarian imperatives but also contributed to an orderly internment. Initially, four Public Health Service nurses and one physician, utilizing one barrack, provided medical care. By 1945, medical facilities occupied nine small buildings and included a tuberculosis ward with a separate kitchen, a pharmacy, dental clinic, laboratory, and seventy-four-bed hospital, staffed by internee physicians, five nurses, and a surgeon from the Public Health Service. Local physicians, under contract, provided care for major surgery, ophthalmology, and some dentistry. In twenty-eight months of operation, there were twenty-six deaths, with the chief causes listed as carcinoma, cerebral hemorrhage, heart disease, and tuberculosis.[30]

In the area of mental health, relief from the boredom and monotony of camp life could be derived from work assignments. The Geneva Convention stated that internees could be required to perform work associated with the operation of their internment camp, without pay, provided that they were physically fit for such work. Aside from the required and routine maintenance work, such as trash collection and janitorial duties in the barracks, mess halls, and other buildings, volunteer work not directly connected with camp upkeep, such as work on the poultry farm, was paid at the rate of eighty cents per eight-hour day. The work program included everything from carpenters to cobblers, from laundrymen to lab technicians, and from plumbers to physicians, all drawn from a list of volunteers. Workers were more plentiful than jobs, and there was never a shortage of competent workers in any field. Nor did unrest among the internees ever seriously affect the overall work program. The most serious problem for the administration was the desire among the workers for frequent rotation from one job to another. As the administration realized, this strong desire to work was motivated not by pay but by the diversion it provided.[31] Even so, as in any custodial institution, time passed slowly.

The loss of liberty and the broken human relationships inherent in a custodial institution produce a sense of pain and isolation that may be ameliorated by generous visiting privileges. The Justice Department instructed the INS that visiting hours and regulations for relatives, friends, and legal counsel should be as liberal as local conditions permitted. The camp did receive large numbers of visitors, sometimes as many as forty-five per day. Visitors to the camp could see only one or two individuals per visit, and the INS supervised all visitations, except for those of representatives of the protecting power or of the Department of State. At one point, when two internees charged that the camp did not meet Geneva Convention provisions, the administration retaliated by reducing visiting hours from six hours per week to the minimum allowed by the Justice Department of two hours per week. However, a request from the Spanish Embassy quickly produced an INS directive that visiting hours be extended to twelve hours per week.

The administration could allow an internee to travel, at his own expense and under guard, to the War Relocation Authority projects, usually to visit an ailing relative or to attend a funeral. But there were limitations on this policy. Visits to the WRA camps required the permission of the central office of the INS in Philadelphia or of the director of the AECU in Washington, D.C.; camp authorities were wary lest the privilege of visiting dying relatives be abused.[32]

The administration considered their visitation policy, which they described as one of "wide latitude," to be a great success and noted that "no single act has done more to create a feeling that we are honestly endeavoring to help internees than has the visiting privilege."[33]

From the internee's viewpoint, however, this visiting policy did not overcome the emotional deprivation, loneliness, and pain caused by broken relationships. Internees expressed this sense of loss and anguish through their concern about the issues of parole, repatriation, and family reunion. These issues caused widespread frustration among the internees, reflecting another of the deprivations of a captive society, the loss of autonomy inherent in being subjected to a vast body of rules and commands, often trivial and often unexplained.

Repatriation and parole were linked to the loss of family, for many sought repatriation to rejoin their family in Japan, while others sought parole to join their family in WRA camps or in an unrestricted zone. Those seeking repatriation were doubly frustrated for they contended with a maze of regulations of both governments. The Spanish consul often reminded those waiting impatiently for repatriation that the Japanese government decided who would be accepted. Those who applied for parole were equally impatient for the rehearings that could set them free or send them to a WRA camp. But some internees who feared returning to the outside world with its hostile public and unemployment and housing problems were reluctant to seek parole.[34]

From the time the Santa Fe camp opened in 1942, the internees expressed concern for their families to the Spanish consul in San Francisco, Mr. F. de Amat, who represented the protecting power. As early as April 1942, the camp spokesman asked that the internees be reunited with their families and invoked the issue of reciprocity under the Geneva Convention with the argument that in Japan the families of American civilians were not separated, a point that Edward Ennis conceded in testimony before Congress the following month. In July, seventy-two internees petitioned Consul de Amat to investigate the alleged life-threatening conditions at Poston, Arizona, where their families lived.[35]

By the time the Santa Fe camp reopened in 1943, the men with families had been separated from them for over a year and being reunited was their major concern. Appeals to the protecting power and to the INS were frequent and fervent.[36] Internees could be reunited with their families through release or parole to a WRA camp, or by applying for transfer to special INS family camps at Crystal City and Seagoville, Texas.[37] Some found the slow pace of this process maddening and, in December 1943, 350 disgruntled internees

threatened that if they were not reunited with their families at Crystal City within a month, they would, through the Spanish consul, demand that the Japanese government immediately retaliate against interned U.S. civilians in the Orient by forcibly separating husbands, wives, and children. The Spanish Embassy, which the State Department generally found cooperative, exerted a moderating influence on such requests by pointing out the good-faith efforts of the U.S. government and by noting the practical problems involved in family reunions.[38] Internees who had applied for repatriation could also apply for transfer to Crystal City or, provided that they were neither "actively pro-Japanese or trouble-makers," they might join their families at Tule Lake.[39] But for the majority of the internees, there would be no family reunion for the duration, and no relief from this anguish.

To the extent that the inmates do not control their own lives and have only a limited number of choices, they are placed in a weak and dependent status, which in turn undermines their self-image as responsible adults. At the Santa Fe camp, the Justice Department ameliorated the situation with regulations requiring the internees to establish their own camp administration with elected officials to manage their own internal affairs and to represent them to the INS and to the protecting power. The internees established a comprehensive form of self-government, led by the spokesman and vice-spokesman and including a camp council, department heads, barracks captains, treasurer, and postmaster. Camp politics centered on the efforts of various factions to control the elected positions and to oust their opponents.[40]

This system served the interests of the camp authorities who found it conducive to an orderly administration. Camp administrators viewed the spokesmen as reasonable and understanding men, most of whom steered a middle course between the wishes of the internees and the requirements of the administration. They also believed that the internees responded best when given logical and straightforward responses to their questions or complaints, and that compromise was generally possible, so long as the internees achieved some portion of their goals. Nonetheless, it is undeniable that the internees had lost autonomous control of the most fundamental decisions of life and that this was a seriously felt deprivation.[41]

Another characteristic of the Santa Fe camp was that, like all custodial institutions, it was an authoritarian society in which the administration exercised power to control and order the internees' behavior. The exercise of that power may be based on authority, with authority being defined as a complex social relationship, in which one group is recognized as possessing a legitimate right to issue commands or regulations and in which those who receive these commands feel duty bound to obey. In general, prison administrators do not exercise authority in this sense, for while prison inmates may concede that their guards have a legitimate right to issue orders, as inmates they feel no sense of duty to obey.[42] Whether the internees at Santa Fe recognized the administration as having this legitimate authority is problematical; nonetheless, the administration did have another form of power, a form based on the ability to reward and punish. However, there are limitations to coercive power, both societal and practical, on the nature and effectiveness of the rewards and punishments that may be used in a custodial institution. For example, the Justice Department prohibited brutality, force, and violence, and provided specific and detailed instructions defining the appropriate punishment for unacceptable behavior. There were six punishable offenses: insubordination toward camp authorities or elected camp leaders; refusal to perform legally required work; escapes or attempted escapes; offenses against fellow internees or disruptive conduct; malicious destruction of property; and serious infractions of the camp rules.[43]

The officer-in-charge imposed punishment within specified limitations. Internees could be punished only by closer confinement and isolation, not to exceed thirty days for any single offense, and they could not be punished more than once for the same offense. The Justice Department stipulated that the guardhouse or detention cell was to be light, dry, warm, and ventilated, and that prisoners must be given two hours of outdoor exercise daily. Although the camp had two detention cells, one of which could hold two people and another which could hold fifteen, disciplinary problems were rare and they were seldom used. Fighting between individuals sometimes occurred as did occasional overindulgence in beer at the canteen, but the internees handled their own affairs and seldom brought such matters to the authorities unless the incident was serious.[44]

Camp authorities preferred to exercise control through rewards, rather than by punishment. Granting extra privileges beyond the requirements of the Geneva Convention not only raised morale and encouraged a spirit of cooperation but also provided an effective means of control. The suggestion that a privilege might be withdrawn threatened the entire group, and thus curbed the individual behavior that provoked the threat. Like any system of self-censorship or self-criticism, this placed a heavy burden on the internees.[45]

Overall security was not a problem. The only known attempted escape was unsuccessful. According to the guard's report, on November 10, 1945, Otomatsu Kimura scaled the fence and climbed the light pole to the top of a guard tower and then jumped to the road below. When told to get down from the fence, Kimura reportedly asked the guards to shoot him. He was hospitalized with possible fractures of the vertebrae and pelvis.[46]

The administration believed that the forbidding countryside and fear of the hostile local citizens convinced the internees that they were safer inside the camp and that escape was unwise. In general, the Santa Fe camp was tranquil and orderly, with few security problems, until March 1945, when a serious disorder occurred.[47]

This crisis did not originate at Santa Fe, but at the WRA center at Tule Lake, which the government used as a segregation center for all evacuees designated as disloyal. In November 1943, unable to govern the camp in an orderly fashion, the WRA suppressed the internee's elected representatives, and through January 1944, the army ran the camp under martial law. From this turmoil emerged an antiadministration, resegregationist group insisting that all individuals loyal to the United States be removed from Tule Lake; this would leave only those who supported Japan and they would be free to express this allegiance openly. The resegregationists organized two major groups: the Sokuji Kikoku Hoshi-dan (the Hoshi-dan), the Organization to Return Immediately to the Homeland to Serve, composed largely of Issei, and the Hokoku Seinen-dan (the Hokoku) or Young Men's Organization to Serve Our Mother Country, composed largely of Nisei. Both groups practiced nationalistic activities with military overtones, including marching and drilling, bugle calls, playing the Japanese national anthem, celebrating the eighth of each month in commemoration of the attack on Pearl Harbor, wearing short military-style haircuts, and wearing rising-sun emblems on their coats and shirts. They were also implicated in acts of intimidation, coercion, and physical violence against their opponents. In July 1944, the president signed the Denaturalization Bill (Public Law 405 of the 78th Congress) allowing U.S. nationals to renounce their citizenship in time of war while still residing within the U.S. This devious law, when combined with the lifting of the West Coast exclusion orders in December 1944, the announcement that the WRA camps would close in one year, and with the emotional atmosphere of Tule Lake, produced a crisis in which over 5,000 individuals renounced their U.S. citizenship. The resegregationists sought to profit from this situation believing that increased turmoil would force the WRA to accede to their demands.[48]

In December 1944, John L. Burling, the assistant

director of the AECU, arrived at Tule Lake to investigate the impact of the Denaturalization Bill and the activities of the resegregationist group.[49] After extensive interviews with internees, Burling decided to remove the leaders and the entire membership of the more active "subversive groups" and send them to INS camps for the duration of the war. This would quell the openly pro-Japanese activities at Tule Lake. Burling reasoned that

> It is . . . extremely difficult to control the conduct of people within Tule Lake because of the great number of persons assembled in one camp. For this reason, about the only way in which these activities can be surpressed [sic] at Tule Lake is to remove and intern those who engage in them. The threat of internment will be a far more effective deterrent to pro-Japanese activities at Tule Lake, however, if it is clear that those who are interned will be effectively prevented from such activities. It is for this reason that I believe it is particularly important that the remaining residents at Tule Lake hear from internees, that activities comparable to those of the two organizations are not permitted at camps of the Immigration and Naturalization Service.[50]

Leaders and active members of the two resegregationist organizations were dispersed to Fort Lincoln and Santa Fe between December 1944 and March 1945. In a sense, they won a victory, for they were resegregated and, when the first of three groups left for Santa Fe, they departed to a spectacular farewell celebration with marching formations, patriotic songs, bugles, and shouts of "banzai." The first group of seventy included two men (Zenshiro Tachibana and a Mr. Wakayama) identified by Burling as "probably the two principal leaders of this entire movement."[51] A second group of 171 departed for Santa Fe, with a similar farewell, on January 26, 1945. This group included a leader of the Hokoku Seinen-dan (Tsutomi Higashi), identified by Burling and others as one of the most militant members of the organization. A third group of 125 left for Santa Fe on March 4. An Associated Press dispatch reported that this group included the president of the Hoshi-dan (Shigeyoshi Kawabata), and the president of the Hokoku Seinen-dan (Minoru Hinoki). Santa Fe had thus inherited 366 of the most active resegregationist leaders of the troubled Tule Lake Segregation Center.[52]

At Santa Fe, the Tuleans displayed an attitude that camp authorities described as arrogant, headstrong, and uncooperative. The administration charged that they violated established camp rules and attempted to spread confusion, dissention, and dissatisfaction among others. An anonymous group called the Suicide Squad threatened the camp censors with death. But these activities failed to move the established residents of the camp, who resented the newcomers' behavior so much that, contrary to all past experiences, informers sent anonymous letters to the administration naming the troublemakers and pointing out situations that needed attention. Although the INS, from the camp's earliest days, had offered to pay informers five dollars for information relating to planned escapes, there is no evidence that such payments had ever been made, and this was not the motive of those who informed on the Tuleans. The anonymous letter writers always claimed that they wrote in the interest of the peaceful, harmonious operation of the camp and of good relations between the internees and the administration.[53]

The INS and the camp authorities did take precautions both at Santa Fe and elsewhere before the Tule Lake internees arrived. Following a suggestion made in 1943 by the officer-in-charge at Santa Fe, the INS had established a small disciplinary camp for incorrigible agitators at Fort Stanton, New Mexico, which they named "Japanese Segregation Camp #1." Using fear and uncertainty as a means of control, the INS kept the location but not the existence of this camp secret from the internees. The agency informed the Spanish Embassy of the camp and gave assurances that the standards of the Geneva Convention would be followed, but requested, for psychological and disciplinary reasons, that the Spanish government not divulge the location of the segregation camp. The INS did not mention to the Spanish that, although the Geneva standards prevailed, the camp was to be run on a "minimum basis." At Santa Fe, camp administrators enjoined the guards to greater vigilance and met the first group of the new arrivals with a general memorandum stating that they should consult the established internee representatives to learn the camp rules; that their conduct would affect the privileges of the entire camp; that no new arrival could hold a position in the internee government; that their conduct would determine whether they could eventually apply for family reunion; and that "no political, military or other demonstrations are permitted and any violations thereof will be subject to disciplinary action."[54]

On February 21, 1945, Tsutomu Higashi, described by W. F. Kelly, the assistant commissioner of the INS for alien control, as "the leader and the most militant and aggressive member of the younger Japanese subversive organization" (the Hokoku Seinendan), was sentenced to twenty days in the guardhouse for disobedience of orders and insolence to the head nurse and the officer-in-charge. As was his custom, at the expiration of one-half of the sentence, Ivan Williams, the officer-in-charge, offered to suspend the remainder of the sentence if Higashi would cooperate, but "Higashi stated that he had no intention of cooperating and that he would not comply with the camp regulations."[55] On March 8, Kelly authorized Williams to transfer Higashi to the Japanese segregation camp at Fort Stanton.

The previous day, March 7, Williams had ordered the internees to surrender to the chief internal security officer by no later than March 9, all articles of clothing that displayed the emblems of the two societies. After the deadline, anyone showing the emblems would be subject to disciplinary action.[56] The order was specifically aimed at the third group of Tuleans who had just arrived and who annoyed camp authorities by flaunting their rising-sun sweat shirts. Williams asserted that Zenshiro Tachibana was at the bottom of the trouble. Within two days, Kelly authorized Tachibana's transfer to Segregation Camp #1.[57]

On the morning of March 9, three of the recently arrived Tuleans (Aoki, Tamura, and Kameda) requested an interview with the officer-in-charge. Williams later reported that the men asserted that they were not going to surrender their sweat shirts and, when queried, claimed to represent the entire Tule Lake contingent. When Williams asked if it were the consensus of all the Tule Lake group not to comply with the rules and instructions of the internment camp, they answered yes. The officer-in-charge then sent them from the room and called in the camp spokesman and three other prominent Tuleans, Tachibana, Wakayama, and Yoshida. Finally, in the presence of all seven Japanese, Williams asked if the first three (Aoki, Tamura, and Kameda) actually represented the entire Tule Lake group. When it became clear that they did not and that there was disagreement among the internees, Williams told them that the order would stand, that all internees must turn in their sweat shirts. One of the Japanese replied, "We are going to defy you."[58]

After speaking to Kelly at the central office in Philadelphia, Williams called the District Director of the INS at El Paso and secured thirty inspectors from the Border Patrol, who arrived in Santa Fe the night of March 9. The next morning, the guards searched the camp and confiscated several dozen rising-sun sweat shirts and found many more with the emblem cut out. On the morning of March 12, the administration decided to transfer three of the recalcitrant leaders, Tachibana, Tsuha (a Buddhist priest and founder of the Hokoku Seinen-dan), and Higashi to Fort Stanton. As Tachibana and Tsuha were removed, a crowd of about 250 gathered at the gate near the headquarters building, where fifteen patrol inspectors confronted them. Chief Surveillance Officer Clifton M. Monroe approached and spoke to an internee who asked that he

and the others be taken to the same place Tachibana and Tsuha were going. Monroe reported that on at least five occasions over a period of twenty minutes, he ordered the crowd to disperse and, when they did not, he ordered the guards to fire tear-gas grenades. As the crowd retreated, throwing stones, Monroe issued a general call to quarters for all guards and issued submachine guns and riot guns to several patrol inspectors and ordered them to guard strategic locations outside the fence. One group of sixteen patrol inspectors, armed only with billies and gas grenades, entered through the confrontation gate, while six more made for another gate. The patrol inspectors, although almost surrounded, charged the crowd, which retreated, rallied, and then gradually dispersed after a series of scuffles. The entire melee lasted approximately ten minutes. Four internees (Mitsuo Hirashima, Akira Osugi, Gentaro Ono, and Isamu Uchida) were hospitalized with injuries, and 360 were segregated in a wire-enclosed stockade and denied any official standing or recognition.[59]

The crisis was of short duration and rapidly wound down. In a stern statement, Williams reviewed the events since December 1944 and blamed the resegregationist group and Zenshiro Tachibana in particular for the riot. The internees appointed a three-man investigation committee, but Kelly, who had arrived at Santa Fe, would not allow them to interview the four hospitalized internees, whom he called "troublemakers."[60]

By March 21, Kelly noticed a marked improvement in the attitude of the majority of the Tuleans. He concluded that the situation was rapidly improving; the troublemakers had been identified and their imminent transfer to the segregation camp would clear the air, and the other Tuleans could shortly be released from the stockade. In a letter to a State Department official, Kelly stated that

Yesterday I had (Kintoku) Ige, one of the very worst, in here laying the law down to him. He was most meek and submissive; said . . . that they have never previously been told what sort of conduct was expected of them—further that if they had been treated in a more firm way there never would have been any trouble at all.[61]

One year after the riot, in the first interview given to the press at the Santa Fe camp, Williams revealed that seventeen men, believed to be the leaders of the riot, had been sent to the segregation camp at Fort Stanton and subsequently had been repatriated to Japan, while others were given sentences of up to thirty days in the stockade. When a member of the resegregationist group was elected vice-spokesman, Williams set his election aside as contrary to the camp rule that no one transferred for disciplinary reasons could hold elected office. In June, another group of 399 arrived from Tule Lake, but there were no more disturbances in the camp.[62]

In the final months of the war, however, there were moments of uncertainty. Authorities wondered how the internees would react to the news that the war was over and even considered "the remote possibility of a banzai charge by the radical element in this camp, in the event of the unconditional surrender of Japan."[63] But when the internees heard the news and the noise of the celebration in the town, they secluded themselves in their barracks, with some fear that the public might attack them. Public hostility toward the Japanese had grown with the liberation in the Philippines of American prisoners of war and the disclosure of their treatment at Japanese hands, and also with the prospect of Japanese American resettlement in the western states after the war. Although the administration alerted the guards to the possibility of some act of violence against the camp, nothing of the sort occurred.[64]

From the Japanese surrender until April 1946, the Santa Fe camp served as a holding and processing center as the Justice Department closed the other INS camps and released or repatriated the internees. In late October 1945, there were 58 Japanese internees at Fort Stanton and 2,019 at Santa Fe, 1,373 of whom had applied for repatriation. Between November 1945 and April 1946, at least four groups left Santa Fe for the West Coast and repatriation, and the camp population rapidly declined to less than 500. The first group of 894 repatriates left for Seattle on November 21, followed by 330 more in late December, and 57 more on February 20, 1946. On March 1, 1946, 200 men, formerly residents of Tule Lake, arrived from Fort Lincoln, and on April 18, 135 men were transferred to Crystal City. Four days later 89 men left for Terminal Island, California, and repatriation. By the first of May, 1946, only 12 internees were left and the camp closed shortly thereafter.[65]

In the final analysis, it is clear that, although the Santa Fe internment camp shared certain characteristics with other custodial institutions, in other ways it was distinct. Administratively, because it operated under the provisions of the Geneva Convention, it resembled a prisoner-of-war camp. From the internees' viewpoint, because of the frustration and deprivation the camp imposed, it resembled a penitentiary. And because the population was made up entirely of Japanese who were interned because of wartime hysteria, it resembled the WRA camps. Each of these points merits some concluding thoughts.

Surprisingly, the Santa Fe camp perhaps least resembled a WRA camp. Compared to the WRA camps, the population was small and homogeneous: the internees were all male, which simplified the administrator's task, for they did not face the problems of confining women and children. For the internees, however, this meant separation from families and the deprivation of heterosexual relationships. Until the arrival of the renunciates late in the war, the internees were all Issei and, thus, intergenerational conflict was absent. Most were in their late middle-age or on the threshold of old age. In 1943, the average age of the internees was fifty-two and, thus, presumably their age and experience gave them more emotional maturity and stability, compared to a population of much younger individuals. While the original group of internees were all from California, after 1943, the camp included men from the entire West Coast, Hawaii, and Alaska. There were also Issei from WRA camps who had been arrested under presidential warrants as alleged troublemakers and transferred to Santa Fe. Perhaps the most hapless group were the Japanese from South America who were some of the 2,118 deported from the area, mostly from Peru, for internment in the U.S. at Washington's request.[66]

In its administrative regulations, the camp most closely resembled a prisoner-of-war compound. The two most important features of the administration of the camp were that the government had the material resources to provide adequately for the physical needs of the internees, and that the camp operated under the provisions of the Geneva Convention which were quite specific and left little room for uncertainty or confusion on the essential points. In addition, the government's sensitivity to the reciprocity issue produced pressure to avoid giving the internees any grounds for serious complaint that the Japanese government might use as a pretext for mistreatment of Americans in their custody.[67]

Also, unlike some of the WRA camps, the camp administrators at Santa Fe were experienced officers of the INS or Border Patrol, a service with a sense of professional pride and bureaucratic continuity. These men were accustomed to meeting and dealing with aliens of different nationalities, and they did not perceive the internees as Americans who might or might not be disloyal to the United States; they viewed them more dispassionately as noncitizens identified by ancestry with an enemy nation, who had been placed in their safekeeping for the duration of the war. Although the Santa Fe camp and prisoner-of-war camps both operated under the Geneva Convention, clearly there was a difference in the manner in which these regulations were applied. When some of the original 1942 internees returned to Santa Fe in 1943, after a period of army custody at Lordsburg, the Santa Fe authorities found that their attitude had changed appreciably, which they attributed partly to the rigid system of army control.[68]

The deprivations and frustration, resembling those of a penitentiary, that the camp imposed are difficult to evaluate. The difficulty lies not in determining the actual conditions of the camp, for these are evident and have been noted; the difficulty lies in analyzing the effect of the conditions on the internees. There are as many different prisons as there are prisoners, which is to say that each captive or inmate perceives his situation differently. The sociological concept of relative deprivation is quite similar.[69] The effect of deprivation on an individual depends upon his perception of his situation in relation to the condition of others who serve as a reference group. Friends and relatives in WRA camps, as well as people in the free society, served as reference groups for the Santa Fe internees. And in relation to either of these groups, the Santa Fe internee had good reason to feel seriously deprived. Except for the loss of security, the internees experienced the same type, if not the same degree, of deprivations suffered by inmates in a maximum security prison—the loss of liberty, of goods and services, of heterosexual relationships, and of autonomy. However, conditions in the camp sometimes ameliorated these deprivations. The system of internee self-government, as well as their knowledge that they individually had lines of communication to various authorities, lessened the loss of autonomy. Internees could, and frequently did, appeal directly to the officer-in-charge for help with personal problems. They could also contact directly the INS commissioner in Philadelphia, the AECU of the Justice Department, the State Department, the Spanish Embassy, and the International Red Cross.[70] These appeals or complaints might or might not bring the desired result, but the process itself was significant. However, even though one may objectively say that the conditions of the camp mitigated the deprivations, the concept of relative deprivation suggests that the internees nevertheless felt these losses deeply, for the psychological perception may be more important than the actual condition.

From the government's perspective, the Santa Fe camp successfully fulfilled its assigned task of maintaining an orderly internment. The camp was well managed and functioned with a minimum of strife, controversy, and publicity. But this short-range success begs the question. Viewed from the wider perspective of American civil liberties, the entire program of alien enemy control by the Justice Department must be judged a travesty and a failure. It was not just that the government succumbed to hysteria and used its power

in an arbitrary and abusive manner, which it did. Nor was the program a failure because the conditions of internment were brutal and inhumane, for they were not. The flaw that made this program a mockery of justice was fundamental and lay close to the heart of American society; it was the failure that Gunnar Myrdal in 1944 called the American Dilemma—the gap between our highest national ideals and our behavior.[71] Like black Americans, people of Japanese ancestry had been denied full acceptance as Americans and as individuals. The Issei, like characters in Joseph Heller's war novel *Catch-22*, were trapped in an illogical bureaucratic web. They were interned because they were enemy aliens, but they were aliens because discriminatory laws denied them naturalized citizenship. However, even if the Issei had been citizens, as the Nisei were, they would have been incarcerated on the basis of ancestry. This denial of naturalization rights and the racist assumptions upon which it rested were the fundamental injustices which the Justice Department incorporated uncritically into its enemy alien control program. The nature of the hearings the Issei received before the Alien Enemy Hearing Boards and the deprivations endured in the camps merely piled injustice on injustice.

Just as Woodrow Wilson's administration in World War I failed to meet the test that Wilson himself had posed, so the Roosevelt administration in World War II failed to meet the same test—the challenge of winning the war greatly and worthily, showing the real quality of our purpose and of our highest national ideals.

NOTES

1. Albert Shaw, ed., *The Messages and Papers of Woodrow Wilson*, 2 vols. (New York: Review of Reviews Corporation, 1924), 1: 486.

2. Francis Biddle, *Democratic Thinking and the War: The William H. White Lectures at the University of Virginia* (New York: Charles Scribner's Sons, 1944), 55.

3. For a sampling of how the Justice Department program has been treated in the literature, see Francis Biddle, *In Brief Authority* (Garden City, N.Y.: Doubleday and Company, 1962); Jacobus tenBroek, Edward N. Barnhart, and Floyd W. Matson, *Prejudice, War and the Constitution* (Berkeley: University of California Press, 1954); Roger Daniels, *Concentration Camps, USA: Japanese Americans and World War II* (New York: Holt, Rinehart and Winston, 1972); Morton Grodzins, *Americans Betrayed: Politics and the Japanese Evacuation* (Chicago: University of Chicago Press, 1949); Dorothy Swaine Thomas and Richard S. Nishimoto, *The Spoilage: Japanese-American Evacuation and Resettlement During World War II* (Berkeley: University of California Press, 1946); and Michi Weglyn, *Years of Infamy: The Untold Story of America's Concentration Camps* (New York: William Morrow, 1976).

4. *Ozawa v. United States*, 260 U.S. 178; Milton R. Konvitz, *The Alien and the Asiatic in American Law* (Ithaca: Cornell Univer-

sity Press, 1946), 79–88; Roger Daniels, *The Politics of Prejudice*, 2nd ed. (Berkeley: University of California, 1977), 98.

5. tenBroek et al., 101; Grodzins, 231–32; J. Edgar Hoover, "Alien Enemy Control," *Iowa Law Review* 29 (March 1944): 396–97; Bob Kumamoto, "The Search for Spies: American Counterintelligence and the Japanese American Community 1931–1942," *Amerasia Journal* 6 (Fall, 1979): 52, 58; testimony of Edward J. Ennis, director of the Alien Enemy Control Unit, March 20, 1942, in U.S. Congress, House Subcommittee of the Committee on Appropriations, *Hearings on the Sixth Supplemental National Defense Appropriation Bill for 1942, Part 1, Navy Department and General Appropriations*, 77th Cong., 2d sess., 1942, 391–94. Hereafter SSA.

6. Alien Registration Act of June 28, 1940, 54 Stat. 670; *Annual Report of the Attorney General of the United States, for the Fiscal Year Ended June 30, 1941* (Washington, D.C.: Government Printing Office, 1942), 237–38, 242–43; Zechariah Chafee, Jr., *Free Speech in the United States* (Cambridge: Harvard University Press, 1954), 440–90; Osmond K. Fraenkel, *Our Civil Liberties*, 2d ed. (Port Washington, N.Y.: Kennikat Press, 1969), 36, 85–86.

7. U.S. Department of Labor, *Twenty-Eighth Annual Report of the Secretary of Labor, for the Fiscal Year Ended June 30, 1940* (Washington, D.C.: Government Printing Office, 1940), 102.

8. U.S. Code, Title 50, Section 21; U.S., Cong., House, *National Defense Migration*, 77th Cong., 2d sess., 1942, H. Rept. 2124, 157–59; Grodzins, 234–35.

9. Hoover, 398–99.

10. *Code of Federal Regulations: Title 3, The President, 1938–1943 Compilation* (Washington, D.C.: Office of the Federal Register, 1968), 273, 276, 278.

11. Hoover, 401–2.

12. For the quote from Biddle see *New York Times*, December 11, 1941, p. 24; Francis Biddle, "Identification of Alien Enemies: Let Us Not Persecute These People," *Vital Speeches of the Day* 8 (February 15, 1942): 279–80, and Grodzins, 233–34.

13. SSA, 233; *Annual Report of the Attorney General of the United States, for the Fiscal Year Ended June 30, 1946* (Washington, D.C.: Government Printing Office, 1946), 12.

14. For an overview see: U.S. Federal Security Agency, Social Security Board, *Policies and Procedures Governing the Administration of Services and Assistance to Enemy Aliens Affected by Governmental Action: A Handbook for State Agencies* (Washington, D.C.: Bureau of Public Assistance, 1942), and "Limitations on Enemy Alien Activity," January 31, 1944, File No. 1300/R, Enemy Alien Internment World War II, Records of the Immigration and Naturalization Service, Record Group 85, National Archives, General Archives Division, Suitland, Maryland. Hereafter RG 85 Suitland.

15. The best descriptions of the entire process are: Francis Biddle, "Circular 3616, Supplement No. 1, Instructions to Alien Enemy Hearing Boards," January 7, 1942, File No. 1300/Y, RG 85 Suitland, and "Instructions to United States Attorneys Re: Alien Enemies," n.d., File No. 1300/R, RG 85 Suitland.

16. For the brief quotations from Ennis see: SSA, 393–94, and for his general views see, Ennis to Special Defense Unit, Department of State, August 22, 1942, File No. 740.00115 PW/852, General Records, Department of State, Record Group 59, National Archives, Washington, D.C. Hereafter RG 59 Washington.

17. U.S. Department of Commerce, Bureau of the Census, *Sixteenth Census of the United States, 1940: Population*, vol. 1, Number of Inhabitants, 695, 702.

18. Jensen to Kelly, "Description of Santa Fe Camp," January 20, 1944, File No. 1300, RG 85 Suitland; Williams to Kelly, "History of the Santa Fe Internment Camp," August 9, 1945, File No. 1300, RG 85 Suitland; "Memorandum to Mr. Jerre Mangione," October 14, 1943, File No. 1300/L, RG 85 Suitland.

19. Jensen to Kelly, "Description of Santa Fe Camp," January 20, 1944, File No. 1300, RG 85 Suitland; Hudson to Kelly, March 14, 1942, File No. 1300, RG 85 Suitland; H. J. Walls, "Radiogram," May 9, 1942, File No. 1300/L, RG 85 Suitland; Williams to Kelly, "History of the Santa Fe Internment Camp," August 9, 1945, File No. 1300, RG 85 Suitland; Ennis to Grantham, March 23, 1942, File No. 1300/Y, RG 85 Suitland; Grantham to Palmer and Hennessy, April 2, 1945, File No. 1300/Y, RG 85 Suitland; Bryan to Commanding General, Eighth Corps Area, June 11, 1942, File No. 1300/R-3, RG 85 Suitland.

20. Jensen to Kelly, "Description of the Santa Fe Camp," January 20, 1944, File No. 1300, RG 85 Suitland; Miller to Bryan, March 13, 1943, File No. 1300/R, RG 85 Suitland; Jensen, "Report of Detentions," June 15, 1943, File No. 13430/10, RG 85 Suitland; Jaeger to Central Office, INS, August 30, 1943, File No. 1300/Z, RG 85 Suitland; Schreiber to Kelly, October 23, 1945, File No. 1300/Z-1, RG 85 Suitland; Jensen to Central Office, INS, March 24, 1943, File No. 13430/10, RG 85 Suitland; U.S. Justice Department, *Annual Report of the Attorney General of the United States, for the Fiscal Year Ended June 30, 1943* (Washington, D.C.: Government Printing Office, 1944), 10; *Santa Fe New Mexican*, "Jap Camp Will Close April 19," March 20, 1946, in Scrapbook, vol. 73, "Social Effects, Book 2, Aliens and Internment Camps, Crime, Vice, and Delinquency, Population Movements," State Records Center and Archives, Santa Fe, New Mexico. Hereafter Scrapbook 73 Santa Fe.

21. This discussion of custodial institutions and deprivations is based on Gresham M. Sykes, *The Society of Captives: A Study of a Maximum Security Prison* (Princeton: Princeton University Press, 1958), 63–83.

22. INS Internment Camp, Santa Fe, "General Rules," n.d., File No. 1300/R3-b, RG 85 Suitland.

23. "Memorandum to Mr. Jerre Mangione," October 14, 1943, File No. 1300/L, RG 85 Suitland; Williams to Kelly, "History of the Santa Fe Internment Camp," August 9, 1945, File No. 1300, RG 85 Suitland.

24. Schofield to INS, "Instruction No. 58," April 28, 1942, File No. 1300, RG 85 Suitland; "Memorandum to Mr. Jerre Mangione," October 14, 1943, File No. 1300/L, RG 85 Suitland; Jensen to Kondo, August 17, 1943, File No. 1300/R, RG 85 Suitland; Jensen to Kelly, "Description of the Santa Fe Camp," January 20, 1944, File No. 1300, RG 85 Suitland.

25. "Memorandum to Mr. Jerre Mangione," October 14, 1943, File No. 1300/L, RG 85 Suitland; Williams to Kelly, "History of the Santa Fe Internment Camp," August 9, 1945, File No. 1300, RG 85 Suitland.

26. Williams to Kelly, "History of the Santa Fe Internment Camp," August 9, 1945, File No. 1300, RG 85 Suitland; Schofield to INS, "Instruction No. 58," April 28, 1942, File No. 1300, RG 85 Suitland. For food shipments from Japan see: Meyer to Officer-in-Charge, December 9, 1943, File 1 No. 1300/R, RG 85 Suitland; Savoretti to Officers-in-Charge, September 25, 1942, File No. 1300/L, RG 85 Suitland; Marc Peter to Officer-in-Charge, September 28, 1942, File No. 1300/L, RG 85 Suitland.

27. Okado and Nakamura to Biddle, June 10, 1942, File No. 1300/R-3, RG 85 Suitland.

28. Gufler and Herrick, "Report on Civilian Detention Camp, Santa Fe," May 26, 1942, File No. 740.00115 PW/758, RG

59 Washington; Groth, "Memorandum," July 27, 1942, File No. 740.00115 PW/757, RG 59 Washington.

29. Shimano to Jensen, August 9, 1943, File No. 1300/L RG 85 Suitland; Williams to Kelly, "History of the Santa Fe Internment Camp," August 9, 1945, File No. 1300, RG 85 Suitland. Celebrations of Japanese holidays, such as the anniversary of the coronation of the Emperor Meiji, also produced entertainment. See: Jensen to Kelly, November 4, 1943, File No. 1300/L, RG 85 Suitland; Hudson to Wells, March 19, 1942, File No. 13210, RG 85 Suitland; "Memorandum to Mr. Jerre Mangione," October 14, 1943, File No. 1300/L, RG 85 Suitland; Jensen to Kelly, "Description of Santa Fe Camp," January 20, 1944, File No. 1300, RG 85 Suitland.

30. Jensen to Kelly, "Description of the Santa Fe Camp," January 20, 1944, File No. 1300, RG 85 Suitland; Williams to Kelly, "History of the Santa Fe Internment Camp," August 9, 1945, File No. 1300, RG 85 Suitland.

31. Schofield to INS, "Instruction No. 58," April 28, 1942, File No. 1300, RG 85 Suitland; Williams to Kelly, "History of the Santa Fe Internment Camp," August 9, 1945, File No. 1300, RG 85 Suitland; INS Internment Camp, Santa Fe, "General Rules," n.d., File No. 1300/R3-b, RG 85 Suitland. For an example of the number and type of workers, see: Jensen to Kelly, August 23, 1943, File No. 1300/R, RG 85 Suitland; for an account of the poultry farm operations, see: Morago to Jensen, May 20, 1944, File No. 13209, RG 85 Suitland.

32. "Memorandum to Mr. Jerre Mangione," October 14, 1943, File No. 1300/L, RG 85 Suitland; Schofield to INS, "Instruction No. 58," April 28, 1942, File No. 1300, RG 85 Suitland; Ishimaru to Jensen, July 28, 1943, with enclosure, File No. 1300/L, RG 85 Suitland; Jensen to WRA Project Directors, October 6, 1943, File No. 1300/R-2, RG 85 Suitland; Jensen to Kondo, August 4, 1943, File No. 1300/L, RG 85 Suitland; Jensen to Oyama, August 16, 1943, File No. 13200/L, RG 85 Suitland; Collaer to Officers-in-Charge, November 20, 1943, File No. 1300/R, RG 85 Suitland; Jensen to Okamoto, July 19, 1943, File No. 1300/K, RG 85 Suitland; Jensen to Officer-in-Charge, Fort Missoula, December 18, 1943, File No. 1300/R, RG 85 Suitland.

33. "Memorandum to Mr. Jerre Mangione," October 14, 1943, File No. 1300/L, RG 85 Suitland.

34. Williams to Kelly, "History of the Santa Fe Internment Camp," August 9, 1945, File No. 1300, RG 85 Suitland; Kelly to Officer-in-Charge, June 16, 1943, File No. 1300/R, RG 85 Suitland; Jensen to District Director, September 15, 1942, File No. 1300, RG 85 Suitland; Jensen to Douglass, January 31, 1944, File No. 1300/R-2, RG 85 Suitland; de Molina to Kawasaki, October 21, 1943, File No. 1300/Z, RG 85 Suitland; Jensen to Kelly, November 11, 1943, File No. 1300/Z, RG 85 Suitland.

35. Okado to de Amat, June 2, 1942, File No. 1300/L, RG 85 Suitland; Japanese detainees to de Amat, July 9, 1942, File No. 1300/L, RG 85 Suitland; Okado to Biddle, April 2, 1942, File No. 1300/L, RG 85 Suitland; SSA, 398.

36. Jensen to Kelly, August 6, 1943, File No. 1300/R, RG 85 Suitland; Spanish Embassy to Department of State, November 12, 1943, File No. 740.00115 PW/1991, RG 59 Washington.

37. Savoretti to Officers-in-Charge, June 22, 1943, File No. 1300/R, RG 85 Suitland; Jensen to Kelly, October 11, 1943, File No. 1300/R, RG 85 Suitland; Biddle to Harrison, January 11, 1943, File No. 3022/A-7, RG 85 Suitland.

38. Kondo to de Molina, December 28, 1943, File No. 1300/R, RG 85 Suitland; Japanese detainees to Ennis, December 28, 1943, File No. 1300/R, RG 85 Suitland; de Molina to Kawasaki, October 21, 1943, File No. 1300/Z, RG 85 Suitland; Gufler to Lyon, July 23, 1942, File No. 740.00115 PW/782, RG 59 Washington.

39. Jensen to Kelly, July 13, 1943, with enclosures, File No. 1300/L, RG 85 Suitland; Barrows to Merritt, October 28, 1943, File No. 1300/R, RG 85 Suitland; Williams to Mukaeda, February 6, 1945, File No. 1300/R-3b, RG 85 Suitland.

40. "Memorandum to Mr. Jerre Mangione," October 14, 1943, File No. 1300/L, RG 85 Suitland; Okado to Kelly, April 14, 1942, File No. 1300/L, RG 85 Suitland; Williams to Kelly, "History of the Santa Fe Internment Camp," August 9, 1945, File No. 1300, RG 85 Suitland.

41. Williams to Kelly, "History of the Santa Fe Internment Camp," August 9, 1945, File No. 1300, RG 85 Suitland.

42. Sykes, 46-53; Geoffrey Duncan Mitchell, ed., A New Dictionary of the Social Sciences (New York: Aldine Publishing Company, 1979), 12–15.

43. INS Internment Camp, Santa Fe, "General Rules," n.d., File No. 1300/R3-b, RG 85 Suitland.

44. Schofield to INS, "Instruction No. 58," April 28, 1942, File No. 1300, RG 85 Suitland; Williams to Kelly, "History of the Santa Fe Internment Camp," August 9, 1945, File No. 1300, RG 85 Suitland.

45. Williams to Kelly, "History of the Santa Fe Internment Camp," August 9, 1945, File No. 1300, RG 85 Suitland; "Memorandum to Mr. Jerre Mangione," October 14, 1943, File No. 1300/L, RG 85 Suitland.

46. Williams to Kelly, January 12, 1945, File No. 1303, RG 85 Suitland; Schreiber to INS, Philadelphia, November 12, 1945, File No. 1303, RG 85 Suitland; Davy to Monroe, November 11, 1945, File No. 1303, RG 85 Suitland; Jensen to Charlton, April 5, 1943, File No. 1303, RG 85 Suitland.

47. Williams to Kelly, "History of the Santa Fe Internment Camp," August 9, 1945, File No. 1300, RG 85 Suitland. For the public reaction to Germans and Italians who escaped from one of the POW camps within the state, see: Santa Fe New Mexican, "Nazi Escapes [sic] Recaptured; 1 is Wounded," November 4, 1942, Scrapbook 73 Santa Fe; Health City Sun, "The Way to Handle Them," November 6, 1942, Scrapbook 73 Santa Fe; Roswell Daily Record, "Three Prisoners Escape From Roswell Internment Camp, One Was Killed and The Others Captured Near Artesia," January 11, 1943, Scrapbook 73 Santa Fe; Albuquerque Journal, "Californian Nabs Fugitive Nazis From New Mexico," April 30, 1944, Scrapbook 73 Santa Fe; Las Cruces Sun-News, "Prisoner of War Dies of Wounds," February 8, 1945, Scrapbook 73 Santa Fe.

48. "The Segregation Program: A Statement For Appointed Personnel in W.R.A. Centers," n.d., File No. 1300/R, RG 85 Suitland; Donald E. Collins, "Disloyalty and Renunciation of United States Citizenship By Japanese Americans During World War II" (Ph.D. diss., University of Georgia, 1975), 2, 23ff., 88–93; see also: Thomas and Nishimoto, 303ff. and 333ff.; Weglyn, 156ff. and 229ff.; and tenBroek, et al., 175–76.

49. Collins, 110 and 208, n. 5.

50. Burling to Kelly, "Japanese Subversive Organizations at Tule Lake," February 7, 1945, File No. 1300/P, RG 85 Suitland (page 4 of this document is missing).

51. Burling to Kelly, "Japanese Subversive Organizations at Tule Lake," February 7, 1945, File No. 1300/P, RG 85 Suitland.

52. Burling to Kelly, "Japanese Subversive Organizations at Tule Lake," February 7, 1945, File No. 1300/P, RG 85 Suitland; Collins, 119, 127–29; Clovis News-Journal, March 5, 1945, Scrapbook 73 Santa Fe.

53. Williams to Kelly, "History of the Santa Fe Internment Camp," August 9, 1945, File No. 1300, RG 85 Suitland; Williams to Kelly, March 3, 1945, File No. 13255, RG 85 Suitland; Wagner to Jensen, July 20, 1942, File No. 1303, RG 85 Suitland; Waller to Officer-in-Charge, July 2, 1945, File No. 1303, RG 85 Suitland.

54. "Memorandum to Mr. Jerre Mangione," October 14, 1943, File No. 1300/L, RG 85 Suitland; Kelly to Gufler, March 10, 1945, File No. 740.00115 PW/1-1045, with enclosures, RG 59 Washington; "Memorandum of Bernard Gufler," March 7, 1945, File No. 740.00115 PW/3-245, RG 59 Washington; "Officer-in-Charge to All New Internees," December 31, 1944, File No. 1300/R3-b, RG 85 Suitland; Monroe to Staff, January 20, 1945, File No. 13325/1, RG 85 Suitland; Langston to Staff, February 28, 1945, File No. 13325/1, RG 85 Suitland.

55. Monroe to Staff, February 21, 1945, File No. 13325/1, RG 85 Suitland; for both quotations see: Kelly to Gufler, March 10, 1945, File No. 740.00115 PW/3-1045, with enclosures, RG 59 Washington.

56. Monroe to Staff, "Internment Order No. 6," March 8, 1945, File No. 13325/1, RG 85 Suitland.

57. Kelly to Gufler, March 10, 1945, File No. 740.00115 PW/3-1045, RG 59 Washington.

58. Williams to Kelly, "Report Concerning Demonstration at the Santa Fe Internment Camp, March 12, 1945," March 30, 1945, File No. 1300/P, RG 85 Suitland (sanitized by NARS); Ono to Spanish Embassador [sic], n.d., File No. 740.00115 PW/3-1945, RG 59 Washington (contains names of participants). There is a brief discussion of the riot and interviews with Katsuma Mukaeda, a camp spokesman, and Abner Schreiber, a camp administrator, in: Paul F. Clark, "Those Other Camps: An Oral History Analysis of Japanese Alien Enemy Internment During World War II," (M.A. thesis, California State University, Fullerton, 1980).

59. Williams to Kelly, "Report Concerning Demonstration at the Santa Fe Internment Camp, March 12, 1945," March 30, 1945, File No. 1300/P, RG 85 Suitland; Monroe to Williams, "Exhibit U," March 21, 1945, File No. 1300/P, RG 85 Suitland; Schreiber to Williams, "Exhibit S," March 14, File No. 1300/P, RG 85 Suitland; Hospital Report, "Exhibit V," March 14, 1945, File No. 1300/P, RG 85 Suitland; Jones to Williams, "Exhibit R," March 26, 1945, File No. 1300/P, RG 85 Suitland; Kelly to INS, March 16, 1945, File No. 1300/P, RG 85 Suitland; Kelly to Gufler, March 19, 1945, File No. 740.00115 PW/3-1945, RG 59 Washington; Ono to Spanish Embassador [sic], n.d., File No. 740.00115 PW/3-1945, RG 59 Washington.

60. Ivan Williams, "To Each Internee," March 15, 1945, File No. 740.00115 PW/3-1945, RG 59 Washington; Kelly to Saki, March 21, 1945, File No. 740.00115 PW/3-21-45, RG 59 Washington; for Kelly's statement see, Kelly to Gufler, March 21, 1945, File No. 740.00115 PW3-21-45, RG 59 Washington.

61. Kelly to Gufler, March 21, 1945, File No. 740.00115 PW/3-21-45, RG 59 Washington; for the quotation see handwritten letter of Kelly to Gufler, March 21, 1945, File No. 740.00115 PW/3-21-45, RG 59 Washington.

62. Santa Fe New Mexican, "Jap Camp Will Close April 19," March 20, 1946, Scrapbook 73 Santa Fe; Williams to Officer-in-Charge, Fort Stanton, June 30, 1945, File No. 1300/P-1, RG 85 Suitland; Williams to Kelly, June 30, 1945, File No. 1300/B, RG 85 Suitland. Williams to Saiki, Spokesman, May 18, 1945, File No. 1300/R-36, RG 85 Suitland.

63. Williams to Kelly, "Confidential," August 7, 1945, File No. [indecipherable], RG 85 Suitland.

64. For the reaction of the internees to news that the war was over, see: Albuquerque Journal, "Santa Fe Jap Internees Receive the News Calmly," August 16, 1945, Scrapbook 73 Santa Fe; Santa Fe New Mexican, "Nobody Will Mourn End of Camp Where Thousands of Japs Held," March 21, 1946, Scrapbook 73 Santa Fe. For hostility toward the Japanese, see: Las Cruces Sun-News, "Valley Farmers Move to Enforce Jap Exclusion," September 16, 1945, Scrapbook 73 Santa Fe; Las Cruces Sun-News, "State Law Cited in Resolutions; Urge Alien Deportation," October 2, 1945, Scrapbook 73 Santa Fe; Waldo D. Todd, "Memo to Surveillance Group," January 28, 1944, File No. 13325/1, RG 85 Suitland; Monroe to Staff, November 11, 1945, File No. 13325/1, RG 85 Suitland; Williams to Kelly, "History of the Santa Fe Internment Camp," August 9, 1945, File No. 1300, RG 85 Suitland. Jerre Mangione, who worked in the alien affairs division of the Justice Department, states that in the spring of 1942 an armed mob of local citizens marched on the camp intent on murder, but Williams persuaded them to disperse. I have found no other report of this incident. See: Jerre Mangione, An Ethnic At Large: A Memoir of America in the Thirties and Forties (New York: G.P. Putnam's Sons, 1978), 323.

65. Schreiber to Kelly, October 23, 1945, File No. 1300/Z, RG 85 Suitland; Schreiber to Bonham, November 21, 1945, File No. 1300/Z, RG 85 Suitland; Schreiber to Department Heads, December 29, 1945, File No. 1300, RG 85 Suitland; Schreiber to Central Office, INS, January 3, 1946, File No. 13430/10, RG 85 Suitland; Santa Fe New Mexican, "Santa Fe Japs Know Who Won War; Others Don't," December 29, 1945, Scrapbook 73 Santa Fe; Santa Fe New Mexican, "57 More Leave Jap Camp Here For Homeland," February 20, 1946, Scrapbook 73 Santa Fe; Roswell Daily-Record, "Send Young Japs From Nebraska to Camp at Santa Fe," February 21, 1946, Scrapbook 73 Santa Fe; Santa Fe New Mexican, "Jap Camp Will Close April 19," March 20, 1946, Scrapbook 73 Santa Fe; Santa Fe New Mexican, "Last of Japanese Internees to Be Transferred Soon," May 1, 1946, Scrapbook 73 Santa Fe; Williams to Officer-in-Charge, Terminal Island, California, April 22, 1946, File No. 1300/B, RG 85 Suitland; Ivan Williams, "Report of Detentions," May 1, 1946, File No. 13430/10, RG 85 Suitland. All told, between May 1945 and June 1946, 9,331 alien enemies were repatriated to Germany, Italy, and Japan. Approximately 8,000 were sent to Japan. See: U.S. Justice Department, Annual Report of the Attorney General of the United States, for the Fiscal Year Ended June 30, 1946 (Washington, D.C.: Government Printing Office, 1946), 12.

66. Williams to Kelly, "History of the Santa Fe Internment Camp," August 9, 1945, File No. 1300, RG 85 Suitland; "Memorandum to Mr. Jerre Mangione," October 14, 1943, File No. 1300/L, RG 85 Suitland. In 1942 the median age of all Issei males was fifty-five, see: Dorothy Swaine Thomas, The Salvage (Berkeley: University of California Press, 1952), 578; Black to Meyer, April 12, 1944, File No. 1300/A, RG 85 Suitland; Meyer to the Attorney General, May 2, 1944, File No. 1300/A, RG 85 Suitland; Biddle to Director, FBI, "Warrant," May 17, 1944, File No. 1300/A, RG 85 Suitland; Francis Biddle, "Order," May 27, 1944, File No. 1300/A, RG 85 Suitland; and U.S. Congress, Senate, Subcommittee of the Committee on Military Affairs, Hearings, War Relocation Centers, 78th Cong., 1st sess., 1943, S. Rept. 444, 40; Clinton Harvey Gardiner, The Japanese and Peru 1873–1973 (Albuquerque: University of New Mexico Press, 1975), 81ff., and Clinton Harvey Gardiner, Pawns in a Triangle of Hate: The Peruvian Japanese and the United States (Seattle: University of Washington Press, 1981).

67. For an example of the State Department's sensitivity on the issue of reciprocity, see: Santa Fe New Mexican, "Anti-Jap Stories Roil Department," April 23, 1942, Scrapbook 73 Santa Fe.

68. "Memorandum to Mr. Jerre Mangione," October 14, 1943, File No. 1300/L, RG 85 Suitland.

69. The concept or term "relative deprivation" was first used by Samuel A. Stouffer in 1950 (S.A. Stouffer, ed., *The American Soldier* [Princeton: Princeton University Press, 1950]), and later formalized by Robert King Merton in *Social Theory and Social Structure* (Glencoe, Ill.: The Free Press, 1961); see also: Mitchell, 157.

70. "Memorandum to Mr. Jerre Mangione," October 14, 1943, File No. 1300/L, RG 85 Suitland. Internees could send uncensored, unread, and sealed letters directly to the INS Commissioner, see: Miller to Officers-in-Charge, "Direct Correspondence by Internees," August 7, 1943, File No. 1300/R, RG 85 Suitland.

71. Gunnar Myrdal, *An American Dilemma: The Negro Problem in Modern Democracy*, 2 vols. (New York: Harper and Brothers, 1944).

The Forced Migrations of West Coast Japanese Americans, 1942–1946: A Quantitative Note

Roger Daniels

It is often assumed that all Japanese Americans suffered a common fate during World War II: imprisonment in a War Relocation Authority concentration camp. This was not the case; the purpose of this note is to indicate the variety of Japanese American experiences during the war and to establish a uniform terminology.

According to the Census of 1940, there were 126,947 persons of Japanese ancestry living in the United States, another 157,905 in the Territory of Hawaii, and 263 in the Territory of Alaska, for a total of 285,115 persons. More than two-thirds of these were native-born American citizens. Because, except for a few World War I veterans, no Japanese person could be naturalized, there were close to 100,000 aliens of Japanese birth who became, after Pearl Harbor, enemy aliens.

Some of these enemy aliens were the first forced migrants of the war. Starting on December 7, some 3,000 adult aliens, almost all of them male, were arrested by the FBI and interned in such places as Missoula, Montana, or Lordsburg, New Mexico. This was a well-established governmental policy, recognized in international law, and represented no innovative action. The men were interned under military guard but were in the custody of the Immigration and Naturalization Service (INS), part of the Department of Justice. Eventually, each man interned received a hearing, and some were freed as a result of those hearings. The vast majority of adult male enemy aliens were not interned, nor were any women and children. Several hundred of the internees were repatriated during the war on the exchange ship *Gripsholm*, a Swedish passenger liner.

In December and January 1941–42, most, but not all, of the more than 3,000 Japanese American citizens who had been inducted into the armed forces since the institution of the draft in October 1940, were discharged because of their ancestry, and they, and all other Japanese Americans were placed in a special category, IV-C, normally reserved for enemy aliens, and making them ineligible for military service.

After the promulgation of Executive Order 9066 by President Franklin D. Roosevelt on February 19, 1942, the U.S. Army took control of all persons of Japanese ancestry—aliens and citizens, men, women, and children—who lived in California, in the western parts of Oregon and Washington, and in part of Arizona, and forced them to leave their homes for the duration of hostilities. According to the 1940 census, 111,938 persons lived in what became the forbidden zone. In the more than two years between the census and the forced removal, that population gained from natural increases and was also affected by voluntary migration. According to the army's statistics, 117,116 persons were "eligible" for *incarceration* between March and October 1942. But it took charge of only 110,723. They were *incarcerated*, first in assembly centers under the jurisdiction of the army, and then in relocation centers under the jurisdiction of the War Relocation Authority.

This process has been given many names. Franklin Roosevelt was willing to call the places of confinement *concentration camps*. The War Relocation Authority abhorred that term and preferred to talk about the process as "relocation," although it sometimes referred to its prisoners as "evacuated" or "impounded people." The problem with the word "relocation," apart from its euphemistic nature, is that it also has been used to describe the process by which some Japanese Americans "voluntarily" moved out of the forbidden zone, and to the process by which, during and just after the war, thousands of Japanese Americans moved out of the camps to new homes and businesses in the interior of the United States. To further the semantic confusion, it has become common in recent years to speak of the "internment" of Japanese Americans as describing all the procedures affecting aliens and citizens, a practice that has been given official sanction by Congress, which created the Commission on the Wartime Relocation and Internment of Civilians (CWRIC) in 1980.

Most of the few thousand Japanese Americans resident on the West Coast who were neither interned nor incarcerated were allowed to migrate voluntarily outside of the forbidden zone. Japanese Americans who already lived in such places as Salt Lake City, Chicago, or New York were, if they were not interned,

A difficult farewell as the train departs from the Oakland railroad terminal during evacuation. Photo by Dorothea Lange. Courtesy Bernard K. Johnpoll.

left in nervous liberty. The army's data indicate that nearly 5,000 voluntarily migrated east between March and October 1942. Clearly, others had already done so between December 7 and the beginning of March, but there are no good data on the numbers involved.

To complicate matters further, some Japanese Americans not subject to incarceration because of their residence returned to the forbidden zone to join their families, as did some discharged servicemen. In addition, some 1,000 persons were in various institutions, medical and penal, and not otherwise incarcerated; however, some patients were concentrated into a few institutions, such as Hillcrest Sanitorium outside of Los Angeles.

According to the War Relocation Authority, it had, at one time or another, 120,313 individuals in custody. It received 111,236 from the army, 1,118 from Hawaii, 1,735 who were transferred from INS internment camps, 219 "voluntary residents" (mostly individuals who joined families already in camp), and 24 from various institutions. In addition, 5,981 U.S. citizens were born to incarcerated mothers.

The overwhelming majority of Hawaiian Japanese Americans were left at liberty; all but a few thousand of the mainland Japanese Americans were interned or incarcerated, as was every such person who had lived in Alaska. The conditions of life behind barbed wire are described in several of the essays that follow. Here, I merely want to outline the migrations of the 120,000 persons incarcerated by the WRA.

At the very outset, even before the relocation centers had been filled, several hundred persons received "work release furloughs" to assist in harvesting crops, such as sugar beets in the western states outside of the forbidden zone. Others were allowed to volunteer for service with military intelligence units of the U.S. Army. In the fall of 1942, hundreds of students were allowed to leave to attend colleges and universities outside of the forbidden zone. And, particularly after the beginning of 1943, a process of controlled resettlement in the interior states was encouraged.

Thousands were moved from camp to camp: while some transfers were to reunite families and others at the convenience of the government, the major reason for intercamp migration was caused by a desire to *segregate* those considered disloyal in one camp—Tule Lake, California. Loyalty was largely determined by inmate answers to a questionnaire administered to all adults in WRA custody early in 1943. The two crucial questions asked were:

27. Are you willing to serve in the armed forces of the United States on combat duty, wherever ordered?

28. Will you swear unqualified allegiance to the United States of America from any or all attack by foreign or domestic forces, and forswear any form of allegiance or obedience to the Japanese emperor, to any other foreign government, power or organization?

Those who answered "No" to one or both questions—some 6,700 of the 75,000 respondents—were considered disloyal and most of them were segregated

in the camp at Tule Lake. This segregation involved moving some 13,000 inmates, for about 6,200 "loyal" persons were moved from Tule Lake to other camps and some 6,800 persons were moved to Tule Lake.

By the end of the war almost half of the incarcerated people were out of camp, having received what the WRA came to call "leave clearance" to work, to go to college, or to enter the armed forces. By March 20, 1946, the last camp was empty. The following table shows the movement of people in and out of the camps.

INPUT-OUTPUT DATA FOR WRA CENTERS, 1942–1946

FROM		TO	
90,491	assembly centers	54,127	return to West Coast
17,491	direct evacuation	52,798	relocated to interior
5,918	born in camp	4,724	Japan
1,735	INS internment camps	3,121	INS internment camps
1,579	seasonal workers (furloughed from assembly centers to work crops, then to camp)	2,355	armed forces
1,275	penal and medical institutions	1,862	died
1,118	Hawaii	1,322	to institutions
219	voluntary residents (mostly non-Japanese spouses)	4	unauthorized departures
120,313	Total population ever under WRA control	120,313	

PART IV

Reactions to the Camps

Although the relocation and incarceration of the Japanese Americans remains a major blot on the democratic record of recent American history, in another sense it was quite "democratic": that is, it was highly popular with the overwhelming majority of the American people. It may well have been the most popular home-front action of the federal government during the entire war. The same public that supported Executive Order 9066, leading to relocation and incarceration, was less than enthusiastic about a truly democratic Executive Order 8802, issued on June 25, 1941, which established the first federal Fair Employment Practices Committee. Although most residents of the states in which Japanese Americans were relocated objected to the presence of what they regarded as "California's problem," farmers and beet sugar producers who needed their labor welcomed their availability, as they welcomed the migrant Mexican labor brought in under the Bracero program.

In the essays that follow Geoffrey S. Smith skillfully and ingeniously relates the impulses that brought about the relocation to earlier and contemporary searches for other kinds of "subversives." F. Alan Coombs concentrates his examination on the reactions of Congress to the whole relocation program, making it quite clear that such congressional criticism that existed was only that the WRA's rules and regulations tended to coddle Japanese Americans. In three parallel essays, Leonard J. Arrington, Robert C. Sims, and Roger Daniels explore the reactions of three of the host states, Utah, Idaho, and Wyoming, showing that although personalities and events were different, a basic hostility was common to all three. In an extraordinary example of how public school teachers can introduce their students to a controversial event with contemporary relevance, Jane Beckwith relates the way in which her students at Delta High School investigated the wartime ordeal of the Japanese American people at the nearby Topaz Relocation Center and how the camp affected their own community and the lives of their parents and grandparents. Those of us who went to Delta in March 1983, along with a few of the people who had been incarcerated there, will always remember the ways in which the students of the 1980s related to the victims of the 1940s.

Among the few voices to protest the relocation of the Japanese were spokesmen from the West Coast churches. Some of these were former missionaries to Japan who worked with Japanese Protestant churches in these states. Others were men and women of goodwill and conscience appalled by the violation of civil liberties and the principles of justice and fair play.

Did these people of religious conviction do enough? Floyd Schmoe, an outstanding opponent of relocation whose work with the Quakers in Seattle did much to ease the pain for Japanese Americans in that area, speaks of his personal experiences with the churches. He is critical of the unwillingness of most Christians to speak out for their fellowmen. Sandra C. Taylor analyzes the work of Protestants and Catholics, and while critical of the indifference of the mass of church members, points out the good that some of them did, especially in aiding the internees in resettling outside the camps.

The best possible introduction to the study of public opinion and the Japanese Americans is a perusal of contemporary magazines, local newspapers—especially for the West Coast states that exported Japanese and the interior states that received them—and, of course, the *Congressional Record* and the hearings cited by Coombs. The most convenient listing of contemporary articles is the bibliography which comprises Appendix II of Edward H. Spicer, Asael T. Hansen, Katherine Luomala, and Marvin K. Opler, *Impounded People: Japanese-Americans in the Relocation Centers* (Tucson: University of Arizona Press, 1969). For public opinion and nativism, generally, see Geoffrey S. Smith, *To Save a Nation: American Countersubversives, the New Deal and the Coming of World War II* (New York: Basic Books, 1973). The best study of the "home front" remains Richard Polenberg, *War and Society: The United States, 1941–1945* (Philadelphia: Lippincott, 1972), but see also John Morton Blum, *V Was for Victory: Politics and American Culture during World War II* (New York: Harcourt Brace Jovanovich, 1976). Somewhat conflicting studies of public opinion as a factor in the relocation may be seen in Morton Grodzins, *Americans Betrayed: Politics and the Japanese Evacuation* (Chicago: University of Chicago Press, 1949) and Jacobus tenBroek, Edward N. Barnhart, and Floyd W. Matson, *Prejudice, War and the Constitution* (Berkeley and Los Angeles: University of California Press, 1958). Unfortunately, historians of the American West and of the western states have paid little attention to the Asians in their midst; for an outstanding exception, see T. A. Larson, *Wyoming's War Years* (Stanford: Stanford University Press for the University of Wyoming, 1954).

Roger Daniels

Racial Nativism and Origins
of Japanese American Relocation

Geoffrey S. Smith

On October 20, 1938, the Columbia Broadcasting System aired an adaptation of H. G. Wells's *War of the Worlds*. With its spare narrative, Orson Welles's production of a fictional invasion of New Jersey by hostile Martians proved for many listeners indistinguishable from a live broadcast of real events.

To the astonishment of everyone, hundreds of thousands of Americans accepted the scenario; indeed, no other broadcast in history had produced commensurate panic.[1] The response to the *War of the Worlds* prompted observers to question the potential effect of radio on a gullible populace. A *New York Times* writer observed that a voice "as dramatic as that of Orson Welles is a powerful instrument; it must learn to handle 'news' without the slightest color of melodrama."[2]

Behind such advice lay suspicion that propaganda might lull citizens into dangerous slumber, or lure them into unwise political action. European totalitarianism had kindled in America fears of misleading political sophistry and the threat of dictatorship in America. In this context Franklin D. Roosevelt's emphasis upon public relations, epitomized by his press conferences and fireside chats, raised the threat of manipulated opinion. With war in Europe a definite possibility by October 1938, supporters and adversaries of continental democracy—and the Roosevelt administration itself—showed concern with fifth-column groups and subversive ideas. Thus it was not surprising that the broadcast grated upon a populace anxious to remain aloof from global turmoil.[3]

At first glance, the *War of the Worlds* may seem a bizarre way to introduce an analysis of the origins of the tragedy that befell 120,000 Japanese Americans. Yet judging from the fear, irrational arguments, and overreaction that characterized government decision making and a large majority of citizens, especially on the West Coast, the comparison is suggestive.

Pearl Harbor resurrected the image of Pacific Coast Japanese as advance agents of the dreaded "Yellow Peril," and subjected them, ultimately, to the most broadly based and effective nativist crusade in American history. The decisions to evacuate and to incarcerate the Japanese Americans illuminate several key sources of a powerful nativism that made this ethnic minority a likely if not inevitable target. The intense opposition of Americans to the Japanese was racially based, but also contained themes of ethnic and cultural countersubversion that tied the anti-Japanese crusade to previous nativist episodes.[4]

Scholars suggest the difficulty in isolating any one factor as the basis of the nativism that resulted in evacuation.[5] Nonetheless, one must underline the significance of Pearl Harbor—the worst defeat ever inflicted upon this country. That event produced a mix of disbelief, outrage, and anxiety in the United States, emotions that grew in the ensuing weeks as Japan dealt Allied forces in the Western Pacific an unexpected series of military reversals.

These developments revealed complacency in both Washington and London, and the underrating of Japan by government leaders in both countries. Roosevelt, Secretary of War Henry L. Stimson, and British Prime Minister Winston Churchill, among others, concluded that a mere flexing of Anglo-Saxon muscle might restrain Tokyo. Adolf Hitler was public enemy number one—and the Boy Scouts could handle the Pacific.[6]

Cultural hubris thus precluded both British and American leaders from recognizing that Japan's attack on Hawaii represented not only a quest for national survival but, equally important, a deep-rooted East Asian revolt against the values of the western world—a pursuit similar to earlier Boxer and Filipino rebellions. Japan's military successes in 1942, in fact, etched in bold relief its Pan-Asian aspirations and their threat to western white prestige. This anticolonialism held important implications for India, Africa, Southeast Asia—and for American blacks.[7]

What Japanese policymakers termed defensive measures to stem western imperialism, many Americans—especially on the West Coast—saw as evidence of something they had suspected since the early 1900s. Americans faced in the "Japs" an enemy that was perceived as a different species, "whose skull pattern," as Roosevelt put it, "being less developed than that of the Caucasians, might be responsible for their aggressive behavior."[8] The fact remained, however, that a colored nation had defeated the world's leading Anglo-Saxon powers.

In the shadow of Pearl Harbor the fear of an actual invasion by Japan became acute. This concern was voiced by Secretary of the Navy Frank Knox, who reviewed the damage and condemned Hawaiian Japanese "traitors" for "the most effective fifth-column work that's come out of this war except in Norway."[9] Knox left the impression, born out by subsequent opinion polls, that the Issei and Nisei were, like their Hawaiian counterparts, a "treacherous," "sly," "cruel," and "warlike" people.[10]

A week later the official committee of inquiry, led by Supreme Court Justice Owen J. Roberts, released its report. The board criticized naval laxity at Pearl Harbor but also fingered Japanese secret agents as facilitating the attack.[11] This assertion had no basis, but it fanned American antagonism toward Japanese Americans. The Roberts Commission report also suggested that the FBI had been hindered prior to Pearl Harbor by adhering too closely to constitutional guarantees of civil liberties.

With the federal government priming Americans with tales of Japanese Hawaiian perfidy, it did not matter that Japanese Americans in California comprised a paltry 1.4 percent of that state's total population. Nor did it register that a secret government investigation before Pearl Harbor, headed by journalist C. B. Munson, discovered a "remarkable, even extraordinary degree of loyalty" among the Hawaiian and West Coast Japanese. Nor, finally, did it merit consideration that the Pacific Coast Nisei, through the Japanese American Citizens League, strongly defended their loyalty to the United States.[12]

What weighed most in shaping regional and national opinion during the two months before FDR signed Executive Order 9066 was the simple fact that

the nation had been "pushed around by a slant-eyed people to whom [it felt] racially superior."[13] Quickly, racial nativism burgeoned, spearheaded by regional patriotic organizations, agricultural and fishing interests, and by "commercial buzzards" eager to take over Japanese American enterprise. These groups, with a long history as agitators, were joined by several influential publishers, editors, and columnists, as well as by reformers, labor leaders, and politicians.

In Los Angeles radio commentator John B. Hughes warned that "ninety percent or more of American-born Japanese are primarily loyal to Japan." Obedient and poised to strike, the Japanese would "die joyously for the honor of Japan." Seeking support for evacuation, Hughes predicted that unless authorities formulated an adequate policy, Californians would invoke vigilante law, with its code of "shoot first and argue later."[14] Hearst columnist Henry McLemore observed that the war marked the end of the melting pot. "I am for immediate removal of every Japanese on the West Coast to a point deep in the interior," he wrote. "Herd 'em up, pack 'em off and give 'em the inside room in the badlands. Let 'em be pinched, hurt, hungry, and dead against it. . . . Personally, I hate the Japanese. And that goes for all of them."[15]

Calm prevailed immediately after Pearl Harbor, but by late January pandemonium enveloped the West Coast. Though J. Edgar Hoover opposed evacuation, feeling that the FBI already had identified "supposed" Japanese agents, the bureau exacerbated fears by publicizing such seized "contraband" as cameras, binoculars, hunting knives, and the dynamite used by farmers to clear their land of tree stumps.[16] Soon, most California newspapers deprived the imputed Asian fifth columnists of all humanity, describing them as "yellow men," "mad dogs," "Nips," and "yellow vermin." A Native Daughter of the Golden West inquired, "Did God make the Jap as he did the snake, did you hear the hiss before the words left his mouth? Were his eyes made slanting and the hiss put between his lips to warn us to be on our guard?" A mortician announced his preference to "do business with a Jap than an American." Thousands of dust-bowl refugees, meanwhile, themselves hapless victims of circumstance scant years before, joined the clamor, finding in the "yellow bellies" a group that allowed them new social respectability.[17]

Demands for evacuation soon began to flow into Washington from California's congressional delegation. In the process, any goodwill the Japanese Americans possessed soon dissipated. Governor Culbert Olson, a liberal, epitomized the movement of "friends" of the Japanese, from support to condemnation. Before Pearl Harbor he insisted that even if war came, the state's Japanese retain equal protection under the law—a basic constitutional guarantee. But on December 8 he proposed that the Japanese observe house arrest "to avoid riot and disturbance." A few weeks later, Olson approved the abrupt firing of hundreds of Nisei civil servants and also called for evacuation.[18]

Similarly, a month after denouncing Mississippi congressman John Rankin who called for deporting all Japanese Americans, California Republican congressman Leland Ford changed his mind. Perhaps influenced by a telegram from actor Leo Carillo, he counseled Stimson to place "all Japanese, whether citizens or not . . . in inland concentration camps."[19]

For the duration of the war, federal and state authorities found not one act of espionage or sabotage within either the mainland or Hawaiian Japanese communities. Nevertheless, California Attorney General Earl Warren emphasized this point to the Tolan Committee in late February, after evacuation had been determined. A contender for governor, Warren knew that an anti-Japanese policy would be popular, and in his testimony he confirmed the interpretation that innocent circumstances should be considered ominous. He warned of the danger to security posed by the propinquity of Japanese American enclaves to dams, bridges, harbors, power stations, airports, and aviation factories. He did not mention that in most instances these residences preceded those facilities; he seemed, in fact, to designate any place where the Japanese settled as "strategic."

What counted most was the absence of sabotage in coastal regions. "The fifth column activities that we are to get," he claimed, "are timed just like Pearl Harbor was timed and just like the invasion of France, and of Denmark, and of Norway, and all of those other countries." Californians had been "lulled into a false sense of security," and "the only reason we haven't had disaster in California is because it has been timed for a different date." Evacuation was "absolutely constitutional." Warren concluded in wartime "every citizen must give up some of his rights."[20] Although Warren was not a crucial figure in the decision to relocate the Japanese, and much later recanted his statements, his attitude typified those of pragmatic liberals nationwide.

Racist pressure groups and politicians on the Pacific Coast were by no means alone in their outcry. In the South and Southwest, conservative congressmen Martin Dies of Texas and John Rankin of Mississippi and Senator Tom Stewart of Tennessee demonstrated their own belief in white supremacy. Rankin had earned the reputation of a negrophobe and anti-Semite during the 1930s, and in mid-February he reiterated the "war-of-the-worlds" theme by observing: "Once a Jap always a Jap. You cannot change him. You cannot make a silk purse out of a sow's ear." World War II was "a race war," he concluded. "The white man's civilization has come into conflict with Japanese barbarism [and] one of them must be destroyed." Using an argument that he turned against alleged communists later in the decade, he observed that the Japanese "are pagan in their philosophy, atheistic in their beliefs, alien in their allegiance, and antagonistic to everything for which we stand."[21] Rankin's comments received strong backing from congressmen William F. Norrell of Arkansas, Jennings Randolph of West Virginia, and Schuyler O. Bland of Virginia.

Dies, the chairman of the House Un-American Activities Committee, had made an industry during the preceding four years of chasing fifth columns. A great self-promoter, he announced on January 28 that had his committee been allowed to reveal "facts" it possessed the previous September, "Pearl Harbor might have been averted." Unless Washington alerted itself to the problem, there would occur on the West Coast "a tragedy that will make Pearl Harbor sink into insignificance with it."[22] On February 9, Dies lamented anew that Washington remained "lax, tolerant, and soft toward the Japanese who have violated American hospitality; Shinto Temples still operate; propaganda outlets still disseminate propaganda material; and Japanese, both alien and American citizens, still spy for the Japanese government."[23]

One is tempted to dismiss such claptrap as a prime example of the paranoid style in American politics—the monopoly of fringe groups that exert little impact upon national policy. But, unfortunately, similar nativist sentiments infused the entire political spectrum, encompassing liberals like Warren, Mayor Fiorello La Guardia of New York, journalist Walter Lippmann, and Representative John Dingell of Michigan (who *before* Pearl Harbor suggested incarcerating 10,000 Hawaiian Japanese as hostages to ensure Tokyo's good behavior), and leftists like Vito Marcantonio and Carey McWilliams, and the editors of the Communist *Daily Worker* and *People's World*, each of whom found the fight against militarism and fascism more important than the civil liberties of Japanese Americans.[24]

Hatred directed at the suspected (and powerless) Asian adversary within provided both a vicarious means of striking back at an unexpectedly awesome enemy and a source of unity and welcome consensus after the great foreign policy debate of 1941. Condemnation of the Japanese Americans could create strange bedfellows, as exemplified in the consensus between Lippmann, the dean of liberal journalism, and Westbrook Pegler, a Scripps-Howard columnist whose venomous style anticipated the *National Inquirer*. When Lippmann declared the Pacific Coast a combat zone and stated that "nobody ought to be on a battle-field who has not good reason for being there," Pegler responded with glee. "Do you get what he says?" he wrote. "This is a high-grade fellow with a heavy sense of responsibility. . . . The Japanese in California should be under armed guard to the last man and woman right now—and to hell with habeas corpus until the danger is over. . . . If it isn't true, we can take it out on Lippmann, but on his reputation I will bet it is all true."[25]

The most respected journalist of his day, Lippmann assessed "The Fifth Column on the Coast" after meeting Lieutenant General John L. DeWitt, head of the Western Defense Command, entrusted by Roosevelt with the defense of the Pacific Coast. This elderly bureaucrat had more experience in supply than in combat and drew little respect from other army brass. He was cautious, indecisive, galled, no doubt, by seeing younger officers promoted throughout the army, and panic stricken lest he suffer a fate similar to his Hawaiian counterpart, Lieutenant General Walter C. Short. Yet in the month after Pearl Harbor, DeWitt appeared content to leave the problem of enemy aliens to the Justice Department.[26]

DeWitt initially approved "any preferential treatment to any alien irrespective of race," but his position shifted during the next six weeks.[27] There were, to be sure, some scruples to overcome—for example, a policy emphasizing enemy ethnicity instead of race, per se, precluded action against Japanese aliens not also taken against German and Italian aliens. Yet the size of the latter groups, their political power, and their high degree of assimilation, made evacuation unthinkable. Moreover, action only against enemy aliens would prevent moving against the Nisei who were, after all, citizens. The Nisei were considered a greater threat than the Issei by some, but they could not be evacuated and their elderly parents left behind.[28]

As late as February 3, Stimson observed that "we cannot discriminate among our citizens on the ground of racial origin."[29] These views soon became casualties in the battle for control of the issue between the War and Justice departments. In this contest DeWitt became an important pawn, a spokesman for Major Karl R. Bendetsen, chief of the Aliens Division, Provost Marshal General's Office, and the latter's superior, Allen Gullion, who strongly desired not only removal of the Japanese from the West Coast but also sought to wrest control of enemy aliens from Attorney General Francis Biddle. Throughout the decision-making period, Gullion called the shots while Chief of Staff George C. Marshall "had little to do during January and February with the plans and decisions for Japanese evacuation."[30]

The DeWitt clique became, in fact, the *diabolus ex machina* of relocation. "Military necessity" was the doctrine invoked—a transparent mantle, it soon became clear, for an elite nativism that ultimately breached the Bill of Rights "on a scale so large as to beggar the sum total of all such violations from the beginnings of the United States down to that time."[31] By mid-February the professional soldiers and their civilian superiors—especially Stimson and his assistant, John J. McCloy—had reached conclusions about the Nisei "problem" that were indistinguishable from the warnings from western politicians and patriotic organizations, labor unions, and observers like Lippmann.[32]

Bendetsen, who with Gullion exerted strong pressure on McCloy and Stimson, felt certain that a Japanese invasion was possible and doubted that the Nisei "could withstand the ties of race and affinity" with the land of their fathers.[33] Stimson himself needed little prodding. Doubting the capacities and patriotism of brown, yellow, and black Americans, he noted in his diary on February 10 that "an invisible deadline was approaching" and the "racial characteristics" of the Nisei predisposed them to potential disloyal behavior.[34]

Influenced by Bendetsen and Gullion, DeWitt reacted similarly. "In the war in which we are now engaged," he wrote Stimson on February 14, "racial affinities are not severed by migration. The Japanese race is an enemy race, and while many second- and third-generation Japanese born on United States soil, possessed of United States citizenship, have become 'Americanized,' the racial strains are undiluted. . . . It therefore follows that along the vital Pacific Coast over 112,000 potential enemies of Japanese extraction are at large today." "A Jap's a Jap," he proclaimed later, "and that's all there is to it."[35]

Through the War Department, anti-Japanese racial nativism became national policy on February 19, when FDR authorized the military to evacuate "dangerous persons" from specified coastal areas and to erect inland concentration camps to hold them. Attorney General Biddle failed to prevent the issue from passing to War Department control, feeling—perhaps because he was new to the cabinet—unready to oppose Stimson, "whose wisdom and integrity I greatly respected."[36] FDR, meanwhile, expressed satisfaction that the question had reached Stimson's hands.

The decision for relocation becomes clearer when viewed as part of the administration's quest for national unity, which after Pearl Harbor became a sine qua non of both domestic policy and the Anglo-American alliance. This drive had as its earliest quarry American communists, who offered FDR unsolicited support in the 1936 campaign, and such "fascists" as Father Coughlin and Silver-Shirt leader William Dudley Pelley. In 1936 and again in 1939, Roosevelt used FBI and military and naval intelligence to probe subversive activities. In November 1939 the FBI began assembling a "custodial detention index" of persons with "strong" Nazi or communist "tendencies," whose liberty during war "would constitute a menace."[37]

By mid-1940 the fear of fifth-column activities amounted to a "little red scare," uniting intellectuals like Lewis Mumford, the editors of *The Nation*, Roosevelt, and Hoover.[38] After the Nazi-Soviet Pact of August 1939, which linked communism and fascism in American minds, concern with subversive intrigue grew markedly. With Dies's House Un-American Activities Committee decrying leftist influences within the administration, the loyalty issue became partisan, and all the more important to the president. Despite his attorney general's disagreement in May 1940, FDR approved FBI surveillance of "persons suspected of subversive activities," a directive that soon encompassed the right to open suspicious mail entering or leaving the country.[39] When "sabotage, assassination, and 'fifth-column' activities are completed," Roosevelt observed, referring to Europe, it might be too late to act.[40] In September, after passage of the Smith Act, Attorney General Frank Murphy (generally regarded as a friend of civil liberties) agreed. "Unless we are pudding-headed," he stated, "we shall drive from the land the hirelings here to undo the labors of our fathers."[41]

After the Soviet Union entered the European war in June 1941, and FDR increased naval support to Britain, the administration viewed its critics as just the sort of "hirelings" to whom Murphy referred. The president was convinced, for example, that the nation's leading isolationist lobby, America First, drew sustenance from illicit sources. Roosevelt also achieved success on another front. For, while Coughlin and other anti-Semites suggested that international Jews and communists dictated "Rosenfeld" foreign policy, interventionists linked the domestic "fascists" to such noninterventionists as Senator Gerald P. Nye and Charles Lindbergh, and to America First, and identified them with Nazi Germany. Guilt by association paid dividends in September when Lindbergh broached the forbidden theme of anti-Semitism in a speech at Des Moines, where he indicted the Jews as one of three major groups secretly taking the nation to war.[42]

In linking its adversaries with Berlin, however,

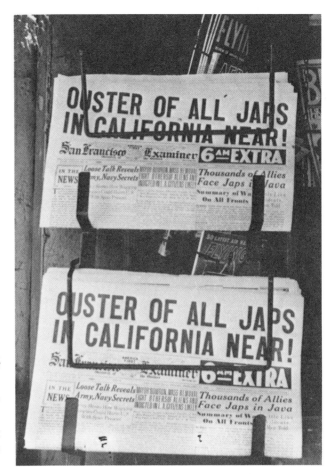

Headlines in San Francisco newspapers on the day before the order to evacuate. Courtesy Bernard K. Johnpoll.

the administration did not establish clear moral superiority over them. While denouncing their opponents as Nazis, interventionists found it impolitic to admit that their own house was permeated by a genteel, albeit powerful, anti-Semitism. The fate of the Wagner-Rogers bill in February 1939 indicated that a large segment of the populace opposed Jewish immigration, hardly surprising in a nation still reeling from economic woes. Two-thirds of those polled opposed the measure to admit 20,000 additional Jewish refugee children beyond the annual quota of 27,000 persons from Germany and Austria. Critical Americans saw the bill as "a wedge for thousands more," while several Jewish leaders worried that passage would strengthen anti-Semitism.[43]

The State Department's restrictive immigration policy after 1938 also reflected a belief shared by Hoover, FDR, and Undersecretary of State Breckinridge Long that Jewish refugees might themselves be part of a German fifth column recruited to subvert the United States. Long personally disliked Jews, and he and the president were known to share a chuckle at anti-

Semitic jokes. One should not conclude from this that anti-Semitism dominated the White House, but it is clear that it became an expedient rather than an ethical issue during the Great Debate.[44]

Indeed, in private moments Roosevelt himself exhibited some dubious views on race, including thoughts about crossbreeding Europeans and Asians to extinguish Japanese deliquency. On one occasion he told Treasury Secretary Henry Morgenthau that "you either have to castrate the German people or you have to treat them in such a manner that they can't just go on reproducing people who want to continue the way they have in the past." FDR also scorned the Burmese as "dislikeable," and he would inform Joseph Stalin at Yalta that the Vietnamese were "a people of small stature . . . and not warlike." On another occasion, while discussing with associates the apparently excessive Puerto Rican birthrate, the president suggested, jokingly, the need to utilize "the methods which Hitler used effectively," in this case an electric current, "very simple and painless," that would "sterilize subjects in about twenty seconds."[45]

FDR was no political cousin of the Beast of Berchtesgaden, but his views underline D. W. Brogan's observation that "in the years between the wars, the United States was only outdistanced by Germany as a market for race theories, some of them crude enough to have suited Hitler."[46] Thus Roosevelt's correspondence with Dr. Ales Hrdlicka, an idiosyncratic anthropologist at the Smithsonian, commands more than passing interest. Throughout the 1930s Hrdlicka warned him that Japan's leaders were "utterly egotistic, tricky, and ruthless" men, "working steadily towards the exclusion of all, and particularly the white man, from the Pacific and Eastern Asia." In the summer of 1941, Hrdlicka urged Roosevelt to "rouse our people. Rouse the women, the young, the very children, regardless of obstruction," to oppose Japan.[47] Although not endorsing Hrdlicka's extremism, FDR did ask him in the early weeks of the war to undertake a study of race-crossing of Asian and European stocks. If the Japanese could be driven back to their islands, Roosevelt believed, perhaps their aggressive characteristics might be bred out of them.[48]

If the connection between this assumption and Executive Order 9066 remains debatable, FDR's racial perspectives did make it easier for him to deprive Japanese Americans of their liberties. In fact, questions of race and civil liberties became interlocking expedients as the administration moved to cement national unity after Pearl Harbor. Having reiterated often the Trojan horse analogy after May 1940, with Pearl Harbor Roosevelt stepped up his demand that Hoover and Attorney General Biddle get rid of all

traitors. Although Biddle hoped to avoid the "extravagant" civil liberties abuses of World War I, FDR peppered him and Hoover with ultimata about the disloyal. The president saw "no valid reason" why "suspected subversive activities" by congressmen should be immune from investigation, and soon adversaries like Father Coughlin and Pelley were silenced and some thirty other seditionists were headed for a trial that became a bizarre circus.[49] Still, these worthies did receive varying measures of due process.

By discrediting perceptive noninterventionists, the administration identified its opponents as subversives. After Pearl Harbor Roosevelt told Churchill that a free press had become an additional burden, urged Biddle to get grand juries into action against his critics, and asked Hoover several times whether the director had cleared the Washington hotels of their "alien waiters."[50]

The decision to relocate the Japanese Americans was consistent with the administration's prewar attitudes and policies toward objectionable minorities. Having proscribed the ideological marketplace, the federal government found it easy to shut down the ethnic marketplace for a group ill-equipped to defend itself. In fact, relocation was the tribute that administration pragmatism paid expediency. The quest for domestic unity early in 1942 had become both less and more of a problem: If isolationism lay buried with the fleet at Pearl Harbor, most Americans—two-thirds according to one poll—called upon the president to direct U.S. forces against Japan before counterattacking in Europe. Public opinion thus jeopardized Roosevelt's desire for a smoothly functioning Anglo-American alliance, as well as the conviction that European operations should precede any large-scale response in the Pacific.[51]

While defending the Allied war effort as part of "the great upsurge of human liberty of the Bill of Rights and individual freedom against Nazi barbarism," the president did not take unity for granted. Roosevelt recognized the need to strike symbolic and substantive blows against Tokyo to counter what he construed as a mood of public demoralization. Toward these ends he ordered supplies flown to Chiang Kai-shek, made plans for sixteen B-25s to bomb Tokyo, and ordered General Douglas MacArthur to Australia to assume command of American forces in the Southwest Pacific.[52]

And four days after the fall of Singapore, FDR signed Executive Order 9066, finding still another way "to relieve feelings of powerlessness towards Japan, and to quiet a potentially divisive issue."[53] Recognizing that relocation centers were essentially concentration camps, Roosevelt realized the shaky constitutional ground he occupied and cautioned the army "to be as reasonable as you can."[54] From the lack of opposition to the measure, Roosevelt knew that it would be popular, and, besides, 1942 was an election year. If relocation might help western Democrats in their quest for re-election, the move would strengthen bipartisanship since the cabinet's Republican appointees, Knox and Stimson, remained adamant for evacuation. In addition, the measure promised to mollify American Sinophiles and "Asia Firsters," to let Chiang know that Washington valued China's role in the future of the Far East, to allow the president maneuverability to strengthen his ties with Churchill, and for both men to secure their Europe-first strategy.

In all these considerations, the quest for national unity remained paramount. If the army proved mistaken about the West Coast Japanese, FDR felt that was too bad; the military was fighting the war, and to oppose the military would be to court disunity and disaster.[55]

The sundering of the constitutional rights of the Japanese minority had its origins in three centuries of American racial nativism. The episode might be compared to other forced relocations—those of American Indians during the nineteenth and twentieth centuries and of African blacks during the eighteenth and nineteenth. In the case of the Japanese, as with other minorities, legal status was defined by the dynamic of Caucasian hegemony interacting with expectant capitalism—with few countervailing forces to oppose Roosevelt's executive order and the forces that lay behind it.

Socialist leader Norman Thomas, American Civil Liberties Union attorney A. L. Wirin, and a few others demonstrated courage in opposing relocation, but the power at their command was merely moral, and their impact proved even less telling than the opposition against the earlier majorities mustered by the abolitionists, friends of the native Americans, or, for that matter, anti-imperialists at the turn of the century. California, apparently, remained the white "racial frontier" so celebrated since the days of the Gold Rush.[56]

Knowing little or nothing of the diversities within Japanese American culture, nativists ascribed to this vulnerable, "middleman" minority a tightly knit organization that did not exist; a single-minded allegiance to a hostile power; a nonexistent incredible fecundity; an imaginary economic rapacity; and an unwillingness to become "Americanized," which existed because the Caucasian majority deemed that it should.[57]

Perhaps, as Mayor Fletcher Bowron of Los Angeles conceded on February 6, 1942, the Japanese could not be trusted in the present emergency precisely because of the discrimination Californians had visited upon them.[58] From the perspective of four decades, however, such an observation provides no consolation. In attempting to understand the origins of relocation, one cannot avoid seeing a chilling prologue to several trends that became central to subsequent U.S. foreign policymaking: a concern with internal security that would have been laughable had it not wreaked such devastation between the late 1940s and 1970s; the concomitant growth of a national security bureaucracy that swiftly outstripped the checks originally designed to guide it; augmented civilian deference to military decision makers; a continuing failure to recognize the important nexus between culture and diplomacy; the imputation of the most demonic characteristics (often, with racial overtones) to the nation's adversaries; and, the greatest illusion of all—the self-appointed moral superiority of the United States in a bipolar world. Wells and Welles had been right. *The War of the Worlds* was more than a metaphor.

NOTES

1. Hadley Cantril, *The Invasion from Mars* (Princeton: Princeton University Press, 1940), 58–67.

2. Orrin E. Dunlap, "Message from Mars," *New York Times*, November 6, 1938, 12.

3. See David Culbert, *News for Everyone: Radio and Foreign Affairs in Thirties America* (Westport, Conn.: Greenwood Press, 1976); Michael Leigh, *Mobilizing Consent: Public Opinion and American Foreign Policy, 1937–1947* (Westport, Conn.: Greenwood Press, 1976); and Geoffrey S. Smith, *To Save a Nation: American Countersubversives, the New Deal, and the Coming of World War II* (New York: Basic Books, 1973).

4. For definitions of nativism see John Higham, *Strangers in the Land: Patterns of American Nativism, 1860–1925* (New York: Atheneum, 1963). See also, Geoffrey S. Smith, "Nativism," in *Encyclopedia of American Foreign Policy: Studies of the Principal Movements and Ideas*, ed. Alexander DeConde, 3 vols. (New York: Charles Scribner's, 1978), 2: 651–67.

5. See Roger Daniels, "American Historians and East Asian Immigrants," *Pacific Historical Review* 43 (November 1974): 449–72.

6. Christopher Thorne, *Allies of a Kind: The United States, Britain, and the War Against Japan, 1941–1945* (New York: Oxford University Press, 1978), 4–5.

7. See Akira Iriye, *Pacific Estrangement* (Cambridge: Harvard University Press, 1972), 159; Gunnar Myrdal, *An American Dilemma* (New York: Harper's, 1944), 1006; and Richard Polenberg, *One Nation Divisible: Class, Race, and Ethnicity in the United States since 1938* (New York: Penguin, 1980), 71–72.

8. The wording is Thorne's. See Thorne, 8.

9. Cited in Roger Daniels, *Concentration Camps North America: Japanese in the United States and Canada during World War II* (Malabar, Fla.: R. E. Krieger, 1981), 35. See also Knox to Tolan, March 24, 1942, in House of Representatives, *Fourth Interim Report of the Select Committee Investigating National Defense Migration*, 77:2 (Washington, 1942), 48–49.

10. Roger Daniels, "Westerners from the East: Oriental Immigrants Reappraised," *Pacific Historical Review* 25 (November 1966): 380–81.

11. *Pearl Harbor Attack*. Hearings before the Joint Committee on the Investigation of the Pearl Harbor Attack, *Part 39* (Washington: Government Printing Office, 1946), 12.

12. Michi Weglyn, *Years of Infamy: The Untold Story of America's Concentration Camps* (New York: William Morrow, 1976), 33–53; Daniels, *Camps: North America*, 24–25.

13. William Lydgate, *What America Thinks* (New York: Crowell, 1944), 52–53.

14. Hughes to Biddle, January 19, 1942, cited in Jacobus tenBroek, Edward N. Barnhart, and Floyd W. Matson, *Prejudice, War and the Constitution* (Berkeley: University of California Press, 1954), 74.

15. *San Francisco Examiner*, January 20, 1942.

16. Ibid., January 30, 1942; Bob Kuamamoto, "The Search for Spies: American Counterintelligence and the Japanese American Community, 1932–1941," *Amerasia Journal* 6 (1979): 45–75.

17. *Los Angeles Times*, December 19, 1941; *Life* 11 (December 22, 1941): 81–82.

18. Weglyn, 93; Daniels, *Camps: North America*, 43.

19. Daniels, 47; tenBroek et al., 77.

20. *Hearings Before the Select Committee Investigating National Defense Migration*, Part 29, 77:2, San Francisco, February 21, 1942 (Washington, 1942), 11009–21.

21. *Congressional Record*, 77:2, February 14, 1942, A691–92.

22. *Congressional Record*, 77:2, January 15, 1942, 420; February 26, 1942, 1682–83; Special Committee on Un-American Activities, *Appendix, Part VI, Report on Japanese Activities* (Washington, 1942); *Part VIII* (Washington, 1943).

23. Drew Pearson, "Washington Merry-go-Round," February 7, 1942, cited in tenBroek, et al., 88; *San Francisco Chronicle*, February 9, 1942.

24. William Petersen, *Japanese-Americans: Oppression and Success* (New York: Random House, 1971), 75–76, 79–81; Daniels, *Camps USA*, 69–70, 79; Thomas Sowell, *Ethnic America: A History* (New York: Basic Books, 1981), 172. Dingell to Roosevelt, August 18, 1941, Official File 197, Franklin D. Roosevelt Library, Hyde Park.

25. Walter Lippmann, *New York Herald-Tribune*, February 12, 1942. For Pegler's reaction, see Westbrook Pegler, *Washington Post*, February 15, 1942, in *Congressional Record*, 77:2, February 17, 1942, 568–69.

26. Francis Biddle, *In Brief Authority* (Garden City: Doubleday, 1962), 215.

27. Stetson Conn, "Japanese Evacuation from the West Coast," in *The United States Army in World War II: The Western Hemisphere: Guarding the United States and its Outposts*, ed. Stetson Conn, Rose C. Engleman, and Byron Fairchild (Washington: Government Printing Office, 1964), 136–37.

28. Polenberg, 80.

29. Henry L. Stimson Diary, February 3, 1942, Stimson MSS, Sterling Memorial Library, Yale University.

30. Stetson Conn, "The Decision to Evacuate the Japanese from the Pacific Coast," in *Command Decisions*, ed. Kent R. Greenfield (New York: Harcourt Brace, 1959), 92.

31. James J. Martin, *Revisionist Viewpoints: Essays in a Dissident Historical Tradition* (Colorado Springs: Ralph Myles, 1971), 32n.

32. Like Lippmann, McCloy had no subsequent change of heart about relocation, as his letter in Appendix 3 indicates. He felt relocation was "reasonably undertaken and humanely conducted." The war, McCloy also observed, "caused disruption for the boys who died at Pearl Harbor." See Alan Brinkley, "Minister Without Portfolio," *Harper's* 266 (February 1983): 35; and Geoffrey S. Smith, "Doing Justice: Relocation and Equity in Public Policy," *The Public Historian* 6 (Summer 1984): 90–91.

33. United States Department of the Interior, *WRA: A Story of Human Conservation* (Washington: Government Printing Office, 1946), 181.

34. Stimson Diary, February 10, 1942; Polenberg, 80.

35. United States Department of War, *Final Report: Japanese Evacuation from the West Coast, 1942* (Washington: Government Printing Office, 1943), 34; *Los Angeles Times*, April 14, 1943.

36. Biddle, 226.

37. United States Senate, Select Committee to Study Governmental Operations with Respect to Intelligence Activities, *Final Report: Supplementary Detailed Staff Report on Intelligence Activities and the Rights of Americans, Book III*, S963-3, 94:2 (Washington: Government Printing Office, 1976), 393, 404–5, 413–15; Leo Ribuffo, "Civil Liberties for Villains? The Roosevelt Administration and the Far Right," paper delivered to Organization of American Historians, New Orleans, 1979, 6. See also, Athan Theoharis, *Spying on Americans: Political Surveillance from Hoover to the Huston Plan* (Philadelphia: Temple University Press, 1978), 40–41; and Frank Donner, *The Age of Surveillance: The Aims and Methods of America's Political Intelligence System* (New York: Knopf, 1980), 52–78. Interestingly, neither book includes the Japanese Americans among citizens whose civil liberties were violated by the Roosevelt administration.

38. Polenberg, 42–45; "Our Enemies Within," *Nation* 150 (June 22, 1940): 745–46; Lewis Mumford, *Faith for Living* (New York: Harcourt Brace, 1940), 106–7.

39. United States Senate, *Report on Intelligence Activities, III*, 413–14, 421–22; Theoharis, 65.

40. Robert Dallek, *Franklin D. Roosevelt and American Foreign Policy, 1932–1945* (New York: Oxford University Press, 1979), 224–25.

41. Murphy to Hoover, September 7, 1940, quoted in J. Woodford Howard, *Mr. Justice Murphy: A Political Biography* (Princeton, N.J.: Princeton University Press, 1968), 207.

42. Ribuffo, "Civil Liberties," 9; Wayne S. Cole, *Charles A. Lindbergh and the Battle Against American Intervention in World War II* (New York: Harcourt Brace Jovanovich, 1974), 161–62; Smith, *Nation*, 174–81; and Geoffrey S. Smith, "Isolationism, the Devil, and the Advent of the Second World War: Variations on a Theme," *International History Review* 4 (February 1982): 81–84, 87.

43. Polenberg, 41–42; Saul Friedman, *No Haven for the Oppressed* (Detroit: Wayne State University Press, 1973), 102.

44. See David Wyman, *Paper Walls: America and the Refugee Crisis, 1938–1941* (Amherst: University of Massachusetts Press, 1968); and Henry Feingold, *The Politics of Rescue: The Roosevelt Administration and the Holocaust, 1938–1945* (New Brunswick: Rutgers University Press, 1971).

45. Thorne, 8, 159.

46. D. W. Brogan, *The Price of Revolution* (London: H. Hamilton, 1951), 144.

47. Hrdlicka to Roosevelt, February 25, 1933; December 18, 1937; August 29, 1941; Smithsonian Institution MSS.

48. Thorne, 168n.

49. Ribuffo, "Civil Liberties," 9; Biddle, 234–47. A full account of the "great sedition trial" (which never reached a verdict) may be found in Norman Dorsen and Leon Friedman, *Disorder in the Court* (New York: Pantheon, 1973). See also, Leo Ribuffo, *The Old Christian Right: The Protestant Far Right from the Great Depression to the Cold War* (Philadelphia: Temple University Press, 1983), 194–215.

50. Biddle, 237–38; Francis L. Lowenheim, Harold D. Langley, and Manfred Jonas, eds., *Roosevelt and Churchill: Their Secret Wartime Correspondence* (London: Barrie and Jenkins, 1975), 194–95; Dallek, 335.

51. Dallek, 321, 327–31; Richard W. Steele, *The First Offensive, 1942* (Bloomington: Indiana University Press, 1973), 46–53, 81–93.

52. Dallek, 317, 336; Stimson Diary, January 29, February 3, 1942.

53. Dallek, 334.

54. Conn, "Japanese Evacuation," 131–32.

55. Biddle, 219.

56. Sherburne F. Cook, "The California Indian and Anglo-American Culture," in *Ethnic Conflict in California History*, ed. Charles Wollenberg (Los Angeles: Tinnon-Brown, 1970), 23–42.

57. Harry H. L. Kitano, "Japanese Americans: The Development of a Middleman Minority," *Pacific Historical Review* 63 (November 1974): 500–519; and Hubert Blalock Jr., *Toward a Theory of Minority Group Rule* (New York: Wiley, 1967), 82.

58. *Congressional Record*, 72:2, February 9, 1942, A547–48.

Congressional Opinion and War Relocation, 1943

F. Alan Coombs

Much of the historical focus in studying the relocation of Japanese Americans during the Second World War has been on the experience itself, on what it meant for the people who had to endure it, and upon the administrative arrangements through which it was carried out. War itself is largely an executive function once the shooting has begun, and the relocation was an enterprise of the executive branch of the federal government. The initial program grew out of a presidential executive order implemented initially by the army; the War Relocation Authority was created to supervise the long-term operation by another executive order in mid-March 1942. So the legislative branch was only incidentally involved.

However, congressional sources and records provide additional insight in an effort to gain a comprehensive view of the event. Congress, for better or worse, generally reflects American public opinion (if not necessarily the national interest) more accurately than the other parts of the federal establishment. The Congress in 1942–43 was, as always, made up of highly political people who had strong opinions about a program as significant as the one designed to remove Americans of Japanese ancestry from the West Coast to "less sensitive areas."

As Morton Grodzins and others have shown, there was a great deal of pressure from Congress to "do something" about the West Coast Japanese, and that pressure was certainly a factor in the promulgation of Executive Order 9066 on February 19, 1942.[1] Nor did 9066 halt congressional anti-Japanese initiatives. On March 3, 1942, Representative Homer D. Angell, Republican of Oregon, again called attention to the "serious menace confronting the Pacific coast areas by reason of the large number of Japanese located there" and entered into the *Congressional Record* a resolution from a Portland American Legion post urging "that immediate action be taken to evacuate all Japanese, citizens and aliens alike, from the entire Pacific coast area, and place them in protective custody in a location completely removed from these necessary war activities carried on on the Pacific coast."[2]

A few days later, California Republican Carl Hinshaw warned the House that

> If our administrative officials do not stop diddling around with this Japanese problem on the west coast and get down to quick action to evacuate all Japanese and all

other enemy aliens immediately—and that means now and not day after tomorrow—they may, by inaction, have committed so great a sin that even history may never forgive them.[3]

On March 19, the Senate and the House quickly approved a bill "to provide a penalty for violation of restrictions or orders with respect to persons entering, remaining in, or leaving or committing any act in military areas or zones." When Representative Andrew J. May of Kentucky requested the unanimous consent of the House to take up the measure, he was asked for an explanation of the bill and specifically whether its purpose was to implement the president's executive order. Somewhat reluctantly he acknowledged that it was "intended to apply particularly to the situation that exists on the west coast at this time." Representative John Sparkman of Alabama then noted that when "our committee was out on the west coast studying this problem," Lieutenant General John L. DeWitt had informed them that, although he had the executive order, "he had no way of enforcing the order by penalty if anyone violated it. All he could do was to move them. . . . If they came back, there was no penalty provided by law. He asked for this specific legislation. It is needed immediately because that evacuation is taking place now."[4]

So relocation proceeded. The camps were built, but their operation continued to receive congressional scrutiny. When some members became dissatisfied with the civilian War Relocation Authority, it was manifested in the early days of the Seventy-eighth Congress. On January 18, 1943, Senator Mon C. Wallgren, Democrat from Washington, introduced for himself and Senator Rufus C. Holman, Oregon Republican, a bill "providing for the transfer of certain functions of the War Relocation Authority to the War Department." The motive behind the proposal was clear. As Wallgren later explained, "we felt that under the Army we had a better chance . . . of getting proper discipline and a proper segregation than we have under the existing set up."[5] The implication was that the WRA had been too "soft" in the treatment of its charges and insufficiently rigorous in ferreting out those in the camps who were truly disloyal to the United States.

In a sense, Wallgren and Holman could be seen as representative of "Middle America" in the early 1940s.

The senator from Washington, an optometrist and jeweler by training, counted himself a proud member of the American Legion and was a Mason, an Elk, an Eagle, and a Rotarian. Rufus Holman had started as a farmer before becoming a paper box manufacturer; he too was an active Mason and had been a director of the Portland Rotary organization.

Between January 20 and March 6, 1943, a subcommittee of the Senate Committee on Military Affairs under the chairmanship of the colorful Albert B. "Happy" Chandler of Kentucky held hearings on their bill. The attitudes voiced during those hearings by various members of the subcommittee reveal a great deal about the state of mind that spawned the relocation program and that kept it in operation. They also reveal that some people were troubled that this program was so much at variance with the principles of freedom, dedication to civil liberties, and equal protection of the law that America was supposedly fighting to preserve.

When the hearings opened on January 20, the first witness was Dillon S. Myer, director of the WRA. Myer gave a brief history of his agency and discussed the actual construction of the camps and the work that went on inside them. But the real interest of some members of the committee was in exposing "troublemakers" among the evacuees, and they were especially concerned about repetition of the riots that had occurred at Manzanar and Poston. Myer tried to quiet fears, pointing out that local residents had had little experience with people of Japanese ancestry prior to the establishment of the centers and were understandably nervous about "things and people they don't know." Nevertheless, he continued, although some of the older residents of the camps might be alien in their culture, "very few of them are dangerous people."[6]

That was hardly what sponsors of the bill wanted to hear. After the director said he had been "amazed that we have not had more trouble" in the camps and characterized the number of crimes committed there as "amazingly few," he then described the procedures adopted under the guidance of the Department of Justice for determining which evacuees were and were not "sound from the standpoint of internal security." Mon Wallgren expressed his doubts:

> You know, a Jap would be an awfully good dog right up to the point that he can pull something. Naturally he is going to be a very, very obedient prisoner or evacuee. He will be just as nice as he possibly can be in order to get an opportunity to do that job that he wants to do for [Japan]. . . . They will use [e]very trick in the world in order to throw you off your guard, and then they will stab you in the back, and we had an experience at Pearl Harbor that ought to really be a lesson to anyone, and yet we are going to still continue to grant them leaves of absence, where they might be able to go out some place and blow up maybe Coulee Dam or Bonneville, or maybe some large munitions plant.[7]

With some frustration, Myer tried to explain that the WRA was administering the program under certain assumptions: That most of the evacuees, both aliens and citizens, would continue to live in the United States; that the relocation centers should not be viewed "as internment camps or concentration camps," rather that they were "established as places to provide reasonably minimum living conditions until the evacuees could get relocated in other areas of the country." He felt Japanese Americans had a significant contribution to make to the manpower program during the war.[8]

In addition, the WRA director pointed out what a different kind of program could mean. "I sincerely believe, gentlemen," he told the committee, "that if we don't handle this problem in a way to get these people absorbed as best we can while the war is going on, we may have something akin to Indian reservations after the war, which will be a problem that will be with us for years and years. We will have a racial issue which I don't think we need to have. . . ." He felt strongly that the WRA approach was "very closely related to what we are fighting for," and further warned: "The Japanese militaristic government has been trying to prove for some time that this is a racial war, that it is the orientals against the whites. I don't think that we should contribute to their theory by making this a racial issue."[9]

However reasonable—or naive—that argument may sound in the 1980s, whatever validity it had in 1943 was largely lost on several members of the subcommittee. The WRA's attitude on the question bothered Senator Edwin C. Johnson of Colorado. "Is it your underlying idea," he asked Myer, "that the Jap, no matter how long he is here, will finally merge with our citizenship the same as any white man? . . . Of course, you know that no Pacific States allow intermarriage. They are always going to be brown men. Do you think they will finally merge and just be accepted in every way like a white man?"[10] Senator Johnson obviously did not.

A little of that kind of rhetoric suffices to make the point. Of equal or greater interest is the fact that Dillon Myer was *not* lacking support on the subcommittee; at least one member, Senator Joseph C. O'Mahoney of Wyoming, a Democrat, could be considered a friend. The two men had worked closely together the previous fall to supply labor from the relocation center at Heart

Mountain, Wyoming, to help harvest the sugar beet crop—some 1,500 workers, constituting roughly 15 percent of the total population of the camp and nearly all of the able-bodied men between the ages of eighteen and forty-five, had taken part in that endeavor. In the wake of that project, O'Mahoney had written Myer a warm letter of thanks.[11] Now, as the hearings progressed, the senator took the lead in asking the director questions designed to elicit information about the positive accomplishments of the relocation program under civilian authority.

It is also apparent that constitutional issues were on O'Mahoney's mind:

> There is a question involved here for which the War Relocation Authority cannot be held responsible. Congress has not provided any law or any direction to the Army, to the Navy, or to the War Relocation Authority to govern the handling of American citizens of Japanese ancestry. They are, under our law and under the Supreme Court's interpretation of the Constitution, citizens, entitled to go and come just as the members of this committee are entitled to go and come. The War Department, because of the great danger involved, with the approval of the President, undertook to remove all of these Japanese, whether citizens or aliens, from the west coast and, not having any guidance from Congress as to what to do with them, . . . the War Relocation Authority was set up by the President to handle these Japs in relocation centers.[12]

Those who were taking the WRA to task for coddling the evacuees should remember, O'Mahoney continued, "that the War Relocation Authority cannot make prisoners of these people unless Congress, by law, takes away their rights as citizens." Attacked by Senators Chan Gurney and "Happy" Chandler, O'Mahoney was compelled to give ground, and reaffirmed his support for the evacuation.[13]

If O'Mahoney required further convincing that the Wallgren-Holman bill was a bad idea, he received it a few days later at the hearing of January 28, when the lead witness was the former ambassador to Tokyo, Joseph Grew. Again the Wyoming senator's questioning was friendly. After asking Grew about the Japanese national character and whether it was trustworthy, O'Mahoney asked the ambassador if he concurred that "we ought to follow the policy of not condemning all of these Japs, but of seeking to find out those who cannot be trusted." Grew agreed.[14]

Apparently O'Mahoney found that kind of testimony reassuring, for he later referred to Grew's remarks as "rather persuasive" and made reference to them in his letters to constituents who complained about the "luxuries" being showered upon the residents of the camps. "Most of these evacuees," he told one such

correspondent, "about 60%, are under the law citizens of the United States who were moved away from their homes, from the lands which they owned and the businesses which they operated to be placed in these camps."[15]

He also expressed pleasure that the inspection of the relocation centers by the Spanish consular representatives handling Japanese affairs in this country during the war had been favorable, and he cautioned the project director at Heart Mountain that "the treatment which we accord Americans of Japanese ancestry and every alien Japanese has a direct bearing upon the treatment of our own people in the hands of the Japanese."

The Wyoming senator inserted in the record of the hearings President Roosevelt's letter to Secretary of War Henry Stimson approving the proposal to organize an all-Nisei combat team in February 1943. He pointed out to an old colleague in Wyoming, former Congressman Paul Greever, that "some of the most effective work which has been done for the Navy in Hawaii . . . has been done by Japanese born in Hawaii."[16] He concluded the subcommittee's hearing of January 28, 1943, with a short lecture stressing the need to encourage Germans and Japanese to develop democratic traits.[17]

When Dillon Myer made a return appearance before the subcommittee on February 11, 1943, O'Mahoney elicited from him the information that the director knew of no cases whatsoever of sabotage by evacuees and had received no reports of sabotage from the FBI, the army, or any other agency.

It would be easy to overemphasize the degree of O'Mahoney's sensitivity to the injustice of relocation; he introduced no legislation to dismantle the camps or to send the evacuees home after reacquiring the property they had been forced to surrender. In the short run, however, it may have been helpful merely to have a voice of moderation on the military affairs subcommittee considering the Wallgren-Holman bill.

When Colonel William P. Scobey of the U.S. Army General Staff testified that the War Department opposed the measure because it would give [the Department] "a responsibility which it is not particularly qualified to handle, because the objective to be accomplished is of a social nature rather than a military nature," the immediate threat to the WRA's more humane orientation was blunted.[18] Although Senator Chandler made a whirlwind tour of a number of the camps in March and, quite predictably, found alarming evidence of disloyalty, the Wallgren-Holman bill was not materially aided by that effort.

When the war agencies appropriations bill came

before the Senate in June 1943, Chandler again castigated the WRA for treating its function "as a social experiment at the expense of the people of the United States." He concluded, "I feel that every Jap in those camps who said he was against the United States was against the United States. Many of them, too, who said they were for us are against us."[19]

There was little likelihood that Senator Chandler's mind would be changed. But control of the program remained in the hands of Dillon Myer and his associates and, in his reminiscence, *Uprooted Americans*, Myer said he believed O'Mahoney had helped keep the subcommittee's report "temperate."[20]

Getting into the contemporary records and source materials on relocation for the first time can be an eerie experience for a researcher. One starts with the knowledge that it was a disgraceful episode, unwarranted and sad, and that there could be explanations but ultimately no excuses. Yet it is distressing to find new evidence to fulfill our darkest visions of the mind set, the fear, and the hatred of that period. The next temptation is to look for other evidence—of what Abraham Lincoln called "the better angels of our nature," some sign that not everyone succumbed totally to hysteria and racial prejudice. Fortunately, there is some of this too.

The constant challenge for the historian is to evaluate human behavior by the standards of its own time and in its own context. In that sense, it should not be surprising that the courage to speak out against the injustice being done was rare, for public opinion surveys in March 1942 showed 93 percent of those questioned approved of the relocation of Japanese aliens and nearly three-fifths favored the same treatment for "the Japanese who were born in this country and are United States citizens." Also, nearly two-thirds of the respondents felt "they should be kept under strict guard as prisoners of war" and should not be "allowed to go about fairly freely in their new community." Even four years later, nine months after the war had ended, 66 percent of those asked in one poll believed that "the Japanese who lived in this country" had been involved in espionage activities for the Japanese government.[21]

Those public servants who were willing to brave that kind of suspicion and prejudice should not be forgotten, even if their efforts did not prevail. They would be among the first to endorse the spirit of this volume and the firm resolve to learn from the tragic experience of the 1940s so its like will never happen again.

NOTES

1. Morton Grodzins, *Americans Betrayed: Politics and The Japanese Evacuation* (Chicago: University of Chicago Press, 1949).

2. *Congressional Record*, 77th Cong., 2d sess., 3 March 1942, 88, pt. 2:1916–17.

3. Ibid., 7 March 1942, 88, pt. 2:2032.

4. Ibid., 19 March 1942, 88, pt. 2:2729–30.

5. S. 444, *A Bill Providing for the Transfer of Certain Functions of the War Relocation Authority to the War Department*, introduced by Senator Mon C. Wallgren for himself and Senator Rufus C. Holman, *Congressional Record*, 78th Cong., 1st sess., 18 January 1943, 89, pt. 1:197; Senate Committee on Military Affairs, *War Relocation Centers*, Hearings before a Subcommittee of the Committee on Military Affairs on S. 444, 78th Cong., 1st sess., 28 January 1943, 18 (hereafter cited as *War Relocation Centers*).

6. *War Relocation Centers*, 29 January 1943, 21.

7. Ibid., 25–26, 41.

8. Ibid., 36–37.

9. Ibid., 53.

10. Ibid., 55.

11. Myer to O'Mahoney, 21 October 1942, and O'Mahoney to Myer, 24 October 1942, box 67, Joseph C. O'Mahoney Collection, Western History Research Center, University of Wyoming, Laramie, Wyoming (hereafter cited as O'Mahoney MSS). See also Douglas W. Nelson, *Heart Mountain: The History of an American Concentration Camp* (Madison: The State Historical Society of Wisconsin for the Department of History, University of Wisconsin, 1976), 15–39, and T. A. Larson, *Wyoming's War Years, 1941–1945*, (Laramie: University of Wyoming, 1954).

12. *War Relocation Centers*, 20 January 1943, 45.

13. Ibid., 45–46.

14. Ibid., 28 January 1943, 112.

15. Ibid., 127; O'Mahoney to W. B. Johnson, 5 February 1943, box 77, O'Mahoney MSS.

16. O'Mahoney to Guy Robertson, 17 February 1943, box 74, O'Mahoney MSS; *War Relocation Centers*, 11 February 1943, 158, O'Mahoney to Paul R. Greever, 6 February 1943, box 74, O'Mahoney MSS.

17. *War Relocation Centers*, 28 January 1943, 128.

18. Ibid., 20 January 1943, 83.

19. Senator Robert R. Reynolds introducing S. Res. 101 authorizing "the Committee on Military Affairs or any subcommittee thereof duly appointed . . . to visit, for the purpose of inspection, . . . the Japanese relocation centers in the United States," *Congressional Record*, 78th Cong., 1st sess., 11 February 1943, 89, pt. 1:821; S. Res. 101 amended on 25 February 1943 by S. Res. 111, adding the words "accompanied by one investigator," *Congressional Record*, 78th Cong., 1st sess., 89, pt. 1:1286. See also Senator Chandler's remarks on the WRA, *Congressional Record*, 78th Cong., 1st sess., 30 June 1943, 89, pt. 5:6834–35.

20. Dillon S. Myer, *Uprooted Americans: The Japanese Americans and the War Relocation Authority During World War II* (Tucson: University of Arizona Press, 1971), 93–95.

21. National Opinion Research Center surveys, 28 March 1942 and May 1946, in Hadley Cantril, ed., *Public Opinion 1935–1946* (Princeton, N.J.: Princeton University Press, 1951), 380–81.

Utah's Ambiguous Reception:
The Relocated Japanese Americans

Leonard J. Arrington

There is reason to believe that Utah's reaction to the arrival of Japanese evacuees might have been different from those of its contiguous states. My task is to assess whether this, in fact, was true—whether the Utah reaction was substantially different from that of Wyoming, Idaho, Nevada, Colorado, and the other inland western states. Let us consider the reasons why the response might have differed.

Historically, the Mormon settlers of Utah generally admired the Japanese. For 100 years or so, the Latter-day Saints had sought to establish a separate Kingdom of God in the Great Basin; that is, they had attempted to establish a predominantly, if not exclusively, Mormon commonwealth unified in its economics and politics, as well as in its religion. They did not completely succeed in these efforts, but their Great Basin Kingdom did achieve a high degree of economic independence, and the preservation of their own peculiar values caused the Latter-day Saints to admire nations and peoples who, like the Japanese, were attempting the same.

After the Meiji Restoration in 1868, a number of Japanese came to the United States as observers. Perhaps a dozen of these groups visited the Mormon communities in the valley of the Great Salt Lake. The Mormon church newspaper, the *Deseret News*, unfailingly reported these visits favorably and included with some pride a quotation or two from the visitors pointing out the similarities between Mormon and Japanese value systems. One of these quotations was to the effect that the Mormons, like the Japanese, were people of vision: they were planning not for the next year or for the next five years or even for the next generation, but for a hundred years in the future. In the last third of the nineteenth century, when Mormon leaders were seeking to counteract the attempts of the federal government to force them to adopt the non-Mormon, predominant American values and practices, they often brought up the image of the Japanese—"We are trying to do what the Japanese are doing," they repeatedly asserted; "we are building the basis for a better future for our children and our children's children."[1] These and other references suggest that the Latter-day Saints had a great admiration for the Japanese—for their industry, patience, frugality, strong family ties, and their willingness to sacrifice for the future of their people.[2] Some people have suggested

another reason why the Mormons admired the Japanese—their permissiveness with respect to polygamy and the way they kept their wives in place. At the end of World War II, a *Stars and Stripes* reporter interviewed a number of American servicemen in Tokyo and asked them what they thought of the Japanese. One of those interviewed was a Mormon from Utah, and his comments were to the effect that American women could learn a lot about faithfulness from Japanese women. Another quality which American women might learn, he declared, was obedience. "When Japanese men tell the women to do something," he explained, "Japanese women snap to."

In addition, ties had been established between key Utah leaders and the Japanese people after the Mormons established a proselyting mission in Japan in 1901. Many articles on Japan appeared in Utah and Mormon newspapers. Considering the transportation and means of communication of the time, the excitement in Utah during the early years of the Mormon mission in Japan was somewhat analogous to excitement over early space flights. Here was a direct contact with an exotic land and culture about which Utahns knew very little and wanted to know more. Some Mormon writings of the time even suggested that the Japanese people were related to the chosen people of God whose story was told in the Book of Mormon.[3]

The leader of this first Mormon mission to Japan was Heber J. Grant, one of the twelve apostles of the Mormon church. Again, it is significant that he was president and prophet of the Mormons during the 1940s when the evacuation occurred. A review of his sermons and letters during the 1940s suggests that this Latter-day Saint prophet could not find it in his heart to hate the Japanese, even if America was at war with Japan. In the papers of Governor Herbert Maw in the Utah State Archives is a news release signed by President Grant entitled "They are God's Children Also":

> Reports coming to this office declare that in outlying districts these Japanese-Americans find a lack of warmth . . . not evident in the more urban communities. . . . [P]rotests have been registered against leasing land to Japanese or those of Japanese ancestry. . . . [T]he ranchers needed labor this fall, and were willing to have Japanese labor imported, but . . . did not want the Japanese boys and girls attending . . . schools where their own children were students.

[P]rejudices went ever farther. . . . In one community efforts made to raise money . . . [for] more books . . . [were experiencing] difficulty. . . . Finally someone thought of going to two or three Japanese families . . . for funds, and the response of these people was so generous that the solicitors decided there must be something crooked in it and reported the generous donations to the sheriff.

Americans who are loyal are good Americans whether their ancestors came from Great Britain or Japan, the Scandinavian countries or Germany. Let us, therefore, endeavor to banish these foolish prejudices from our natures and let us attempt to see that all good and loyal Americans are treated as such.[4]

Among the early Latter-day Saint missionaries to Japan was Elbert D. Thomas, Utah's senior senator during World War II. Senator Thomas maintained close relationships with many Japanese, both in Japan and in the United States; after his return from his Japanese mission, he even wrote a book in Japanese. Because of his love for and understanding of the Japanese people, Senator Thomas was one of the few voices of reason during the fear and frenzy that followed the attack on Pearl Harbor. At the end of the war, Senator Thomas was appointed high commissioner for formerly Japanese-held islands in the Pacific—Saipan, Tinian, and other trust territories.

Finally, Utah's governor in 1942 was Herbert B. Maw, a liberal Democrat, a Mormon church official, and a humanitarian who had love and compassion for all peoples and particularly toward persons who experienced discrimination. Unfortunately, one must add that he was also a politician, anxious to retain his support and to be reelected; sometimes his compassion was overruled or tempered by political necessity. At a governor's conference in Salt Lake City in April 1942,[5] Maw suggested giving each state a quota of evacuees and letting each handle them in its own way. This was really a political bid to get funding for a state-run program that could be efficiently managed and, simultaneously, assure jobs for his supporters.

Japanese began migrating to Utah shortly after 1900. First, there was the immigration of Japanese Mormon converts.[6] Second, copper mining in Bingham Canyon began, and several hundred single Japanese men were imported to assist in this giant enterprise. Many of these remained only long enough to accumulate enough money to return to Japan, to marry and settle down there with a small competence. Third, several hundred Japanese, including both single men and families, had migrated to Box Elder County to work in the sugar beet fields when the Garland refinery was opened in 1903. Others went to Salt Lake County when another refinery was opened in 1916. Most stayed, purchased or leased land, and became perma-

nent residents. Many of their descendants are still in Utah. Many became Mormons and were assimilated into the life of the local village. Others later moved to areas where new beet sugar factories were established and where labor was scarce—particularly to the Upper Snake River Valley in southeastern Idaho, where many of their descendants remain today.

During the agricultural depression that began in 1920, the industrious Japanese shifted from the cultivation of sugar beets to lettuce, celery, tomatoes, and fruit. They developed an important export market for these commodities, and Utah enjoyed a wide reputation for its fine celery and lettuce.

Another group to migrate to Utah were families who came to Salt Lake City to practice a profession or to establish restaurants, stores, and other businesses to service the persons of Japanese ancestry and the Utah community at large. There were already more than one hundred by 1913; they formed the Japanese Association of Utah and held regular meetings in the Latter-day Saint Fourteenth Ward chapel in Salt Lake City. According to news reports, they sang the Japanese national anthem at the opening of their meetings and the "Star Spangled Banner" at the close. Elbert Thomas, during these years a professor of political science at the University of Utah, was a frequent visitor and speaker. The association opened a Japanese school, to which Japanese boys and girls went for an hour after the public schools let out, and also published a tri-weekly newspaper, the *Rocky Mountain Times*, and later a daily, *The Utah Nippo*. By the 1920s each had a circulation of about 1,000. The stated purpose of the association was "to bring all Japanese living in the area to a correct understanding and appreciation of the American spirit and life, and at the same time contribute to the intellectual, social and moral development of the Japanese themselves."[7] Certainly no Utahn would have taken exception to that objective.

This is not to suggest that there was universal appreciation and admiration for all these adopted Utahns. There were a few interracial marriages but not many as Utah law prohibited them. The children went to public school, but they were not always welcomed or, at least, not by every Utah resident, although some of the Japanese students were athletes and student officers. One indication of Utah's favorable attitude was the occasion in 1921 when Governor William D. Stephens of California was trying to drum up national support for the prohibition of further Japanese immigration. Utah's Governor Charles R. Mabey responded negatively.[8] A second indication was the invitation extended to Professor Tomoyoshi Mutai of Tokyo in January 1928 to give a major address on Japanese culture and religion in the Mormon Tabernacle in Salt Lake City. His talk, approximately an hour in length, was subsequently published in full in the *Deseret News*. The representative of the Mormon church who introduced him, Levi Edgar Young, arose at the end of the address to say, "We agree with all he has said."[9]

Another example of pro-Japanese sentiment was the reaction in Utah generally to a series of raids or night rides by a group of vigilantes in the Salt River Valley in Arizona who were attempting to rid the valley of the industrious Japanese farmers who had settled there. Utah newspapers published some editorials expressing righteous indignation that fellow westerners would act in such an uncivilized and undemocratic manner. "Arizonians," admonished one newspaper, "ought to observe the law and insist on fair play. It isn't exactly fair or manly to gallop through the darkness hurling bombs indiscriminately among brown women and children with the same right to live and enjoy life as white women and children have."[10]

When Pearl Harbor was bombed, 2,210 persons of Japanese ancestry resided in Utah, nearly all of them in Box Elder, Weber, Davis, Salt Lake, and Utah counties, the counties comprising northern Utah. While an elaborate breakdown is not available, one analysis for an earlier period indicates that there were five Japanese medical doctors, a dozen journalists, and several dozen merchants in Utah. Some of the latter were members of the Salt Lake Chamber of Commerce, made contributions to political parties, and took an active part in community affairs. Most were workingmen, of course; many belonged to labor unions. There were six Japanese boardinghouses, six restaurants preparing only Japanese dishes, and about a dozen stores handling mostly Japanese foodstuffs. Many Japanese also operated American-style restaurants. Most of the Japanese, according to the report, ate one meal of native food daily. About 70 percent were said to be living in Utah to make money, the remainder coming for the ideal of liberty or because they preferred American life. There were about twenty Japanese students in Utah high schools and another dozen in Utah universities. They had a gymnasium of their own in Salt Lake City where they fenced, played basketball, and practiced the ancient art of jujitsu; they also had a baseball team. About 10 percent, according to the report, were Christians, the remainder mostly unaffiliated.[11]

Among the Utahns of Japanese ancestry who attained status in the Salt Lake Valley were Mike and Joe Grant Masaoka. They were graduates of West High School in Salt Lake City, and Mike graduated with honors from the University of Utah in 1937; they were active in the Japanese American Citizens League, which had been founded in 1928 and had 20,000 members by 1942. Because of his personality, intelligence, and energy, Mike became national secretary and field executive of the JACL and served as such during the war. The JACL national weekly newspaper, *The Pacific Citizen*, was published in Salt Lake City during the war and had a circulation of 7,000.

If the above factors suggest reasons why Utahns might have been more receptive to the influx of Japanese evacuees in early 1942, a number of other factors suggest that the Utah reception would not be substantially different from that of the other western states—and some of these also stem from the Mormon character.

The first of these goes back to the last half of the nineteenth century, a long period of conflict between Mormons and other Americans. Ostensibly, the quarrel was over polygamy, but historians in recent years have demonstrated that the real quarrel was over politics and economics—the power to control the state. Eventually in the course of the struggle, Congress removed all Mormon territorial officers from office, prohibited loyal Mormons from voting in territorial elections, placed the government of the territory in the hands of a presidential commission, confiscated the property of the Mormon church (including the Salt Lake Temple), and proceeded to place several hundred Mormon leaders in the penitentiary. This situation ended only when the Mormons agreed to halt the practice of plural marriage (1890), dissolved the church's People's Party and supported non-Mormon candidates for about half the key offices of the territory (1891), and discontinued the exclusivist economic program that had made entry into the commercial life of the community difficult for non-Mormon businessmen and industrialists (1887).

Having made the firm and irreversible decision to bow to the national will, the Mormons from that date on seem determined to establish and prove their patriotism. With a little hesitancy, the Mormons joined the national clamor during the Spanish-American War, and they played an enthusiastic and proud role in both world wars. The per capita rate of army volunteers in both World War I and World War II was exceptionally high. A tendency for some to become "superpatriots" has been suggested. Although their reaction to the Pearl Harbor attack was not significantly different from that of other westerners and, although it would not be accurate to say that they hated the Japanese, Utah Mormons did wish to demonstrate that the Latter-day Saints loved America as much as anyone and, if the Japanese were America's enemies, they did not want to welcome people who posed threats to America's survival. To put it another way, the degree to which Mormons were alarmed by the entrance of the

Japanese into Utah is the degree to which the Mormons by this time were "Americanized."

A second reason one might expect opposition to the relocation of Japanese Americans to Utah is that some Mormons objected to the immigration of every non-Mormon group. The Mormons wanted to keep their culture as pure as possible and, just as they objected to the coming of railroad construction workers in the 1860s, miners in the 1870s, and to soldiers at any time, so they objected to "invasions," as they regarded them, of Missourians, Texans, Mexicans, Chinese, Japanese, and every other group of "outsiders." Not all of this was religiously oriented: there were only a few valleys in Utah where water could be had for farming; there was hardly room and resources for the Mormons themselves to make a living, let alone outsiders.

Related to this is the fact that Utah had gone through two decades of depression and still suffered substantial underemployment in rural areas in 1942. Utah has always maintained a high birthrate, its manufacturing was still undeveloped, and its farms had been subdivided through successive generations to the point that too many were trying to make a living from inadequate resources. Although a heavy outmigration to California took place in the 1920s and 1930s, there was still unemployment in Utah and Utahns were fearful that the voluntary evacuees, those Japanese who came to Utah in the months after Pearl Harbor, by their industry and ingenuity, might preempt opportunities needed by native Utahns. To sum it up, there are reasons to suggest that Utah would be reasonably receptive to incoming evacuees; while others indicate Utahns might oppose their coming.

The diverse attitudes of Utahns are reflected in more than two hundred letters written to Governor Maw. These letters—more than two hundred of which are to be found in his papers—range from ardent opposition to the warmest reception. There were the haters and zealots:

Once a Jap, always a Jap. I suppose if my cat had kittens in a fish hatchery they would be fish?

We will not tolerate Japanese here to sabotage and blast our industries, water systems, defense plants, and beautiful cities. . . .

How can we afford to enlist our own good American boys, whom we have raised for purposes other than war, to fight Japanese aggression and at the same time allow these people to roam at will within our country?

We as citizens are willing to go into the fields, but we don't want to mingle with Japs. The sugar company wants to put them in here; I suggest the sugar officials put them in their own back yards and not in ours. . . .

I've heard club women talking of boycotting farmers all over the state who hire Japs to protect their families from possible poisoned produce.

Governor, I hope you will keep these ruthless barbarians, these plague-dispensing savages far removed from our homes and farms and industries. [This man suggested that they all be removed to some of the islands west of California and required to support themselves there in isolation.]

We have fifty-six Japs living in our town limits and others are coming. Fourteen percent of our school children are Japs and the Japanese children tell our youngsters that they will show them who is boss as soon as those California kids get here. If we must have these Japs in our communities, let's have them in camps and under strict supervision.[12]

There were the predictable resolutions protesting the importation of California Japanese drawn up by patriotic and economic organizations. These were usually worded to suggest that they were drawn up nationally and distributed to local leaders for their own vote and signatures. They include resolutions from the locals of the United Mine Workers, the American Legion, the Independent Order of Odd Fellows Lodges, the Federation of Women's Clubs, the auxiliary of the Grand Army of the Republic, the Veterans of Foreign Wars, the United Veterans Council, some city councils, and some local labor unions, all protesting the influx of Japanese. These were not from all such organizations in all communities, but from perhaps 10 percent of them, and one may hypothesize that only a minority of these organizations in Utah really opposed volunteer evacuees coming to Utah.[13]

There are also letters, telegrams, and statements from county commissioners who, at the request of the governor, canvassed opinion in their counties about possible Japanese resettlement. Their reports in all instances showed at least token or political opposition. Privately, however, some wrote the governor that there were those who needed laborers and would welcome Japanese evacuees; but when publicly asked, "Does your county want Japanese citizens and aliens?" all had answered negatively.[14]

Surprisingly, a letter from one of the local Japanese American Citizens Leagues (one hesitates to identify it) stated its "emphatic and sincere" opposition to the entrance and settlement of Japanese evacuees from restricted coastal areas. Our local "Japanese of first and second generation," the letter noted, "have established a reputation through industry and good behavior. . . . It appears exceedingly unwise to disturb and disrupt this status. . . . Strangers from other localities might be undesirable in adjustment to these settled conditions."[15]

Also, many letters suggested opportune places in Utah for Japanese evacuees to settle and offered them work or land:

I own one of the best farms in Emery County. . . . There are forty acres of cultivated land with excellent water rights. . . . It has a good home, with city water piped in and electricity, a barn and some farm equipment. Since a lot of Japanese people are being removed from the Pacific Coast area, it occurred to me that my farm could be of service to some of these people, and through their efforts could be of more productive service to our country during this war.[16]

I . . . would like to get some good farmers on our place . . . in Duchesne County. We have two extry houses . . . 14 milk cows, . . . teams, 3 wagons, mower and rake. . . . Hoping you can do us some good, and that I haven't caused you any trouble.[17]

There are similar letters from Morgan, Uintah, Iron, Wasatch, Cache, and Millard counties. An Orem man summed up the general attitude:

It seems to me it will be far better to let some of these people come in and do our work, thus producing food, than it will to let our work go undone, producing nothing. Some of the best and most dependable help I ever had was Japs. . . . Personally, I think it is better to put these people to productive labor on our farms than to put them in some concentration camp where they will need a lot of supervision and produce nothing.[18]

Another man from Logan wrote with much the same thought, adding:

For over fifteen years I have been in daily contact with Japanese. They worked on our farm, have lived in the same house, eaten at the same table. Their customs and habits I am quite familiar with. They are industrious, intelligent, and clean. They are good farmers and adapt themselves readily to surrounding conditions. Many . . . would give a good account of themselves. . . . Let [them] serve our country's needs. . . . We need [their] labor now more than ever before.[19]

Finally, there are letters of appreciation from persons with Japanese names, thanking the governor and others for favors shown them in locating in Utah. They are full of expressions of loyalty, of willingness to sacrifice and suffer, and of the desire to serve "this great free Republic." "All we ask is a chance to live, work, and prove our loyalty. . . . [We want] to make the people of Utah proud of us."[20] One of the letters must have given special satisfaction to Governor Maw; it was from the head of a Japanese family the governor had placed on his own farm in Provo.

Much of the credit for the not completely unfavorable Utah reaction to voluntary evacuation to Utah was due to the brilliant and courageous leadership of Mike Masaoka. He met frequently with the governor to strengthen his hand, assisted with resettlement, constantly pledged obedience to and cooperation with the U.S. government, and publicly deplored the efforts of enemy Japanese to turn the hostilities into a race war. In an official statement of the Japanese American Citizens League, he said,

Tokyo hopes to pervert this struggle between ruthless aggressor powers and the forces of democracy and decency into an all-out race war. Our Japanese Americans in service are disproving Tokyo's racist propaganda. . . . We think, feel, act like Americans. The Axis Aggressors must be crushed and we are anxious to participate fully in that struggle. . . . The Japanese Americans have pledged their efforts toward achieving victory, and the American men of Japanese ancestry fighting today on the Pacific and European fronts . . . are living proof of that pledge.

The statement ends with the request that Americans work toward the unconditional surrender of the "murderers of the Axis."[21]

Utah did receive 1,500 refugees during the period of voluntary evacuation; the largest number of these settled in a Nihonmachi or "Japan Town" in downtown Salt Lake City. A group of 130 Nisei from the Oakland area under the leadership of produce dealer Fred Wada leased the 4,000-acre George A. Fisher ranch in Keetley, Wasatch County, and raised vegetables and other produce. They lived in a two-story apartment building originally erected for miners. Intensely patriotic, they erected "Food for Freedom" billboards along the highway. Another group of migrants worked on a cooperative basis for the Chipman Livestock Company.

In August 1942, before the opening of the relocation center at Topaz, and during the period when extensive agricultural leaves were granted, the WRA asked the Western Institute of Public Opinion in Los Angeles to make a public opinion survey in Utah on "the Japanese question." In a poll of 5,000 Utahns, 66 percent expressed approval of a policy permitting citizen Japanese to leave the relocation centers and accept outside employment. Only 18 percent approved of permitting alien-Japanese to work outside the centers. Of those who favored permitting Nisei to work outside the center, 52 percent favored having them in the immediate vicinity of where the interview took place.[22]

Unfortunately, there is no way to compare this with the attitudes elsewhere, since no similar surveys were taken in other states. Various WRA administrators, however, were convinced that the reception in Utah would be and was relatively friendly.

Approximately a thousand evacuees from the Topaz Relocation Center were permitted to work in Utah during the fall of 1942 in the sugar beet fields, harvesting fruit, in construction, and performing other labor. After their return to camp in January 1943, a questionnaire circulated among them asking what kind of a reception they had found in the communities and on the farms in Utah and southern Idaho. Approximately 85 percent indicated they had a "good"—as compared with 12 percent "fair" and 3 percent "poor"—reception. Since Topazans were preponderantly urban and industrial in their origins and backgrounds, their chief complaint was that economic opportunities in Utah were not more diversified.

Several thousand internees from the relocation centers remained in Utah for a while after the closure of the camps, but because of the lack of economic opportunities, and perhaps for other reasons, many of them later left the state. There were in 1980, about 5,500 persons of Japanese ancestry in Utah.

The most reasonable conclusion seems to be that the reception of Japanese Americans in Utah may have been somewhat better than in other western states because of voices of reason and calmness, friendship, and tolerance. Even if this was true, this was no reason for complacency or self-congratulation. Raymond S. Uno, a native Utahn, a circuit court judge, and a former national president of the Japanese American Citizens League, pointed out in a 1971 letter to the *Salt Lake Tribune* that racism still existed, particularly in subtle ways, such as employment, relative pay, promotions, and in the rarity with which minorities, such as Japanese Americans, held high-paying positions in Utah. "We in this country," wrote Judge Uno, "have the best opportunity to conquer racism, and we must make an irrevocable compact with government, religion, business, and the American people to do it—now!"[23]

Army volunteers, Topaz Relocation Center. Courtesy of the Bancroft Library.

NOTES

1. These statements are based upon my long-time perusal of nineteenth-century Utah newspapers: *Deseret News, Salt Lake Tribune*, and such news magazines as *Woman's Exponent, The Contributor*, and the *Improvement Era*.

2. *Salt Lake Telegram*, May 6, 1946.

3. *Deseret News* (Salt Lake City), June 19, 1901.

4. *Deseret News*, December 4, 1945.

5. War Relocation Authority, San Francisco Office, "Report on Meeting, April 7, at Salt Lake City, with Governors . . . of 10 Western States," April 8, 1942, 19. Typescript in Herbert Maw Collection, Utah State Archives, Salt Lake City.

6. Journal History of the Church, June 2, 1920, 2, MS., Historical Department, The Church of Jesus Christ of Latter-day Saints, Salt Lake City, Utah.

7. Their activities are reported in the *Deseret Evening News*, November 1, 1913, November 20, 1917, and the *Salt Lake Telegram*, February 17, 1918.

8. *Deseret News*, April 21, 1921. See also papers of Governor Charles Mabey, Utah State Archives, Salt Lake City.

9. Murai's address was printed in full in the *Deseret News*, February 4, 1928. See also ibid., January 30, 1928.

10. *Salt Lake Tribune*, December 6, 1934; also *Deseret News*, August 29, 1934.

11. A. Ray Olpin, "Japanese in Utah," *Deseret News*, January 26, 1924.

12. The letters in which these and subsequent quotations are found were confidential communications to the governor. Although the letters are available in the Maw Collection, Utah State Archives, Salt Lake City, they are not cited here by name of the writer. Similar letters, incidentally, may be found in daily issues of the *Salt Lake Tribune* and *Deseret News*, particularly for February and March 1942. In some instances I have taken some liberties with the idiosyncratic punctuation of letters.

13. Letters of these organizations containing these resolutions, sometimes signed by several dozen people, are in the Maw Collection. Again, I have not used the names of the signers.

14. Letters from the various county commissions are in the Maw Collection.

15. The letter, dated March 23, 1942, emphasized that the region was a Central Defense Area, had problems of housing, and "the influx of new Japanese inhabitants would be a hazard to these already established here." Maw Collection.

16. Confidential letter to Governor Maw, Salt Lake City, March 7, 1942.

17. Confidential letter to Governor Maw, Bridgeland, Utah, March 10, 1942.

18. Confidential letter to Governor Maw, Orem, Utah, March 24, 1942.

19. Confidential letter to Governor Maw, Logan, Utah, March 27, 1942.

20. Fred Wada to Governor Maw, Keetley, Utah, April 23, 1942.

21. *Deseret News*, April 9, 1942; April 29, 1943.

22. Leonard J. Arrington, *The Price of Prejudice: The Japanese-American Relocation Center in Utah during World War II* (Logan: Utah State University Faculty Association, 1962), 37, n. 27.

23. *Salt Lake Tribune*, August 12, 1971.

Residents of Topaz being entertained by Delta High School band, May 11, 1943. Photo by Tom Parker. Courtesy National Archives, Washington, D.C.

Forty Years Later:
Delta High School Students Look at Topaz

Jane Beckwith

In 1982–83 my students at Delta High School, in Utah, studied the Topaz camp. This project really began many years ago. As a child growing up in Delta, I learned about the camp from my parents—not facts and details as much as the emotion of it, the sorrow. That came, too, from family visits to the site where we walked and talked, almost reverently. My father would refer to an employee from the camp with respect—for him and for his work. My other contact with the camp came on rainy days. I liked to lean against the bookcase in our living room and look through the Topaz yearbook that had been given to my father. The names always transported me to faraway places.

Naively, I believed that everyone, at least everyone in Delta, shared my feeling of sorrow. But when a friend who had traveled to Delta to see the campsite and asked directions at a local service station recounted his conversation to me, with its bigoted overtones by the attendant, I could hardly believe what he said until I, too, had had similar conversations. Still, I didn't think the pervasive opinion was one of bigotry.

When I returned to Delta in 1976 to teach English and journalism in the high school, I encouraged the newspaper staff to write about Topaz and other topics of local interest. They did, of course; but they were just "articles," nothing more.

Then, about three years ago, I was invited to tour the Intermountain Power Plant site with city and county officials and their wives. As we were returning to Delta, one woman said, out of the blue, "I don't know how anyone can think those Japs had it so bad. A lot of people here didn't have running water or indoor plumbing then either. I get pretty tired of hearing how bad off they were." No one in the van said anything. And neither did I. The woman had been a teacher of mine—and I'd always liked her.

All at once I was back in elementary school, hoping that someone would change the subject or the bell would ring. Instead, she repeated her statement, and her husband concurred. Before I knew what I was doing, I said, "But you weren't forced to live in a house that wasn't your own. And there was no barbed wire around it." She didn't grab my ear and march me to the principal, but my heart was beating so loudly I couldn't hear what the next topic of conversation was.

From that point on, my motivation for a project on Topaz came much faster. In the fall, three exchange students from Japan enrolled at Delta High. By about the third week of school, they were lonesome and lost in a maze of difficult assignments in English; and for the first time they realized they were the only Japanese for miles.

Coincidentally, a Japanese reporter dropped into my sister's newspaper office downtown; he was researching information on the race-track basing mode for the MX missile. The three of us talked about the irony of placing the track so close to the Topaz camp, and he decided to include that in his story. When he planned a trip to the camp, I asked if the three students from school could go along, thinking that it might ease their homesickness. When they returned to school, it seemed to have worked.

Several months passed and then one host parent called me to say that the camp visit was the worst possible thing I could have done. He said that all the host families had decided to never mention the camp to the students. Now that she knew, one of the girls was having terrible headaches because of the camp. (I felt a more accurate explanation would be that she was unprepared for her classes. According to the other two students, a headache was an easy way to get out of class.)

By the fall of 1982, one more small conversation propelled us into the study that was to keep my class interested and working for almost a year: another friend had told me that there might be funds available from the Japanese American Citizens League for students who wrote articles on internment topics. I relayed the information to Wendy Walker, editor of *MoDel*, the school newspaper and she liked the idea.

The next day I presented our discussion to the journalism class, and the response was incredible. I knew I had a class with potential, but their reaction and enthusiasm were astounding. All period long we discussed the directions our study could go, while I wrote key ideas on the board. At the beginning of class, they were intrigued by the idea of doing schoolwork for money, but that soon melted into a genuine interest. Those who knew about the camp started to explain to those who had never heard of it. By the end of the period, the entire board was filled with leads, as if they had been planning a celebration instead of work. I had never in twelve years of teaching found something that caught on so intensely. It made me nervous about whether I would be able to sustain and promote their excitement.

I was even more amazed the next day when interest was just as high; it hadn't soured overnight as so many things do. Before the bell rang for class, I had students standing around the desk talking about the project; and, as the bell rang, one girl who had not been particularly interested the day before leaped into the room and said, "I talked with my dad last night, and he helped build that camp." Psychologically, that became one of the turning points of the project. Now that she was with us, we were all in it together.

That day we refined our directions: we were going to devote an entire edition of the school newspaper to the camp. Information would come from interviews of people who had had some connection with it. We would photograph the camp as it looks today, trace barracks that had been turned into houses or sheds, compile a bibliography that we could use for reference, photocopy the local newspaper from 1942–43, and invite people to lecture in our class. We listed all the people we knew who had a Topaz story. I rummaged through the closet for cassette tapes, passed those out, made other assignments, stated deadlines, and we were off. I left that tangle of planning on the blackboard for weeks, just because I liked to look at it.

While the work was being done outside class, we returned to our regular classwork, but it was punctuated with references to Topaz and progress reports. I sent a proposal to Frank Yoshimura of the Japanese American Citizens League, and, on December 7, 1982, we received a check from his committee for $430 to use for supplies and for the production of our project. Renewed, the students set off on their research with increased vigor.

We planned a field trip to Topaz for the students who had never been there. It was a miserably cold Saturday, but that too led to a poignant moment: "Can you imagine how cold those barracks must have been!" In spite of the wind, the students continued to walk over the camp, picking up remnants and listening to Wendy's father, Roger Walker, talk about the camp. He had been fighting in the Pacific, came home from the war, and had a job as a fireman at the camp before it closed. He said, "Every freedom I had been fighting for was violated in my own back yard." He showed us the floor of the firehouse, pointed out the administration building foundation, and noted that the Japanese gardeners were even able to grow flowers there in the alkali soil!

Back at school, the pace quickened. The class invited several community members in to speak. Scott Bassett, a fourth-grade teacher who always taught a unit on the camp, brought copies of Leonard Arring-

ton's book *The Price of Prejudice*; we also read *Trek*, the camp literary magazine, and *Citizen 13660*. Beth Brown, a former secretary in the administration building, discussed her experiences while working at the camp. She also brought copies of pamphlets she had saved. One, entitled "Welcome to Topaz," had been written as an orientation for new workers.

David Styler, a college student, had just completed a paper on the camp and shared his work with us. His lecture precipitated a very interesting discussion. One of the controversies in class had centered on what we should call the camp: an internment or concentration or relocation camp. When Mr. Styler finished his lecture, he asked the students questions, and the controversy resurfaced. One student objected to using the word "concentration" in connection with the camps. A lively debate followed among class members, including an exchange student from Germany. Up to this time she hadn't said much regarding the project. Now she told the class that in Germany tiny children see movies and study the Nazi camps. She was surprised to learn that the United States had had any camps at all, even though they weren't like Germany's. But she was more surprised that some people in America didn't know about the camps within their own country. She ended the discussion by saying, "Germans realize that what they did was horrible, but unless every generation knows, it might happen again."

By Christmas vacation, the students had completed their interviews, including a tape of former wartime Governor Herbert B. Maw and Dr. Wanda Robertson, a school administrator, a civilian guard, a grocery store owner who had leased a portion of his store to a young Japanese American, a rancher in charge of the cattle operation at the camp, the camp fireman, a real estate broker who negotiated the sale of the land to the government, and others.

They had viewed the movie *Guilty by Reason of Race* and had read documents sent from all over. They had written to college and university libraries in Utah for bibliographic information. We had decided that the final material from our project would be donated to our school library. We had also planned to enter the Utah History Fair, so from that point on only five students worked on the project: George Henrie, Lance Atkinson, Tonya Jeffery, Kyla Overson, and Jayleen Wright.

In March, the same day as the regional history fair in Nephi, the University of Utah opened its Relocation and Redress Conference at Topaz. Two buses brought people to the site for a short ceremony, and then to Delta High School to hear Leonard Arrington speak. It was a big day for my students. They returned to the school from the fair just before the buses arrived

Lawson Inada, poet and writer, speaks to Jane Beckwith's class at Delta High School, April 28, 1983.

from Topaz with the good news that they had won a superior rating. As soon as the people from the bus started looking at our display, the events of the day and the camp became even more important. Before that, the students had had tapes and letters and books and newspapers in their hands, but now they shook hands with the people who were at the camp, people whose lives were churned because of the camps. My students were born in 1964—some in 1966—but that day they met people who had been their age in 1942. The historical gap closed, and my students learned the humanity of history.

The following day, after a bit of bureaucratic juggling, sixteen students and I boarded a bus to attend some sessions of the conference at the University of Utah. At first, I was worried that the papers read would be too academic: adolescents sometimes have a low tolerance for intellectual discourses. But they were at least stretching themselves in a healthy direction. They heard Governor Maw in person this time, listened to discussions about education in the camps, and saw Guilty by Reason of Race again. In Lawson Inada's session on camp literature, we heard about Toshio Mori, who had been at Topaz, and heard Inada praise Trek, the camp literary magazine.

It was a stimulating day for me, but, quite frankly, my students were about "camped out." By late afternoon, they wanted to go home and even suggested that if I wanted to stay for the evening activities, I'd have to find another way home: they were commandeering the

bus. Fortunately, my twelve years of disciplining paid off and I volleyed a threat that compelled them to be at the Alta Club that evening to hear Minoru Yasui speak. I had listened to his story at another conference held at the university and wanted the students to hear it, too.

That evening half of the group showed up on the steps of the Alta Club as scheduled and I broke the bad news to them: we weren't really dressed for the occasion or the place. The news was not well received, but I opened the door and ushered them inside. Once in the lobby, an employee explained very kindly that rules of the club, while not his rules, were necessary; therefore, he asked us, if we wouldn't mind, for our own comfort, waiting in a room prepared for us. It was a pretty gloomy sight, seeing the elevator close in front of sullen faces. I waited for the second half of the group to arrive and went upstairs with them. When we entered the room, one of the students already there said, "Welcome to Tanforan." The students were sipping apple juice and sitting on the floor in "make-believe horse stalls!" There was a lot of talk about being "second-class citizens." Some wondered whose fault it was . . . not the man at the desk . . he was just doing his job. The subject of concern changed from the distant past of Tanforan to a more immediate freedom-of-speech controversy at school. Soon the group moved from the room of "Tanforan" to the stairs of "Topaz." Sitting on the stairs made it impossible for most to see the speaker, but they heard him.

Afterwards, heading to the bus, the same student who had suggested I find my own ride home said, "I'm glad we stayed. He was great."

Within the next week, plans were started to have poet Lawson Inada teach in Delta. Through funding from the Utah Endowment for the Humanities, he came the end of April. During the four-day residency, he lectured to a small group, including teachers from Spanish Fork, seventy miles away. Later that week he taught in the high school, middle, and elementary schools, talking about creative writing, Topaz, Japanese, and Japanese American literature. He conducted an adult education workshop and composed a program mixing excerpts from newspaper accounts, student writing, and his own poetry.

At the Utah History Fair, the students and their project had won a superior rating and the right to compete in the National History Fair in Baltimore. Even the fact that they had to raise nearly $3000 for the trip didn't dampen their excitement. So we began raising the funds. The Millard School District offered $1500 and the rest was collected from community members and from Japanese American citizens who had heard about our work; one donation came from Japan. When members of the Buddhist Temple in Salt Lake City visited the site, they donated.

By June we were set, with almost $100 extra and a trunk weighing over seventy pounds holding photographs, a slide/tape show, memorabilia, newspapers, articles, oral histories, and—a skate board. (We lashed *that* to the trunk so we could scoot through the hills of the University of Maryland campus.)

We did well in the competition, scoring 86 out of 100 points. The students were proud of themselves and rightly so: they had learned about a desperate period of U.S. history; they had become teachers for the entire community; they had done quality work. And for that, they had inner satisfaction. Besides, they had toured Washington, D.C., ridden a mass transit express, eaten space ice cream, and seen Fonzie's jacket!

But of all the things they still talk about, the time that they seem to refer to time and time again was the day that the Japanese Americans came to Delta High School and talked and joked with them as people. Once while we were working together, Lance Atkinson said, "Every time I see a Japanese American, I want to talk with him, ask if his parents were in a camp, and which camp." All the other students agreed.

I can't guarantee that this project will ensure that my students will never deny another citizen his rights, that they will be personally committed to the ideals of freedom, or will even think; but for this particular piece of history, they know that it was wrong to negate the delicate balance of justice, even in war. I hope they know that ignoring issues won't make them go away.

Every student in the state and in the country deserves the same encounter with internment that these students had. And instead of looking away, discounting its importance, they should investigate and probe; not that they can fix anything; not to demean the ideal of America, but so that they come away with a better understanding of themselves and the intricacies of the human heart.

Japanese Americans in Idaho

Robert C. Sims

On April 23, 1942, the U.S. Army announced that a relocation center for Japanese Americans would be established on the Minidoka reclamation project in southeastern Jerome County, near the town of Eden, approximately sixteen miles from Twin Falls, Idaho. The center occupied a federally controlled site approximately two and one-half miles long and one mile wide adjacent to a large irrigation canal.[1] Minidoka, or Hunt, as the camp was called, affected both the state and the region in both positive and negative ways. Because the evacuation occurred at a time when emotions were high and reason often wanting, inevitably injustices took place. Ultimately we are left with only inadequate explanations for the removal of more than 70,000 American citizens from their homes and for their placement in detention camps. The total effect of that program may never be known, but in recent years historians have probed for explanations for why it happened. The Minidoka experience may provide some insights into that question.

Relocating 10,000 Japanese Americans in a county with only slightly more than 9,000 residents was bound to cause disruption. However, Japanese were not unknown in this region—about 1,200 lived in Idaho in 1940.[2] Two things had attracted them—railroad construction and farming. Virtually all of Idaho's early Japanese residents came with the development and extension of railroad lines in the 1890s, serving as a principal source of railroad labor until 1910.

Beginning in 1903 and continuing until about 1912, when a factory was built at Burley, the developing beet sugar industry attracted Japanese Americans to the state. Cassia County, which had eight Japanese residents in 1910, had forty-one a decade later. Twin Falls County, with forty-four in 1910, almost doubled that figure by 1920.[3] Although these early residents helped meet important economic needs for the developing region, they often encountered contempt and opposition, and their presence was sometimes seen as a threat to local residents. Almost from the beginning, they met instances of discrimination and occasional acts of violence.

By the second decade of the twentieth century, Japanese had become increasingly successful as merchants and farmers in Idaho and throughout the West. This success triggered opposition that first found expression in California in 1913 when a law was passed prohibiting aliens ineligible for citizenship from owning agricultural land. The Idaho legislature soon began considering similar bills and, by 1923, Idaho also had such a law. In the 1917 legislative session, when the bill was debated in the Idaho House of Representatives, a Wendell newspaper editor commented: "Members of the House [in voting unanimously for the bill] declared unequivocally for Americanism and American rights over those of foreign birth who do not, while in this country and enjoying its rights and benefits, become naturalized citizens."[4] This reflects several important aspects concerning anti-Japanese attitudes in this period, but primarily it reveals the misunderstanding that prevailed, for Japanese could not become naturalized citizens.

Idaho's Japanese continued to thrive, however, in spite of misunderstandings and overt discrimination. By 1940, the Japanese community of the Twin Falls, or Magic Valley, region had grown to about 150 to 200, with approximately 65 percent of these native-born Americans.[5] Like other Japanese American communities, the Magic Valley Japanese Americans experienced some tension between their identity as Japanese and as Americans. In the 1930s, when the Japanese American Citizens League began its organizing efforts in south-central Idaho, there were spirited discussions about efforts to become Americanized at the cost of losing one's Japanese cultural heritage. Although some counseled that local Japanese should create a "little Japan," others resisted.[6] The lack of a large Japanese population center and the dispersed nature of Idaho's Japanese enhanced their "Americanization."

In 1936, an article in the *Japanese-American Courier*, a Seattle paper, commented on the Idaho Nisei: "The majority of the second generation are engaged in farming. The general outlook for them seems bright in this field and many who at one time believed the work both hard and tedious, are now finding it profitable and best suited to them."[7] Life in Idaho in the mid-1930s involved association with other Japanese. Japanese youths from communities throughout the state participated in sports tournaments, and various cultural events drew Idaho Nikkei from a wide region.

For both the first and second generations, the developing tension between the United States and Japan was a constant source of concern. Older Japanese were faced with the dilemma of supporting their chosen land, which, while offering them some eco-

Eden, Idaho. Baggage for evacuees from Puyallup, Washington, being sorted and trucked to evacuee apartments at Minidoka. Photo by Francis Stewart. Courtesy National Archives, Washington, D.C.

nomic opportunity, denied them the rights of citizenship, or maintaining some loyalty for the land of their birth. For the Nisei, the choice was already made: they were Americans. In November 1940, when the new Selective Service act went into effect, the first Idaho Japanese to volunteer for army duty was a young man from Rupert, a graduate of the University of Idaho.[8]

On the West Coast, the more than 110,000 people of Japanese ancestry living there felt the approaching war sharply. Agitation against their presence on the coast continued to build in the weeks after Pearl Harbor, soon received official support, and, in February 1942, the decision came to remove all Japanese Americans from the West Coast. The specific nature of the removal program was determined during the following weeks: Japanese would be placed in ten camps in the interior, one to be located in Idaho.

Attitudes among Idaho's residents toward Japanese Americans were mixed. Governor Chase Clark contributed considerably to anti-Japanese feelings by generally displaying a racist attitude toward Japanese

and Japanese Americans alike. Before the decision was made to relocate the Japanese to the camps, an early proposal called for voluntary relocation on an individual basis. Clark strongly opposed this plan and became personally involved in thwarting several cases of attempted relocation. His rhetoric contributed to an anti-Japanese attitude.[9]

One of the most important effects relocation had on Idaho was in providing labor for the state's agriculture industry. Idaho farmers, faced with an increased demand for farm products and a sharply reduced labor supply, had a serious problem. The first reaction to the possibility of using Nikkei labor was largely negative. At a farmers' congress in Twin Falls in late February 1942, south-central Idaho farmers voted 371 to 41 against using such labor. According to a newspaper account, "One man . . . voted . . . against the importation of alien labor under any circumstances. His reason was short and to the point. He put three words after his mark where he voted against enemy alien labor. Those three words were 'Remember Pearl Harbor.' "[10]

However, not all were opposed; representatives of area sugar companies also attended that farmers' congress and one "stated that his company had no objections to the use of Japanese labor in beet fields, if properly guarded."[11]

The decision to place a relocation camp in Idaho came amid an atmosphere of strong anti-Japanese feeling. When one reads the local newspapers, it is apparent that most of the excitement about the war, especially animosity directed toward the enemy, was aimed at Japan rather than at the other Axis powers. In early 1942, a nationwide Gallup poll survey showed "that while hatred for Germany is concentrated largely on a few public figures such as Hitler, Goebbels, Himmler, Japanese war leaders have not been clearly identified in the public mind."[12] Thus, for Germany and Italy, Americans tended to think of evil leaders; for Japan, they thought in terms of a hated race. It is possible to see this attitude reflected in Idaho in a newspaper article about the discontinuation of a Christmas decoration contest, which would not be held for the duration because of War Production Board requests to conserve energy. "When Hitler, Mussolini, and the Japs have been blacked out, the project will again shine forth with renewed energy."[13]

This attitude found expression in other ways as well. In a controversy over melting down the cannon on the statehouse lawn to make "bullets," Governor Clark referred to their use for killing "Japs." He later sought to scrap the iron fence around the Soldiers' Home in Boise, "so the metal can be converted to bullets. They [the residents of the home] hate to look at it, they say, when they realize that it could be used for bullets to kill the Japs."[14] Wartime hatred coupled with general inability of Idahoans to distinguish between Japanese in Japan and those in America, including those who were American citizens, created difficulties for Idaho's Japanese.

Clark, who actively sought to prevent West Coast Japanese from relocating in Idaho during the period of voluntary evacuation, applauded the Twin Falls Chamber of Commerce for supporting his position. In a letter to the chamber he asked them to "keep up the good work" in restraining Japanese from settling permanently in Idaho.[15]

An important event affecting Idahoans' feelings toward Japanese was the capture of more than 1,000 Idaho civilians who were employed by the Boise-based Morrison Knudsen construction company at their Pacific sites on Wake Island and elsewhere. Their treatment by the Japanese army was a source of strong anti-Japanese feelings on the part of their friends and relatives, feelings too easily transferred to Japanese Americans.

Unfortunately, the treatment of those who came to Idaho also reflects this attitude, for individuals and groups in Idaho joined their voices to the chorus of anti-Japanese sentiments. In a meeting in late February, members of American Legion posts for five south-central Idaho counties recommended concentration camps for Japanese brought into the state, a sentiment the Twin Falls Chamber of Commerce supported. The justification for such treatment was that Japanese were assumed to be a threat to the country's security; that is, they were expected to support Japan in case of an attack on American soil.[16]

Magic Valley strongly adhered to this assumption. When it was first suggested that Japanese might be brought there, the chairman of the Twin Falls Chamber of Commerce pointed out the danger of being too sympathetic and thus too lenient on any Japanese brought into the state. "Sympathy for Japanese," he said, "will make it easier to sabotage the Magic Valley Irrigation system."[17] The president of the Idaho Farm Bureau opposed their use as farm laborers and declared that "Japanese should be treated as prisoners of war. We have no more use for them in Idaho than they have for them on the coast."[18]

About the same time that decisions were being made regarding relocation, Idaho farmers received some important news: Acreage restrictions were removed on sugar beet production and Idaho farmers were "implored to raise 100,000 acres in 1942 as compared with 48,000 the previous year."[19] This led to speculation about using relocated Japanese as farm laborers. Almost immediately two Idaho sugar beet refineries "indicated that they could use about 1,000 Japanese apiece during the season," according to one account.[20]

One of the first public reactions to the April 23 decision to build the Minidoka camp came from the farmers in the Gooding area who were concerned about irrigation water. They thought that water was already too scarce, that the development of the camp would "deprive permanent residents of long-used water rights," according to a report. Governor Clark responded by holding a meeting in Gooding on April 29 that resulted in "adamant opposition to diversion of irrigation water from the Gooding area," by the 200 farmers present.[21] Yet this had no apparent effect on the War Relocation Authority.

Although impending construction of the camp upset farmers, area businessmen were more favorably inclined. An item in the Twin Falls Times-News pointed out that "the camp [was] expected to add materially to South Central Idaho business."[22]

For the construction of the camp, the Morrison Knudsen company, the contractor, needed a crew of about 3,000 men, which immediately affected area labor supply and wage rates, a consideration not always viewed favorably by the region's employers. In addition was the problem of housing the workers. Twin Falls and Jerome responded by providing housing for 1,500 workers each, billeting them in fairground camps and private residences.[23]

The pressures generated by camp construction were added to the growing demand for acquiring Japanese evacuees as sugar beet workers. While waiting for the relocation centers to be built, West Coast Japanese Americans had been gathered in assembly centers. From these, evacuees were recruited for the sugar beet fields. Malheur County, Oregon, adjacent to southwestern Idaho, became the first area to use such labor. By early May, Idaho sugar beet companies received approval to use evacuee labor, an approval contingent on acceptance of a specific plan by state and local officials. A number of groups in Magic Valley voiced strenuous objections to releasing evacuees. The American Legion post at Hazelton, for example, passed a resolution urging that any Japanese released to work on area farms be strictly guarded.[24]

By mid-May, state and federal officials had sent a plan to fifteen Idaho counties for the use of Japanese labor in the beet fields. The county officials were given final say as to whether the evacuees would be used. Governor Clark, relenting ever so reluctantly, declared, "We will not permit Japanese to go into any county that does not want them."[25]

Three counties in eastern Idaho responded immediately with labor requests, the south-central counties following the next day. On May 19, it was predicted that 1,000 workers would be brought into Magic Valley as beet crew labor and that 600 of them would be housed in the labor camp south of Twin Falls. They were to work the approximately 19,000 acres in Twin Falls, Cassia, and Minidoka counties.[26]

But, because of the governor's anti-Japanese expressions and vocal opposition by individuals and groups in Idaho, the Japanese Americans in the assembly centers were reluctant to enter the state. In early May, the governor had given a speech at Grangeville, characterizing the Japanese as people "who live like rats, and act like rats," and adding that Idahoans did not want them. When sugar beet company representatives went to assembly centers to recruit workers for Idaho, they found newspaper clippings of Clark's comments on the bulletin boards and a notable lack of enthusiasm among the evacuees for coming to the state.[27]

The governor and others sought to undo the damage, Clark stating that any Japanese willing to "prove their loyalty" by assisting Idaho farmers would be excluded from his earlier remarks. This apology of sorts resulted in part from local pressures. In an attempt to create a better atmosphere, the Twin Falls *Times-News* called for a "square deal" for Japanese workers: "Japanese workers are not prisoners and come into this area of their own free will. Citizens are urged to see that they are allowed all considerations."[28]

But the mood continued to be uncertain, with some area residents concerned about potential problems if the evacuees came. Not convinced that the federal government was capable of solving all problems, the Jerome County sheriff asked county residents to turn in their "high-powered firearms, to be used in case of emergency."[29]

Nevertheless, by the end of May, meetings with county officials, farm organizations, chambers of commerce, and similar groups "officially opened" every county in south-central Idaho to relocatees. Those at the meeting had to vote favorably and to agree to a "written guarantee" signed by the "county commissioners, Prosecuting Attorney, Sheriff, and others."[30]

As evacuee laborers began arriving in early June to work on area farms, construction continued on the camp. Although somewhat behind schedule, the job was nearly complete in late August and early September. An advance party of relocated Japanese Americans arrived in early August; the rest of the camp's occupants began arriving on the sixteenth and came at the rate of approximately 500 a day through the middle of September. A member of the advance crew recorded his impressions upon his arrival that reflect astonishing optimism. After noting that "the great intensity and extent of work that needs to be done here cannot be overemphasized," he went on to say that "there is no denying the fact that the place is a desert now but it can be made into a model community and will certainly be worth a try."[31]

Another of the same group wrote: "The train stopped at the end of the tracks which was right in the midst of sage-brushes, and dust. It was a desolate looking place and down in the bottom of my heart, I started feeling homesick for the green trees [and] . . . the Puget Sound. . . . I could feel the struggle inside of me to keep the tears from coming up."[32]

A reporter from an area newspaper visited the camp in mid-August and wrote:

Fourteen miles from Eden as a truck rolls through sagebrush, and an incalculable distance from anything resembling the garden of the same name, a new home is being built for Tojo. In official circles it is the Minidoka War Relocation Area Project. The common name is Jap Camp. . . .

If Tojos now on the grounds forget why they are 12 miles north of Eden, they can have their memories jogged by looking at a billboard near camp headquarters. It says, "Remember Pearl Harbor."[33]

A crew of sugar beet toppers from Minidoka working for Berlin Fought near Burley, Idaho, October 15, 1943. The young women cooked their own meals. Courtesy National Archives, Washington, D.C.

Minidoka, December 10, 1942. Mud from rain and melting snow. Photo by Francis Stewart. Courtesy National Archives, Washington, D.C.

It may be impossible to appreciate completely the experience of the evacuees. Many seemed committed to making the most of the situation. This is seen in the following editorial from the camp newspaper:

Minidoka . . . is a vast stretch of sagebrush stubble and shifting, swirling sand—a dreary, forbidding, flat expanse of arid wilderness. Minidoka, in September of 1942, is the sort of place people would normally traverse only to get through to another destination. . . . We, the ten thousand, then, can have but one resolve; to apply our combined energies and efforts to the grim task of conquering the elements and converting a wasteland into an inhabitable community. Our obligation to ourselves is to wrest the nearest possible approximation of normalcy out of an abnormal situation. . . . Our great adventure is a 'repetition of the frontier struggle of pioneers against the land and its elements.' Our future will be what we make it; and there is no reason to despair.[34]

Committed to making a viable community at the camp, they soon found that work leave, while it had certain advantages, created serious problems for maintaining an element of regularity in the camp itself. Nowhere was this seen more clearly than in the school situation. Although a staff was recruited and buildings, however inadequate, were ready, classes did not begin for the high school students at Hunt until mid-November, for several reasons, chief of which was the absence of many students on agricultural leave until early November.

That first autumn, some 2,000 evacuees left Minidoka to work in agricultural areas in Idaho, Wyoming, and Utah. As a result, center residents and camp administrators alike got an early taste of one continuing contradiction of early camp life—that of trying to make a community within the camp while supplying agricultural labor for the region.[35]

To accomplish the latter, many Minidoka residents left the center and worked out of regional labor camps, such as those at Rupert and Twin Falls. Thus, some evacuees began to have contacts with local residents. Often they were unpleasant encounters. By early October 1942, because of such encounters, area towns began imposing curfews on Japanese workers. Burley, Paul, and Rupert were among the communities making such restrictions.[36]

But the contacts were not all bad and, as area residents became more familiar with the workers, there seemed to be an easing in relations. A group of JACL officials, on a tour of beet areas in late October 1942, visited the camp at Rupert and found the morale high. According to their report, they "learned that the boys . . . were receiving considerate treatment from the Caucasian people of the area." In Filer, the report continued, "we called upon a group of young people quartered at the Fair Grounds. The treatment they were receiving from the town and farm people was apparently as good as could be expected." Overall, these officials noted "a growing dissension against the Sugar Companies for their practice of coercion, intimidation, and other tactics, to force the boys to work after their contract had been fulfilled. . . . [O]ften the term is employed, 'You have an obligation as patriotic American citizens to save the beet crop.' The boys feel that exploitation of patriotism on the part of sugar companies is not patriotic in itself."[37]

One relocatee gave this version of the experience:

This spring, most of the Idaho farmers resented our coming and things were hard on us. The caucasian friend for whom I am working was threatened; they said that they would tar and feather him if he continued to use us. Due to the good work of the evacuees and to the public relations work of such companies as the Amalgamated Sugar, the local people have finally been won over. They are now demanding that we be used. Of course, the shortage of workers may have something to do with this change in attitude; the important thing is that they now want us to work for them. Some barber shops, pool halls, and theatres have discriminated against us, but things are looking up. I predict that very healthy conditions will prevail next spring."[38]

In spite of the difficulties of that first year, it appears that his assessment was correct. The role the evacuees played in saving the sugar beet crop in 1942 was extremely important in gaining acceptance. An editorial in the camp newspaper expressed it this way: "Barred from participation in defense industries, evacuated by 'military necessity' to relocation centers and hooted at, even assaulted by unthinking outsiders the Japanese here have, nevertheless, contributed in no small way to the nation's victory program and have proven they . . . are loyal Americans."[39]

Another editorial in the camp newspaper expressed a related view:

Fear and distrust are born of ignorance and the unknown. Once this factor is destroyed, better relationships follow. Those evacuees leaving the center are urged to dispel all false rumors concerning persons of Japanese ancestry. Prove to the people the sincerity of your purpose. . . . By building, brick upon brick and stone upon stone, we may rest assured that the majority of the racist, the hypocrite, and the ignorant will be drowned out by straight shooting Americans.[40]

Although acceptance of the evacuees gradually improved in the Twin Falls area, there were occasional incidents that reflected an abiding anti-Japanese attitude. One example of this occurred during the election campaign in the fall of 1942. In that campaign the eventually successful challenger of the incumbent county treasurer placed a political advertisement in a local paper criticizing her for employing a young Japanese American woman in her office, claiming that the treasurer obviously did not understand the feelings of the parents of "boys who lost their lives at Pearl Harbor, Wake Island, Midway, Guam and [the] Solomon Islands . . . when they have to walk into the county Treasurers' office and pay their taxes to a Japanese." In response, the incumbent pointed out that the young woman in question was an American citizen, a native of Twin Falls, and a recent honor graduate of the local high school. But even this did not satisfy those who made no distinction between Japanese in Japan and Americans of Japanese ancestry.[41]

Camp administrators, aware of the need for some positive contacts with the community, actively pursued a policy of providing them. One thing that did help improve the relationship between camp and community was the practice of sending student groups to area schools to entertain. Also, camp musical groups, such as the Harmonaires, proved quite popular in the surrounding towns. This group, working out of the Twin Falls labor camp in the late summer and early fall of 1942, developed quite a following after playing at a Halloween dance at the Odd Fellows Hall and appearing at the formal Thanksgiving dance at Filer High School.[42] In January and February 1943, the Minidoka Mass Choir of eighty-nine voices gave a number of concerts in area towns, including a concert in the First Methodist Church in Twin Falls. In addition, a Hunt High School talent review visited several schools and received warm responses.[43]

Sports provided another form of contact with residents of the region. Baseball teams from Hunt played an extensive schedule with surrounding towns during the summer of 1943. However, it is questionable how much they did for public relations since they had the decidedly undiplomatic knack of defeating most of their opponents.

Also, with "the promotion of better relationship between the center residents and the people on the outside as its aim, an arts and handicraft exhibit, displaying original work of Hunt residents," was held at the Twin Falls Public Library in June 1943.[44]

While all these efforts apparently improved the camp and community relationship, problems remained. In the spring of 1943, because of a number of incidents in Twin Falls, the local Kiwanis Club passed a resolution protesting the "public use of the languages of countries with which the United States is at war." The resolution condemned such actions as tending to "create suspicion and distrust," and recommended that "ways and means be devised to inform [these people] in no uncertain terms that the spoken words of our enemies grate upon our senses."[45]

This incident also revealed another serious problem. Japanese Americans who were long-time residents of the area often were linked in the public mind with the evacuees and, when the latter created problems, this reflected upon all. In a letter to the camp newspaper, an officer of the Magic Valley chapter of JACL asked that something be done about those from the camp who were coming into Twin Falls and other towns and "getting intoxicated and making scenes in public." "This small group," according to the writer, "is making our public relations work extremely difficult."[46]

Another element of discrimination against

The First Communion class of the Catholic church at Minidoka with the Rev. Leopold H. Tibesar, pastor. Tibesar followed his Japanese American parishioners from Seattle after they were evacuated. Courtesy National Archives, Washington, D.C.

Japanese Americans was the practice of local school districts charging tuition for the evacuee children. When this was challenged in 1943, the Idaho attorney general upheld it. When WRA officials and the state superintendent of public instruction continued to complain about it some school districts relented. The state superintendent called the practice "astonishing . . . in the face of the contribution the evacuated people have made to Idaho's outstanding record of agricultural production in war time." With a change in the attorney general's office in 1945 evacuee tuition was abandoned. Twin Falls, which charged tuition during the 1942–43 school year, dropped it the following year.[47]

Nothing did more for the eventual acceptance of Japanese Americans in Idaho or elsewhere than the military record of the 100th Battalion and the 442nd Regimental Combat Team, two Japanese American units that fought in Europe. Shortly after the war began, Selective Service no longer inducted Japanese. But the War Department soon conceived the idea of these special combat units, and plans for such groups were formalized in late 1942. In early 1943 recruitment

began at all the centers. Minidoka led all the camps in the number of volunteers for the 442nd and, by late 1943, Japanese American units were fighting in Italy. There and in the campaigns that followed they distinguished themselves with their valor and became the most decorated American unit in the war.

It is impossible to overemphasize what this did for acceptance of Japanese Americans. The Minidoka *Irrigator* expressed this feeling, noting that because of the excellent record of these units, people of Japanese ancestry were viewed with "a little more respect, a little more courtesy, and a little more equality."[48]

This situation seemed a sharp contrast to that of their parents, many of whom remained in camps until the end of the war. In 1945, four mothers from Magic Valley were six-star mothers, so-called because they each had six sons in the armed services and were entitled to display small flags with six stars. One of these flags hung in the Twin Falls Migratory Labor Camp temporary home of Mr. and Mrs. Takeo Sakuma.[49]

Through their contributions as laborers, their military service, and their overcoming the hardships of relocation, Japanese Americans gradually won considerable respect and support. And, as the editorial writer of the Minidoka *Irrigator* stated, "Day by day the American public is beginning to realize which side of the fence we are on."[50]

In January 1945, the ban excluding Japanese Americans from the West Coast was lifted and those who wished returned to their former homes. By that time the Magic Valley region had come to depend upon evacuee labor and some were reluctant for them to leave. The Burley *Herald* praised the labor and conduct of the evacuees:

> The Japanese men and women who have worked in Burley have performed a great service. They have thinned, cultivated, and harvested the beets; they have irrigated, picked up and sorted the potatoes, they have tended sheep in the winter and herded the fattening beef in the summer. They have cooked and served food in the cafes.... We doubt if any other group of Americans would have acted any better under the circumstances. Next year... the need for these good workers will be acute here. We hope many of the present residents will want to remain here to help us.... We have come to understand and appreciate them, and we admit we need them."[51]

In early 1945, it was decided that all the centers would be closed by the end of the year.[52] As the closing process continued, some evacuees returned to their former homes while many relocated in other areas. Most of those deciding to remain in Idaho chose eastern and southwestern Idaho, with the smallest concentration remaining in Magic Valley. The last family left Minidoka in October 1945 and by that time few evacuees remained in the Twin Falls area. By January 1946, only about 150 Japanese Americans remained at the Twin Falls labor camp, a number that declined rapidly thereafter.[53]

In 1947, camp land began to be divided into homesteads for which veterans could file. Along with their allotments, each received two buildings from Hunt, and the process of its dismantling continued.[54] Today many of these buildings still stand in the camp area, but there are few other visible remains. However, other traces persist. The memories of those who lived through that experience—the evacuees, the camp personnel, and the area residents as well—people whose lives were touched by Minidoka show that for them the camp in the Magic Valley region was of major significance in their lives.

For many years those involved in that experience were content to leave it unexamined. Reopening that part of the past is not intended to reopen old wounds, but rather to shed light on those experiences. Perhaps by doing that we might better understand ourselves as well.

NOTES

1. Twin Falls *Times-News*, April 23, 1942, 1.

2. U.S. Department of Commerce, *Sixteenth Census of the United States: 1940, Population*, Vol. II. *Characteristics of the Population*, Part 2: *Florida-Iowa*. (Washington, D.C.: Government Printing Office, 1943), 440.

3. Ibid.

4. Wendell *Irrigationist*, February 1, 1917, 11.

5. *Sixteenth Census*, 440.

6. Letter to James Sakamoto, December, 1935. Box 1-21, Sakamoto MSS, University of Washington Library.

7. *Japanese-American Courier*, November 26, 1936, 4.

8. *Idaho Daily Statesman*, November 30, 1940, 7.

9. Clark's role in the relocation program is examined in: Robert C. Sims, " 'A Fearless, Patriotic, Clean-Cut Stand': Idaho's Governor Clark and Japanese American Relocation in World War II," *Pacific Northwest Quarterly* (April 1979): 75–81.

10. Portland *Oregonian*, February 28, 1942, 10; and, Twin Falls *Times-News*, March 1, 1942, 3.

11. "Survey of Public Opinion in Western States on Japanese Evacuation." "Idaho" (A 16.03) 6, Japanese American Evacuation and Resettlement Collection, Bancroft Library, University of California, Berkeley.

12. *Idaho Daily Statesman*, July 2, 1942, 5.

13. Ibid., November 25, 1942, 4.

14. Ibid., September 18, 1942, 2.

15. Twin Falls *Times-News*, April 1, 1942, 1.

16. Ibid., February 25, 1942, 1.

17. Ibid., February 24, 1942, 1.

18. Ibid., February 23, 1942, 2.

19. *Idaho Daily Statesman*, February 18, 1942, 4.

20. Ibid., February 26, 1942, 5.

21. *Idaho Daily Statesmen*, April 30, 1942, 1.

22. Twin Falls *Times-News*, April 28, 1942, 10.

23. Ibid., May 4, 1942, 1.

24. Ibid., May 4, 1942, 1; May 10, 1942, 10.

25. *Idaho Daily Statesman*, May 16, 1942, 2.

26. Twin Falls *Times-News*, May 19, 1942, 1; May 20, 1942, 3.

27. *Idaho Daily Statesman*, May 23, 1942, 1–2; May 26, 1942, 8.

28. Twin Falls *Times-News*, June 2, 1942, 1.

29. *Idaho Daily Statesman*, June 11, 1942, 8.

30. Ernest J. Palmer, "Historical and Personal Narrative," January 1946. JERS, Bancroft Library, University of California, Berkeley.

31. Dyke Miyagawa to Sakamoto, August 10, 1942. Box 10, Sakamoto MSS.

32. Imelda Kinoshita to Sakamoto, August 14, 1942. Box 10, Sakamoto MSS.

33. *Idaho Daily Statesman*, August 14, 1942, 1, 6.

34. Minidoka *Irrigator*, September 10, 1942, 4.

35. Edward H. Spicer, et al., *Impounded People: Japanese Americans in the Relocation Centers* (Tucson: University of Arizona Press, 1969), 128.

36. *The Rupert Farm Labor Camp Laborer*, October 21, 1942, 1.

37. "Minutes," JACL Special Emergency National Conference, November 17–24, 1942, Salt Lake City. Supplement #6, "Beet Field Survey."

38. "Minutes," JACL Special Emergency National Conference, November 17–24, 1942, Salt Lake City, 42.

39. Minidoka *Irrigator*, November 14, 1942, 2.

40. Ibid., October 9, 1943, 2.

41. Twin Falls *Times-News*, October 28, 1942, 3.

42. Ibid., October 30, 1942, 4.

43. Minidoka *Irrigator*, November 25, 1942, 7; January 27, 1943, 7; and March 13, 1943, 6.

44. Ibid., June 19, 1943, 5.

45. Ibid., June 5, 1943, 1.

46. Ibid., June 19, 1943, 4.

47. Ibid., May 29, 1943, 1; *Salt Lake Tribune*, September 8, 1944, n.p., clipping in August Rosqvist MSS., Idaho State Historical Society.

48. Minidoka *Irrigator*, September 16, 1944, 6.

49. Ibid., August 12, 1944, 1.

50. Ibid., November 11, 1944, 2.

51. Ibid., January 20, 1945, 2.

52. Ibid., February 3, 1945, 1.

53. Palmer, 13.

54. *Idaho Daily Statesman*, March 15, 1947, 6.

Western Reaction to the Relocated Japanese Americans: The Case of Wyoming

Roger Daniels

Although it is generally believed that West Coast pressure triggered and shaped the removal and incarceration of the Japanese Americans in the weeks after Pearl Harbor, an important and hitherto almost totally neglected aspect of the relocation process was the nearly uniform hostile attitude expressed by the people and the governments of the western states slated to receive the persons displaced within the United States. The result of this hostility was a relocation program that was even more repressive than those in charge had originally intended it to be. The focus of this essay will be upon the state of Wyoming; yet, the results would probably be the same if any of the other six internment states had been investigated. [1]

Franklin Delano Roosevelt triggered the basic decision to relocate the West Coast Japanese Americans on February 11, 1942. In a brief telephone conversation with his Secretary of War, Henry M. Stimson, the commander in chief gave carte blanche to Stimson and his deputy, John J. McCloy, to do whatever they thought necessary. His only injunction to Stimson was to "be as reasonable as you can." [2] Eight days later, Thursday, February 19, 1942, the real day of infamy as far as the Constitution is concerned, FDR signed Executive Order 9066, giving the War Department the necessary authority to relocate Japanese Americans. A few days later Congress passed what was, essentially, ratifying legislation. What had been decided, to use the words of an old California slogan, was that "the Japs Must Go." What had not been decided was where they were going, what was to be done with them once they got there, and who was to be responsible for arranging the bureaucratic details.

The army as yet had not worked out contingency plans. It was prepared to take care of a few thousand selected "dangerous enemy aliens" of various nationalities whom the FBI rounded up in the days immediately following Pearl Harbor, and it had sketchy plans for handling interned seamen and prisoners of war. But no thought had been given at the highest levels to the problems involved in providing for the custody of more than 100,000 men, women, and children. [3] The West Coast commander, Lieutenant General John L. De-Witt, as early as December 19, had officially recommended that "action be initiated at the earliest practicable date to collect all alien subjects fourteen years of age and over of enemy nations and remove them" to the interior of the United States and to hold them "under restraint after removal." [4] As late as the end of January, he said, "I haven't gone into the details of it, but Hell, it would be no job as far as the evacuation was concerned to move 100,000 people." [5]

A month and a half later, in mid-March, an investigator for the general staff reported to Washington that in DeWitt's command "there was no definite organization for handling . . . the evacuation of enemy aliens." [6] It should be kept in mind that despite talk about "aliens" and "enemy aliens," and despite the various figures that were used, what was in reality being talked about was uprooting and moving approximately 110,000 Japanese Americans, two-thirds of whom were native-born American citizens.

If the West Coast command was totally incapable of planning an evacuation, one army bureaucrat, Major General Allen W. Gullion, the provost marshal general and one of the key architects of the evacuation, had made some rudimentary projections. He and his deputy, Colonel Karl R. Bendetsen, could think of nothing better than to use a large number of existing sites—"agricultural experimental farms, prison farms, migratory labor camps, pauper farms, state parks, abandoned CCC camps, fairgrounds" and the like, and to have the whole program administered by his office. [7] The Gullion-Bendetsen plan would have required a great deal of military manpower—at least the equivalent of a division—something that Chief of Staff George C. Marshall and his advisors found incompatible with their first priority—"the creating and training of an offensive army." [8] Therefore, at Stimson's insistence, a cabinet meeting at the end of February decided that a civilian agency be set up to handle the evacuation. By the middle of March the War Relocation Authority had been established and a young official from the Department of Agriculture, Milton S. Eisenhower, had been named to head it.

Eisenhower, who was forty-one years old, had no knowledge of and few preconceptions about Japanese Americans. A Kansan who had been a Washington bureaucrat since 1926, he also had little knowledge of the western varieties of American racism. Yet he quickly understood, as almost no one else connected with the evacuation did, that it was wrong. On April 1, after two weeks in the West, he wrote privately to his old boss, Secretary of Agriculture Claude Wickard: "I feel most deeply that when this war is over and we consider calmly this unprecedented migration of 120,000 people, we as Americans are going to regret the avoidable injustices that may have been done."[9] Despite lacking sympathy for the program, Eisenhower, like a good bureaucrat, tried to make it work and never made his misgivings public.

In California Eisenhower and the military quickly made some basic decisions. It would be the the the army's responsibility to collect Japanese Americans at assembly points—racetracks, fairgrounds, and the like in the three Pacific Coast states—and the War Relocation Authority would set up and administer places in the interior to which the impounded people could be transferred.

While these plans were being made in late March and early April, rumblings of discontent were heard from the western states selected as relocation sites. Earlier in February and March, a very few Japanese American families had, with the blessings of the government, tried to resettle in the interior. They encountered vigilante action throughout the West; for example, in Wyoming the state highway patrol arrested several families merely for being in the state. As early as February, Governor Nels Smith, a Republican, protested against plans to send "alien Japanese evacuees from the West Coast" to Wyoming, and a leading Republican spokesman expressed fear "that if the government sends these Japs to Wyoming now, we will have them on our hands after the war is over, and Wyoming instead of California will have a Jap problem." When one lone editor, L. L. Newton of Lander, suggested that "Christian principles" be the basis of treatment of any incoming Japanese, a Cheyenne paper asked, apparently for the rest of the state's press, "Has Mr. Newton Gone Berserk?"[10]

In an attempt to quell these growing protests, Eisenhower's WRA and the army called a special informational meeting for western governors and other interested parties in Salt Lake City on April 7. It was an invitational meeting closed to the press. Eisenhower made a long presentation to the assembled officials outlining the still-rudimentary plans of his authority and explaining that the evacuees would do five kinds of work: public work (reclamation, etc.), agriculture, and manufacturing within the relocation centers, and private employment outside the relocation centers. Self-supporting communities might be established outside the relocation centers and provide work for evacuees.

The WRA chief explained a system of wage scales, one for work inside and one for work outside the centers. In the first instance the wage would not exceed the minimum paid American soldiers ($21 a month—actually the top internal wage was soon set at $19), but for the second the WRA would see that the evacuees received the prevailing wage. The purpose of the low wage in the camps—a higher WPA-type wage scale had previously been suggested—was to avoid congressional and public charges of coddling. Though the analogy was ridiculous, these charges came anyway. All evacuees, regardless of skills, were permanent privates by WRA fiat; this included skilled professionals such as doctors, dentists, and nurses. In addition, there were no veterans' benefits for evacuees.

Eisenhower broached the topic that concerned the governors most: What would happen to the evacuees after the war? He promised that the WRA would not transfer or buy land for the evacuees, but did insist that it could not prevent private transactions. That is—and this was a bitter pill for the westerners—the WRA's policy would neither encourage the evacuees to become permanent residents of the states to which they were moved nor encourage them to return to the states from which they came. Eisenhower closed his discussion of public policy with what became a standard WRA myth: "It is not the province of the Authority, other than in the orderly evacuation and relocation of the Japanese, to dictate their lives. They will be encouraged to manage their affairs and their community enterprises to the highest degree."[11]

It seems clear that, even at this late date, Eisenhower and other civilian officials of the WRA still hoped to handle the relocation, once the impounded people had left the coastal area, with a minimum of restraint and duress. Eisenhower probably wanted the relocation sites to be more analogous to the subsistence homesteads of the New Deal (he was, remember, a long-time Department of Agriculture staffer) than to the institutions of totalitarian Europe. Whatever chance there might have been for this kind of solution was scuttled by the reaction Eisenhower's proposals received from the assembled governors. He had ended his presentation with a plea for cooperation and suggestions; what he got was denunciation and indignation.

Herbert B. Maw of Utah led off for the governors. He was disturbed because the people running the show were not westerners and did not know or understand western conditions. Instead of the presumably wasteful federal program, he proposed that each state be given a quota of Japanese—10,000 or 12,000 for Utah—and the federal funds to handle them. Under these circumstances, he insisted, the state of Utah could work them more cheaply and efficiently than could federal bureaucrats. In addition he criticized the army and the WRA for being "much too concerned about the constitutional rights of Japanese American citizens . . . the constitution could be changed."[12]

Chase Clark of Idaho agreed with Maw that the states should handle the Japanese under a federal subsidy. His chief concern was that the Japanese would acquire land in his state. If the army could keep them out of California, he felt that it could also prevent them from buying land in Idaho.

Nels Smith of Wyoming went further than the others. He was concerned lest the Japanese overrun his thinly populated state. Wyomingites, he declared, had a dislike for Orientals and simply would not, as he put it, "stand for being California's dumping ground."[13] Smith, too, was disturbed about possible land acquisition in his state and boasted of telling a delegation of Japanese who had allegedly come to see him that if they bought any land "there would be Japs hanging from every pine tree."[14] All Japanese, he insisted, should be kept in "concentration camps," not the reception centers Eisenhower envisioned. And so it went; almost all the political leaders expressed a desire that any Japanese moved into the area by the federal government be kept under strict guard and that the government guarantee that any Japanese moved in be moved out after the war.[15]

The Salt Lake City conference was thus an important turning point in developing evacuation policy. Although the notion that Japanese Americans would be put into some kind of concentration camp was never far from the minds of most evacuation policy architects, this unarticulated premise had not been made explicit in either the executive order setting up the WRA or in the hasty instructions given to Milton Eisenhower. If the active racism of the West Coast was the initial catalyst for evacuation and the more passive racist climate of the nation as a whole the precondition for its acceptance, the racism of the interior West was the final determinant of WRA policy. Before the Salt Lake City meeting, Eisenhower and his planners assumed that a minimum of restraint would be necessary and that for many, if not most, of the evacuees relocation would be a limited transitional stage leading very quickly to resettlement—as individuals, as families, and as whole communities—within the civilian economy of the interior.

After Salt Lake City it seemed clear to Eisenhower and the other WRA officials that, for the majority of the evacuees, close confinement would be necessary. Had the federal government, in the four months

prior to the Salt Lake City meeting, conducted an educational and propaganda campaign designed to make resettlement acceptable to westerners, a different result might have ensued. Relocation followed by quick resettlement would have indeed been possible, just as a truly voluntary evacuation would have been possible; whether these possibilities would have worked is, of course, unanswerable. They were logical alternatives, but they were never attempted. That they were not tried was not so much a failure of imagination, but rather a direct result of the preconceptions about nonwhites in general and about Japanese in particular held by most Americans, up to and including the commander in chief.

Wyoming then, along with California, Arizona, Utah, Idaho, Colorado, and Arkansas, were slated to become receiving areas for internal refugees. All ten sites eventually chosen can only be described as Godforsaken, places where nobody had lived before and where practically no one has lived since. The army insisted that all camps be "at a safe distance" from strategic installations and the WRA decided for a number of reasons that the sites should be on federal property. The Wyoming site, Heart Mountain, was located in the northwestern part of the state on a partially developed federal reclamation project. That all these areas were still unoccupied and unclaimed in 1942—a half-century after the closing of the frontier—speaks volumes about their attractiveness.

A spectrum of reactions greeted the announcement in late May 1942 that Heart Mountain would be used as a camp for some 10,000 Japanese, reactions which the state historian aptly characterized as running from "hostility to hatred." Even the small voice of organized labor in the state, the *Wyoming Labor Journal*, insisted that "if the Japanese are dangerous in California they would be in Wyoming."[16] In Wyoming, as elsewhere, there were a few exceptions to this general hostility. Apart from the occasional humanitarian groups, special interest groups, largely agricultural, desperately needed labor. In Montana, for example, when it was learned that no camps were planned for the state, the beet sugar producers and others pressured their senators to make sure that they would get some of the available labor.[17] As a spokesman for the Utah Farm Bureau put it, Utah farmers "don't love the Japanese, but we intend to work them if possible."[18]

Correspondence by the state's leading politicians indicates clearly that most Wyomingites shared the prejudices of the state's press. As one couple from Buffalo, Wyoming, wrote the senior senator, Joseph C. O'Mahoney: "If you go to Calif. they search you for fruits or plants or this & that & have their laws about what you can and can't do but they want to dump their aliens onto us." Then, after complaining about the alleged pampering that was going on in Heart Mountain, they suggested what might be termed deprivational genocide: "There should be separate camps for men and women. We don't need more little Japs."[19] While a bit more imaginative than most, this letter is representative of a general view.

Wyomingites most directly affected by relocation were residents of Park County, the site of Heart Mountain. According to the 1940 census, 10,976 persons lived there—approximately the number of Japanese Americans at the relocation center. Almost half the county's population lived in Cody (pop. 2,536) and Powell (pop. 1,948). Politicians, patriotic groups, and labor unions in the county waxed eloquent about the evils of having "Japs" on sacred soil and were often incensed about the relative freedom some evacuees were allowed. In April 1943, the town councils of Powell and Cody adopted identical resolutions demanding that "the visiting of the Japanese in the Towns of Powell and Cody be held to an absolute minimum . . . [but] that this request in no way interfere with or discourage those Japanese on temporary leave who are engaged in gainful employment essential to the war effort and particularly labor on ranches and farms."[20] This resolution puts the Wyoming opinion in a nutshell: work them when we need them, but don't give them any privileges.

The War Relocation Authority at Heart Mountain countered effectively; it declared all of Park County closed or off limits to Japanese, including those who would normally do work on ranches and in homes. This in turn produced protests, both from those who needed Japanese labor and from those who made a profit from the Japanese presence. Typical of the latter was the reaction of a Powell druggist, who wrote Wyoming Governor Lester C. Hunt:

> Neither the Mayor nor any of his councilmen are in the retail business here in Powell, therefore do not come in contact with the Japanese residence [sic] of the Heart Mountain Camp so do not realize what has been and can be spent here in Powell by these Japanese when they are allowed to come here to trade. 90% of the merchants here in Powell have only been able to pay off their old debts and now buy War Bonds since this Relocation Camp was built two years ago. They also have no objection to waiting on Japanese trade in fact most of us would rather wait on them than these Mexician [sic] Nationals brought up from Mexico that can't even talk United States, they steal you blind the minute they come into your store. Another very important fact is that if they are not allowed to trade in Park County then their business goes to Billings, Montana or to the mail order houses in Colorado therefore the State of Wyoming loses the 2%

Sales Tax on each and every dollar sent out of the State. . . .

> Another thing is these people are American born citizens and thru no fault of theirs they were born with slant eyes so who are we to say that they should be denied the right to come to our American cities when the F.B.I. and the War Department say they are O. K.[21]

Not surprisingly the commercial if not the civil libertarian point of view prevailed and the city fathers receded from their local exclusion acts. There were in Park County two recorded instances of assaults against Japanese by white Wyomingites. One resulted in a suspended sentence and the other was never brought to trial.[22]

Elsewhere in the state, contact was minimal. Nisei students, not all from Heart Mountain, were accepted at the University of Wyoming; shortly thereafter, "No Japs Allowed" and "White Only" signs began appearing in Laramie stores.[23] The state government, too, indulged in anti-Japanese activities. The 1943 legislature passed two specifically anti-Japanese measures: one denied the vote to "any citizen . . . interned in a relocation center or a concentration camp" and the other was a California-type alien land act, except that it specifically excluded "Chinese nationals" from its provisions.[24] On an administrative level, the Board of State Medical Examiners refused to license an evacuee physician who wished to help the Park County draft board; happily the U.S. Army was not so choosy. Dr. Robert S. Kinoshita later went to Italy with the 442nd and was awarded a Silver Star, a Bronze Star, and two Purple Hearts.[25] Similarly, the state board of education licensed Japanese American teachers, but only to teach within Heart Mountain.[26]

One could prolong this unhappy tale indefinitely. And, unfortunately, the record would be essentially the same elsewhere. Wyoming, the "Equality State," did not treat the Japanese Americans well, but then neither did neighboring states nor the national government. Despite the fears of Nels Smith and others, few of the relocated Japanese stayed in Wyoming after the war. This was not true of Utah and Colorado. Although present-day Wyoming is no model in race relations, it at least no longer seems haunted by its own version of the "Yellow Peril." The Nixon administration's appointment of a Casper-born Japanese American as assistant U.S. attorney at Cheyenne did not produce a single protest from the state's press.

NOTES

1. This paper is greatly enriched by my having directed the work of a truly gifted graduate student, Douglas W. Nelson. A fuller account of many of these matters may be found in his *Heart Mountain: The History of an American Concentration Camp*, Madi-

son, Wis.: State Historical Society of Wisconsin, 1976. We were both guided by the pioneer treatment in chapter 22, "Heart Mountain," in T. A. Larson, *Wyoming's War Years* (Laramie: University of Wyoming, 1954). I am also indebted to F. Alan Coombs, who is writing a biography of Senator Joseph C. O'Mahoney, for directing me to relevant materials in the senator's papers.

2. Telephone conversation, McCloy to Bendetsen, February 11, 1942, RG 107, National Archives. For a detailed treatment of the decision to evacuate the West Coast Japanese, see my *Concentration Camps, USA: Japanese Americans and World War II* (New York: Holt, Rinehart and Winston, 1971) and *The Decision to Relocate the Japanese Americans* (Philadelphia: Lippincott, 1976).

3. General Brehon Somervell, Memo for the Adjutant General, "Construction of Facilities for the Internment of Alien Enemies . . . ," December 9, 1941, AGO 14.311, RG 407, National Archives. But see R. Daniels, "The Decision to Relocate the West Coast Japanese: Another Look," *Pacific Historical Review* 51 (1982): 71–77.

4. As cited by Stetson Conn, "Japanese Evacuation from the West Coast," in Stetson Conn, Rose C. Engelman, and Byron Fairchild, *United States Army in World War II: The Western Hemisphere: Guarding the United States and Its Outposts* (Washington, D.C.: Government Printing Office, 1964), 116–18.

5. Telephone conversation, DeWitt to Gullion, January 31, 1942, PMG, RG 389, National Archives.

6. Memorandum, Evans to Lutes, March 10, 1942, RG 107, National Archives.

7. Memorandum, Gullion to Chief, Administrative Services, Service of Supply, March 22, 1942, RG 107, National Archives.

8. Quoted from a policy memorandum by Mark W. Clark to Deputy Chief of Staff, January 26, 1942, TAG, RG 407, National Archives.

9. Letter, Eisenhower to Wickard, April 1, 1942, "Correspondence of the Secretary of Agriculture, Foreign Relations, 2–1, Aliens-Refugees," RG 16, National Archives.

10. Larson, 304–5.

11. "Report on Meeting, April 7, at Salt Lake City, with Governors, Attorneys General and other State and Federal Officials of 10 Western States." There are many copies of this report; I quote from a copy (No. 1) in the Department of Agriculture files cited in footnote 9.

12. "Meeting, April 7."

13. Ibid.

14. Ibid.

15. Ibid.

16. Larson, 304–5.

17. There are a number of letters to this effect dated throughout 1942 in RG 107, National Archives.

18. "Meeting, April 7."

19. Letter, C. and M. B. to O'Mahoney, May 11, 1943, Box 74, O'Mahoney MSS., University of Wyoming.

20. Lester C. Hunt MSS., University of Wyoming.

21. Letter, A. R. F. to Hunt, June 21, 1944, Hunt MSS. Report, Bradley, Captain, Wyoming Highway Patrol to Hunt, August 22, 1944, Hunt MSS.

22. Nelson, 81–84.

23. *Branding Iron*, Laramie, May 6, 1943.

24. *Session Laws of Wyoming*, 1943, chapter 27, p. 25 and chapter 35, p. 33.

25. Letters, Kinoshita to Governor of Wyoming, February 3, 1943 and Keith, Secretary, State Board of Medical Examiners to Hunt, February 11, 1943, Hunt MSS.; Kinoshita's war record in Nelson, 56.

26. Nelson, 54–55.

Seattle's Peace Churches and Relocation

Floyd Schmoe

The non-Japanese churches, on the whole, fell far short of their opportunity and responsibility, both in the attempt to prevent the tragedy of relocation and in helping to heal the wounds that resulted from it. Let me cite one instance of that missed opportunity: In February and March of 1942, a government commission headed by Representative John Tolan of California came to the West Coast to investigate "National Defense Migration." Any person concerned, either for or against evacuation, was invited to appear and to testify. At the Seattle hearings, beginning on March 11, 1942, fifty-five people came forth to speak. Of these fifty-five, only twelve were friendly and opposed evacuation and internment, and only eight of these twelve were church-related people. And of the eight, three were Quakers: Bernard Waring of Philadelphia, Robert O'Brien of the University of Washington, and Floyd Schmoe of the American Friends Service Committee (AFSC), a group with a long history of sticking their necks out for oppressed people. No Jewish rabbi, Negro pastor, or Episcopal priest appeared.

THE OUTBREAK OF WAR

It all started for us, on Sunday morning, December 7, 1941, when the Japanese Navy bombed Pearl Harbor and we became involved in all-out war in the Pacific. There were some seven thousand people of Japanese ancestry living in the Puget Sound area, with a few thousand more in the valleys east of the mountains. These were largely the Issei, and their children, the Nisei. At that moment in time more than five hundred of these people were faculty, staff, or students at the University of Washington in Seattle, that is, students and colleagues of mine.

We had five female Nisei students from the Yakima Valley living in our home. When my wife, Ruth, and I returned home from church that morning we found these girls huddled in the basement listening to the radio; they were frightened beyond tears. President Sieg of the university immediately issued a statement that no person at the university was under suspicion and that all students and faculty were secure in their positions. He then set up a campus committee to advise and aid in the transfer of any who wished to leave the area. Dr. Robert O'Brien, a professor of sociology and a Quaker, was chairman of that committee, and I, as secretary of the newly established Regional Office of the American Friends Service Committee, became closely associated with it.

We set up offices at the University Friends Meeting, adjacent to the campus, where we also maintained a hostel. Most of the students living at the Friends Center were Nisei girls. I left teaching at that time to devote full time to the work of the committee. In addition to visiting with students and local Japanese families to offer our sympathy, to advise them, and, where possible, to assist with their problems, I traveled across the country, visiting other colleges and universities outside the restricted zones, seeking acceptance and financial aid wherever possible for our students and faculty members.

Nearly all the schools I visited were sympathetic and willing to accept Japanese American students. Some were fearful and hesitant, but only one, a church school in Idaho, told me bluntly, "We don't want any Japs here."

Our first group of four students were sent off to Guilford College, a Quaker school in North Carolina. By then, an 8:00 p.m. curfew had been ordered in Seattle and their train did not depart King Street Station until 10:00 p.m. We hid our "criminal" students under a blanket in the back seat of the car on our way to the train; their only crime was that they had not been born white. Similar situations were occurring at universities all along the West Coast, and within a few months hundreds of students had been relocated—eventually the number reached more than four thousand.

Of the five girls living with us, one went to the University of Montana at Missoula, one to Wayne State University in Detroit, another secured a job as a music teacher in a Nebraska high school, and the remaining two returned to their homes and were later removed to a relocation center. The girl who went to Wayne later told me, moving to Michigan "was the best thing that ever happened to me. I am now the wife of a Detroit doctor, but if I had remained in the Yakima Valley, I would likely still be chopping beets."

During the war, at least once a week my wife and I visited some of the twenty or thirty people of Japanese ancestry confined to local hospitals. Several of these were young people left behind at the Firlands Tuberculosis Sanitarium. During the internment, a number of these died and their parents were allowed to visit them (or even in some cases to attend the funerals) only under military guard. Our home became a refuge for these people.

EVACUATION

When on February 19, 1942, President Roosevelt signed Executive Order 9066, our work intensified. All sorts of frightening rumors spread. There were direct threats of violence from some individuals and organizations; "No Japs Wanted" signs went up in many restaurants, hotels, barber shops, and even grocery stores; and, of course, there was great fear and uncertainty among the Japanese Americans and other West Coast residents.

In Seattle, the orders came to leave for the Assembly Center at Puyallup on March 2, 1942. On that morning when the people were to gather at designated loading points with only the baggage they could carry, some of us had organized canteens, serving coffee and pastry, and had provided cars for the very old or ill, those for whom the two-hour drive to Puyallup in crowded buses or trucks would be too exhausting. I remember the day well, but I do not remember that, with the exceptions of Frances Vogel of the YWCA, Father Tom Gill of Catholic Charities, and the few Caucasian pastors and deaconesses (mostly former missionaries to Japan) of the local Japanese churches, *any* churchmen were on hand to even bid good-bye to their Japanese neighbors.

During the three to four months in which the people were crowded into tar-paper barracks under the grandstands and into livestock stalls at the assembly centers, a small but dedicated team of churchmen and churchwomen (mainly those mentioned above) spent a great amount of their time visiting families, running errands, attending to neglected property and possessions, and comforting the people.

I should note that, during all this time, those of us thus involved were under the constant scrutiny of government information agents—the FBI and, in Hawaii, Naval Intelligence. We were followed, questioned, and, in my case, subjected to search. In our case neighbors reported to the FBI that we possessed contraband materials and that our house on a high bluff overlooking Lake Washington was "undermined with tunnels and the tunnels were full of Japs." When agents politely searched the premises, they found five frightened girl students, a cheap camera given by one of them to my son, and a potted plant given us for safekeeping by the wife of a Japanese doctor.

Recently under the Freedom of Information Act I obtained my FBI record. It is an interesting document consisting of seventy-one pages of "pertinent" information, such as the statement that I was a "rabid pacifist," but ending with a report from the local representative of the Attorney General that, since I appeared to be sincere in my misguided efforts and since there was no law specifically prohibiting the

visiting or even photographing of assembly and relocation centers, they had decided not to press charges.

RELIGION IN THE CAMPS

At Minidoka in the Idaho desert, sage and greasewood were almost the only natural materials available and a few men, including our former Seattle neighbor Arthur Abe, made a hobby of creating canes, floor lamps, and candlesticks from the gnarled and twisted stems. Sometimes men were permitted to leave the camp briefly to hunt for such material and, on a cold winter day in 1943, Arthur was overtaken by a blizzard while some distance from camp. He did not return that evening and the next day his body was found frozen.

Arthur's funeral, and other similar tragic experiences, brought many people together in the programs of the community churches and temples which had been established within the camps. Pastors and layworkers of all the Protestant churches had joined together in a joint religious program. Buddhist and Catholic priests, mostly Issei, also maintained the services of their faiths. Religious service by churches, or church leaders, fell generally into one of four categories.

First, and most significant, was the service rendered by the churches and temples within the camps and by the ministers and priests, both Buddhist and Christian, who were themselves internees. Each center was well served by this capable leadership. Each of these churches, of several denominations and sects, had their own following. They set up programs of services ranging from worship and Bible study to such social and recreational activities as church dinners, Boy Scout troops, and kindergarten. The majority of the people in each camp participated to some extent in one or another of these programs.

The second and greatest service was that of concerned Caucasian ministers, teachers, and social workers, many of them former missionaries to Japan, who made frequent visits to centers or who in some cases took up residence nearby to help in any way possible with the spiritual needs of the people. Outstanding in this group were Herbert Nicholson, the Pasadena Quaker who spent much time at Manzanar but also visited most of the other centers and prisons as well;[1] Emery Andrews of the Seattle Japanese Baptist Church, who served in similar ways between Seattle and Minidoka; Everett Thompson and his wife, Zoa, of the Seattle Japanese Methodist Church, who moved to Twin Falls for the duration to be near the Minidoka Center; and others in other areas.

The third service was performed by religious leaders who visited the centers on occasion for mass evangelical or inspirational gatherings.[2] Of these, E.

The Rev. E. Stanley Jones, head of the travelling missionary team, addresses assembled audience during visit to an unidentified relocation center. At speaker's table, l–r, are Dr. Skoglund, Rev. E. Stanley Jones, Dave Tatsumo, and Mrs. Charles F. Ernst. Courtesy National Archives, Washington, D.C.

Christmas program put on by the Protestant Sunday school, Topaz. Courtesy National Archives, Washington, D.C.

Stanley Jones, Kirby Page, and Allen Hunter were outstanding examples.

The fourth service was provided by equally dedicated people, who took employment with the War Relocation Authority as social workers, teachers, or nurses, and, residing within the camps or nearby, were in daily contact with the people. Outstanding among them were Ralph and Mary Smeltzer of the Church of the Brethren who taught at Manzanar; Lily Raudebush, a Quaker, also a teacher and counselor at Manzanar; Harold Jacoby, a security officer at Tule Lake; Carl Sandoz, head of social services at Minidoka and his wife, Winifred, who taught in the camp school.

In most of the centers, the administration cooperated with the religious programs of the people. George Townsend, a Quaker in charge of personnel at the Idaho camp, was especially sympathetic and helpful. At one point he secured a government truck to transport church pews, organs, pianos, and hymn books from Seattle churches to the center.

A number of other individuals, church related but motivated by personal concern and out of friendship, tried to be of service to the internees. My wife, Ruth, accompanied me on extensive visits both within the northern camps and to families who had resettled farther east; and my daughter, Esther, then a student at the university, dropped out of school and went to work as a volunteer nurse at the Minidoka Camp hospital. Esther Boyd, a Wapito, Washington, merchant, whose customers had largely been Japanese American farmers, testified favorably before the Tolan Committee, extended credit, contributed materials, and kept in touch with her friends within the camps. She was also very helpful in looking after property left behind and in easing the return home after the camps closed.

HERBERT NICHOLSON

The outstanding example of a single individual who, during the entire period of internment and relocation, gave his entire time and effort to the comfort and material aid of the Japanese American refugees was Herbert Nicholson of Pasadena, California. He did this without official sponsorship and without salary.

Nicholson and his wife had been Quaker missionaries in Japan and spoke the language fluently. Returning home in 1939, Herbert became Assistant Pastor of the West Los Angeles Japanese Methodist Church and, when the army under General John De-Witt began to remove all people of Japanese descent, both citizens and noncitizens, from the West Coast, Nicholson was among the first to spring into action. He immediately called a meeting of the entire Japanese church community of Southern California to plan with them for whatever might occur. He then went to Terminal Island where most of the leaders of the community had already been taken into custody.

Soon after that, my assistant, Tom Bodine, and I met Nicholson in Pasadena and drove up the San Joaquin Valley, across Oregon and Washington, and on to Missoula, Montana, visiting families, Japanese churches and Buddhist temples. At Fort Missoula, where some 600 Japanese alien men had been interned as enemy aliens, we were allowed to meet with the entire group and later with individuals; and Nicholson was asked to remain as counsel and interpreter for a series of hearings involving individual cases. As a result of these hearings, about half the men were eventually allowed to rejoin their families in the relocation camps.

During the three years of internment, Nicholson spent almost all of his time in the camps or on the road, transporting all manner of things—from trucks to pet kittens. At Christmastime he hauled entire truckloads of fruits, candies, and gifts gathered by Los Angeles churches for the children of Manzanar. All told, he drove the 400-mile round-trip some thirty times, with visits in between to the Poston and Gila camps in Arizona; to Tule Lake in Northern California; Minidoka in Idaho; Heart Mountain in Wyoming; and to Amache in Colorado.

EMERY ANDREWS AND OTHERS FROM SEATTLE

In the Seattle area, Emery Andrews, then pastor to the Nisei congregation of the Japanese Baptist Church, performed similar services. With the church's ancient Chevrolet bus, Andy, as he was affectionately called by all who knew him, was constantly on the road, transporting people and their belongings, running errands, visiting the sick, and tending children. During the weeks and months the people waited at the crowded Puyallup Assembly Center, he made almost daily trips and, when all had been transported to Minidoka in Idaho, he drove the 1,200-mile round-trip on many errands of mercy. Rev. Andrews probably performed more Nisei wedding ceremonies and conducted more funerals than any other single minister. After the war, Andy went with me to Hiroshima on two different occasions to build housing for survivors of the atom bomb.

Ray Roberts, a Seattle merchant and member of the Church of the People, not only opposed the evacuation and internment but was most helpful in providing sponsorship and in finding jobs for relocatees. He loaned money interest-free to several families to establish new businesses, and he organized a cooperative farming project near Spokane which served a number of families with income-producing employment and as a hostel for those seeking work.

Arthur Barnett, a Quaker attorney associated with both the American Friends Service Committee and the Council of Churches, was helpful with the legal problems of many people, notably Gordon Hirabayashi's test case which went all the way to the Supreme Court.

Ralph and Mary Smeltzer of the Brethren Service Committee were tireless workers who helped many families find acceptance and employment in Chicago and in the farming areas of the Middle West. With the backing of the Church of the Brethren and the American Friends Service Committee, the Smeltzers, during 1943–45 established and operated a hostel in Chicago and later another in Brooklyn where evacuees could live while seeking employment.

Father Leopold Tibesar of the Maryknoll Mission and other priests and nuns of that order were tireless in their efforts to give moral support and material aid to evacuees both within and beyond the camps. Through their efforts hundreds of people found employment and resettlement upon their release.

Father Thomas Gill (later Bishop Gill) of Catholic Charities provided much comfort and assistance, especially at the time of evacuation and during the frustrating detainment at the Puyallup Assembly Center.

Another agency in Seattle that gave assistance both during the departure and return of Japanese Americans was the Family Services Agency of King County, under the direction of Orvil Roberts.

Staff members of the YWCAs were helpful with housing for young women and job finding during the relocation. For example, Frances Vogel, then secretary of the Seattle YW, was instrumental in helping returning Japanese doctors secure reinstatement within the King County Medical Society. At one point, a delegation from the National Office of the YWCA visited most of the centers to encourage and aid in the resettlement of young people.

Many local churches helped in collecting gifts and clothing at Christmastime, but few churches on the West Coast were enthusiastic in welcoming their neighbors' return. In fact, some Seattle churches actively opposed the reestablishing of the Japanese congregations in that city.

In preparing this statement, I sent fifty questionnaires to churches in the Seattle, Tacoma, Portland, and Yakima areas. I asked what their response had been to the removal and internment of their Japanese American neighbors; what, if anything, they had done to prevent the internment or to aid the relocation. My final statement was, "If I do not have a reply to this inquiry, I will assume that either you were not concerned or that you had no occasion to be." I thought that this statement would surely bring some sort of response. I had a total of five replies: Two said that their church was not in existence at that time; only three, one in Seattle, one in Wenatchee, Washington, and one other told of any concern that they had had or of effort they had made to be of even neighborly assistance.

At the Congressional Hearings on Redress held in Seattle last May, an Issei woman made the statement that the Quakers were the only non-Japanese church that stood by them all through the war. This, of course, was not entirely true, but it is sad to remember how little concern was exhibited by the average person. The hysteria generated by the war, the lies and misinformation, and the fear of adverse public opinion are strong inducements to avoid involvement. And often, it seems, one finds it easier to see and respond to suffering in a distant land than to that which is near at hand.

MY SERVICES

Although I represented the Society of Friends during this period, I personally did not undertake religious services of any sort in the camps. I did attend services within the camps and participated with the worshipers.

I well remember Easter at Heart Mountain in 1944. A sunrise service had been planned and to accommodate the expected crowd a podium had been set up on the baseball field. A certain bishop (I will not use his name or denomination) had been imported all the way from Los Angeles to officiate. On Saturday night I shared a room with His Eminence at the hospital. At dawn Easter morning a blizzard was blowing. I dressed and walked a mile to the ball park where I found several hundred people gathered. The sun did not appear that morning; neither did the bishop. We sang some hymns, someone offered prayers, and we dispersed. It was still snowing. When I returned to my room, the bishop was propped up in bed reading a paperback novel. He did not ask where I had been.

I think the most important service I was able to offer during all the four years of internment was simply in being with the people and doing small errands. I spent three Christmases in camp, having driven each year a car loaded with gifts of clothing, school supplies, toys, etc., contributed by friends in Seattle. I also traveled widely in Montana, Wyoming, and Colorado, and to various eastern cities, visiting families who had relocated. One year I took motion pictures of relocatees in their new homes or businesses and returned to show the film in the camps, where many, especially the older people, had preferred to remain. During this time I also wrote a number of articles on problems of the internment and relocation, which were published in religious periodicals and local newspapers.

POST-WAR RESETTLEMENT

Finally in 1945, we faced the most difficult task of all, that of helping some of the people return to their former homes and reestablish their lives. Much of their property had been lost, homes were vandalized and land often run down and neglected. Worst of all, there was still a great deal of hostility.

We organized volunteer work parties, mostly with university students, to help rework the gardens, replant strawberry fields, paint and repair houses, and find new tools and furnishings. Even some of the personal property that had been stored in the boarded-up Japanese churches had been stolen or destroyed. Also, at this point, a difference of opinion arose as to whether the ethnic churches should be encouraged to reorganize or whether (in the name of integration) it would be best for the people to join and become involved in the non-Japanese church of their choice. This disagreement reached to the highest levels of denominational administration and policy.

In the end, most of the people, both Nisei and Issei, chose to reestablish their former congregations, and all of the Japanese churches in Seattle have prospered upon the return of their congregations. At least three, the Blaine Memorial Methodist Church, the Japanese Presbyterian Church, and the Japanese Congregational Church, have been able to build new and larger facilities. In Seattle, there is an Association of Japanese Protestant Churches, as well as the Japanese Maryknoll Mission, and the temples of three Buddhist sects.

Today, I ask myself why the majority of West Coast churches and their spiritual leaders were—in that time of intense mental and physical suffering—so negligent? Why so seemingly unaware of the plight of their Japanese American neighbors?

In the rural valleys to the south of Seattle and in the valleys to the east of the Cascades where competition with local non-Japanese farmers and businessmen was most intense, the local churches, in some cases reflecting the temper of the community, actually welcomed the removal of the Japanese people. For many outspoken leaders of the hostile communities (most of whom were also influential members of their local churches) the motivation was obviously economic. They wished to remove the competition, and they were eager to secure the use of the rich farmland that would be vacated. This was especially true in some of the California valleys.

From the fifteen or twenty letters of inquiry I sent to Puyallup and Yakima Valley churches in my preparation of this paper, there was *not a single reply*. This may indicate a continuing lack of concern. From my memory of what occurred at the time and from the response—or lack of it—to my present inquiry, I can only conclude that, as a result of the fear and hysteria generated by the war in the Pacific, and because of a reluctance on the part of the white community to risk the censure, these people must have said to themselves, "This is not my war . . . this does not hurt me . . . so why should I become involved?"

In summation, it appears to me that the Japanese Americans as individuals and the Japanese American community as an ethnic minority have had more to contribute to society and to the local church community than the churches have had to offer them. And perhaps this is as it should be, for we have all learned something from the experience. Certainly the churches of America have, on the whole, responded more creatively in the recent crises of the southeast Asian refugees and the displaced people currently arriving from El Salvador.

NOTES

1. For Nicholson's career see two autobiographical volumes, Herbert V. Nicholson, *Treasure in Earthen Vessels: God's Love Overflows in Peace and War* (Whittier, Calif.: Penn Lithographics, Inc., 2nd ed., 1974) and Herbert V. Nicholson and Margaret Wilke, *Comfort All Who Mourn: The Life Story of Herbert and Madeline Nicholson* (Fresno, Calif.: Bookmates International, 1982) plus Michi Weglyn and Betty F. Mitson, eds., *Valiant Odyssey: Herbert Nicholson in and out of America's Concentration Camps* (Upland, Calif.: Bruhn's Printing, 1978).

2. For a compendium listing dozens of clergy who held services for the incarcerated people, see Lester E. Suzuki, *Ministry in the Assembly and Relocation Centers of World War II* (Berkeley: Yardbird Publishing Co., 1979).

"Fellow-Feelers with the Afflicted": The Christian Churches and the Relocation of the Japanese During World War II

Sandra C. Taylor

America's Protestant denominations reacted in a variety of ways to the evacuation, the relocation, and the ultimate resettlement of America's Japanese during World War II. Courageous and sympathetic acts of individual assistance coexisted with the general acceptance of the necessity for evacuation that was based on old stereotyped attitudes about the wily and devious Oriental; yet overall, there was a feeling of regret and humanitarian concern. The role of the churches and their responses to the relocation of the Japanese can be divided into three phases: the initial response to demands for relocation; the assistance provided while the camps were in operation; and the support given during resettlement in 1945–46. Of these, the churches can be faulted for their relative inaction during the first phase, then praised for their contributions during the second two.[1]

Perhaps it was unavoidable that religious leaders, whose calm voices pleaded for justice, would be unheard in the general hysteria that followed Pearl Harbor. Rumors of sabotage and treachery combined with fears of attack and, for many people, the very presence of Americans of Japanese ancestry was an intolerable reminder of the "day that would live in infamy."

Liberal church leaders were anxious to mitigate the violence and lessen the hysteria. The Federal Council of Churches, the Foreign Missions Conference of North America, and the Home Missions Council of North America issued a joint appeal calling for restraint, reminding people of the loyalty of the Japanese, most of whom were citizens who shared the hostility toward the Tokyo government. "We call upon the church people of this country to maintain a Christian composure and charity in their dealings with the Japanese among us," the declaration concluded.[2]

From mid-December to late January, many officials called for tolerance and praised the loyalty of the Japanese Americans, trying to counter the voices of hatred while Washington pondered their fate. Total evacuation was always an option, and it certainly was the solution preferred by economic and political forces on the West Coast who had advocated exclusion and practiced discrimination for the preceding fifty years.[3] Meanwhile, the FBI rounded up suspect enemy aliens,

often the leaders of Issei society, holding them for extended periods in what are best described as concentration camps. Some of those arrested were Christian ministers.[4] The majority of the Japanese Americans, Nisei in their early twenties and younger, suffered from the loss of Issei leadership, from a lack of money because of the freezing of assets in Japanese-owned banks and the loss of jobs, and, above all, from a paralyzing uncertainty about their fate.

The religious community harbored its own share of bigots and "Jap-haters," some in positions of considerable influence. Nevertheless, the attitude of most was one of brotherly concern. Pastors helped the Japanese Christian families in their parishes deprived of husbands and fathers, and urged their congregations to be charitable. Former missionaries to Japan like Herbert Nicholson of Los Angeles and Reverend Everett W. Thompson of Seattle worked closely with the Japanese pastors in trying to aid their panicked congregations.[5] But even the sympathetic did little to try to shape government policy or to forestall mass evacuation. Many pastors and congregations believed the rumors linking the Hawaiian Japanese to sabotage at Pearl Harbor, and most assumed that among the mass of loyal Japanese in this country there undoubtedly lurked saboteurs ready to communicate with and help the enemy. Rumors of crops planted in the shape of arrows to aid enemy navigators had ready believers in those turbulent days.

The fate of the Japanese in America had much to do with people's beliefs about what happened at Pearl Harbor. On January 25, the Roberts Report, a preliminary investigation into the disaster, was published. Although it did not identify specific acts of sabotage, it did not rule them out. Public opinion was again aroused and, in this new climate of hostile opinion, the head of the Western Defense Command, Lieutenant General John DeWitt, and his subordinates were able to persuade the president to issue Executive Order 9066. This order gave the military the authority to carry out extraordinary measures in the name of "military necessity."[6]

Still, by the end of January 1942, specific orders to move people had not yet been issued, and the House

Select Committee Investigating National Defense Migration, headed by Congressman John H. Tolan, arrived on the West Coast to conduct hearings into the proposed total evacuation. Although the Tolan Committee had been invited to the coast by Carey McWilliams, chief of the Division of Immigration and Housing of the California Department of Industrial Relations, whose intent was to clear the air by allowing both sides to be heard, the plan misfired, becoming the setting for a diatribe against Japanese Americans. Testimony spewed forth from politicians, longstanding anti-Japanese groups, the American Legion, and organized labor. What was remarkable was the relative lack of sentiment opposed to the idea of mass evacuation.[7] The committee conducted hearings in Los Angeles, San Francisco, Portland, and Seattle. Only about one-tenth of the witnesses spoke on behalf of the Japanese, and very few Japanese Americans were called upon to testify. A reading of the committee's questions of the witnesses leads one to conclude that its members were probably as supportive of mass evacuation as the vast majority of the people who testified.[8] Not only did voices cry out for exclusion: the more rabid among the witnesses urged disfranchisement, that is, depriving the Japanese American of their citizenship, as well as deportation and even sterilization.[9]

The hearings did provide an opportunity for the voices of reason to be heard. A few churchmen attempted to stem the tide, urging selective evacuation and individual investigation of suspects. In San Francisco, Reverend Galen Fisher of the Pacific Coast Committee for Fair Play stressed the impracticality and the lack of necessity for such massive action and pointed out that, even if a few Japanese Americans had intended to cause trouble, they were highly unlikely to do so because their Issei leaders' had already been interned. He reminded the congressmen that such an action would give Tokyo devastating propaganda to use against the United States.[10] In Seattle, Reverend E. W. Thompson, pastor of the Japanese Methodist Church, stressed the loyalty of the Issei and the need for their continued labor. He too touched on the effect the action would have on the enemy: "It would be defeating democracy, doing what Hitler did to the Jews."[11] The American Friends Service Committee testified in Seattle; its representative Floyd Schmoe advocated voluntary resettlement in an area inland, which was already about one-third Japanese. The AFSC's pacifist aims prevented it from endorsing any war measures, and its concerns were primarily specific—humanitarian and individualistic, rather than general—with the policy as a whole.[12]

The voices of the dozen or so clergy called to testify were sympathetic if futile, but more damning in retrospect was their lack of a strong, united front in opposition. The president of the Church Federation of Los Angeles failed to testify, on the grounds that he was "too busy."[13] The church groups were too late in their protest, their spokesmen were too few to appear as representatives of any ground swell of public opinion, and even among themselves there was division. Some appear to have been Californians first and Christians second, and most Californians in 1942 did not like Japanese, wherever they were born, whatever language they spoke.

As orders for the systematic evacuation of the West Coast were issued and carried out, many Japanese evacuees needed help in preparing for the departure. The Federal Reserve Bank and the Farm Security Administration were authorized to assist individuals in disposing of their personal property and real estate. The Farm Security Administration surveyed the owners of the approximately 5,000 Japanese farms and tooks steps to ensure the continuity of planting and harvesting. The bank hired agents to interview those evacuees who sought their assistance; approximately 26,000 of the 112,000 did. The majority understandably distrusted the government and sought to make their own arrangements. The federal reserve agents did give advice on the sale or leasing of property, and they would even store goods in government warehouses for individuals, although they wouldn't insure them. But their procedures were sloppy and usually their help was given with indifferent haste. They encouraged the evacuees to use their own resources or the commercial services of the community. The secretary of the Berkeley chapter of the Committee on Fair Play to Aliens of Enemy Nationality wrote the San Francisco Federal Reserve Bank proposing a plan to store Japanese goods in private homes. She felt this might reduce white bitterness towards the aliens and Japanese Americans; it would also reassure the evacuees to know that neighbors held their goods for them. The bank official heading the Office of Evacuee Property endorsed the idea.[14]

Such actions were not uncommon in areas where the Protestant churches maintained close ties with their Japanese counterparts. Reverend Frank Herron Smith, chairman of the Seattle Council of Churches, wrote to religious leaders in that area urging them to organize help committees in each church to aid evacuees by storing small valuables for them. Although he was able to offer no financial aid, he encouraged the church people to persuade the Japanese to move beyond the Rockies if they could (voluntary evacuation was briefly encouraged by the army). He also recommended that Japanese pastors transfer the titles of their churches to the Board of Missions of the Methodist Church,[15] a common practice in the larger areas. The Portland Council of Churches set up a subcommittee of their Commission on International Justice and Goodwill to perform similar functions.[16] On April 27, 1942, the *San Francisco Chronicle* printed a letter, signed by twenty-eight Protestant and Jewish clergy, promising assistance to the Japanese American evacuees,[17] and there were many acts of individual charity. Such help was usually restricted to the Japanese Christian community, which represented no more than half of the total evacuee population. The churches also provided storage facilities, as did Buddhist churches, and at least the white Christian community was available for the duration to protect the property entrusted to them.[18] The churches were also of great assistance in the February 17, 1942 evacuation of Terminal Island, Los Angeles, where unfortunate residents had less than forty-eight hours to pack and leave. The Japanese Church Federation appealed for help to aid these victims in finding temporary housing.[19]

As one author has noted, "it took real courage to speak for the unfortunate Japanese-American minority in the spring and summer of 1942."[20] The risks for religious institutions were not as great as for individuals, who might be accused of being "Jap-lovers." The churches acted, rather than spoke, storing goods and assisting individuals with property problems. They dispensed tea, coffee, doughnuts, and sandwiches to the evacuees as they departed for the assembly centers.[21] Reverend Frank Herron Smith noted that "about the only friends standing by are the church people, and they have manifested a fine Christian spirit."[22] He later conducted the Methodist annual conference at the Santa Anita Assembly Center. The Church Council of Sacramento wrote their "Japanese friends and fellow Americans" a letter saying, "We believe in you . . . God bless you and keep you."[23] That group also accepted power of attorney from many Japanese Americans unable to complete property transactions before their departure.

Yet the hostility was there, too, even in the churches. Charles M. Goethe, a Sacramento millionaire, was a financial backer of some virulent anti-Japanese groups and at the same time was very active in the Northern California Council of Churches. Christian brotherhood and charity didn't extend everywhere.[24]

The evacuees were sent first to assembly centers, usually nearby fairgrounds, CCC camps, or racetracks. During the assembly center period, the local churches provided Sunday preachers and other visitors to the residents. The Fellowship of Reconciliation, the American Friends Service Committee, and the YWCA also helped to set up libraries and recreational facilities.[25] The Seattle Council of Churches organized a vacation school for Christian children at Camp Harmony, and they were urged by the area chaplain, Reverend Thomas Okabe, to open it to all children.[26] Denominational boards supplemented the money interned parishioners raised to support their pastors.[27]

The churches, as well as liberal groups in society, were slow to awaken to the tragedy of relocation. In June 1942 the Protestant publication *Christian Century* called them on it: "It is time that all the churches stir themselves to make plain to the nation the tragic mistake it is making . . . the method is not democratic, is not in accord with American traditions, and is not right."[28] These feelings of outrage grew from an increasing sense of guilt at having failed to prevent relocation. A "dear friend" letter from the American Friends Service Committee of northern California urged readers to try to convince people of the loyalty of the Japanese Americans and to work to prevent their disfranchisement. It concluded with the telling sentence: "In sending this letter we are keenly aware of our failure to mold public opinion sufficiently to save Japanese-Americans from their present serious predicament, but we crave your understanding help . . . that we become 'fellow-feelers with the afflicted.' "[29] They urged learning from the experience and working to prevent a resurgence of hatred at the war's end.[30] Other denominations and groups such as the Disciples of Christ, the California Synod of the Presbyterian Church, and the Fellowship of Reconciliation began urging the government to establish hearing boards to determine the loyalty of individual evacuees to pave the way for their resettlement.[31] Galen Fisher termed the evacuation a "military success, social failure, and an international technical blunder."[32] Slowly a sense of guilt and outrage over the needless incarceration of American citizens began to penetrate the Christian conscience.

Although it was too late to stop relocation, many tasks remained. Japanese American and white ministers helped those in the camps by providing Christian religious services; all religious services except Shinto rites were allowed. Christian workers performed acts of individual assistance, such as bringing evacuees needed goods from storage or purchasing items in town. Concerned Christians also worked to prevent even worse outrages, such as the withdrawal of Nisei citizenship. The Quaker Herbert Nicholson traveled to the camps and detention centers on his own limited funds, visiting his Japanese friends and bringing their plight to sympathetic ears in Washington, carrying on a one-man crusade against the injustice.[33] The Catholics, who had established Japanese churches in Los Angeles, San Francisco, and Seattle, continued their ministry in the assembly centers and camps throughout the war. Father Hugh Lavery of Los Angeles was especially active in this work.[34] However, the Salvation Army did not support its Japanese members in the camps; it refused to provide financial assistance to the Protestant Commission for Japanese Service, although all other denominations did so.[35]

The WRA, viewing its job as custodian of the Japanese Americans as temporary, pending their relocation elsewhere, was considering resettling the internees in society even as the camps were filling. Because of the acute labor shortage, schemes were developed to release (or, more accurately, to parole) some of the evacuees to aid in the war effort. Some college students were allowed to resume their education in midwestern or eastern colleges. However, many Japanese Americans hesitated to reenter the white society that had so decisively rejected them; they accepted the security of camp life over the prejudice and racism to be encountered outside. First, the WRA experimented with seasonal, farm-work releases, drawing on the extensive demand for agricultural labor. That success led to a more permanent program of indefinite leave. However, the original requirements for leaving the camps were extremely strict: FBI clearance for loyalty, no past trips to Japan, a guaranteed job outside the jurisdiction of the Western Defense Command, and assurance of favorable community support. The WRA attempted to expedite resettlement by requiring all internees to answer a questionnaire regarding their loyalty and willingness to perform military service, but this misfired, exacerbating old questions about their loyalty and the injustice of relocation itself. In fact, the whole leave program would probably have failed without nongovernmental assistance; as it was, 11 percent were judged eligible for parole and about one-third of this group accepted it.[36]

It was in the program of voluntary resettlement of evacuees into communities in the Midwest and East that the Protestant churches made their most substantial effort. Three of the largest interdenominational groups in the country, the Federal Council of Churches and the Home Missions Board, in cooperation with the Foreign Missions Conference of North America, sponsored the Committee on Resettlement of Japanese Americans. The committee had a twofold task: first, to find jobs for evacuees in locations where they would be accepted; and second, to convince its own constituencies that this was a cause they should support. The Reverend George Aki noted that without the church people resettlement wouldn't even have begun, yet at the same time he found most congregations unwilling to have him speak to them when he toured the country prior to joining the 442nd Regimental Combat Team as its chaplain.[37] The committee cooperated with the WRA, the YMCA, the AFSC, and the Baptist Home Mission Society.[38]

Beginning in April 1943, the committee published a monthly newsletter, entitled *Resettlement Bulletin*, to be distributed in the camps.[39] The *Bulletin* announced the formation of a placement division to match inquiries about workers with people available for relocation. Successive issues of the *Bulletin* reported on specific eastern and midwestern cities, describing the work available, the housing situation, the cost of living, and the prospects for community acceptance. Soon the newsletter was printing testimonials from successfully placed Japanese, which generally stressed how good life was outside the camps. The committee also published provocative pamphlets to break down white prejudice. One entitled "Planning Resettlement of Americans" described the plight of the "70,000 American-born citizens whose only crime is their racial visibility . . . living behind barbed wire, exiles in their native land."[40] They were the products of "a confusion of a problem of national safety with the dogmas of racism."[41]

As a further stimulus to resettlement, the AFSC and the Brethren Service Commitee established hostels. Upon approval of an evacuee's leave request, a hostel would accept an application for a place to reside, and the hostel manager would meet the person and help him or her get settled in the city. They accepted everyone, regardless of religion.[42] Church people also assisted by providing the necessary letters of reference for the evacuees, enabling them to obtain leave clearance for resettlement.[43] The college-educated, the Christian, or the secular nonagricultural Nisei more often sought and had less difficulty obtaining leave clearance, and they also received more encouragement and assistance in resettlement than did Buddhists.[44]

As the war reached its final year, the focus of resettlement shifted. The easily resettled had either left the camps for work or had been drafted, and those who remained were the very young and the very old. Roy Gibbons, the director of the Council for Social Action of the Congregational Churches, visited the camp at Granada, Colorado, and noted that more work needed do be done with the Issei, who were afraid to leave the camps and had reverted to their old Japanese customs.[45] The *Bulletin* urged its readers to remember the little children (who like the old, were left behind), to send gifts for Christmas, and to aid in plans for holiday parties.[46]

Many factors entered into the decision to close the camps. Japan's fading resistance made military necessity appear a hollow pretext for holding loyal citizens; but the heavy West Coast resistance to their return had to be considered. Hate groups had conducted a propaganda campaign opposing their return throughout the war. Even the Pacific Coast Committee for Fair Play was not sure that return was a wise or safe course to encourage, and the Los Angeles Federation of Churches opposed it while the war was still being fought.[47] Nicholson later recalled how he and the strongly pro-Japanese Quaker group, the Friends of the American Way, organized a letter-writing campaign among Christians to convince the government that there was substantial support on the West Coast for releasing everyone from the camps.[48]

Discussions about ending exclusion had begun even before the Supreme Court's historic Endo decision ruled in December 1944 that the involuntary and indefinite detention of loyal citizens was invalid. In fact, according to Howard Ball, the Court deliberately delayed announcement of its decision until the executive was ready to act.[49]

A few carefully selected Japanese Americans had been allowed to return to the West Coast; however, a mass migration of the exiles to their former homes was still a risky proposition. Such a migration began on January 2, 1945, and a few weeks later the Pacific Coast Committee for Fair Play called a conference in San Francisco to plan for their reintegration into community life. Sixteen state and federal agencies sent representatives, as did even more private agencies. This and similar meetings probably contributed significantly to the relative lack of violence on the West Coast.[50] The Committee on Resettlement published a handbook for local committees to assist in helping the returning evacuees to find housing, employment,[51] and moral support when they returned to freedom. By March of that year, the committee urged every church in Los Angeles to become the sponsor of at least one returning family, to provide employment, fellowship, and temporary housing.[52]

The final issue of the *Resettlement Bulletin* expressed its continuing concern that the government delay the final closing of the field offices of the WRA, set for March 1946, and to provide continued assistance for problem cases. It listed ongoing services the churches would provide. The editor also emphasized that the closing of the camps should not mean the end of their efforts. They should now address themselves to the continuing legacy of segregation and discrimination, working to end alien land laws, to prevent the involuntary deportation of some 8,000 protesters from the camps, and to gain compensation for the real and personal property losses the Japanese evacuees had suffered.[53]

Liberal Christians who were willing to work for racial justice had their work cut out for them. In January 1944, Colorado narrowly defeated an amendment that would have prohibited anyone of Japanese ancestry from owning land; the churches were instrumental in this victory.[54] But that legislation was just one symptom of resurgent racism. A study done by the National Opinion Research Center in Denver reported in January 1945 that only 16 percent of the public thought that Japanese in America should have as good a chance as whites to get any kind of job after the war, that 61 percent would give whites first chance, and 21 percent would give equal opportunity only if the Japanese were loyal American citizens.[55]

The return of some 60 percent of the original evacuees to the West Coast did provoke some violence; a few fire bombings and terrorist acts did occur. The situation remained touchy for several months, while a remarkable modification of opinion took place and acceptance replaced hostility. The churches alone cannot claim credit for this transformation, but they helped. A determined and persistent minority of whites, many of whom were church people, were determined to obtain some kind of justice for the Japanese Americans, and they played a significant role in promoting a peaceful return.[56] A changed climate of political opinion, a different government policy, and the remarkable about-face of the leading anti-Japanese newspapers—the Hearst press and the McClatchy chain—were the most influential. The churches did work to modify public opinion and they provided specific assistance in housing, jobs, and resettlement. Seattle was a stellar example. The AFSC's Floyd Schmoe mobilized students to help returning Japanese repair and paint their devastated dwellings. The program developed into summer weekend work camps.[57]

The final reports issued by the district offices of the WRA in 1946 were generally praiseworthy of the churches' efforts. The San Francisco office noted that the schools "tried weakly to combat racism" but the churches did better. The ministers also obtained religious buildings for temporary housing to help ease a desperate situation.[58] In Sacramento, local agricultural leaders were persuaded individually to hire returnees, and canneries and the AFL-CIO cooperated.[59] However, the San Francisco office of the

WRA noted the intense hostility to the returnees in that area and reported that even the schools were unfriendly and the churches apathetic. "As was the case with the schools, much work had to be done in the churches before they were definitely on our side," it reported.[60]

In conclusion, one can say that the Protestant churches represented a cross section of the American people: some actively supported Japanese rights at the outset, others learned to temper their racist attitudes with brotherhood and compassion, and others were indifferent. The more theologically liberal of the denominations were the most tolerant and consequently the most sympathetic to the plight of the Japanese Americans. Quakers, Congregationalists, and Methodists stood out in their efforts to help, while the Church of Jesus Christ of Latter-day Saints (Mormons) and the more fundamentalist sects, particularly those located in the South, were largely silent. Even among the groups who eventually sided with the evacuees, the response to their plight immediately after Pearl Harbor was slow. People were caught off guard, and they were at first disarmed by the catch-all phrase "military necessity." Their willingness to believe the rumors of Japanese sabotage was probably the result of years of prejudice and stereotyping, which led most people to believe the image of the wily and treacherous Oriental. Some clearly never abandoned that image. And Japan's actions in Asia during the previous decades had won her no friends in this country. By the early 1930s even the Japan missionary community had ceased to condone Japanese expansionism. The Japanese had no visible heroes, no Joe DiMaggios whose fame brought toleration not only for his enemy alien parents but for all Italian Americans. The churches were misled into supporting the idea that some evacuation was justified, though some soon repented that decision. From that point on, their actions were reactive and humanitarian in nature, redemptive rather than initiatory, seeking to undo the initial wrong.

One may ask if they might not have done more to become a real voice for toleration and understanding. It is disheartening to conclude that the churches, when pitted against the voice of the military establishment, which cried out so strongly for mass evacuation, were bound to lose. But the two institutions were not pitted against each other, for the churches acquiesced in the military decision. What was needed was foresight and a stronger program to combat prejudice before the act. The churches went along because their members, too, harbored an unconscious racism that permitted them to become dupes of a misguided military policy, and that is the greater misfortune.

NOTES

1. I wish to express my thanks to the Sourisseau Academy of San Jose State University for the research grant for this project, and the Research Committee of the University of Utah for a David P. Gardner Faculty Fellowship that provided the release time. This paper was initially prepared for the luncheon meeting of the Conference on Peace Research History, American Historical Association, Los Angeles, California, December 28, 1981.

2. Toru Matsumoto, *Beyond Prejudice: A Story of the Church and the Japanese Americans* (New York: Friendship Press, 1946), 10.

3. See Roger Daniels, *The Decision to Relocate the Japanese* (Philadelphia, New York, and Toronto: J. B. Lippincott, 1975); Jacobus tenBroek, Edward N. Barnhart, and Floyd W. Matson, *Prejudice, War and the Constitution* (Berkeley and Los Angeles: University of California Press, 1954); and Morton Grodzins, *Americans Betrayed* (Chicago: University of Chicago Press, 1949).

4. Lester E. Suzuki, *Ministry in the Assembly and Relocation Centers of World War II* (Berkeley: Yardbird Publishing Co., 1979), 5–6.

5. See "A Friend of the American Way: An Interview with Herbert V. Nicholson," in *Voices Long Silent: An Oral Inquiry into the Japanese American Evacuation*, ed. Arthur A. Hansen and Betty E. Mitson (Fullerton: California State University, 1974), 110–42.

6. Audrie Girdner and Anne Loftis, *The Great Betrayal: The Evacuation of Japanese Americans During World War II* (New York: MacMillan, 1969) and Roger Daniels, *Concentration Camps, USA* (New York: Holt, Rinehart and Winston, 1972), 52–55.

7. Daniels, 74–78; Girdner and Loftis, 107–8.

8. Allen R. Bosworth, *America's Concentration Camps* (New York: W. W. Norton, 1967), 65–67.

9. Girder and Loftis, 104–5.

10. U.S. Congress, Select Committee Investigating National Defense Migration, *Fourth Interim* Report, 77th Cong., 2d sess. (Washington, D.C.: Government Printing Office, 1942), Part 29, 11195.

11. Ibid., Part 30, 11607–9.

12. Ibid., Part 30, 11526.

13. Matsumoto, citing Rev. Frank Herron Smith, 15.

14. Mrs. H. L. Kingston to R. E. Everson, Federal Reserve Bank, March 26, 1942 and March 28, 1942, Miscellaneous File, Papers of the Evacuee Property Division, Federal Reserve Bank, San Francisco. (Hereafter cited as FRB.) See also Sandra C. Taylor, "Evacuation and Economic Loss: The Relocation of the Japanese and the Role of the Federal Reserve Bank," *The Public Historian* 5 (Winter 1983): 9–30.

15. "Japanese-American Relocation," File 1358, Box 7, Seattle Council of Churches papers, Suzzallo Library, University of Washington. (Hereafter cited as SCC papers, UW.)

16 I. George Nace, Portland Council of Churches, to Gertrude Apel, March 27, 1942, SCC papers, UW.

17. Girdner and Loftis, 126.

18. Matsumoto, 16.

19. Suzuki, 6.

20. Girdner and Loftis, 126.

21. Matsumoto, 22.

22. "Japanese American Relocation, Papers of Dr. Frank Herron Smith," SCC papers, UW; Suzuki, 20–21.

23. Interview File, Sacramento, FRB.

24. Girdner and Loftis, 360.

25. Ibid., 156–57.

26. May 19, 1942, SCC papers, UW.

27. Executive Committee, Western Area Protestant Church Committee for Wartime Japanese Service, Frank Herron Smith papers, UW.

28. "Justice for the Evacuees," *Christian Century*, 750–52, clipping in the Conard-Duveneck collection, Hoover Institution on War, Revolution, and Peace. (Hereafter cited as Conard-Duveneck collection, Hoover.)

29. Letter from American Friends Service Committee, June 4, 1943, Japanese American Evacuation Research Study collection, Bancroft Library, University of California, Berkeley. (Hereafter cited as JERS.)

30. American Friends Service Committee letter, August 4, 1942, Conard-Duveneck collection, Hoover.

31. *The Church Measures the Evacuation: Three Recent Church Statements Opposing Continued Wholesale Detention of America's Japanese*, Fellowship of Reconciliation, Berkeley, October 26, 1942; and Caleb Foote, *Outcasts! The Story of America's Treatment of Her Japanese-American Minority*, Fellowship of Reconciliation, n.d., Conard-Duveneck collection, Hoover.

32. Galen Fisher, "A Balance Sheet on Japanese Evacuation," reprinted from *Christian Century*, August 18 and 25, September 1 and 8, 1943, by Berkeley Committee on American Principles and Fair Play, Conard-Duveneck collection, Hoover.

33. Hansen and Mitson, 130–40.

34. Suzuki, 17.

35. Ibid., 18.

36. Girdner and Loftis, 342–43; tenBroek, 142–43.

37. *Resettlement Bulletin*, Vol. 1, No. 2, April 1, 1943, JERS.

38. Girdner and Loftis, 354.

39. Copies are found in the Japanese Relocation folder, File 1567-2, Box 5, UW, and also in JERS.

40. As described in *Resettlement Bulletin*, Vol. 1, No. 4, July 1943, JERS.

41. Pamphlet by Thomas B. Douglass, *70,000 American Refugees—Made in USA*, Citizens Committee for Resettlement, Congregational Christian Committee for Work with Japanese Evacuees, St. Louis, n.d., JERS.

42. Matsumoto, 71–72.

43. Letters of Gertrude L. Apel, SCC papers, UW.

44. Dorothy Swaine Thomas, *The Salvage* (Berkeley: University of California Press, 1952), 125; and Matsumoto, 58.

45. *Resettlement Bulletin*, Vol. II, No. 6, July 1944, JERS.

46. *Resettlement Bulletin*, Vol. II, No. 9, November 1944, JERS.

47. Girdner and Loftis, 368.

48. Hansen and Mitson, 139–42.

49. See Howard Ball, "Judicial Parsimony and Military Necessity Disinterred: A Re-examination of the Japanese Exclusion Cases, 1943–1944" in this volume.

50. Daniels, 158.

51. *Relocating the Dislocated: First Aid for Wartime Evacuees*, Committee for Resettlement of Japanese Americans, New York, January 1945, JERS.

52. *Resettlement Bulletin*, Vol. III, No. 2, March 1945, JERS.

53. *Resettlement Bulletin*, Final Issue, April 1946, JERS.

54. Matsumoto, 88–96.

55. *Postwar Planning*, War Relocation Authority publication, 1945, RG 210/93.105, National Archives, Washington, D.C.

56. Daniels, 162.

57. *AFSERCO News*, American Friends Service Committee, June–July 1945, in Conard-Duveneck collection, Hoover.

58. *Final Report*, Relocation Division, War Relocation Authority, San Francisco, May 15, 1946, JERS.

59. Ibid.

60. Ibid.

PART V

Incarceration Elsewhere

When the Great Pacific War broke out in December 1941 there were some 600,000 ethnic Japanese in the New World, the result of immigration that had begun in the late nineteenth century. They included perhaps 250,000 to 300,000 in Brazil, 150,000 in the Territory of Hawaii, some 125,000 in the continental United States, about 25,000 each in Canada and Peru, fewer than 10,000 in Mexico, in addition to small settlements and colonies in many Caribbean and Central and South American nations. The New World Japanese did not share a common fate. Those in Brazil and Hawaii—the two largest populations—were left largely at liberty. The United States and Canada exiled men, women, and children to desolate camps; Peru, with the help of the U.S. government, exported much of its Japanese population to the United States, where it was interned. Mexico required its Japanese to resettle in one of two cities—Mexico City or Guadalajara. Some Central American countries sent a few Japanese to the United States, usually in company with Japanese Peruvians, while Cuba required that all adult male Japanese be sent to Havana for incarceration, but allowed women and children to stay at home, which for most was an agricultural settlement on the Isle of Pines (now the Isle of Youth).

In this section the fate of some of the groups of Japanese elsewhere in this hemisphere is considered. Dennis Ogawa and Evarts C. Fox, Jr., tell the story of that minority of Hawaiian Japanese who were either interned or incarcerated. The story they tell is largely unknown, even to residents of the Aloha State. Gordon Hirabayashi, who, like so many American academics, migrated to a Canadian university, tells the more widely known story of the Japanese Canadians. Anyone who believes that the Canadian government was less repressive than the American should ponder Hirabayashi's essay. And, finally, C. Harvey Gardiner tells perhaps the most curious story of all, that of the Japanese Peruvians, persecuted by both their own and the American government.

The literature about the New World Nikkei is both extensive and uneven. For a historiographical and bibliographical essay, see James Tigner, "Japanese Immigration into Latin America: A Survey," *Journal of Interamerican Studies and World Affairs* 23 (1981): 457–82. For the largest group, the Japanese of Brazil, most of the best work is in either Portuguese or Japanese. For a good short summary, in English, of the whole Japanese-Brazilian experience, see Hiroshi Saito, "The Integration and Participation of the Japanese and their Descendants in Brazilian Society," *International Migration* 14 (1976): 183–97.

On Peru, Gardiner's work is definitive: see both his *Pawns in a Triangle of Hate: The Peruvian Japanese and the United States* (Seattle: University of Washington Press, 1981) and *The Japanese and Peru, 1873–1973* (Albuquerque: University of New Mexico Press, 1975). These may be supplemented by the memoirs of the

American diplomat who helped select the Japanese Peruvians to be exported: John K. Emmerson, *The Japanese Thread: A Life in the U.S. Foreign Service* (New York: Holt, Rinehart and Winston, 1978), especially chapter 6, "Japanese and Americans in Peru," 125–49. See also Orazio Ciccarelli, "Peru's Anti-Japanese Campaign in the 1930s: Economic Dependency and Abortive Nationalism," *Canadian Review of Studies in Nationalism* 9 (1982): 113–33.

For the Japanese of Mexico see Chizuko Watanabe, "The Japanese Immigrant Community in Mexico: Its History and Present," unpublished M.A. thesis, California State University, Los Angeles, 1983. A brief account of the Japanese in Cuba may be found in Dennison Nash and Louis C. Schaw, "Achievement and Acculturation: A Japanese Example," in Melford E. Spiro, ed., *Context and Meaning in Cultural Anthropology* (New York: Free Press, 1965), 206–24.

For Canada there is a large literature. The most important books are: Forrest LaViolette, *The Canadian Japanese and World War II* (Toronto: University of Toronto Press, 1948); Ken Adachi, *The Enemy That Never Was: A History of the Japanese Canadians* (Toronto: McClelland and Stewart, 1976): Barry Broadfoot, *Years of Sorrow, Years of Shame* (Toronto: Doubleday, 1977), an undocumented but fascinating oral history; W. Peter Ward, *White Canada Forever: Popular Attitudes and Public Policy Toward Orientals in British Columbia* (Montreal: McGill-Queens University Press, 1978) which goes only to 1942; and Ann Gomer Sunahara, *The Politics of Racism: The Uprooting of Japanese Canadians during the Second World War* (Toronto: James Lorimer, 1978), which is the most detailed account. Roger Daniels, "The Japanese Experience in North America: An Essay in Comparative Racism," *Canadian Ethnic Studies* 9 (1977) 2: 91–100 and *Concentration Camps, North America: Japanese in the United States and Canada during World War II* (Malabar, Fla: Krieger, 1981) make explicit comparisons between the policies of the North American democracies. Students of anti-Asian attitudes and activities in Canada are awaiting a large work from Professor Patricia E. Roy of the University of Victoria, who has published many illuminating articles. See, for example, her "The Soldiers Canada Didn't Want: Her Chinese and Japanese Citizens," *Canadian Historical Review* 59 (1978): 341–58.

For wartime conditions in Hawaii, see J. Garner Anthony, *Hawaii Under Army Rule* (Stanford, Calif.: Stanford University Press, 1955). Thomas D. Murphey, *Ambassadors in Arms* (Honolulu: University of Hawaii Press, 1975), tells the story of the 100th Battalion. For a memoir by Hawaii's senior senator, see Daniel K. Inouye with Lawrence Elliott, *Journey to Washington* (Englewood Cliffs, N.J.: Prentice-Hall, 1967). All of the few hundred Japanese in Alaska, including some of native American cultural heritage, were either interned or incarcerated: see Claus M. Naske, "The Relocation of Alaska's Japanese Residents," *Pacific Northwest Quarterly* 74 (1983): 124–32.

Roger Daniels

Japanese Internment and Relocation: The Hawaii Experience

Dennis M. Ogawa and Evarts C. Fox, Jr.

Much attention has been given to the plight of the Japanese Americans on the mainland during wartime.[1] The concentration camps stand as one of the greatest injustices ever committed by the U.S. government against its own citizens. However, what of the Japanese Americans in Hawaii? They constituted a large portion of Hawaii's population, but little is known about their internment experience, both shortly after the attack on Pearl Harbor and during the war.

An immediate result of the December 7 attack was the declaration of martial law in the Territory of Hawaii, which included the authority to control the civilian population of 421,000, of which 157,000 were persons of Japanese ancestry with about 35,000 aliens and approximately 68,000 individuals holding dual citizenship.[2]

Martial law in the islands lasted from December 7, 1941, to October 24, 1944, when a modified system of military control was placed in effect that allowed civilian control of most governmental functions excepting security and military-related activities. This modified authority existed until October 24, 1945, when it was suspended by the president and all governmental functions reverted to civilian authority.[3] During the period of military control, approximately 10,000 people living in the Hawaiian Islands were investigated for security reasons. These investigations resulted in the apprehension of 1,569 individuals, of whom 1,466 were Japanese.[4] As a result, the number of Japanese interned during the war was 1,250, slightly less than one percent of Hawaii's total Japanese population.[5] Because a significant portion of the territory's economy depended upon Japanese labor, mass internment or relocation based on the West Coast model was not practical. Consequently, most of the Japanese were permitted to remain in the islands and to function under a system of strict control and surveillance.

Although all civilians in the territory were subject to numerous restrictions related to security, travel, curfew, and rationing, the Japanese were required to comply with additional regulations and restrictions. These included turning in weapons, ammunition, and explosives; registering as aliens; expanded curfews; reporting foreign military service; restrictions of entry into certain security areas; tighter than normal travel restrictions; restricted access to communications equipment; and a prohibition about writing or printing attacks against the government. In addition, no alien could engage in fishing activities and the Japanese fishing fleet was impounded. However, the Japanese were not prohibited from attending gatherings or meetings, but the population in general was asked to report to the provost marshal any gathering at which aliens were present. Buddhist meetings were specifically mentioned.[6]

Before the attack on Pearl Harbor, counterintelligence agencies investigated the possibility that the local Japanese population might engage in sabotage or espionage. They concluded that active disloyalty by Hawaii's Japanese would only be likely in the case of a Japanese landing and partial or complete occupation of the islands.[7] Nevertheless, they assembled a list of individuals considered potentially dangerous to the United States, dividing them into two categories of suspects. Everyone included on List 1-A was to be apprehended immediately upon the beginning of hostilities between the United States and the Axis powers; those on List 1-B were to be placed under surveillance

The main entrance to the internees' camp showing the building of the women internees' houses completed. Sand Island, Honolulu, T.H., February 13, 1942. Courtesy U.S. Army, Negative No. SC 137290.

and their activities curtailed. Army Intelligence (G-2) estimated that there were about 300 persons in each group, most of them Japanese.

After martial law was declared, Army Counter Intelligence (CIC), assisted by the FBI, the Office of Naval Intelligence (ONI), and the Honolulu Police Reservists began to bring in those on List 1-A. The first arrest took place at 11:00 a.m. December 7, 1941, and by day's end about 200 individuals had been interned at the Honolulu Immigration Station. By December 10, 400 people, three-fourths of them Japanese, were detained at the Immigration Station.[8]

On December 8, 1941, the government activated the Sand Island Detention Camp. Its location in Honolulu Harbor, along with the existing facilities of the Territorial Quarantine Hospital, made the island an attractive first site for a detention camp. Within one week approximately 300 Japanese had been transferred from the Immigration Station to Sand Island.[9]

The Sand Island Detention Camp was used for fifteen months, and during that time about $500,000 was spent on various additions and improvements. The camp was divided into four compounds: two of 250-person capacity for male Japanese, one for 40 women of mixed races, and one for 25 German and Italian men. Although transfers of the internees held at Sand Island to Justice Department camps on the mainland began in early 1942, a number of aliens and Kibei still remained at the facility when it was closed on March 1, 1943 to become part of the expanded Honolulu Port of Embarkation. The Immigration Station, however, continued to be used for the temporary custody of aliens pending interrogation and internment hearings.[10] By March 1, 1943 most internees still at Sand Island were moved to a facility at Honouliuli located in central Oahu or were shipped to the mainland.[11]

Investigations and arrests continued throughout the islands until shortly before the end of the war.

During the period of martial law, the counterintelligence operations had the right of search and seizure in civilian areas and the authority to arrest civilians. Most CIC activity took place during the first year of the war, and the majority of the individuals interned were Buddhist and Shinto priests, consular agents, language school officials, commercial fishermen, and Kibei. Almost all of the 5,000 Kibei living in Hawaii were processed during this time.[12]

Military authorities regarded counterintelligence operations as defensive in nature, in that they disrupted any program of sabotage or espionage the enemy might mount in Hawaii. CIC personnel believed that they apprehended most of the individuals who were possibly dangerous and, most important, they felt that the constant threat of investigation, apprehension, and detention was a powerful deterrent to subversion.[13] The internment of individuals, along with the exercise of strict controls over the remaining Japanese population, was considered to be more effective and more practical than other proposals, which included locking all Japanese in stockades overnight while permitting daytime freedom, or evacuating all Hawaii's Japanese to the mainland or to an isolated part of the islands.[14]

The military authorities were troubled by not knowing what to expect in a given situation from a group comprising almost one-third of the territory's population. Lists of potentially disloyal persons were put together with this problem in mind. They suspected Shinto and Buddhist priests because of their nationalistic and religious ties to Japan. Consular agents who worked at the very active Japanese Consulate in Hawaii were looked upon as, at the least, unofficial imperial conduits to the Japanese people living in Hawaii. These agents regularly registered new births with the consulate, conducted censuses, and helped local Japanese apply for military deferment with the Japanese government. As a result, the consulate had fairly complete records on all Japanese in Hawaii and presumably had a working knowledge of individual qualifications and loyalties. The language school officials taught Japanese and Japanese ideology, possibly strengthening loyalty to the emperor. Members of various organizations and societies, who contributed to Japanese war relief, entertained visiting Japanese naval training vessels, and bought Japanese war bonds, demonstrating questionable loyalty. Japanese businessmen even had their own chamber of commerce. Finally, the Kibei, who had spent their formative years studying in Japan, were considered potentially the most dangerous group. Not only had they been subjected to pure Japanese thought during their schooling, they were young and strong and, therefore, were felt to pose a threat to internal security.

With these considerations in mind, investigations and apprehensions were made until the end of the war. Each person was brought before a hearing board made up of representatives from the CIC, the FBI, and the ONI. If this board decided that someone should be interned, his case was placed before a Civilian Hearing Board made up of two army officers and three civilians. Its recommendations were reviewed by the Intelligence Review Board, which was made up of the heads of the three counterintelligence agencies. This group would either concur or make its own recommendation for disposition. The case then went to the Military Governor's Review Board for a final recommendation. That recommendation, signed by the military governor, ended the procedure: the subject was interned or released.[15]

By February 1942, space became available on the mainland to confine Hawaii internees. Consequently, on February 19, 1942 the first group left Sand Island. Of the 200 individuals in the transfer, 175 were Japanese; a total of six internee transfers occurred during 1942 and 1943, in which 700 aliens went to the mainland. Included in this number were 675 Japanese.[16]

At the outbreak of the war, the authorities had to decide about evacuating civilians of all kinds from Hawaii, for both safety and security considerations. To a War Department inquiry concerning how many Japanese should be evacuated if only military security considerations were involved, General Delos Emmons replied that to guarantee all disloyal individuals were removed would require relocating 100,000 persons.[17] Also, Washington considered the possibility of using Hawaii Japanese in a repatriation agreement between the United States and Japan. But the military authorities in the islands objected to people from Hawaii being included in this exchange on two counts: (1)

Lt. Robert I. Freund interviewing internee Charles I. Hasebe, assisted by interpreter, Mr. Forrest Garnett. Mrs. Irene E. Rogliandi, recorder. The Immigration Station, Honolulu, T. H., February 17, 1942. Courtesy U.S. Army, Negative No. SC 137283.

anyone from Hawaii would have knowledge of military bases in the islands and would likely be able to help Japanese intelligence; (2) repatriation would have a serious effect on the morale of the remaining Japanese living in Hawaii.

However, four more groups of Japanese civilians were evacuated from Hawaii and sent to mainland relocation centers. These individuals were, for the most part, volunteers hoping to be reunited with an interned family member. The first evacuation of 107 individuals took place on November 23, 1942. The second group of 443 individuals left Hawaii on December 28, 1942. Another group of 261 left on January 26, 1943, and a final group of 226 departed for the Topaz Relocation Center in Utah on March 2, 1943.

This latter group arrived at Topaz on March 14, 1943. It included 176 unattached men, Kibei whose average age was between twenty and twenty-three years.[18] The majority of them had recently been graduated from high school in Japan and upon returning to Hawaii were among those detained and interned.[19] Security authorities believed that, because of their recent close ties with Japan, these Kibei were potentially dangerous.

After this last embarkation, the Hawaiian military authorities recommended suspending evacuation of the civilian Japanese population. The War Department concurred and only those to be interned were then sent.[20]

In September 1943, most of the Topaz group from Hawaii, approximately 170 people, were transferred to Tule Lake. These individuals had either answered "no" to questions 27 and 28 on the revised WRA Form 126 or had refused to answer them. Some did so because they wanted to return to Japan, while others protested because they felt that the government had violated their freedom. Ten to fifteen of those persons actually

Topaz. Evacuees from Hawaii being transported to Delta in army trucks, March 14, 1943. A reception was held in their honor by the other residents. Photo by Francis Stewart. Courtesy National Archives, Washington, D.C.

went to Japan, but most chose to return to Hawaii at the end of the war.[21]

During the period of martial law, the hearing board recommended some internees in Hawaii be released on parole. When martial law ended on October 24, 1944, no legal authority to hold American citizens of Japanese ancestry in internment remained. (Executive Order 9066 did not apply to Hawaii, which was outside of the Western Defense Command.) However, Presidential Order 9489, which lifted martial law, gave the commanding general of the Territory of Hawaii authority to exclude anyone from Hawaii who was considered dangerous to security. The order also gave authority to detain individuals pending exclusion. On October 24, 1944, sixty-seven citizens of Japanese ancestry and fifty aliens remained at the Honouliuli. The sixty-seven citizens went to Tule Lake on November 9, 1944, and the fifty aliens were gradually released on parole. On V-J Day, the twenty-two aliens still in camp were released. During 1945, authorities apprehended twelve Japanese civilians and placed them in custody pending exclusion from the territory.[22]

Overall, for the Hawaii experience, less than one percent of the islands' Japanese population was interned during World War II; compared to the mainland episode, such a figure would hardly appear to be significant. However, numbers alone may not indicate

the possible loss and cultural damage internment created, particularly in the area of the humanities, for many of those who were interned were not only the outspoken and distinguished Issei in the Hawaiian community but were also the major leaders in the humanities, the spiritual, cultural, and literary figures of the Japanese population. Their removal may have very well created a major void in the quality of the ethnic cultural life among Hawaii's Japanese and contributed to the problems of ethnic identity and cultural continuity of succeeding generations of Japanese Americans.

NOTES

1. This work was made possible through the assistance of a research grant from the National Endowment for the Humanities.

2. Office of the Chief of Military History, *United States Army Forces Middle Pacific and Predecessor Commands During World War II, 7 December 1941–2 September 1945, History of the Provost Marshal's Office,* Vol. 24, Pt. 1, p. 11.

3. *History of the Provost Marshal's Office,* Vol. 24, Pt. 1, p. 12.

4. Office of the Chief of Military History, *United States Armed Forces Middle Pacific and Predecessor Commands During World War II, 7 December 1941–2 September 1945, Civil Affairs and Military Government,* Vol. 8, Pt. 2, p. 16.

5. Office of the Chief of Military History, *United States Army Forces Middle Pacific and Predecessor Commands During World War II, 7 December 1941–2 September 1945, History of the Provost Marshal's Office,* Vol. 24, Pt. 2, p. 196.

6. *History of the Provost Marshal's Office,* Vol. 24, Pt. 1, pp. 17–26.

7. Office of the Chief of Military History, *United States Army Forces Middle Pacific and Predecessor Commands During World War II, 7 December 1941–2 September 1945, History of G-2 Section,* Vol. 10, Pt. 2, p. 8.

8. *History of G-2 Section,* Vol. 10, Pt. 2, p. 23.

9. *History of the Provost Marshal's Office,* Vol. 24, Pt. 2, p. 188.

10. Ibid., 191.

11. Statement by Iwao Kosaka, Kibei Internee, Editor and Journalist, *Hawaii Hochi,* Personal interview, Honolulu, Hawaii, December 15, 1983.

12. *History of G-2 Section,* Vol. 10, Pt. 2, pp. 24–25.

13. Ibid., Pt. 2, p. 19.

14. Ibid., Pt. 1, p. 7.

15. Ibid., Pt. 2, p. 24.

16. *History of the Provost Marshal's Office,* Vol. 24, Pt. 2, p. 202.

17. *Civil Affairs and Military Government,* p. 7.

18. U.S. Department of Interior, War Relocation Authority, *The Evacuation of a People: A Quantitative Description* (Washington, D.C.: Government Printing Office, 1946), 183.

19. Kosaka Statement, December 1983.

20. *Civil Affairs and Military Government,* pp. 15–16.

21. Kosaka Statement, December 1983.

22. *History of the Provost Marshal's Office,* Vol. 24, Pt. 2, pp. 203, 204.

The Japanese Canadians and World War II

Gordon K. Hirabayashi

The history of Japanese immigration to Canada is similar to that of the United States, with the peak years being the decade of 1900 to 1910. For both countries the year 1907 represented the heaviest single year of immigration.[1] In those days there was little awareness among the immigrants of any national boundary; to them the land across the Pacific was simply "America." In 1977 the Japanese Canadians celebrated the centennial of the arrival of the first known Japanese settler.[2] At the time of World War II, 23,149 persons of Japanese ancestry lived in Canada; in the continental United States in 1940, the Japanese American population totaled 126,947. If the Japanese Americans were heavily concentrated in the three western coastal states (88.5 percent), the concentration of the Japanese Canadians in British Columbia was even greater, (95.5 percent). Further, more than half of the remaining Japanese Canadians lived in the adjoining province of Alberta, with fewer than 500 in all the rest of the country.

The heavy concentration of the Japanese in British Columbia had its political implications. A bad situation was prevented from becoming worse by the Anglo-Japanese Treaty of Commerce and Navigation of 1894, which bound Canada and forced the federal government to contravene and disallow such British Columbia laws as the ones that prohibited employment of Orientals on works authorized by the provincial government.[3] British Columbia was also stymied in its attempt to change the minimum naturalization requirements from three years' residence to ten years for Orientals. As a result, many Japanese were naturalized. By World War II, 16 percent were naturalized Canadians and 58 percent were native born. The remaining 26 percent were Japanese nationals.

Compared to the treatment of the Chinese during the late nineteenth and early twentieth centuries, the state of the Japanese remained relatively favorable, due primarily to the active attention of the Japanese Consulate General, watching both Victoria and Ottawa for anti-Japanese legislation that might emerge contrary to the treaty signed with the British.

Unlike in the United States, some Japanese in Canada were able to become naturalized citizens, but they, along with the native-born Canadians of Japanese ancestry, were barred from franchise in British Columbia. An 1895 act denied the provincial vote to Asians who became British subjects by naturaliza-

tion but, more significantly, it disqualified, on the basis of race, children of immigrant parents born in Canada. Since the provincial voters' lists were used to compile the federal list, this prevented Japanese Canadians from voting in federal elections. As Ken Adachi has noted, "the prior restriction imposed by the provincial authority extended . . . to the federal franchise."[4] This restriction was not repealed until 1948, and voting rights became operationally effective in 1949.

The above restrictions and harassments are but a few selected samples of the general climate confronted by the Japanese in British Columbia, a province that not only openly proclaimed British Columbia to be for whites but mainly for British whites. Moreover, what British Columbia persistently sought were laws such as the anti-alien land laws like those in California, and when the U.S. Immigration Act of 1924 excluded Japanese immigration there, British Columbia busily hounded Ottawa for similar action.

As a part of the British Commonwealth, Canada entered World War II in 1939. After Pearl Harbor, especially in British Columbia, it became the Pacific War, the "real" war, and anti-Japanese feeling shifted into high gear.

Heretofore, Japanese and Canadians had been monitoring the Canadian handling of German and Italian aliens, anticipating that if war in the Pacific came, Japanese aliens would inevitably suffer. Within hours of the attacks on Pearl Harbor and Hong Kong, Canada declared war on Japan for "wantonly and treacherously" attacking British territory and threatening "the defence and freedom of Canada."[5]

The following events quickly occurred in Canada: Some Japanese aliens were taken into custody; others were interviewed and subsequently arrested; language schools were closed; judo instructors, veterans of the Japanese army, and officials of local Japanese associations were placed under surveillance; vernacular Japanese-language newspapers were closed; and all aliens were required to register.

Then followed the impounding of more than a thousand vessels. Rumors persisted that the fishermen were really Japanese naval officers in disguise, had detailed maps of all inlets and waterways, shortwave radios, and so on. Subsequent Royal Canadian Mounted Police investigations revealed that in all cases the fishermen were Canadians and the maps and radios were their standard equipment. As the successes of the Japanese military campaign in Southeast Asia became known and casualties in Canadian army units in Hong Kong and Singapore mounted, pressures increased toward stricter surveillance and internment not only of aliens but *all* persons of Japanese ancestry.

Of the many politicians urging the removal of all Japanese, the most powerful voice was that of Ian Mackenzie, a member of parliament from British Columbia and a cabinet minister. He headed a group of anti-Japanese MPs from British Columbia. They not only represented themselves as the informed experts on the Japanese, but they also worked on William Lyon Mackenzie King, the prime minister. King wanted to establish conscription in Canada but knew that he must overcome the powerful resistance of the French-Canadian Quebec MPs. The prospect of British Columbia supporting the prime minister on conscription was dangled as a negotiating point. When Canada learned of the American decision to uproot all persons of Japanese ancestry, British Columbia politicians moved forcefully to demand that *all* Japanese be removed from Canada's west coast. In the meantime, not only aliens but all persons of the Japanese "race" had to register.

An important factor should be mentioned here. When the European War began in 1939, Canada invoked the War Measures Act—the first time since World War I. The country was run by orders-in-council of the prime minister and the cabinet. Special government actions could be invoked by cabinet decision, not by the Parliament as a whole. For this reason, the friendship of Ian Mackenzie with Prime Minister King became significant as it related to cabinet decisions.[6]

With the fall of Singapore on February 15, 1942, things came to a head. Although the military held that a Japanese invasion of the west coast was remote compared to the logistical advantage of the Japanese military focus in Southeast Asia, the fears of the press and the public became exploitable again.

In the end, the Japanese Canadians became victims of circumstance: the government actions in uprooting them would "confirm" to the public the imminent dangers on the west coast. By February 19, 1942, Ian Mackenzie had persuaded the cabinet to agree to the removal of all male Japanese from the west coast to areas at least 100 miles inland. Five days later, on February 24, the cabinet passed an order-in-council similar in effect to the American order: Order in Council P.C. 1486 empowered the minister of justice to remove and detain "any and all persons" from any designated "protected area" in Canada. While the powers were broad enough to be applied to citizens or aliens, white or nonwhite, individuals or groups, they were to be applied only to persons of Japanese ancestry.[7] The conscription bill was later enacted. The removal of the Japanese from the west coast was clearly not dictated by concerns over national security.

Japanese Canadians were moved to interior British Columbia, to partially abandoned mining towns, lumber camps, and to some special camps where the internees built their huts. Physically, the conditions were worse than in America, but an ameliorating factor was the maintenance of a family center in those situations where the men were not away in road camps. There were no mess halls; the family ate together.

Even before the war there were a few Japanese Canadians who had struggled for their rights. Most of these earlier protests were lonely affairs, without broad support, and they were not very successful.

After the war Japanese Americans could opt for deportation or expatriation. Those approximately five thousand renunciants who elected to go to Japan did so for various reasons, such as disillusionment, anger, keeping the family together, alienation, or the loss of hope in the United States. These people were moved to the Tule Lake camp and, as ships became available, left for Japan in 1946.

The story in Canada was in stark contrast. To get rid of the Japanese was not just a product of wartime hysteria but was part of a fifty-year campaign to make British Columbia safe for English white people. Therefore, the deportation of all Japanese was a continuing, long-term goal. How one could deport Canadian citizens already living in their home country, their country of origin, was a small technicality that did not bother deportation advocates.

Thus, in the fall of 1945, the cabinet issued an order-in-council for the deportation of 10,000 Japanese Canadians, including all persons sixteen years or over, Japanese nationals, "naturalized British subjects of Japanese race," and "natural born British subjects, who have made requests for repatriation or have been in detention in one of the holding camps." It also allowed for children under sixteen and wives to accompany the repatriate. In the chauvinist fashion of that era, only the men were asked to declare. It was clearly evident that this "option" for repatriation was to be administered in a no-nonsense style, virtually a forced deportation.[8]

Earlier, when the Japanese had begun to arrive in Toronto from the ghost towns and camps, a citizens group had been organized to assist with the settlement, especially of the single young women. As settlement moved along successfully, the Cooperative Committee for Japanese Canadians (CCJC), with Nisei advisors, began to express concern over government actions that were coercive and smelled of injustice. The CCJC distributed 75,000 copies of a pamphlet entitled "From Citizens to Refugees—It's Happening Here." Another group, the Vancouver Consultative Council, published and circulated a leaflet: "Orders-in-Council Threaten Your Citizenship." An Issei-Nisei group, the Citizenship Defense Commission, met in Toronto to raise funds to fight the forced deportation.

In December 1945, after four years of restricted and uprooted living, some Japanese celebrated a peacetime Christmas but found they had to fight for their lives again—"But at least they had friends this time around."[9] Other groups of Nikkei began to organize: a Civil Rights Defense Committee in Winnipeg, a Joint Committee of Southern Alberta, and citizens' groups from the Tashme and Slocan camps. These joined forces with CCJC and other groups. Their lawyer, Andrew Brewin, issued writs in the names of two Nikkei on December 27 against the attorney general to test the legality of the deportation orders. On their behalf, "the CCJC claimed that the deportation orders were invalid, illegal and beyond the powers of the Cabinet and, further, that the repatriation forms which they had signed in August of that year were illegal, invalid and of no effect because the Cabinet was not authorized by the War Measures Act or by any other valid statute or law to take such an action."[10]

Meanwhile, the protest movement against "repatriation" reached a summit at a packed meeting in a Toronto college. A senator stated: "I do not advocate a witch hunt among German or Italian Canadians, but I ask why are the Japanese singled out since the highest authority assures us no act of sabotage has been uncovered? Non-cooperation with the government is being used as grounds for deportation. . . ." He concluded, "May I ask when non-cooperation with government became a ground for deportation?"

A rabbi had the final word: "I am here on behalf of six million Jews who were slaughtered . . . for no reason other than being Jews. . . . The ghost of Hitler still walks in Canada. The thing for which Hitler stood has been inscribed on the order-in-council which punishes little children for crimes they couldn't commit."[11]

The Canadian supreme court justices were badly divided. Deportation of the aliens and naturalized Japanese Canadians was unanimously declared legal; however, they split five to two in favor of deporting some Nisei, and four to two against deporting the unwilling dependents of the male deportees. The judicial division greatly embarrassed the government. And with the fading influence of Ian Mackenzie and the rising protest of the Canadian public in support of the Japanese, cabinet members indicated that if a little of the pro-Japanese clamor had been raised earlier, they could have forced Mackenzie down.

An immediate change of policy did not happen. Nearly a fifth of the Japanese Canadian population, almost 4,000 persons, did leave before King stopped the program in January 1947. And only on April 1, 1949 were Japanese Canadians permitted to return to coastal British Columbia.

The management of a wartime crisis shows that human rights and citizens' rights can easily be abrogated, especially in a climate of hysteria. In this climate, pro-Japanese sentiment remained quiet. Because of the low level of support for the Japanese during the dark days after Pearl Harbor, a number of unpleasant events occurred, violating Canada's traditional style of justice. However, when citizens raised concern about these injustices and the more vocal and active Japanese Canadians began to take stands, they made a considerable impact on governmental policies and actions.

NOTES

1. Among other sources for Japanese Americans, see Michi Weglyn, *Years of Infamy: The Untold Story of America's Concentration Camps* (New York: William Morrow, 1976); Roger Daniels, *The Decision to Relocate the Japanese Americans* (New York: Lippincott, 1975) and *Concentration Camps, USA* (New York: Holt, Rinehart and Winston, 1971); Bill Hosokawa, *Nisei: The Quiet Americans* (New York: William Morrow, 1969); Bill Hosokawa and Robert Wilson, *East to America* (New York: William Morrow, 1980); and Ann R. Fisher, *Exile of a Race* (Seattle: F & T Publishers, 1965). For Japanese Canadians, Ken Adachi, *The Enemy That Never Was: A History of the Japanese Canadians* (Toronto: McClelland & Stewart, 1976); Ann Gomer Sunahara, *The Politics of Racism* (Toronto: Lorimer, 1981); Barry Broadfoot, *Years of Sorrow, Years of Shame* (Toronto: Doubleday, 1977).

2. *A Dream of Riches* (Vancouver: The Japanese Canadian Centennial Project, 1978).

3. Adachi, 41.

4. Ibid., 52.

5. Sunahara, 27.

6. Ibid., 41. Ian Mackenzie by this time was also chair of the newly created cabinet committee on Japanese questions, a three-member group set up to advise the cabinet on Japanese Canadian policy.

7. Ibid., 47.

8. Adachi, 291, 309–15.

9. Ibid., 310.

10. Ibid., 311.

11. *Toronto Star*, January 21, 1946.

The Latin-American Japanese and World War II

C. Harvey Gardiner

During World War II the United States was a co-conspirator and participant in a program that seized, shipped, and interned 2,264 Latin-American Japanese, against none of whom was a charge of espionage, sabotage, or subversion ever leveled. Residents of twelve Latin-American countries, they experienced the violation of their civil and legal rights, both by their country of residence and by various branches of the American government.[1]

The ignorance, prejudice, hate, fear, and disregard for legal norms that accompanied American abuse of Japanese Americans reached out to include Japanese Latin Americans living on the Pacific side, from Mexico to Chile. Brazil, with more Japanese than all the rest of Latin America, was not involved by virtue of its facing the Atlantic. The same was true of Argentina. One country, Peru, was home to approximately 75 percent of the people of Japanese ancestry on the Pacific side of Latin America; however, even though Peru, a primary focus of U.S. policy, deserves our major attention, the program did not originate there, nor did it begin with the United States. In fact, it did not even begin with World War II.

The tiny country of Panama played a precedent-making role regarding enemy aliens that influenced the internment-repatriation program of the entire hemisphere. On October 17–18, 1941, the American ambassador and the Panamanian foreign minister discussed the internment of the Japanese in the event of war. After reviewing the record of U.S.-Panamanian cooperation during World War I, they concluded that Panama would arrest the ethnic Japanese on Panamanian soil and intern them on Taboga Island, nine miles off the Pacific end of the canal. The United States would bear all expenses and assume full responsibility should any claims arise. The two governments never reduced these arrangements to a written document.

For months Panamanian authorities, aided by American officials—especially FBI agents—had been refining their lists of potentially subversive aliens. On December 7, 1941, in a matter of hours, they took those Axis aliens into custody. An analysis of Japanese apprehended indicates that 94 percent were arrested that very day; 71 percent in the city of Panama, 23 percent in Colon.

Ambassador Edwin C. Wilson urged the immediate construction in Panama of an internment camp. Particularly pleasing to Washington was the speed with which Panama had arrested and interned its Axis aliens, declared war against the Axis states, and frozen Axis funds. Soon, however, the internment issue provoked a different approach. After enumerating the problems attendant upon the construction, maintenance, and operation of an internment camp, American authorities suggested that the enemy aliens be sent to the United States "as was done during the last war." Panama agreed.[2]

So it came about that, before Christmas 1941, the progressive steps whereby enemy aliens were apprehended, interned, and shipped from Panama to the United States reflected close adherence to, if not conscious duplication of the experience of 1917–1918, when Germans first went to Taboga Island and then were shipped north. In both instances, the specter of lax Panamanian control of internees sped the process. The U.S.-Panamanian precedent bred the program of 1941–1942 and it, in turn, established the American approach to the control of presumably dangerous aliens from the rest of Latin America where, also, no agreements were reduced to writing.

On December 9—less than forty-eight hours after the bombing at Pearl Harbor—American efforts aimed at economic strangulation through a government-sponsored boycott that listed 159 Japanese businesses in Peru. This blacklist was euphemistically termed "The Proclaimed List of Certain Blocked Nationals." Probably that fuzzy avoidance of truth was conceived by some of the same minds that avoided the term "concentration camps" when they referred to the handling of Japanese Americans.

After the January 1942 meeting in Rio de Janeiro of Western Hemisphere foreign ministers, numerous Latin-American governments broke diplomatic ties with Japan and prepared to repatriate their enemy aliens, diplomatic and consular personnel, and private citizens, via the United States. In April 1942 they arrived in the United States from Panama, Costa Rica, Colombia, Ecuador, Peru, and Bolivia. The initial ousting and repatriating of Japanese who were not formal representatives of Japan along with the diplomats opened the door to continuing these practices.

Basic responsibility for deportation and internment programs rested with the chief executives of the various countries. "When the security of the state requires it," Article 70 of the Peruvian Constitution read, "the Executive can suspend totally or partially . . . the guarantees set down in Articles 56, 61, 62, 67 and 68." That meant that Peruvian homes could be invaded and individuals detained without written authorization, that people could neither congregate nor move about freely, and finally, that they could be removed from the country without legal recourse. Other Latin-American constitutions and laws were similar.

At the same time, in the United States the Alien Enemy Act of 1798 permitted the summary apprehension and internment of nationals of states at war with the United States. However, to apply this 143-year-old law to Latin-American Japanese, someone would have to seize those enemy aliens and bring them within range of American legal authority. That, in turn, called for U.S.-Latin American cooperation at the executive level.

Between April 1942 and April 1945 approximately 1,800 Peruvian Japanese were interned in the United States. They represented 80 percent of all the Latin-American Japanese interned here. The deportation-internment program involving the Latin-American Japanese was totally unrelated to the relocation-internment program of the War Relocation Authority. The Immigration and Naturalization Service held the people from Latin America in Texas, at Kenedy in a one-time CCC camp; at Seagoville in a federal reformatory for women; and at Crystal City in a migrant labor camp.

As soon as the first shipment of enemy aliens arrived from Panama, the question of keeping the internee families together quickly entered U.S.-Peruvian relations. When the State Department and the Peruvian Foreign Office agreed that family unity should be preserved, one was left to wonder how much of the decision stemmed from elementary humanitarianism and how much reflected the expedient control of even larger numbers of aliens. After all, the U.S. ambassador in Lima, R. Henry Norweb, had declared, "We may be able to assist the Peruvian Government by making available information and suggestions based upon our handling of Japanese residents of the United States."[3]

The embassy staff in Lima included John K. Emmerson, probably the only person with a command of Japanese at any American diplomatic mission in all Latin America. Thirty-five years later he would declare, "During my period of service in the embassy we found no reliable evidence of planned or contemplated acts of sabotage, subversion, or espionage."[4] Nonetheless, Japanese assets were frozen and successive issues of the American blacklist targeted more businesses. Fears multiplied as the Japanese witnessed the increasing alignment of Peru with American wartime aims. As the press mounted attacks on the Japanese, the Peruvian police fashioned lists of prospective deportees that encouraged the solicitation and acceptance of bribes in return for the opportunity to escape deportation temporarily.

In early 1942, in both Latin America and the United States, more uncertainty and tension beset those of Japanese ancestry. Then the American government corralled them in the horse barns of Santa Anita and other assembly centers en route to desolate relocation centers. In the same period, those in Peru scheduled for internment, they knew not where, were fretting in the jails of Lima and other cities.

In the Lima embassy, Emmerson concluded that the Japanese posed a very serious problem. He considered the colony in Peru, led by a relatively small number of powerful individuals, to be dangerous, thoroughly organized, and intensely patriotic. To defuse the potential danger associated with the colony, he recommended that "Japanese leaders believed to be dangerous should be expelled from Peru. These include," Emmerson declared, "officers of Japanese associations, businessmen who have been active in the Japanese colony, journalists, directors of educational and propaganda organizations, and teachers in Japanese schools."[5] The State Department quickly established these recommendations as the cornerstone of the ensuing deportation program.

Pivotal in this statement of criteria for expulsion were the words "believed to be dangerous." Many individuals named by Peruvian authorities could well be the objects of economic envy, cultural detestation, irrational and emotional outbursts, and whimsical dislike. To Peruvians, the Japanese constituted social and economic, not military, dangers, and the designation of "dangerous" men by Peru largely ignored American concerns about the conduct of a war. Inasmuch as Emmerson's expulsion criteria required no proof that a person was dangerous, American authorities were willing to ally themselves with Peruvians in a program that honored blind prejudice and emotion, ignoring legal rights and formalities. It was happening that way with the Japanese Americans in the United States, so why not in Peru?

By mid-June 1942, three ships had transported Japanese from west coast South American countries to the United States. One vessel, the *Etolin*, docked at San Francisco; the other two, the *Acadia* and the *Shawnee*, transited the canal and docked at New Orleans. Among the passengers on the three ships were more than 500 Peruvian Japanese, all of whom were sent to the Texas camps. Preceding them was a ship bearing Panamanian and Central-American Japanese.

A multifaceted sequence had promoted the inclusion and movement of many nonofficial Japanese from Latin America to the United States. Along with the widening scope of the war and the insistent desire of both Japan and the United States that their officials be exchanged, there were such factors as the desire of loyal Japanese to return to Japan, the U.S. desire to retrieve the many American civilians in Japanese hands, the desire of Latin American governments to rid themselves of unwanted aliens, as well as the American fear that the Latin-American governments would not be able to control prospective saboteurs. One thing had led to another and, as a capstone to all else, the large size of the ships used suggested the inclusion of other Japanese in addition to the diplomatic officials in the exchange program.

By mid-1942, battlefield casualties did not constitute the only body count. For the Japanese-held Americans who were eligible to be sent to the United States, an equal number of Japanese had to be sent to Japan. When the United States put men, women, and children from Costa Rica and Panama and numerous men from Peru aboard the exchange vessel *Gripsholm*, those Latin-American Japanese represented pawns in a human traffic Washington hoped to continue. Before the completion of the first exchange, American officials had compiled lists for future exchanges, believing they would quickly follow.

In that frame of mind, it was easy for the Washington authorities to accept the line of thought propounded by Ambassador Norweb in Lima: "the removal . . . to the United States of all persons in Peru of the Japanese race."[6] Backing him were the conclusions of his staff—Emmerson, the commercial attache, the legal attache, and the military and naval attaches. All had produced copious files on the Japanese individually and collectively. Norweb's proposal to remove everybody of Japanese ancestry from Peru involved no fewer than 25,000 people.

In August 1942, Secretary of State Cordell Hull expanded the wartime role of his department. Calculating that there were 3,300 American citizens in China alone who desired to return to the U.S., he told President Roosevelt, "In exchange for them we will have to send out Japanese in the same quantity." To do so, he urged the continuance of "our exchange agreement with the Japanese" and "our efforts to remove *all* the Japanese from these American Republic countries for internment in the United States."[7]

When fifteen months elapsed between the first and second repatriation voyages of the *Gripsholm*, official American disappointment set in. And when that second shipload left the United States in September 1943, Latin-American Japanese represented 55 percent of the passenger list.

In the meantime, four more shiploads of Axis aliens, including 500 Peruvian Japanese, had landed in the United States. The helplessness of those men, and indeed of all the Latin-American Japanese, became immediately apparent the moment they set foot on American soil. In lines they moved slowly toward the tables, behind which sat Immigration and Naturalization Service officials. As a man reached the front of the line, he heard the question, "Do you have a passport?" Inasmuch as all passports and other identifying documents had been confiscated en route to this country and never returned, each man responded, with varying degrees of concealed bitterness, "No." Lacking the precious document, each heard an official declare, "You must recognize the fact that your entry into the United States is illegal."

It was a weird world in which the kidnapper was telling the kidnapped that the wrong was of his doing. From the beginning the U.S. government had considered such individuals as pawns. Upon reaching the United States, the Latin-American Japanese realized that this was indeed so.

The second voyage of the *Gripsholm* proved to be the last wartime exchange with Japan, and as more and more Axis aliens came north from Latin America the United States, instead of serving as a way station in a repatriation program, increasingly became an internee depository. The operation of internment centers, for which the State Department had neither the experience nor the facilities and the Immigration and Naturalization Service had but limited experience, spawned bureaucratic bungling on all fronts.

One example will illustrate the problem. During his first two weeks in Texas, Taiichi Onishi, a thirty-seven-year-old Lima merchant, attempted suicide four times. The Immigration and Naturalization Service, holding the State Department responsible for his presence in the United States, tried to relieve itself of the troubled internee. But the State Department, lacking the needed facility, suggested that the War Department, experienced in handling insane soldiers, surely had the needed capability. This buck-passing continued until finally a Texas state hospital admitted the ailing man.

Of the pattern of life ten shiploads of people experienced in the Texas camps from 1942 to 1946—indeed, well beyond the end of the war—little need be said. It essentially resembled the experience of the Japanese Americans in the WRA centers. It should be recognized, however, that the Latin-American Japanese had an even more bewildering experience because their countries were not fighting Japan; they were interned in a foreign land whose language and laws were strange to all of them; and their camps, never publicized, drew neither public scrutiny nor the attention of humanitarian agencies. As elsewhere, a general listlessness born of boredom undermined staid and sober people, rendering them frivolous. Life behind barbed wire and watchtowers reduced otherwise dignified individuals to scandal mongering that fueled hates and jealousies. Hypochondria set in. Family ties weakened and parental discipline broke down. The camps bred rivalries that even produced confrontations between social gangs. But at the same time, the docile side of their Japanese nature readily prompted their coming to terms with their jailers.

Between November 1945 and June 1946, approximately 750 Peruvian Japanese were shipped to Japan, the country of their choice once they learned that Peru would not readmit them and the United States did not want them. Approximately 100 gained reentry into Peru, thanks to special circumstances such as marriage to a Peruvian woman or Peruvian citizenship. However, hundreds of Peruvian Japanese, denied reentry by Peru and refusing to go to Japan, lived in limbo. In August 1946, they were paroled to Seabrook, New Jersey. An amendment to the Immigration Act of 1917 gave them some hope, as did the stubborn aid of American Civil Liberties Union attorney Wayne Collins and others. In June 1952, Public Law 414 made them, some of whom had virtually been stateless for a decade, eligible for U.S. citizenship. They and their children remain in this country.

Unlike the story of the deported and interned Latin-American Japanese, no full account of the wartime experiences of the Japanese that remained in Latin America will emerge. Unknown is the precise number of men whose pocketbooks and influential contacts enabled them to escape deportation. Unknown is the total amount of money paid as bribes. Unknown is the complete record of property transfers, confiscations, and other maneuvers by which the Japanese were victimized. On every count, officially and unofficially, the Latin-American countries prefer to forget—even more, to ignore—a chapter that lends no distinction to their history.

In conclusion, anyone who thoughtfully reflects upon certain events of the 1940s will conclude that they were unnecessary militarily, inept politically, and inhumane socially. But there is to be no consolation derived from the fact that they are part of the dead past in which the Alien Act of 1798, President Roosevelt's Executive Order 9066, General DeWitt's orders on our West Coast, and the program of American ambassadors in Latin America fostered gross abuse of elementary human rights.

Why not? Because "the uncertain future that precipitates other tense and fear-laden moments may unfortunately find American law, an American president, the American military, and American diplomats equally able and willing to violate the human rights of innocent men, women and children."[8]

BIBLIOGRAPHICAL NOTE

The primary source for this paper has been the writer's *Pawns in a Triangle of Hate: The Peruvian Japanese and the United States* (Seattle: University of Washington Press, 1981), a volume based upon research in Department of State diplomatic files, correspondence, and memoranda; interdepartmental correspondence of the departments of State, Justice, War, and Navy; FBI reports, many of which had to be declassified; Immigration and Naturalization Service records; passenger lists; internment camp records; court proceedings; files of attorneys and philanthropic organizations; and personal recollections of former internees and officials. The research required wide travel in the United States, Peru, and Japan.

Also related to the present theme are Gardiner's other publications: *The Japanese and Peru, 1873–1973* (Albuquerque: University of New Mexico Press, 1975); "Gaikokujin kara mita nihonjin no iju (The Foreign Perception of the International Emigration of the Japanese People)," in *Kaigai iju no igi wo motomete (Seeking the Meaning of Overseas Emigration)* (Tokyo: Japanese Foreign Office, 1979), 294–311; and "The Panamanian Japanese and World War II," *Iberoamericana* 4 (January 1982): 25–41.

NOTES

1. C. Harvey Gardiner, "The Panamanian Japanese and World War II," *Iberoamericana* 4 (January 1982): 37.

2. Ibid., 32.

3. C. Harvey Gardiner, *Pawns in a Triangle of Hate: The Peruvian Japanese and the United States* (Seattle: University of Washington Press, 1981), 13.

4. Ibid., 22.

5. Ibid., 40.

6. Ibid., 54.

7. Ibid., 56.

8. Ibid., 176.

PART VI

Effects of Incarceration Analyzed

As is the case with any significant historical event, the effects of the relocation and incarceration of the Japanese American people are ongoing: both the larger society and the ethnic community continue to react and reverberate to the events that began over four decades ago. On April 27, 1985, for example, the camp at Manzanar was designated a National Historic Landmark by the National Park Service; California had made it a state landmark thirteen years before. Speaking for the National Park Service, its associate director noted that Manzanar was

> representative of the atmosphere of racial prejudice, mistrust, and fear, that resulted in American citizens being uprooted from their homes, denied their constitutional rights, and with neither accusation, indictment, nor conviction, moved to remote relocation camps for most of the duration of the war. Manzanar is symbolic of a tragic event in American history, an event that reminds us that a democratic nation must constantly guard and honor the concept of freedom and the rights of its citizens.[1]

This was, of course, merely the most recent in a long series of official "regrets."

The essays in this section are concerned with a different set of effects, effects that are much more difficult to analyze. Their authors seek to delineate some of the long-term impact that the whole complex of events that we call the relocation has had on the Japanese American people, including persons not yet born when it took place. Such a reckoning is bound to be controversial and inconclusive. There are writers, of whom former Senator S. I. Hayakawa and economist Thomas Sowell are the most well known, who argue that, somehow, the relocation was "good" for the Japanese American people. One analyst has contended, for example, that "most [Japanese American] families were not weakened but strengthened by the indignities they suffered."[2] Such fatuous views are not held by any of the authors represented here.

In 1982 and 1983 the Commission on Wartime Relocation and Internment of Civilians made two independent attempts to arrive at an assessment of impact. It first convoked a group of social scientists and one historian led by Professor S. Frank Miyamoto to consider the psychic impact. All agreed that it was severe and largely negative: none was able to suggest any easy method of measurement, although it was generally agreed that a large-scale comparative epidemiological study of the survivors and their families might well have great value. The CWRIC also hired a consulting firm to estimate the economic effects of what it called "exclusion and detention." The result was a long and "iffy" guesstimate whose parameters were so broad that they almost certainly encompassed the "truth." The consultants assumed three kinds of economic loss: income loss, real and personal property loss, and human capital loss. It estimated losses in only the first two categories. Its findings are best expressed in the following table:[3]

	Income Losses	Property Losses	Total
Loss in 1945 dollars	$136 million	$67 million to $116 million	$203 million to $251 million
Losses in 1983 dollars			
Inflation adjustment only	$738 million	$365 million to $628 million	$1.1 billion to $1.4 billion
Corporate bond rate adjustment	$1.1 billion	$553 million to $952 million	$1.7 billion to $2.1 billion
3% interest plus inflation	$2.3 billion	$1.1 billion to $1.9 billion	$3.4 billion to $4.2 billion

Our authors' attempts are much more modest and realistic. Harry Kitano uses that unique blend of scholarship and personal experience that has been the hallmark of so much of his work. In this essay he very suggestively tries to relate the Japanese American experience before, during, and after the incarceration to various models of behavioral relationships between what Albert Memmi called the colonizers and the colonized. Amy Mass uses evidence from her own clinical practice among contemporary Japanese Americans and her observations of the CWRIC hearings to arrive at an assessment of psychological effects. Sandra Taylor's treatment of economic loss asks rather than answers questions. Her earlier investigation of the wartime role of the Federal Reserve Bank of San Francisco has demolished one of the minor myths of the evacuation: the oft-cited $400-million property loss. Here she outlines the kinds of research that would have to be done before one could arrive at a reasonable estimate of property losses. A portion of that kind of work has been done by Gary Okihiro and David Drummond. It is not necessary to agree with one of their major premises—that "economic gain" was "the principal aim of exclusionism"—to recognize that they have taken a careful and valuable beginning step toward answering the economic questions raised by Taylor. In the final essay in this section, Howard Ball, using the private papers of the justices, examines in detail the inner workings of the Supreme Court in adjudicating the Japanese American cases of 1943–44. An authority on Justice Hugo Black, about whom he has published an admiring book, Ball judges the Alabaman and his liberal colleague, William O. Douglas, particularly culpable in helping to craft decisions that Eugene V. Rostow correctly labelled "a disaster" forty years ago.

Taken as a group, these essays pose the basic questions—or most of them—about the effects of the wartime experience. Just asking them is another way of trying to come to grips with the enormity of what was done. While it is true, as Morton Grodzins suggests, that the whole incarceration process betrayed "all Americans," it was and is Japanese Americans who have borne the burdens of that betrayal.

Roger Daniels

Harry Kitano and Minoru Yasui at Topaz, March 1983. Courtesy Sandra C. Taylor.

Participants in Conference on Relocation and Redress arriving at Topaz in March 1983. Sandra Taylor and Roger Daniels at center of photo. Courtesy Sandra C. Taylor.

NOTES

1. "Remarks by Jerry L. Rogers, Associate Director, National Park Service at Manzanar National Historic Landmark Designation Ceremony, April 27, 1985, Lone Pine, California." I am indebted to Edwin C. Bearss, chief historian, National Park Service, for this and other information.

2. Edith Blicksilver, "The Japanese-American Woman, the Second World War, and the Relocation Camp Experience," *Women's Studies International Forum* 5 (1982): 351–53.

3. Frank S. Arnold, Michael C. Barth, and Gilah Langer, *Economic Losses of Ethnic Japanese as a Result of Exclusion and Detention, 1942–1946* (Washington, D.C.: ICF Incorporated, June 1983), 5.

The Effects of the Evacuation
on the
Japanese Americans

Harry H. L. Kitano

What were the effects of the evacuation on the Japanese American evacuees? The question is often asked, but is very difficult to answer. The problem of measuring the results of an event that occurred over forty years ago is complicated by intervening years, a lack of relevant material, a complexity of the many interacting variables that affect behavior, the vagaries of memory, and the near impossibility of reconstructing an event not designed for evaluative purposes.

If a "mad" social scientist had been in charge of the evacuation, he might have designed the program differently. He would have administered a battery of tests as a baseline measure, randomly assigned the evacuees to different centers as a part of the "treatment" design; he would have randomly assigned another sample to a normal life without any evacuation (the control group) and then measured the effects of the incarceration on a variety of "after" measures, which might include some testing—even up to the present time. There could have been a variety of "treatments" in each of the camps so that intact families and communities could be a part of one experimental treatment as opposed to separated families and disorganized communities in another. Under such procedures, research-based answers on the effects of the incarceration might have been forthcoming.

Fortunately, mad social scientists were not in charge of the camps, although the behavior of some politicians and appointed officials and their successful attempts to manipulate the legal system cannot be cited as one of the more glorious or saner periods in America's treatment of its minorities.

It is probably impossible to answer the question, if the task is to measure precisely its effects on the present-day population. The best answers would no doubt include a broad generalization such as "some were affected and others were not"; more precise answers would be time related, such as, "it changed the course of my life at that time," while other responses would include personal recollections of friendships, hardships, and unusual events. Therefore, although we acknowledge that there are developmental, longitudinal sequences in all human behavior and that there are no doubt threads of current attitudes and behaviors which can be traced back to the evacuation (as well as to other previous events), there is great difficulty in precisely identifying the variables. The "prior events—longitudinal model" may not be the most relevant for evaluating the effects of an event that happened so long ago.

However, there is information about Japanese Americans in the camps that allows their behavior under concentration camp conditions to be compared to their behavior under other conditions. A model based on contrasting environments may be a relevant one for evaluating the evacuation era; in research terms we can evaluate the effects of different "treatments" by comparing behavior under different models of governance. The evacuation, of course, provided the clearest example of a special treatment, since virtually the entire population was subjected to similar conditions; other eras were less rigid in controlling and restricting Japanese American behavior so that the contrasting conditions other than the evacuation may be less precise.

MODEL OF GOVERNANCE

We label this approach the model of governance, that is, the more powerful dominant society sets the parameters of ethnic group life through its ability to erect boundaries and to control the interaction between the groups (Table 1).

Our model selects four different time periods: 1920–1941, 1942–1945, 1946–1959, and 1960–1980, as indicative of different types of governance between the dominant group and the dominated group. The perspective emphasizes the power relationships between the Japanese and the majority group as well as the strength of the family and the community and of the adaptations of Japanese Americans under different types of governance. The independent variable is dominant group governance; the intervening variables are power and the Japanese family and community; and the dependent variable, Japanese American adaptation.

Table I

Years	1920–1941	1942–1945	1946–1959	1960–1980
Model of Governance	Domination	Domestic Colonialism	Transition Period	Liberal Pluralism
Intervening variables	Relative power of the ethnic community; role of the ethnic family and community			
Adaptation	Japanese American Attitudes, Expectations, and Behavior			

The model hypothesizes different attitudes, expectations, and behavior under each of the different models of governance. Governance also affects the relative power of the ethnic community and family. In general, the power of the ethnic community and family to shape and control behavior is hypothesized to be the strongest under dominance and the weakest under liberal pluralism.

The basic assumption of the model is that the type of governance shapes and controls the behavior of the minority group. The more pervasive and powerful the restrictions the dominant group places on the minority group, the clearer its effect on minority group attitudes, expectations, and behavior. The ethnic community and family must translate the realities of life in America to its members and socialize them with appropriate norms, values, and cultural wisdom. The most obvious example of the power of the dominant group to enforce its will on the minority was the wartime evacuation when the government virtually controlled the lives of the Japanese Americans.

The model of governance emphasizes the interaction between the majority and minority communities in shaping behavior. The more powerful dominant group sets the parameters and boundaries; the less powerful minority group attempts to adapt to the "realities."

PERIOD I: DOMINATION (1920–1942)

The domination model is shown in Table 2. The stratification reflects "Anglo" dominance and Japanese Americans as the dominated. The two categories are based on a scheme by Max Weber, who differentiated between those who rule and those who are ruled.[1] Status groups tend to draw lines around themselves to restrict interaction, so that social systems are characterized by rankings and hierarchies based on class, status, and power. In this case, the Japanese were placed at the bottom with the white society on top.

Table 2

Model I

DOMINATION

		Act	Mechanism	Effect
Dominant Groups	1.	Prejudice	Stereotypes	Avoidance
	2.	Discrimination	Laws, norms	Disadvantage
Japanese Americans	3.	Segregation	Laws, norms	Isolation

The maintenance of the boundaries between the groups includes such actions as prejudice, discrimination, and segregation, reinforced by stereotypes and laws. There is ample evidence of the boundary maintenance mechanisms keeping the Japanese in the lower half of the stratification system. Laws were passed restricting almost every phase of Japanese American life; citizenship, land ownership, interracial marriage, licensing, housing, and immigration were among the targets. There were restrictions in employment and in the use of public accommodations and facilities, so that the Japanese American was avoided, disadvantaged, and isolated from the dominant group. The position of Japanese Americans could best be ascertained by asking a number of rhetorical questions: Who lives in the better homes in the better neighborhoods? Who has the more desirable and higher paying jobs? Who has access to the political system? Who has the resources and wealth? Who holds the power?

More severe actions against the dominated group can occur during crisis situations. The perception that a minority group is a threat to the system, whether real or imagined, can lead to concentration camps, expulsion, or extermination.

ADAPTATION TO DOMINANCE

One of the effects of the interaction between the majority group and the minority group during this period was that the Japanese Americans were considered a "problem minority." The Carnegie Corporation commissioned a special study in 1929, directed by Edward A. Strong, who fittingly titled his findings *The Second Generation Japanese Problem*.[2] The study evaluated the Japanese Americans and their character, including their honesty and trustworthiness, as well as studying their criminality and delinquency, and their performance on various achievement, psychological, and I.Q. tests.

Interviews from Strong's study illustrated the feelings of many Nisei of this period. A college-educated Nisei reported:

> Our community is not self-sufficient. We can't stand off and live our own lives. We've got to find a place in the American society to survive. And yet, no matter what our qualifications may be, evidently the only place where we are wanted is in positions that no American would care to fill—menial positions as house-servants, gardeners, vegetable peddlers, continually "yes, ma'ming."[3]

Another Nisei wrote: "So many of my friends are giving up the fight. Why get an education . . . why try to do anything at all? . . . we are meant to be just a servile class. We can't help it, so let's make the best of a bad bargain."[4]

Strong recognized that a "new, shiftless, pleasure-seeking, second-generation element" was appearing in the heretofore industrious, thrifty Japanese community. He notes that some "nicer" individuals had turned to the church and to religion to gain some comfort and relief from their economic and social misery.

> They hold a cheaply optimistic, goody-goody idea that if they stay in their place, work hard, and please the Americans and remain happy in the position where God has placed them, surely the Christian Americans, out of the generosity of their hearts, will throw out to them a few more crumbs to ease their condition."[5]

Most Issei felt they could never achieve equality in America—many of them returned to Japan, while others placed their hopes and expectations on their Nisei children. But it is interesting to note that many Nisei also felt they were a sacrificial generation. An editorial in the *Japanese American Courier*, quoted by Strong, shows that some Nisei felt they were pioneers and would have to sacrifice themselves for a better future for the next Sansei generation: "The second generation is filled into a sacrificial position, as pioneers to blaze the trail into American life to effect the proper recognition of themselves as genuine American citizens, to help the proper and easier amalgamation of the third generation into American life."[6]

A Nisei reported becoming aware of racial difference when his high school teacher discouraged him from applying in fields that his Caucasian friends were entering:

> Then the teacher told me outright in a very nice way that there was not much of a chance for an Oriental to get a job in these fields. . . . I began to see that they took us a little differently and we were really not quite American in their eyes in spite of the things they taught us in the classes about equality and so forth.[7]

Another Nisei, who graduated from college in 1939, knew that Japanese Americans were not accepted in jobs outside of the Japanese community:

> Many of the Nisei went to work as salesmen in Oriental art goods stores on Grant Avenue (San Francisco), or else they became gardeners or laborers. The Nisei used to joke that their only destination after getting their diploma was to work for cheap wages in a small Japanese store. They did not have the optimism of the usual Caucasian graduates because they knew there was no demand for their services.[8]

A common Nisei adaptation was to lower expectations and to hope that somehow things would get better. But there were also signs of the development of the problems associated with dominated populations. Some were giving up; there were groups of gangs, such as zoot-suiters; there was a developing hedonism (why save for tomorrow?) and a Nisei stratification system based partly on a popular song of the era, "Goody-Goody."

The goody-goodies were those who believed and preached faith in the American system. Others felt that the American dream was a sham, that the Japanese could never be more than second-class citizens, so working hard and going to college would have little effect on their status.

Strong's main conclusion was that the major problem was not with the Japanese Americans but with the barriers set up by the whites in terms of racial discrimination. His prescription was the "lift yourself up by the bootstraps" model. He said, "If they show the same adaptability and success in later life that they have already evidenced in school and in behaving themselves out of school, they will find the attitude toward themselves changing for the better."[9]

Severe disorganization and alienation occurs under the following conditions:

1. Length of time under domination;
2. Severity of prejudice, discrimination, and segregation restricting mobility and enhancing disadvantage;
3. Disorganized families and communities; and
4. Lack of alternatives.

The saving grace for the Japanese lay in the strength of their ethnic community and families. The community offered parallel occupational and social opportunities through ethnic networks so that social control was maintained even during the depression period.

The Japanese family was probably the strongest during this era. Part of the unity came from the need to survive; income from all members was a necessity. Outside hostility drew family and community members closer; the Nisei were young and inexperienced so that the wisdom and advice of the older generation was generally heeded in a fashion that would not be true a generation later.

Although the Nisei were undergoing acculturation, goals such as equality and full participation in the American society were more dreams than reality. Some, seeing little future in America, chose careers in Japan, although the majority maintained hope that somehow conditions would change for the better.

The most damaging consequence of living under inequality is the internalization of second-class citizenship and acceptance of the role prescriptions of the dominant society. Individuals and groups believing in their own inferiority are apt to behave accordingly, even when the external environment changes.

PERIOD II: DOMESTIC COLONIALISM (1942–1945)

The Japanese attack on Pearl Harbor brought changes in governance of the Japanese. It shifted from dominance to domestic colonialism, resembling the apartheid model of South Africa. The transition to a colonial model is not that extreme, since the population has already been socialized into "a less than equal" position, and this may be one reason why the wartime evacuation progressed relatively smoothly. Nevertheless, evacuation meant registration, the assignment of family identification by numbers, barbed-wire enclosures, armed guards, segregation, and the need for governmental clearance in order to leave the camps. Robert Blauner[10] presents several conditions that are a part of the colonial model:

1. There is forced, involuntary entry.
2. There are forceful attempts towards acculturation, in contrast to the more natural processes of intergroup interaction. The colonizing power carries out a policy that constrains and transforms the indigenous values, orientations, and ways of life of the indigenous population.
3. Members of the colonized group are administered and controlled by representatives of the dominant group.
4. There is racism.

The evacuation met each of these conditions. The approximately 110,000 West Coast Japanese were forced into relocation camps; there was an attempt to acculturate and Americanize them rapidly; the administrators and decision makers were whites, representing the federal government; and only "the Japanese race" experienced the evacuation.

Japanese behavior under this model reflected the vast differences in power and the helpless feelings of the trapped residents. Most evacuees resigned themselves to their pariah position but there were also riots, revolts, murders, internal struggles for power, attempts to emulate and to please those in power, frustration, aggression, hedonism, and gambling. Others gave up; there was the casual use and misuse of government property. There was resistance to military service, the turning on each other, and the searching for scapegoats.

Interviews compiled in *The Salvage*[11] and *The Spoilage*[12] provide a flavor of life in a concentration camp. One male youth said, "We swiped everything in sight."[13] He also commented on the number of gang fights and the ambivalence of being an American with a Japanese face.

The helpless feelings can be summed up by reactions to an incident when a guard shot an evacuee. "What can we do. . . . We're only Japs. All we can do is take it."[14] In terms of the many conflicts, one evacuee commented: "There were Issei-Nisei conflicts, conflicts between northeasterners and Californians, JACL vs. non-JACLers, fights between church groups, fights between Nisei cliques."[15]

Several factors limited the development of a "permanent" colonized minority, although it should be noted that the government had some difficulty in closing the camps because some residents, for a variety of reasons, did not want to leave. One anonymous evacuee with limited funds, having been in camp for three years, said: "I've got 6 children . . . wife, my father and mother. To go outside [of camp] you have to have a certain kind of home. . . . [All they say is] America's going to help you. . . . That's not dependable. . . . By staying here, I'll have a roof over my children's heads and enough to eat, although I don't like the food."[16]

Camp behavior was generally similar to the behavior of any group placed under similar conditions, with modifications based on historical circumstances and the culture of the group. Some group and family norms were immediately modified; for example, eating at the mess halls called for lining up outside (the sound of the mess-hall bell was a stimulus for salivating). Growing adolescents gulped down food so that they could go for possible second servings. Peer groups and friends replaced the family unit as eating companions. Block norms and peer group norms often replaced family controls, weakening the family role. Many heads of families resigned themselves to some of the consequences of their loss of control; children applied for clearance to leave camp against parental advice; some defied their parents and volunteered for the U.S. Army. The loyalty questionnaire found family members on different sides of the issue, and the normal means of control—providing food and housing—were taken over by the U.S. government. More functional norms appropriate to living under concentration camp conditions emerged: hoarding of coal, "stealing" government property to erect additional partitions and shelves, currying favor of those closer to influence and power, intimidation, and a more relaxed attitude towards hard work where the pay was from $16 to $19 per month. A particularly destructive behavior was the search for "informers" (called *inu*, or dogs), collaborators, and scapegoats, since such actions often ended in violence and long-lasting hostility. For example, some former evacuees still retain an anti-Japanese American Citizens League posture because of incidents in the camps.

Segregated, colonial conditions provide unusual contrasts for the colonized. On the one hand there was a complete lack of power to determine the broader issues of one's life—one could not leave the premises, one could only move freely in restricted areas. Yet, on a smaller scale, there was the freedom to compete with other inmates for jobs and positions in a manner unavailable in life on the outside under domination. In high school, Nisei became class officers, athletic heroes, and social "ins," positions usually reserved for Caucasians in West Coast schools. Similarly, competitors for camp jobs were other Japanese, minimizing racial discrimination. So Nisei became firemen, policemen, garbagemen, timekeepers, and schoolteachers, positions not a usual part of occupational life in the outside world. These opportunities warded off monotony and gave structure and meaning to camp life. There was time for indulging in hobbies and for developing friendships, many of which have endured to the present day. As a consequence, a still familiar greeting among a group of middle-aged and older Japanese Americans is, "What camp were you in?"

The camps were not completely closed systems. With governmental clearance, individuals could leave; some went to college, many others left for sea-

Harry Kitano practices high school football. From *Ramblings 1944*, the Topaz yearbook. Courtesy of Grace Oshita, Salt Lake City.

sonal or permanent employment, while some chose repatriation to Japan. Generally, the evacuation left family groups and community life intact, though many facets of camp life strained family and community solidarity.

The majority of the camps operated from 1942 to 1945, so that the factor of time was important in limiting any long-lasting effects, although there were undoubtedly individuals who were permanently scarred by the experience.

Dorothy Thomas and Richard Nishimoto, in discussing the events at Tule Lake, where some of the gravest conflicts occurred, concluded:

With mass renunciation of citizenship by Nisei and Kibei, the cycle which began with evacuation was complete. . . . They . . . had been deprived of rights . . . charged with no offense, but (were) victims. . . . They had been at the mercy of administrative agencies . . . had yielded to parental compulsion in order to hold the family intact. They had been intimidated by . . . pressure groups in camp . . . become terrified by reports of the continuing hostility of the American public.[17]

NISEI SOLDIERS

Another example focusing on the relationship between dominant group treatment and the adaptation of a minority was that of the Japanese Americans in the armed forces. The heroism and the valor of all-Nisei fighting units during World War II are beyond question. But Tamotsu Shibutani examined another group of Nisei soldiers who earned the dubious distinction of being one of the worst companies in World War II.[18] Although they were from the same ethnic group and had the potential to be excellent soldiers, discrimination, poor leadership, inept communication, unclear goals, and the failure of their leader to acknowledge Nisei norms led to low morale, excessive drinking, violence, insubordination, sloppiness, and disruptiveness. The significance of governance was clearly demonstrated; potentially constructive behavior was turned into disorganized, alienated units with high rates of deviant behavior.

The broader question when assessing the concentration camp period relates to the removal of individuals, families, or groups from "normal" settings and placing them in "artificial" environments. In this context, the internment camps have much in common with prisons, with civilians drafted into the armed services, and even with children attending summer camps. All involve the acquisition of a new set of norms; of assessing power, enforcement, and social control mechanisms; and of the degree of identification and commitment to the new setting. Variables such as the continuity of the new setting with previous experiences and with life upon release are important, as are the length of the conditions, the forced nature of the commitment, and the number of options.

Finally, there are the strengths of the governed and the wisdom, purpose, and goals of the governors to be included, so that there obviously can be no simple and facile generalizations concerning the effects of this period upon the Japanese Americans.

PERIOD III: THE TRANSITION PERIOD (1945–1959)

The years that followed the closing of the camps to 1959 were transition years, with changes in the dominant group, in its patterns of governance, and in Japanese American adaptation. Many of the discriminatory practices were undergoing change; there was the rise of ethnic awareness and of a sense of identity and a reexamination of the goals of the American society.

For Nisei who had voluntarily left the camps, their new environment was often radically different from both camp life environment and the life they had experienced in California. It was a much more open and friendly society; one Nisei in the Midwest relates, "There wasn't any prejudice at all in the public recreation places and I never heard of a single case of discrimination. . . . Nisei received invitations to private homes and they seemed to respond very well. . . . [They] were eager to get accepted into the community life."[19]

The Nisei responded to these changing circumstances. There was much job mobility: a Nisei in Chicago might change jobs several times in one year if he or she could find higher-paying and more appropriate employment. Such job mobility was atypical of Japanese American life in prewar California.

PERIOD IV: LIBERAL PLURALISM (1960–1980)

The era beginning in the late 1950s and early 1960s provided a vastly different model of governance between the dominant group and the minority. It was a period of less direct control and of the removal of most boundaries restricting Japanese American opportunity. It included the federal government taking an active role in civil rights and addressing racial inequality. There was federal money for education and job training; employment opportunities were enhanced through fair employment legislation and affirmative action programs. A new generation of Japanese Americans who had not experienced life under the domination and colonial periods found jobs appropriate to their training and education. It was the era when terms such as a "model minority" or "successful minority" described what in the 1930s was a "problem minority."

It is interesting to speculate how "successful" the Japanese would be today if they were still adapting to a stratification system based on dominance and colonialism. Conversely, would the Japanese Americans have been a problem minority or a model minority in the 1930s if the model of governance had been based on liberal pluralism?

PRESENTISM AND PASTISM

By presenting the interaction between the dominant group and the Japanese American under three models of governance we are able to clarify a number of issues. For example, many younger Japanese Americans question the cooperative behavior with the governmental authorities of their parents and grandparents during the trying days of World War II. Conversely, many who grew up prior to 1941 find it difficult to understand the relatively carefree behavior of the present-day generation.

The error is that of *presentism* and *pastism*. Michael Banton defines *presentism* as the tendency "to interpret other historical periods in terms of the concepts, values and understanding of the present."[20] Therefore, Japanese Americans growing up in an era of free speech, dissent, confrontation, and legal redress find it difficult to understand behavior from another era where the interaction was based primarily on domination.

Pastism refers to the tendency to interpret the present in terms of the concepts, values, and governance of the past. As opposed to presentism, it sees yesterday's model as the present-day reality. Therefore, individuals who grew up under domination find it difficult to face the changes in the patterns of governance and expect and behave in a fashion more appropriate to a past era. For example, some Nisei find it difficult to talk about the wartime evacuation and to support a call for financial redress, partly because of the fear that taking a stand on "unpopular issues" would be treated in the same manner that they had experienced in the 1930s.

The sequence from domination to apartheid can also help to explain the generally cooperative behavior of the Japanese in responding to evacuation. A population conditioned to domination will act in a much more conforming manner than one raised under a liberal, pluralistic model. It should be added that the family, the community, and the culture of the Japanese Americans will also be involved in any adaptive response.

In summary, it is difficult to answer what the effects of the wartime evacuation were on the Japanese American. Traces of the experience are probably still a part of every person who went through the trauma, but the identification of its effects, in the context of all other experiences, before and after relocation are much too complex for simple generalizations.

But, there is evidence of their behavior in the camps, as well as under contrasting models of governance. Japanese American behavior under the colonial model appears as similar to all groups placed under colonial conditions. A new set of functional norms developed, norms based on the reality of camp life and on the changes upon release from camp conditions. Its relatively short period of time, the opportunity for some to leave the camps, and the ability of the group to maintain a semblance of group and family organization limited the severity of the concentration camp experience.

In closing I would like to quote Brewton Berry and Henry Tischler, who provide numerous examples of dominated groups from all over the world who nevertheless retain their cheerfulness and loyalty. They marvel at the ability of minority groups to adjust to difficult

Harry Kitano at Topaz in 1983. Courtesy Roger Daniels.

situations and comment, "It is an amazing fact . . . that some human beings have an infinite capacity to endure injustice without retaliation, and apparently without resentment against their oppressors."[21]

But the basic message of the evacuation should be aimed at the ruling elements of any system, that it is their models of governance that provide the structure for minority group adaptation. An open system with a minimal amount of discriminatory boundaries appears to be the best model of governance.

NOTES

1. Max Weber, "Class, Status, Party" in *Max Weber, Essays in Sociology,* ed. and trans. by H. H. Gerth and C. Wright Mills (New York: Oxford University Press, 1946).

2. Edward Strong, *The Second Generation Japanese Problem* (Stanford, Calif.: Stanford University Press, 1934).

3. Strong, 2.

4. Ibid., 12.

5. Ibid.

6. Ibid., 13.

7. Dorothy S. Thomas, *The Salvage* (Berkeley and Los Angeles: University of California Press, 1946), 239–40.

8. Thomas, 215.

9. Strong, 253–54.

10. Robert Blauner, *Racial Oppression in America* (New York: Harper and Row, 1972).

11. Thomas.

12. Dorothy S. Thomas and Richard S. Nishimoto, *The Spoilage* (Berkeley and Los Angeles: University of California Press, 1946).

13. Thomas, 276.

14. Thomas and Nishimoto, 361.

15. Thomas, 560.

16. Thomas and Nishimoto, 344.

17. Ibid., 361.

18. Tamotsu Shibutani, *The Derelicts of Company K* (Berkeley and Los Angeles: University of California Press, 1978).

19. Thomas, 261.

20. Michael Banton, *Racial and Ethnic Competition* (Cambridge: Cambridge University Press, 1983).

21. Brewton Berry and Henry L. Tischler, *Race and Ethnic Relations* (Boston: Houghton Mifflin Co., 1978).

Everyone had an identification tag. Japanese Americans at the Oakland railroad terminal. Photo by Dorothea Lange. Courtesy Bernard K. Johnpoll.

Psychological Effects of the Camps on Japanese Americans

Amy Iwasaki Mass

This paper will discuss the psychological effects of the concentration camp experience on Japanese Americans in an effort to explain the profound impact it had on our self-image and then the psychological defense mechanisms that were used to maintain a sense of integrity and worth. My ideas are a synthesis of the observations and insights made from working with Japanese Americans in clinical practice over the past twelve years as a consultant to Asian American clinics and community service organizations, from talking with Japanese Americans who testified at the hearings of the Commission on Wartime Relocation and Internment of Civilians, and more recently from research interviews with Issei, Nisei, and Sansei in Southern California.

The Japanese are a proud people, and their concern for honor is a significant influence in guiding their personal behavior. Our Issei ancestors carried with them a concern that we Japanese Americans behave in a way that would bring honor and esteem to the race. Individual wrongdoing brought shame not just to the individual and his family but to the Japanese community, the Japanese nation, and all Japanese people. Perhaps that is why we had such mixed feelings of guilt and shame, as well as horror and anger, when Japan attacked Pearl Harbor. As Americans, we were angry and horrified that any country would attack America; as Japanese Americans, we were dismayed, guilty, and ashamed because of our Japanese heritage. We had been taught that when one Japanese does wrong, we are all disgraced.

As human beings grow and develop psychologically, our self-concept is determined by how other people who are important to our lives treat us and respond to us. The way our families and friends view us influences how we see ourselves. Another major source that affects our self-concept is how the society we live in views us. When the news media, the government, employers, shopkeepers, and the man-on-the-street treat us with respect, we feel a sense of worth. If, on the other hand, the majority consistently speaks and acts as if there is something wrong with us because of our race, we will eventually succumb to that message and can begin believing we are inferior.

Prior to World War II, the white American majority clearly dominated the Japanese American community. Prejudice against Japanese Americans was an accepted fact of life. Issei were not allowed to own land or to become naturalized citizens, and Nisei graduates from university professional programs were unable to compete in the so-called "free" market of the majority society. College graduates worked in produce markets and as gardeners. Restrictive covenants forced us into ghettos or marginal communities, and a strong color barrier stood against dating or marrying whites.

Under conditions of domination one common psychological response of the dominated group is identification with the aggressor. The emotional anguish of being a victim is handled by an unconscious process in which the victim identifies with the aggressor by taking on the aggressor's ideas, behavior, and points of view. This process limits the victim's anxiety by creating the illusion of no longer being the victim. Nisei educated in the American schools internalized American values and identified with the U.S. government as the strong, good, righteous authority. The myth of the United States as a harmonious melting pot where everyone is equal regardless of race or creed was not questioned. Under the prewar model of dominance Japanese Americans believed the government could do no wrong.

World War II had a tremendous impact on Nisei self-image.[1] We were stunned—along with the rest of the country—with the news of the attack on Pearl Harbor. The ensuing weeks and months became a period of intense fear, confusion, and anxiety for West Coast Japanese. Community leaders, schoolteachers, Buddhist priests, and anyone with any recent affiliations with imperial Japan were taken by FBI agents to internment camps. Children were afraid they might wake up in the morning to find a parent gone. The FBI picked up my best friend's mother, a schoolteacher. Since her father, a Buddhist priest, was traveling in another city, my friend was left without parents, worrying whether her father would be arrested, too.

Attempts to demonstrate loyalty to America were seen in the pictures of Abraham Lincoln and George Washington that appeared on the walls of Japanese American homes. Issei and Nisei wore American-flag pins saying "I am an American" on coat lapels hoping to convince society of their loyalty. Given the pervasive hostile, racist views expressed in the wartime propaganda of newspapers, radio broadcasts, and other media reports, Japanese American attempts to assert a positive American identity were made in vain.

As one Nisei who was fifteen at the time he went to Manzanar stated, "Suddenly, I became an explicit Jap, a beast, a lecherous threat to white womanhood, a person without ethics, totally devious and sneaky, ugly, and hated. . . . It was Jap, Jap, Jap, and it permeated popular radio shows, newspapers, government pronouncements."[2]

President Roosevelt's decision to incarcerate all Japanese Americans on the West Coast during World War II created an identity crisis, for our parents had told many of us to take pride in the strength and beauty of our ethnic heritage. It was extremely difficult to maintain a positive identity during the racial hostility, propaganda, and hysteria of World War II. Our ideals about America were also shattered. We had believed the American dream of freedom in a democratic nation. We had been socialized to believe that by working hard and being good citizens we, too, could realize the American dream.

Executive Order 9066 confirmed our worst fears. The psychological impact of the forced evacuation and detention was deep and devastating. For the honor-conscious Issei, it was the repudiation of many years of effort and hard work in this country. For the Nisei, it was a rejection by the nation we loved, the nation to which we had pledged our allegiance. Even for the very young Sansei, the impact of spending those early years in a concentration camp has been an undeniable aspect of their identities and has affected their self-concepts throughout life. One of my friends was the last baby born at Manzanar Relocation Center. "Where were you born?" is a question people commonly ask of each other. For my friend, the answer is Manzanar.

One of the age groups most vulnerable to the impact of the incarceration were adolescents. Adolescence is a transitional period of development when questions about one's identity are of major concern; for Japanese American adolescents in 1942, the problems were especially painful and difficult.

> Up to then [May 1942] I had felt quite Americanized and accepted. . . . [O]nce in camp and for the three remaining years of that experience of being incarcerated . . . as an "enemy of the United States" my outlook toward Anglo people and their social institutions changed. Perhaps I could describe this period of my adolescence as the "fallen idol" period. No longer was I looking to be a member of the Boy Scouts of America.
>
> Also, by being with all Japanese peers, my attitudes towards education and teachers changed. I no longer wanted to achieve and be first—to stand out. It was better to slide by. Furthermore, the teachers, especially the non-Japanese faculty, no longer could be trusted . . . most adults I soon found [had] "clay feet." Even the adult Japanese were no longer idols. . . . The usual adolescence

period is not so stressful and, if one is in great pain, usually family, friends, or at least one adult can be of assistance. With all of my support systems incarcerated and exposed as vulnerable and "put down" as undesirable, what was left? Furthermore, to confuse and make my process of identity restructuring difficult was the institutionalizing effect of camp itself. Any person institutionalized is affected in many ways. We were looked upon as untrustworthy, disloyal, sneaky, etc., and perhaps most of all, not really someone with an identity—only a number.[3]

The memories of this man's adolescence reflect the confusion, depression, and negative impact of incarceration on his struggle to form a sense of his own identity. They also hint of the "I don't care," "why struggle" attitude typical of colonized people who have no optimism about the future.

For many years, the majority of Japanese Americans accepted the incarceration as an inevitable wartime necessity. Many still minimize the negative aspects of the camp experience and speak of the positive results. We were told we were being put away for our own safety, a patriotic sacrifice necessary for national security. By believing the government propaganda, we felt virtuous that we helped the war effort. By believing the propaganda, we could feel safe in the care of a benevolent, protective Uncle Sam.

The truth was that the government we trusted had betrayed us. Acknowledging such a reality was so difficult that our natural feelings of rage, fear, and helplessness were turned inward and buried. When human beings experience betrayal by a trusted source, it leads to deep depression, a sense of shame, a sense of "there must be something wrong with me." We were ashamed and humiliated; it was too painful to see that the government was not helping us, but was in fact against us. We used psychological defense mechanisms such as repression, denial, rationalization, and identification with the aggressor to defend ourselves against the devastating reality of what was being done to us.

Human beings use defense mechanisms to protect against psychologically painful, unacceptable material and to maintain a sense of integrity and worth. Repression is an unconscious process. In contrast to suppression—where we are consciously aware of something we don't want to think of, and deliberately put it out of our minds—repression is an unconscious, automatic process by which our psyche protects us from being aware of experiences and insights that are too painful or unacceptable. We cannot recall repressed material by sheer willpower or the conscious wish to do so. For example, recently my older sister and I were talking about some of our going to camp experiences. She remembered vividly that the hardest part of leaving home for me was taking my pet to our neighbor's house. She went with me to the neighbors and remembered my reactions. To this day I still cannot recall that specific experience. It was one I repressed because it was indeed too painful to remember.

We adopted rationalization as a psychological defense, and it fit well with the propaganda of the government. Statements such as "camp was good for us," "it saved us from being murdered by hostile whites," and "the government was doing it for our own good" are examples of the use of rationalization as a psychological defense.

Seeing the government as right and ourselves as somehow "not O.K." is the same psychological response that abused children use in viewing their relationships with their abusive parents. Abused children suffer depression and shame. Mental health experts have found that abused children prefer to believe they, themselves, are bad rather than to believe their parents are bad. In this way the child hopes that by acting properly, his parents will love him and treat him well. Like the abused child who still wants his parents to love him and hopes by acting correctly he will be accepted, Japanese Americans chose the cooperative, obedient, quiet American facade to cope with an overly hostile, racist America during World War II. By trying to prove we were 110 percent American, we hoped to be accepted.

Acceptance by submission, however, exacts a high price at the expense of the individual's sense of true self-worth. Though others may see us as model Americans, we have paid a tremendous psychological price for this acceptance. As long as we defend ourselves against our conflicting feelings about our race, our sense of betrayal, our anger and hurt, we cannot come to terms with a sense of our true self-worth.

For the last twenty years, we have been living in a period of liberal pluralism. In the 1960s, the federal government assumed responsibility in the area of civil rights. As Japanese Americans, we found it possible to examine our own history in relation to civil rights. During this period the consciousness-raising activities of groups such as the Manzanar Committee and the political and legal actions of organizations such as the Japanese American Citizens League and National Council for Japanese American Redress have provided channels through which we could express the hurt, anger, and frustration we experienced during World War II. The activities of these groups contributed to the creation of the Commission on Wartime Relocation and Internment of Civilians.

The recent findings of that Commission indicate a

Leaving Topaz. Courtesy of the Bancroft Library.

"grave injustice" was done to Japanese Americans.[4] This finding has the potential for making a significant impact on Japanese Americans struggling to come to terms with their feelings about the camp experience. When abusive parents acknowledge that they have done wrong, it allows children to feel safe and to examine their true feelings about reality. There is a parallel in the psychological dynamics of Japanese Americans who were wronged by the U.S. government during World War II. One way to resolve our feelings is to have the government admit its wrongdoings. When the federal government assumes responsibility for injustice, Japanese Americans can feel safer in examining how they feel. Denial and rationalization are no longer necessary defenses. Japanese Americans can feel an inner sense of honor and integrity that is validated and confirmed by the larger society.

Scientific studies have not been done to measure the psychological effects of the camps on a quantitative level. Full assessment may be difficult as many former evacuees still use the defense mechanism of repression and denial. The pain and trauma of the camp experience is not available to them at a conscious level, and thus they are unaware of any effect it has on their current lives. Time and the intrusion of many other life experiences also make it difficult to isolate the camp experience when assessing current effects.

However, as I listened to the testimonies at the CWRIC hearings in August 1981, I recognized the inescapable fact that everyone who went through the camp experience had suffered. The overall impression of psychological damage is clear to anyone who listens.

Forced detention under any circumstance is stressful to the human psyche. The effects of racism are destructive and cruel. The fact that many Japanese Americans coped with this by utilizing protective defense mechanisms is indicative of the significant psychological impact these experiences posed. A sense of self-worth is vital to mental health. The CWRIC findings provide a significant impetus in this direction for Japanese Americans who suffered the injustices of the concentration camp experience.

NOTES

1. Amy Iwasaki Mass, "Asians as Individuals: the Japanese Community," *Social Casework* 57 (March 1976) 3: 162.

2. William Hohri. Personal communication, February 1983.

3. P. Chikahisa. Testimony before a panel of mental health professionals, Commission on Wartime Relocation and Internment of Civilians, August 6, 1981.

4. Commission on Wartime Relocation and Internment of Civilians, *Personal Justice Denied* (Washington, D.C.: Government Printing Office, 1982), 18.

Evacuation and Economic Loss: Questions and Perspectives

Sandra C. Taylor

The question of how much economic loss the evacuated Japanese Americans sustained as a result of relocation has assumed new importance because of the redress movement. Redress was long assumed to be a closed issue, resolved, if unsatisfactorily, by the Evacuation Claims Act in 1948. Soon after that time the figure $400 million appeared, and until 1983 virtually all writers took that amount as an accurate representation. But as the redress movement gained headway and various plans were advanced in the Japanese community for financial compensation for their losses, the question of exactly how much the victims of relocation had lost became more than academic. It is useful, therefore, to determine how the figure of $400 million was reached, and then look at the component parts of the question of economic loss. We can then consider the recommendations of the Commission on Wartime Relocation and Internment of Civilians (CWRIC) in this broader light.

Even as people of Japanese ancestry were being removed from the West Coast, federal officials knew that some economic loss would occur. The War Relocation Authority, responsible for the camps, admitted as much in its first *Quarterly Report*, issued on June 30, 1942. "In a movement of this kind . . . it was probably inevitable that some mistakes would be made and that some people would suffer." That report then cited Milton Eisenhower, first director of the WRA, who reported to the House of Representatives shortly after evacuation that "there is no doubt that the evacuees made many financial sacrifices. That was inherent in the situation."[1]

The WRA in its *Final Report* concluded that the handling of evacuee property was poorly done. Japanese lost much in the initial days after Pearl Harbor through panic sales, and more was sacrificed as fear and hysteria mounted, particularly in the period between the issuance of Executive Order 9066 on February 19, 1942, and the granting of authority to the Federal Reserve on March 6. Responsibility for safeguarding evacuee property "bounced from agency to agency" before it came to rest with the WRA, by which time— June through August 1942—evacuation had already occurred. Initial losses were compounded by vandalism and the local officials' indifference to protecting Japanese property. The WRA concluded that "wartime handling of evacuee property is a sorry part of the war record."[2]

While administrators and bureaucrats responsible for the speedy removal of Japanese Americans from the West Coast could, at the time, afford to be cavalier about the financial hardships their victims would suffer through relocation, such is not the case today. In the wake of the findings of the CWRIC that the evacuation of the Japanese was not justified by military necessity, but was rather the result of wartime hysteria, fears, and racist policymaking by military leaders and high government officials, the issue of economic loss assumes new importance.

For thirty years, however, it was assumed that the Japanese evacuees had lost, in total, $400 million, a figure attributed to the Federal Reserve Bank (FRB). Most histories of relocation written between 1950 and 1980 mention that figure and often cite one another as evidence. However, no documentation has ever proven that the fabled $400 million has any basis in fact. When the CWRIC began its work in 1981 the figure came under immediate scrutiny and the Federal Reserve Bank in San Francisco was contacted for documentation.

The San Francisco FRB did play a minor role in relocation. Prior to the establishment of the War Relocation Authority, the Treasury Department froze the bank assets of all enemy aliens. It was also charged with establishing, through the Federal Reserve, a voluntary system of "aid" for the Japanese in disposing of their property before relocation. Shortly thereafter President Roosevelt signed an executive order establishing an office of Alien Property Custodian to handle the material possessions and property of all enemy aliens, including the noncitizen Issei. To avoid confusion the Alien Property Custodian delegated his authority to the Treasury and the Federal Reserve Bank. The Federal Reserve established an Evacuee Property Division in San Francisco in early March 1942 and opened field offices throughout the area to be vacated. The service established was voluntary, open to assist anyone requesting help in disposing of personal property or urban real estate. The Farm Security Administration was assigned the task of assisting evacuees with farm properties.

Federal Reserve Bank records, however, do not

Fishing boats owned by Japanese Americans, abandoned by internees, and later sold for a fraction of their value. Photo by Dorothea Lange. Courtesy Bernard K. Johnpoll.

yield any final figure as to economic loss. The archives of the San Francisco FRB contain interview records on the nearly 27,000 evacuees who sought help from the field agents, in addition to correspondence from administrators of the program and directives from Washington. These records are often exceedingly vague. The people who sought the bank's assistance did not bring their total property problems to the agent's attention, only those items they were unable to resolve themselves. This might be merely an automobile on which installments were being paid, or a large appliance that the store owner wished to repossess without compensating the purchaser for his equity. No mention was made of the home already sold, the lease abandoned, the possessions sold for a fraction of their cost. Transactions once completed, regardless of the circumstances surrounding them, were generally considered closed, and many had panicked and sold at great loss before the bank's program went into operation. The field agents were pressed for time and gener-

ally reported their interviews in cursory fashion, despite instructions to record all pertinent details. When they did record dollar amounts they accepted the evacuee's statements at face value without documentation, and these too were often vague. For example, the owners of a camellia nursery in Sacramento evaluated stock at $13,500 and reported it sold for $10,000, according to the local field agent's report. Even that type of reporting was rare, however; the majority of case files did not cite specific figures. The major exception was in cases involving automobiles, where the blue book appraised value was easier to determine.[3] The very self-congratulatory *Final Report* the Federal Reserve issued in December 1942 documented quite precisely the amount of money expended in running the Evacuee Property Division, but it did not venture a guess as to how much money the evacuees themselves had lost. There is no indication that its poorly run, ill-conceived program was even concerned with that question.

The Federal Reserve's publication *Monthly Review* published several articles on the operation, including one entitled "Economic Implications." While it noted that in 1940 Japanese farmers in the three Pacific Coast states operated 6,118 farms containing 258,074 acres and valued at $72,641,934, the article did not attempt to estimate the value of property or production of the 55 percent of Japanese workers who were not in agriculture.[4] The author, in fact, was primarily concerned with the economic implications of removal of the Japanese upon the economy of the state as a whole. He concluded that while the transfer of Japanese agricultural properties to other operators was designed to have a minimal effect on production, the "departure" of the Japanese would aggravate the labor shortage for domestic help and would disrupt the economy of existing communities with large Japanese populations.

If the Federal Reserve did not issue a statement that the losses were $400 million, who did? In an attempt to track down the elusive figure Roger Daniels researched the existing literature. He found that Leonard Broom and Ruth Riemer had estimated in 1949 the total of both income and property losses would exceed $350 million.[5] However, their calculations were based on interviews with a small group of Japanese Americans who had returned to Los Angeles after the war, and they reached their total by estimating average individual and family losses and multiplying.

An article in the *New York Times* of August 20, 1945 mentioned that alien property of former German and Japanese residents was valued at $450 million plus another $220 million in cash assets. But since this figure also covered German aliens, it could not have been the source for Japanese losses.

Daniels reports that the first person citing the $400-million figure publicly was Mike Masaoka, Washington representative of the Japanese American Citizens League. He first mentioned it in a personal document entitled "Final Report," dated April 22, 1944, just prior to leaving overseas for military service. At that time he did not attribute his source.[6] In 1954 at hearings before a subcommittee of the Committee on the Judiciary, House of Representatives, he stated that "the Federal Reserve Bank of San Francisco . . . estimated that there was a loss of $400 million in actual money losses out of the evacuation."[7] Although he did not cite a source for the figure, his statement appears to have been taken as authoritative by historians following him. Daniels believes the "Final Report" to be the "crucial document."

Works written in the 1960s followed Masaoka in crediting the figure to the Federal Reserve. Allan R. Bosworth in *America's Concentration Camps* accepted the $400 million, citing Masaoka in the JACL paper *Pacific Citizen*, while Audrie Girdner and Anne Loftis in *The Great Betrayal* also used $400 million, again attributing it to the Federal Reserve. Bill Hosokawa did likewise in *Nisei: The Quiet Americans*, as did Roger Daniels in *Concentration Camps, USA: Japanese Americans and World War II*. Michi Weglyn repeated the figure in *Years of Infamy*.[8]

The Federal Reserve Bank has disavowed any connection with the figure, since their researchers could not track it down in any of their materials. The FRB's archivist also traced the statement as far back as the subcommittee meeting of the Judiciary Committee of the House of Representatives in 1954, but found the trail grew cold beyond that point.[9] Roger Daniels recently concluded that he was now convinced that a bank statement about property losses stemming from evacuation was never made, "at least not in that form."[10]

If the $400-million figure is shrouded in myth, what then can one conclude about the losses Japanese Americans suffered in America's concentration camps? Many variables must be taken into account. Actual property losses suffered between 1942 and 1945 represent only one item, albeit an important one. More work needs to be done with the Federal Reserve material. A thorough study of the interview forms of the Federal Reserve Bank, accurately sampled, might yield an estimate arrived at on the basis of the figures included in the data. However, bank data is probably an inadequate measure; a better source would be tax records. Unfortunately, by 1944 the Internal Revenue Service had destroyed most of the 1939 to 1942 tax records of the evacuees.[11]

Information on agricultural losses is also a key ingredient. As noted earlier, the Farm Security Administration administered transfers of farm properties, and its procedures were somewhat different from those the Federal Reserve Bank followed. The FSA's primary goal was to keep land in production, so it did not wait for anxious farmers to come to it for assistance. Its agents took a census, querying each farmer about the ownership of his land and the value of crops planted on it, his machinery, and other property. These data were compiled on cards which are now part of the National Archives' massive documentation on relocation. While they are not readily available to scholars because of the Right to Privacy Act, they will someday provide one more measure of assessing economic loss in a key sector. Farm losses represent one of the most potentially fruitful areas for detailed research on this problem.

War Relocation Authority records are another documentary source. Each of the ten camps had an office of evacuee property, where the people interned could work with a WRA official in an attempt to resolve property problems. Data from the quarterly camp reports also give some indication of the ongoing nature of loss. Much property not lost at the time of removal was lost during incarceration through nonpayment of taxes. In some instances this resulted from deliberate neglect on the part of people who had leased it from its Japanese owners. Land that had prospered under the care of the skilled, hardworking Japanese often failed to produce for its new, less adept managers, and it was often abandoned. Independent scholars reporting shortly after the war echo this finding. Dorothy Swaine Thomas wrote that "every evacuee incurred some loss . . . many of them suffered severe and irreparable losses, both tangible and intangible."[12]

Any final tallying must go beyond the monetary losses of personal and real property and look at other factors. Considering the evacuees who remained in the camps for the duration of the war earned between $12 and $19 per month for the work they did—less money than an army private—their losses in potential income are considerable. While most of the internees were agricultural workers, or small tradesmen, or service people, some were professionals whose careers were stunted. While younger evacuees were not yet of working age, many Nisei were just approaching it, and one must attempt to calculate how the camp experience affected their potential.

Other incidental losses are even harder to calculate. The CWRIC's conclusion that the internment of the Japanese American community served no military purpose makes clear that the evacuees were victims of wrongful incarceration. Not only did they lose their freedom, they were dishonored. The reception of those who left the camps to return to their old homes on the West Coast was even more hostile than the attitude at the time of their departure, testimony to the increased prejudice and racism engendered by their very incarceration. Internment convinced many Americans that the Japanese, even if American citizens, must indeed have been guilty of something. It took years for the white community to extend acceptance, and according to recent studies, a persistent racism still affects their economic mobility.[13]

Even those born after the war suffered from the consequences of relocation. Those that suffered the indignity tried to forget and keep silent, but even their children could not escape its impact. Mrs. Montana Marumoto of Portland, Oregon, testified before the CWRIC that her son learned in junior high school that Japanese Americans had been interned because they were traitors. Fellow students subsequently harrassed and beat him. Phillip Marumoto said the internment had "left an indelible stamp" on his life even though he had never been interned.[14] Certainly he was not alone. Relocation also affected those Japanese Americans who lived outside the military zones. Existing communities had to make room for new residents or transients leaving the camps on work release programs, and the stimulus to existing prejudice that the relocation provided affected their lives too. The ramifications of internment knew few boundaries of time and place.

The Japanese American Citizens League has recommended that the CWRIC study property losses based on 1940 county assessor's tax lists. It suggests that these cases be examined to determine their 1941 market value, and that the same properties be studied on tax records for 1945, 1950, and 1960 to determine what the increased valuation of the lost property was over the years. Such a study would undoubtedly give a much more accurate portrayal of the losses of the Japanese community than has heretofore existed.[15]

The CWRIC did study economic losses in preparing its massive report. Contracting the work out to ICF Incorporated, the commission uncovered considerable data. Their report first reviewed the attempts at compensation made through the 1948 Evacuation Claims Act and noted that the approximately $37 million the government disbursed was grossly inadequate. They concluded that "the difficulty of providing persuasive evidence of claimants' losses, the evidentiary standards followed by the Justice Department and a compromise authority which encouraged the reduction of many claims . . . result[ed] in settlements well below the actual value of losses."[16] The testimony the CWRIC amassed bore witness to countless examples of uncompensated loss. When the commission issued its recommendations, it prefaced them with a statement that the ethnic Japanese had lost between $108 and $164 million in income and between $11 and $206 million in property "for which no compensation was made after the war."[17] Ironically, the total of the larger of the two figures in each category comes to $370 million, not far from the elusive $400 million. However, the commission noted that if these figures were adjusted for inflation, the total losses would "fall between $810 million and $2 billion in 1983 dollars." The ICF study placed the total uncompensated losses at between $1.2 billion and $3.1 billion, and, at a 3 percent interest rate adjusted for inflation, from $2.5 billion to $6.2 billion.[18]

The CWRIC's recommendations include appropriations of $1.5 billion to be made to a fund for personal redress to those who were relocated, a one-time compensatory per capita payment of $20,000 to each of the approximately 60,000 survivors of the camps. The remainder of the fund would be used for public educational purposes.[19]

Economic loss is inextricably tied to the even knottier question of compensation. The CWRIC's proposals are minimal compared to the amount the National Council for Japanese American Redress requested, yet the matter of any financial compensation is a sensitive one on which many people in the Nikkei community disagree. The JACL booklet on redress notes, "Restitution does not put a price tag on freedom or justice. This issue is not to recover what cannot be recovered. The issue is to acknowledge the mistake by providing proper redress for the victims of injustice, and thereby make such injustices less likely to recur."[20] Proper redress must take into account economic loss. As many have noted, ours is a society that often equates real worth with economic value. If this is true, financial compensation of some form is indeed essential in remedying the outrage of relocation.

NOTES

1. *First Quarterly Report*, March 18 to June 30, 1942, War Relocation Authority, Washington, D.C.

2. United States Department of the Interior, *The Wartime Handling of Evacuee Property* (Washington, D.C.: Government Printing Office, 1946), 3–4.

3. Federal Reserve Bank of San Francisco, *Final Report*, December 30, 1942. On the role of the Federal Reserve Bank, see Sandra C. Taylor, "The Federal Reserve Bank and the Relocation of the Japanese in 1942," *The Public Historian* 5 (Winter 1983): 9–30.

4. "Economic Implications of Japanese Evacuation," *Monthly Review*, Federal Reserve Bank of San Francisco, April 1, 1942.

5. Leonard Broom and Ruth Riemer, *Removal and Return: Socio-Economic Effects of the War on Japanese Americans* (Berkeley: University of California Press, 1949).

6. Mike Masaoka, "Final Report," April 22, 1944, Japanese American Relocation Study (JERS), Bancroft Library, University of California, Berkeley, as cited in letter to the author from Roger Daniels, March 27, 1982.

7. Hearings of Subcommittee No. 5 of the Committee on the Judiciary, House of Representatives, 83rd Cong., 2d sess., 1954, 15–16.

8. Audrie Girdner and Anne Loftis, *The Great Betrayal* (New York: Macmillan, 1969); Allan R. Bosworth, *America's Concentration Camps* (New York: Norton, 1967); Bill Hosokawa, *Nisei: The Quiet Americans* (New York: William Morrow, 1969); Roger Daniels, *Concentration Camps, USA: Japanese Americans and World War II* (New York: Holt, Rinehart and Winston, 1971); Michi Weglyn, *Years of Infamy: The Untold Story of America's Concentration Camps* (New York: William Morrow, 1976). The JACL also used the figure in its publication, *The Japanese American Incarceration: A Case for Redress* (San Francisco: JACL, 1978). The number was also used in the Washington hearings of the Commission on Redress, July 1981. This question is also discussed in *Personal Justice Denied* (Washington, D.C.: Government Printing Office, 1982), 120.

9. Letter to the author from Helene Briggs, former archivist, Federal Reserve Bank, San Francisco, May 12, 1981.

10. Roger Daniels to Patricia Rea, Associate Librarian, Research Library, Federal Reserve Bank of San Francisco.

11. Department of Justice, unpublished internal report of the Japanese Claims Section on the administration of the Japanese Evacuation Claims Act, undated (ca. 1959), as cited in *Personal Justice Denied*, 118.

12. Dorothy S. Thomas and Richard S. Nishimoto, *The Spoilage* (Berkeley and Los Angeles: University of California Press, 1946), 16.

13. See Darrel Montero, *Japanese-Americans: Changing Patterns of Ethnic Affiliation over Three Generations* (Boulder, Colo.: Westview Press, 1980).

14. *The Oregonian*, September 12, 1981.

15. Telephone conversation with John Tateishi, Japanese American Citizens League, February 25, 1983.

16. *Personal Justice Denied*, 121.

17. *Personal Justice Denied*, Summary and Recommendations of the Commission on Wartime Relocation and Internment of Civilians (San Francisco: JACL, 1983), 27.

18. Ibid., 27.

19. Ibid., 28–29.

20. *The Japanese American Incarceration: A Case for Redress*.

The Concentration Camps and Japanese Economic Losses in California Agriculture, 1900–1942

Gary Y. Okihiro

David Drummond

Considerations about the losses sustained by the Japanese as a result of their relocation to concentration camps generally begin with their mass removal in 1942. That has at least one limitation: it fails to place the camps and their consequences and meaning to Japanese Americans within the wider context of the anti-Japanese movement. Further, little attention is usually given to the reciprocal nature of their losses and others' gains.

Who profited from the Japanese in America, from the anti-Japanese movement, and from the concentration camps? An examination of that question not only provides insights into the methods and the extent of the losses, but also brings a proper historical perspective to the subject. Additionally, the "economic losses" should not be confined to property losses or lost opportunities but should be defined in their widest sense as "economic exploitation." This paper examines the losses the Japanese incurred during World War II, but it also perceives those losses to have been progressions in the anti-Japanese movement. Its emphasis, Japanese involvement in California agriculture, offers an example of how certain groups profited from their removal. In turn, it sheds light on the generalized process of exclusionism and internal colonialism or economic exploitation.

Scholars have long held that the camps were a result of the anti-Asian movement.[1] A more recent refinement of that thesis uses the models provided by studies on internal colonialism and the world economy. Essentially, this interpretation depicts Asian immigration as migrant labor, that is, the movement of labor from areas of low-capital concentration and underdevelopment to areas of high-capital concentration and development. The advantages of that system to the United States and other capitalist countries include a gain of cheap, vulnerable, but reliable workers without the costs of reproduction. Various mechanisms maintained and sustained the system of migrant labor, such as individual acts of coercion, institutionalized controls through legislative and judicial means, racism, and xenophobia.

The maintenance of migrant labor comprised one end of the exclusionist spectrum of the anti-Asian movement; the other end held for their complete expulsion. Exclusionism of the former variety held four basic goals: first, to regulate the influx and internal movement of the migrant laborers; second, to limit their reproduction; third, to control their economic activities; and fourth, to encourage sojourning and their eventual repatriation after their usefulness had passed.[2] California Attorney General Ulysses S. Webb, author of the 1913 Alien Land Law, made explicit the exclusionist intent of the act when he said,

> The fundamental basis of all legislation upon this subject, State and Federal, has been and is, race undesirability. It is unimportant and foreign to the question under discussion whether a particular race is inferior. The simple and single question is, is the race desirable. . . . It [the law] seeks to limit their presence by curtailing their privileges which they may enjoy here; for they will not come in large numbers and long abide with us if they may not acquire land. And it seeks to limit the numbers who will come by limiting the opportunities for their activity here when they arrive.[3]

Asian labor was useful to the large landholders; their upward mobility represented a loss of human capital and posed a political liability insofar as they competed with the small growers. The various alien land laws provided a way to restrict and channel Japanese economic activities for the maintenance of migrant labor. Thus, for example, California enacted alien land laws in 1913, which deprived the Issei of land ownership; in 1920, which denied them lease-holding rights; and in 1923, which prevented them from sharecropping.

The period of exclusionism in California agriculture began in 1900 with the early involvement of Japanese labor in farming and ended in 1924 with the exclusion of Japanese workers. Those first twenty-four years were characterized by a system of migrant labor, by the means for its support, and by wage and labor discrimination. The latter form of economic exploitation remained substantial until at least as late as 1909. In that year, a study by the California commissioner of labor found that white agricultural workers earned an average $1.80 per day, while Japanese laborers earned $1.54. A 1909 U.S. Immigration Commission report confirmed that finding and concluded that "there is a discrimination of about 25 cents per day in favor of white men as against Japanese and other Asiatics engaged in the same work."[4] By 1915, according to Robert Higgs, because of various factors including the general market tendency, wages had become equal for Japanese and white agricultural workers. Another significant reason for that shift was the rise in Japanese farm operators who preferred Japanese laborers to white and who generally paid higher wages than their white counterparts.[5] Although the Japanese were leaving wage labor for farm tenancy during the first two decades of the twentieth century, and despite the restrictive provisions of the 1907–1908 Gentlemen's Agreement prohibiting laborers from emigrating to the United States, Japanese workers still constituted an important source of migrant labor for California's fields. That was evident in their continued immigration. Between 1913 and 1920 when there was a relaxation of the Gentlemen's Agreement, over 70,000 Japanese immigrated, "among whom the farmers and farm laborers formed the largest group."[6] The exclusion act of 1924, however, clearly signalled the end of the period of Japanese migrant labor.

Table 1
Japanese Farm Operators in California[7]

Date	Number of Farms	Acreage
1900	37	4,698
1910	1,816	156,901
1920	5,152	361,276
1930	3,956	191,427
1940	5,135	220,094

The second period of Japanese involvement in California agriculture, 1924–1942, marked the transition from migrant labor to internal colonialism. Several factors accounted for that change. First, the immigration of Japanese women during the "picture bride" era, 1908–1920, had resulted in the eventual transformation of the Japanese community from one of sojourners to that of settlers. Second, despite the means employed to restrict upward mobility, the number of Japanese farm operators swelled from 1900 to 1920 and coincided with increasingly harsher exclusionist controls. Table 1 documents that growth. Third, indications are that Japanese farm labor was growing increasingly expensive,[8] and the restrictive 1924 exclusion act limited the pool of Japanese laborers. Further, Filipinos and Mexicans were replacing the Japanese during the 1920s as the preferred source of migrant labor.[9] And fourth, Japanese farm tenancy offered another means to secure that community's economic dependence and an opportunity for profit. Non-

Japanese capitalists achieved gains through a racial rent premium, Japanese investments in and management of farm property, unconventional land tenure arrangements, and loans issued on crop liens.

The racial rent premium required Japanese tenants to pay a higher rent per acre. The 1909 U.S. Immigration Commission report observed that "the offer of comparatively high rents, though not universal, is fairly general,"[10] and Theodore Saloutos, in his study of immigrants in West Coast agriculture, noted that "the large landowners found it more profitable to have Japanese as tenants because they produced larger crops, worked longer hours, used family labor, employed scientific techniques, paid higher rents, and were content with smaller profits."[11] This suggests the Japanese were of greater value to the large landowners as tenants than as laborers. Table 2 illustrates the racial rent premium in selected California counties from a 1920 agricultural census.

Table 2
Average Cash Rent/Acre, White and Japanese,
Selected California Counties, 1920[12]

County	Average Cash Rent/Acre	
	White	Japanese
Alameda	$ 5.19	$27.00
Imperial	19.96	27.08
Los Angeles	12.88	23.06
Sacramento	5.96	24.45
San Joaquin	12.53	23.67
Santa Clara	8.95	23.29
MEAN	$10.91	$24.75

Of greater significance is the fact that the Japanese paid higher rents relative to the value of the land, which Higgs estimates to have been 1 or 2 percent of the land's value.[13] Large landowners also found Japanese tenants profitable because their labor increased the property value[14] and they served to ensure the required labor. "In many instances," wrote Iwata, "California farmers resorted to leasing their holdings to the Japanese as a means of securing the nucleus of a labor supply and of transferring to the tenants the task of obtaining the other laborers needed."[15]

Unconventional land tenure arrangements were designed to evade alien land laws. Iwata observed that many Issei moved to short-term tenure and truck farming, which required a small capital investment for buildings and perennial crops. That form of agriculture "probably contributed to establishing an unstable tenure pattern among the Issei agriculturalists with the associated undesirable features inherent in short-term leasing, insecurity of land occupancy, and high tenant mobility."[16]

Writing in 1913, Ichihashi made that same point of Japanese vulnerability: "While many of the Japanese farmers have accumulated considerable property and have become fairly independent in the conduct of their holdings, the largest number have little property and many of them have a form of tenancy which limits their freedom in production."[17] Ichihashi described one such form of tenancy as "quasi-leasing" in which the lessee agreed to pay the lessor a fixed cash rent, yet the lessor maintained "an absolute control over the management of the industry as well as the disposition of the crops." Thus, while the lessor shared in the profits, he did not share the risks. Concluded Ichihashi, "All these systems were initiated by white farmers for their own convenience and economic gains to them were thus secured."[18]

The alien land laws were a critical component in the maintenance of Japanese tenancy. Although ostensibly designed to drive the Japanese out of agriculture, they were not generally enforced. Wrote Carey McWilliams in 1935, "The act is a dead letter. It is no longer enforced nor is there any sentiment for its enforcement."[19] Writing several years later he noted:

> Enforcement of the Alien Land Law of 1920 was vested in local law-enforcement officials. The act was easily evaded: title to a farm land was placed in the names of Hawaiian or American-born Japanese; verbal agreements were entered into that ran counter to the terms of written documents; Japanese were employed as "managers" instead of as "tenants." By these and other devices, and with the connivance of law-enforcement officials, the act was blithely ignored. The amount of land escheated to the state under this statute is wholly negligible.[20]

Both McWilliams and Higgs recognized that the reason for the ineffectual enforcement of the alien land law was that the removal of the Japanese from farm tenancy would have severely damaged the interests of the large landowners. "They are now," wrote McWilliams, "partners in an unholy and highly profitable conspiracy to violate the very measure that binds them together."[21] At the same time, those forms of tenancy were not in the best interests of the Japanese, for they ensured Japanese dependency. Japanese tenants were subject to prosecution under the law and were thus made susceptible to economic exploitation. Table 3

shows the Japanese had not improved their position substantially between 1910 and 1940, given the fact that 86 percent were tenants or managers in 1910 and 74 percent were still tenants or managers in 1940. During the same time the California Nisei population, citizens and thus potential landholders, increased from 3,172 in 1910 to 60,148 in 1940.

Few have examined the subject of economic gain derived from the expulsion of the Japanese following Pearl Harbor. McWilliams cites several examples of the transfer of farm properties from Japanese to non-Japanese operators, including "numerous small Japanese properties" taken over by dust-bowl migrants and eager city dwellers engaging in "week-end ventures."[23] He also suggests that larger, organized groups seized upon this opportunity to enrich themselves: "The grossest imposition was practised upon the Japanese, ranging from petty chiseling to large-scale fraud. . . . In Santa Maria—in Santa Barbara County—local interests have been charged with bilking the Japanese out of holdings valued at $500,000."[24] Economic self-interest forms an important motivation for pressure groups in Grodzins's study of the causes for the concentration camps. In support of that contention, Grodzins quotes Austin Anson, managing secretary of the Grower-Shipper Vegetable Association:

> We're charged with wanting to get rid of the Japs for selfish reasons. We might as well be honest. We do. It's a question of whether the white man lives on the Pacific Coast or the brown men. . . . If all the Japs were removed tomorrow, we'd never miss them in two weeks, because the white farmers can take over and produce everything the Jap grows. And we don't want them back when the war ends either.[25]

In their critique of Grodzins's pressure group theory, tenBroek, et al., call into question Grodzins's evidence and argue that "his interpretation of his alleged evidence of its [Grower-Shipper Vegetable Association] proevacuation activity in December is open to serious question, and his charge that it secretly fomented trouble is wholly without foundation."[26] They point out that growing and marketing organizations were not uniformly in favor of ridding the Pacific Coast of the Japanese and that several groups, such as the Washington Produce Shippers Association, tes-

Table 3
Japanese Farm Owners, Tenants, and Managers in California, 1910–1940[22]

Date	Owners (% of Total)		Managers (% of Total)		Tenants (% of Total)	
1910	233	(12%)	36	(1%)	1,547	(85%)
1920	506	(9%)	113	(2%)	4,533	(87%)
1930	560	(14%)	1,616	(43%)	1,580	(42%)
1940	1,290	(25%)	249	(4%)	3,596	(70%)

tified before the Tolan Committee that "wholesale evacuation would be an economic waste and a stupid error."[27]

Although agricultural groups might not have caused the mass removal of the Japanese, there is very little question that many of them stood to gain from their elimination. As Grodzins observed, the Western Growers Protective Association saw the occasion as an opportunity for economic profit. In the February 1942 issue of its journal, the *Western Grower and Shipper*, the author noted that "the alien Japanese element are going out of the wholesale produce trade in Los Angeles, and many of the large farms are on the market for a few cents on the dollar."[28] The association's managing secretary, in reviewing 1942, reported that considerable profits were realized by the growers and shippers because of the Japanese removal, and that the local vegetable supply had been produced "by the large scale operator, who is again shipping to the Los Angeles and San Francisco market commodities which have for almost a generation been grown on suburban market gardens [by Japanese]."[29]

Besides those means for profit, the California legislature, in a reversion to the exclusionist sentiment of the 1900–1924 period, worked for stricter enforcement of the alien land law and for the appropriation of Japanese farms operating in violation of the law. On December 22, 1941, it authorized a study of "the operation, effect, applicability, and enforcement of the Alien Land Law."[30] In 1943, nine bills were introduced to prohibit land ownership by both Japanese aliens and citizens and to provide for the sale of the escheated property. Eight additional bills were introduced in 1945 to prohibit further Japanese land ownership, and, in that same year, the legislature apropriated $200,000 to investigate and vigorously enforce the 1920 alien land law. By late 1946, more than sixty new escheat cases were filed against the Japanese in California and, between 1944 and 1948, eighty such cases were actively being pursued.[31] "The intent of the law," concluded Chuman, "was clearly to drive the Japanese farmers out of agricultural activities."[32]

The immediate wartime situation and the planned removal of the West Coast Japanese, however, posed a problem to certain agricultural interests. Ironically, the dependence of Japanese farm operators on the capitalist landholders led to the latter's discomfiture. A method employed to obtain Japanese dependency was the issuing of advances on their crops.

The Japanese also seemed to have had an easier time obtaining financing. The capital requirements of the tenants in some kinds of production were minimal because most of the equipment was furnished by the land-

lords, while in sugar-beet production the companies advanced most of the capital; in fruits and vegetables the commission merchants lent money and supplies and took liens on their crops. Where the competition was keen shippers made large advances to the tenants and in some instances leased and subleased land to other farmers.[33]

The profitable arrangements of the earlier period placed those packers and shippers in an unenviable position in the spring and summer of 1942 with the mass removal of Japanese labor and tenants before the harvest. The immediate concern was the very real possibility of the Japanese tenants defaulting on the loans issued and, further, the loss of what promised to be a very bountiful agricultural season.

The remainder of this paper chronicles the subsequent machinations of the landholders and the government designed to benefit themselves at the expense of the Japanese in California agriculture.

The army and the Wartime Civil Control Administration (WCCA) seemed less attentive to the needs of the companies than to the summary mass removal of all Japanese from the designated military zones, consistent with their justification of "military necessity." They did provide, nonetheless, for the handling of evacuee property. Assistant Secretary of War John J. McCloy, in a memorandum to Lieutenant General John DeWitt dated February 20, 1942, stressed the need for protecting evacuee property "consistent with safety," but placed the principal burden on the Japanese themselves.[34]

A further concern, perhaps more vital to the government, was the possible disruption of West Coast agriculture and, hence, an impediment to the war effort. In fact, the contrast in the government's handling of evacuees' property between the protection of that property to minimize Japanese losses and the custodianship of that property to reduce agricultural dislocation is striking and reveals the government's real interest.

The various agencies responsible for evacuee property recognized the immense losses the Japanese sustained and sought to minimize and explain them. DeWitt's final report on the Japanese evacuation contains the most optimistic assessment. He noted

that substitute management and operation [had] been achieved for 99 percent of Japanese farms; . . . farm equipment [had] been utilized, consistent with fair dealing and protection of evacuee interests, to the greatest advantage of the war effort; . . . [and] the use of land, the nature of crops, and the quantity of production underwent a minimum of change as the result of the evacuation of Japanese owners, operators, and labor.[35]

The War Relocation Authority (WRA) offered a more critical appraisal of the army's performance and identified several problems created in the handling of evacuee property. The report cited the prevailing West Coast sentiment, which was opposed "to any recognition of the rights and privileges of this little known and habitually misrepresented minority," including local and state law enforcement officials who have shown "a considerable indifference to vandalism and even to arson committed upon evacuee property." It accused the federal government of being slow in setting up the machinery for minimizing Japanese losses, "thus allowing an interval of golden opportunity to swindlers and tricksters who had a terrified group of people at their mercy." And finally, to absolve the WRA of the losses incurred, the report noted that responsibility for evacuee property "bounced from agency to agency," devolving on the WRA in August 1942, after the removal had been accomplished.[36]

Despite perfunctory genuflection toward property rights, the government's primary interest was economic stability. Hearings of the House Select Committee Investigating National Defense Migration[37] and government handling of Japanese farm property exhibited this.

The Farm Security Administration (FSA), on March 15, 1942, was given the responsibility of ensuring the continued proper use of Japanese farms and for providing for an equitable transfer from Japanese to non-Japanese operators.[38] Some of the dilemmas the FSA encountered in carrying out both those directives are summarized in the following:

> Situations were encountered in which landlords by virtue of non-assignability clauses in leases sought to deprive Japanese farm operators of their crops and forfeit rental payments, . . . by preventing transfers between Japanese tenants and substitute farm operators offering fair prices . . . conditional contract settlers were ready to exercise forfeitures based upon breaches made necessary by the forced evacuation of Japanese. Landlords, creditors and prospective purchasers also appeared ready to take advantage of the adverse bargaining position of the Japanese evacuees even at the cost of a serious loss of agricultural production. Further, there was a possibility that Japanese operators would abandon farm land, would discontinue normal agricultural operations or would refuse to consummate transfers of their agricultural properties.[39]

Surely another hypocrisy of the concentration camp experience is the perception of reluctant Japanese farm operators as un-American and the conjoining of the government with white exploiters who moved on the basis of self-interest at the expense of the war effort. The merging of those interests, of the government and capital, transpired in the following manner.

In March 1942, the FSA faced the enormous task of securing the transfer of over 6,000 Japanese farms to non-Japanese operators while achieving the major program objective of maintaining "the continuation without serious interruption of agricultural production."[40] That charge was even more challenging given the urgency of the ripening crops, which demanded a timely harvest. Certain agricultural interests, on the other hand, faced the possibility of losses from loans advanced to Japanese farmers as liens on their crops and the loss of a substantial portion of the season's harvest for canners and shippers. Thus several of those groups, including Newcastle Fruit Company, Loomis Fruit Growers Association, and the American Fruit Growers, urged a delay in the removal of Japanese farmers in their area until after the harvest.[41]

While that request was being made of the military authorities, members of the California Deciduous Growers' League met with the WCCA and FSA to seek a solution to the problems of both groups. They found it in farm corporations. The FSA offered the following explanation: "Frequently the prevailing sizes of Japanese farm enterprises made successful operation by individual substitute operators uneconomical, and consequently some consolidation of the operation of these small farms was found to be necessary." Additionally, the report noted:

> Since many agricultural interests had a stake in the agricultural production from Japanese-operated farms . . . it was logical for them to find substitute operators to . . . provide for the handling of these properties. In instances where existing agricultural concerns did not care to involve their packing or processing organizations with the task of and financial responsibility for agricultural production or the management of properties, special operating corporations were organized.[42]

At the same time, those agricultural interests sought to avoid the risks of managing those properties. Thus, "although the Fruit Companies were interested in operating evacuees' farms, and although they were anxious to protect the interest they had vested, directly or indirectly, in these farms, they were also anxious to avoid any risk in operating these farms. Formation of a *parent* corporation financed by the government was the solution sought and obtained."[43] Farm corporations, thus formed, were

> non-profit . . . subsidiaries to already existing "successful corporations," and operating on government loans. Thus, the financial inviolability of their "mother" orga-

nizations was assured. These were indeed "dummy" corporations, for their officers were the employees of different fruit shipping and canning companies operating in some of the areas evacuated.[44]

Apparently the farm corporations met the needs of both the government and the capitalists.

At first, the FSA had difficulty securing substitute operators for the small Japanese farms, especially in Sacramento and Placer counties; by May 1, over a month since beginning operations, 51.5 percent of the Japanese farms in those areas had yet to be transferred. By May 22, however, "thanks to the Farm Corporation," nearly 85 percent were transferred, and by June 5, 96.6 percent of the Japanese-operated farms in the two counties had been transferred.[45] The fruit companies obtained generous, risk-free government loans to subsidize their operation (loans were secured on the assets of the Japanese farms), acquired the full use of the farm machinery on those farms at no cost, and, in most cases, shared half of the profits on the sale of the 1942 crops.[46] Recalled the director of the California Fruit Exchange, "All of us understood that if there were any losses on any individual ranches or ranch—the corporations or individuals would not be held responsible. . . . [Otherwise] I wouldn't have stuck my name on those papers."[47]

In northern California, nine farm corporations operated 196 Japanese farms totaling 5,772 acres[48] listed in Table 4. In all, fifteen farm corporations received over $1 million in FSA loans to operate 250 Japanese farms of some 6,000 acres.[49] Besides the extremely favorable terms of the farm corporations' arrangement, companies were provided with an additional means for profit at the expense of the Japanese. First, the companies and their farm corporations held, in effect, a monopoly of the Japanese producers under their control. The swiftness of the "evacuation," the registration and transfer of Japanese farms by the FSA to the farm corporations, and the complete removal of

Japanese growers from their farms and their subsequent confinement helped ensure that monopoly. Second, the farm corporation structure held little incentive for maximizing farm profits apart from recovering the cash advances made to those farms. The normal relationship between producer and middleman did not exist here; in this instance, the middleman held control over production, although these costs in turn were borne by the producers. Further, the middlemen, the farm corporations, were daughter agencies of the manufacturers/distributors—the packing and shipping companies—and, thus, the dictum for middlemen, "buy cheap and sell dear," did not apply. The operating procedure became "buy cheap, sell cheap." Finally, farm profits, normally divided evenly between Japanese grower and farm corporation, provided scant incentive for showing farm profits when the full gain could be realized simply by charging the Japanese producers for services rendered. The tendency thus was to inflate the costs; the farm corporations on paper would accordingly realize little or negative gain, while in reality they would be parasitically drawing from the Japanese farms.

Northern Farms illustrates that process. The parent company, Nash-de-Camp, charged Northern Farms—in effect itself—$7,209.86 for supervision and overhead and $20,602.64 for the "commercial packing of fruit," among other costs. Those charges in turn were passed on to the Japanese as "growing and harvesting costs," including $1,437.76 for "tractor hire," despite the fact that Northern Farms, per the agreement, had full use of the Japanese farm equipment.[51] The summary of Northern Farms' 1942 operations in Table 5 clarifies the method employed. The ledger reveals that despite showing a profit of $2,017.19 for the twenty Japanese farms under its custody, they were charged $6,591.44, the balance due on the government loan, resulting in a net loss of $4,574.25 for the year. Similarly, Florin Farms reported that of the thirty-nine Japanese farms operated, only four showed a

Table 4
Northern California Farm Corporations[50]

Farm Corporation	Parent Company	Loan	Units	Acreage
California Fruit Canners	California Packing Corporation	$ 76,221	2	305
Deciduous Farm Lands	Pacific Fruit Exchange	247,401	59	742
Florin Farms	Florin Fruit Growers Association	89,409	39	1,000
Fruit Farms	California Fruit Exchange	148,471	20	756
Loomis Agencies	Loomis Fruit Growers	61,935	12	524
Northern Farms	Nash-de-Camp	98,077	20	910
Placer Farms	American Fruit Growers	45,661	18	524
Placer Orchards	Heggblade Marguleas	87,757	13	600
Tokay	S. A. Gerrard	42,230	13	440

return of $688.24, while the remaining thirty-five realized a net loss of $17,322.18.[53] Explained G. W. Freil, manager of Florin Farms, in a letter to Wayne Phelps, WRA evacuee property supervisor, dated November 25, 1942:

Table 5
Northern Farms, Inc., 1942 Operations[52]

Receipts:	government loan		$ 98,077.38
	fruit sales		70,247.03
	state gasoline tax refund		35.69
			$168,360.10
Disbursements:	repaid on government loan		$ 91,485.94
	growing/harvesting costs		74,831.97
	state franchise tax		25.00
			$166,342.91
Balance:		2,017.19	
Assets:	cash held in trust		
	for Japanese		$ 2,017.19
	net due from Japanese growers		6,591.44
			$ 8,608.63
Liabilities:	due to Japanese (50% balance)		$ 2,017.19
	bills payable to U.S. govt.		6,591.44
			$ 8,608.63

For your information the operations of Florin Farms, Inc. will definitely be in the red, but the amount of loss involved this year will not be available until the final accounting. The present figures indicate, however, that the total loss will probably be around $20,000.00. The crop has turned out to be approximately ½ of normal and so with a normal crop the operations of these farms would have been profitable to all concerned.[54]

Clearly, to the Japanese farmers the results must have been devastating, especially since most of them were small growers. Conversely, to capital, the arrangement was, in the language of an earlier cited report of the Western Growers Protective Association, "most satisfactory." To preserve their profitable position, at the end of 1942, "most fruit shippers and canners refused to operate for the next year unless they could be financed by the government under the same conditions."[55]

J. J. Woodin, general manager of Fruit Farms, Inc., wrote menacingly to Russel Robinson, WRA chief evacuee property supervisor:

If Gov't money is not available, and by this I mean that the Gov't take the financial risk in the operation of the ranches, then it will be necessary for us of Fruit Farms, Inc. to terminate the leases with the Japanese owners at the conclusion of the 1942 operations. If Gov't money is going to be available, then details should be worked out, certainly by early October, 1942; otherwise the ranches will undoubtedly suffer considerably for lack of care.[56]

The government decided against issuing the FSA loans, and as a result, most companies dissolved their subsidiary farm corporations. Abandonment and foreclosure of Japanese farms followed.[57]

Although the farm corporations' arrangement between the government and capital provided a singular opportunity, the process and end result were neither extraordinary nor unique. Exclusionism, as noted earlier, sought the maintenance of migrant labor. That profitable system of labor prevailed from 1900 to 1924. Immigration laws, antimiscegenation statutes, the denial of naturalization to the Issei, alien land laws, and the ideology of racism were the means taken to ensure Japanese migrant labor. Besides gaining an efficient labor force, capital profited from wage-labor discrimination, by weakening class consciousness, and by avoiding the costs of reproduction. Despite the impediments to their upward mobility, many Japanese moved from the ranks of labor to farm tenancy.

The period 1924–1942 witnessed the transformation of the Japanese community from one of migrant labor to one of an internal colony, a resident minority labor force. Some factors leading to this change included the immigration of Japanese women and the rise of families, the increase in the number of Japanese farm operators, the preference for Filipino and Mexican migrant workers, and the potential for profits from Japanese tenancy. A racial rent premium, Japanese management of farm properties, and unconventional land tenure arrangements secured those gains. The alien land laws served to maintain Japanese tenancy and thus their economic dependence.

Pearl Harbor sparked a return to exclusionism and offered an opportunity for immediate profit and the expulsion of the Japanese from the level of farm operators. Escheat actions, most vehemently applied between 1944 and 1948, revealed the genuine exclusionist intent of the removal and confinement of the Japanese, for they bore little relationship to the needs of national security. The mass removal of the Japanese provided a fortuitous opening for achieving the principal aim of exclusionism and internal colonialism—economic gain. This paper records just one such occasion: the farm corporations met the immediate needs of both government and capital. For the government, they enabled the rapid transfer of farms from Japanese to non-Japanese operators and preserved the 1942 agricultural season without serious economic dislocation. For the capitalists, they provided an extremely favorable avenue for quick profit. Unfortunately for the Japanese, the farm corporations functioned at their expense. That instance of economic exploitation, however, was not inconsistent with the anti-Japanese movement and the concentration camps.

NOTES

1. Morton Grodzins, *Americans Betrayed: Politics and the Japanese Evacuation* (Chicago: University of Chicago Press, 1949); Jacobus tenBroek, Edward N. Barnhart, and Floyd W. Matson, *Prejudice, War and the Constitution* (Berkeley: University of California Press, 1954); and Roger Daniels, *Concentration Camps: North America* (Malabar, Fla.: Robert E. Krieger, 1981).

2. Gary Y. Okihiro, "Japanese Resistance in America's Concentration Camps" (unpublished manuscript), 13–27.

3. As cited in War Relocation Authority, *People in Motion* (Washington, D.C.: Government Printing Office, 1947), 37.

4. Quoted in Robert Higgs, "Landless by Law: Japanese Immigrants in California Agriculture to 1941," *Journal of Economic History* 38 (March 1978): 207–9.

5. Higgs, 209.

6. Masakazu Iwata, "The Japanese Immigrants in California Agriculture," *Agricultural History* 36 (January 1962): 30. Cf. Higgs, 207, 209.

7. Iwata, 29–32.

8. Yamato Ichihashi, *Japanese Immigration: Its Status in California* (San Francisco: The Japanese Association of America, 1913), 26–27 and Higgs, 208–9.

9. Theodore Saloutos, "The Immigrant in Pacific Coast Agriculture, 1880–1940," *Agricultural History* 49 (January 1975): 199–201; Carey McWilliams, *Factories in the Field* (Santa Barbara, 1971), 124–33; and Cletus E. Daniel, *Bitter Harvest: A History of California Farmworkers, 1870–1941* (Ithaca, 1981).

10. Quoted in Higgs, 210.

11. Saloutos, 191. Higgs speculates that the racial rent premium declined during the 1920–1940 period but offers no evidence to support that contention. Higgs, 214.

12. Ibid., 211–12.

13. Ibid., 214.

14. Ibid., 211.

15. Iwata, 28.

16. Ibid., 32.

17. Ichihashi, 29.

18. Ibid., 28.

19. Carey McWilliams, "Once Again the 'Yellow Peril'," *The Nation* 140 (June 26, 1935): 736.

20. Carey McWilliams, *Prejudice: Japanese Americans: Symbol of Racial Intolerance* (Boston: Little, Brown, 1944), 65. See also, Higgs, 214–23.

21. McWilliams, "Yellow Peril," 736. See Higgs, 220.

22. Higgs, 222. Following the 1920 alien land law, the category "manager" was widely used to conceal Japanese tenancy.

23. Carey McWilliams, "Moving the West-Coast Japanese," *Harper's Magazine* 185 (September 1942): 367.

24. McWilliams, *Prejudice*, 139.

25. Grodzins, 27–28. See also, McWilliams, *Prejudice*, 116–17.

26. tenBroek, et al., 191.

27. Ibid., 191–92.

28. As cited in Grodzins, 58.

29. Ibid., 59.

30. California Legislature, *Assembly Journal*, December 22, 1941; and *Journal of the Senate*, 56th Session, March 6, 1945.

31. Frank F. Chuman, *The Bamboo People: The Law and Japanese-Americans* (Del Mar, Calif., 1976), 200–201 and Bill Hosokawa, *Nisei: The Quiet Americans* (New York: William Morrow, 1969), 447–48. See also, War Relocation Authority, *Legal and Constitutional Phases of the WRA Program* (Washington, D.C.: Government Printing Office, 1946), 52 and WRA, *People in Motion*, 41.

32. Chuman, 202.

33. Saloutos, 191.

34. War Relocation Authority, *The Wartime Handling of Evacuee Property* (Washington, D.C.: Government Printing Office, 1946), 14–15.

35. U.S. Department of War, *Final Report: Japanese Evacuation From the West Coast, 1942* (Washington, D.C.: Government Printing Office, 1943), 143–44.

36. WRA, *Wartime Handling*, 3–4; Hosokawa, 446–49; and Daniels, 167-68. War Relocation Authority, *WRA: A Story of Human Conservation* (Washington, D.C.: Government Printing Office, 1946), 161–62. See also, Joseph I. Omachi, "Some Aspects of Economic Losses Suffered by Japanese Evacuees," January 28, 1943, Japanese Evacuation and Resettlement Study (JERS), Bancroft Library, University of California, Berkeley, A 18.06.

37. U.S. House of Representatives, *Hearings Before the Select Committee on National Defense Migration* (Washington, D.C.: Government Printing Office, 1942).

38. Farm Security Administration, *Final Report, March 15, 1942–May 31, 1942*, JERS, A 8.01, 2. Cf., WRA, *Wartime Handling*, 18–36.

39. FSA, *Final Report*, 2–3.

40. Ibid., 42 and Wartime Civil Control Administration, Statistical Section, *Bulletin* 6 (April 11, 1942).

41. "Operation of Evacuated Japanese Farms by Farm Corporations," JERS, A 18.02, 4–8.

42. FSA, *Final Report*, 18.

43. "Operation of Evacuated Japanese Farms," A 18.06, 1–2. See also, Farm Security Administration, *Supplemental Report, June 1, 1942–August 8, 1942*, JERS, A 8.02.

44. "Operation of Evacuated Japanese Farms," A 18.06, 1–2.

45. Ibid., 11. See also FSA, *Final Report*, 32.

46. "Operation of Evacuated Japanese Farms," A 18.06, 15.

47. Ibid., 11.

48. Ibid., 12. Cf., FSA, *Final Report*, 18.

49. "Operation of Evacuated Japanese Farms," A 18.06, 12.

50. "Operation of Evacuated Japanese Farms," A 18.06, 13–14; Philip Neff, "Studies of Post-Pearl Harbor Agriculture," JERS, Carton 3, Folder 2; and FSA, *Final Report*, 18.

51. "Operation of Evacuated Japanese Farms," A 18.06, 16.

52. Neff, "Studies of Post-Pearl Harbor Agriculture."

53. "Operation of Evacuated Japanese Farms," A 18.06, 16; and Neff, "Studies of Post-Pearl Harbor Agriculture."

54. Neff, "Studies of Post-Pearl Harbor Agriculture."

55. "Operation of Evacuated Japanese Farms," A 18.06, 17.

56. Neff, "Studies of Post-Pearl Harbor Agriculture."

57. "Operation of Evacuated Japanese Farms," A 18.06, 17–19; FSA, *Supplemental Report*; and Omachi, "Some Aspects of Economic Losses."

Judicial Parsimony and Military Necessity Disinterred: A Reexamination of the Japanese Exclusion Cases, 1943–44

Howard Ball

Within six months of the attack by Japan, the military authorities placed into operation a three-stage plan to remove from the West Coast all persons of Japanese ancestry. This plan, which originated in the War Department, was, in effect, authorized by President Roosevelt in Executive Order 9066 and by Congress in the act of March 21, 1942, which made it a misdemeanor for a civilian to refuse to obey a military order. First came the curfew order, followed by exclusion from military zones with the accompanying detention in assembly centers. Finally came the forced relocation of over 110,000 persons to internment camps in the interior. Over 70,000 American citizens, without benefit of criminal charges, incrimination, or trial, without the benefit of any hearing at all, and in the guise of national security and military necessity, were forcibly uprooted from their homes and forced to endure years of imprisonment in America's "concentration camps."[1]

THE CURFEW CASE: *HIRABAYASHI V. UNITED STATES*, 320 US 81 (1943)

Gordon K. Hirabayashi, a senior at the University of Washington at the time of his arrest in 1942, was convicted in federal court for "knowingly disregarding the curfew restrictions" and failure to comply with military orders that required all persons of Japanese ancestry to report to assembly centers for eventual movement to more permanent relocation centers away from the West Coast. He appealed his conviction on two grounds: (1) the orders adopted by the military commander were the fruits of an "unconstitutional delegation by Congress of its legislative power" and (2) the restriction on his freedom "unconstitutionally discriminated between citizens of Japanese ancestry and those of other ancestries in violation of the Fifth Amendment."[2]

The Supreme Court heard arguments on the case on May 10–11, 1943. A review of the conference notes and memoranda sent to the justices reveals several things: Judicial deference to military necessity was a primary consideration in their deliberations; great misgivings were voiced by a number of the justices, especially Black and Frankfurter, about the questions and

concerns Douglas raised; and the court majority, especially Black and Frankfurter, refused to modify the Stone opinion in order to pacify the concerns of the concurring justices, most especially Douglas's concurring opinion.

The leading advocates of judicial self-restraint in these Japanese exclusion cases were Justices Black and Frankfurter. These two justices ironically have been portrayed as the embodiment of two different philosophies of judicial behavior—activism (Black) and self-restraint (Frankfurter).[3] However, throughout the decision-making process, from *Hirabayashi* through *Korematsu*, both justices strongly urged judicial deference to military authorities; both justices were influential in developing Chief Justice Stone's *Hirabayashi* opinion and both were able in *Korematsu* to persuade their junior colleague, Douglas, to give up his dissent and join in the majority opinion written by Black.

Shortly after the oral arguments and conference discussion, Justice Black wrote Stone, outlining an important philosophic issue—judicial deference to military leaders—that Black thought should be in the Stone opinion upholding the conviction of Hirabayashi:

> The immediate responsibility for defense must necessarily rest on those who direct our armed forces. . . . Purely military orders, . . . call for the exercise of a military, not judicial judgment. A curfew regulation in a zone of imminent danger is such a regulation. . . . Final authority to say what persons in the area were to be subjected to the curfew regulation was, I think, not in the courts, but in the military department charged with protecting the country against pressing danger. Therefore, I find it unnecessary to appraise possible reasons which might have prompted the order to be issued in the form it was.[4]

Stone responded with a memorandum to the other justices for a discussion at an upcoming conference in early June 1943. Stone indicated that he was willing to modify his draft opinion to reflect Black's suggestion:

> Where, as they did here, the conditions call for the exercise of judgment and discretion and for the choice of means by those branches of the Government on which the Constitution has placed the responsibility of war-

making, it is not for any court to sit in review of the wisdom of their action or substitute its judgment for theirs.[5]

Another equally important principle of judicial restraint is to refrain from examining a question of constitutional law if it is not absolutely necessary to do so to resolve the issues at law before the Supreme Court.[6] In a June 4, 1943 letter to the chief justice, Associate Justice Frankfurter suggested a further "reservation" in the Stone opinion that would make it "eminently clear that we decide nothing that is not before us." Urging the chief justice to limit the substantive issue to the question of the curfew order, Frankfurter argued:

We need not now attempt to define the ultimate boundaries of the war power nor do we intimate any view concerning any issue not now before us. We decide the issue only as we have defined it—we decide only that the curfew order as applied, and at the time it was applied, was within the boundaries of the war power. In this case it is enough that circumstances within the knowledge of those charged with the reponsibility for maintaining the national defense afford a rational basis for the decision which they made. Whether we would have made it is irrelevant.[7]

The Frankfurter suggestion that the Court limit the scope of the *Hirabayashi* opinion to the narrow issue of curfew and ignore the larger issue of evacuation and relocation by force if necessary (and under penalty of imprisonment and then deportation to the relocation centers), was immediately adopted by the chief justice. In a memorandum dated June 4, 1943, Stone revised his draft to reflect the impact of Frankfurter's suggestion; the italicized portions of Stone's memo (my italics) are the exact words taken from Frankfurter's memo sent earlier that day:

We need not now attempt to define the ultimate boundaries of the war powers. Nor do we have any occasion to decide whether circumstances and conditions which may have arisen since petitioner's disobedience of the curfew order, which are not now before us, would afford a basis for judicial inquiry as to petitioner's loyalty or as to any other fact having a bearing on the danger of espionage and sabotage. Whether or to what extent such issues could be adjudicated in the courts, and whether the courts could provide a procedure for determining the loyalty of individual members of the group of citizens of Japanese ancestry, are questions which are likewise not before us in this case. We intimate no views concerning them. *We decide only that the curfew order as applied, and at the time it was applied, was within the boundaries of the war power. In this case it is enough that circumstances within the knowledge of*

those charged with the responsibility for maintaining the national defense afford a rational basis for the decision which they made. Whether we would have made it is irrelevant.[8]

In addition to responding favorably to Frankfurter's suggestion that the Court not examine the broad constitutional issue, Stone also addressed the suggestion that Douglas had tried to have incorporated in the majority opinion—that the Court had to deal with the question of the loyalty of the Japanese Americans forced to evacuate and relocate against their will. Stone rejected Douglas's contention that the Court somehow assist those loyal Japanese Americans in their efforts to come out from under the restrictive military orders.

Justice William O. Douglas's primary fear, as expressed in his notes and concurring opinion in *Hirabayashi*, was that loyalty was being overshadowed by the arguments of the military that the Japanese in America were totally unassimilated and not to be trusted. Loyalty was the issue, stated Douglas, and "a matter of mind and of heart, not of race."[9] For Douglas, there had to be an opportunity for Japanese Americans to show the WRA that they were loyal citizens and that, therefore, they could be released from an unconstitutional and forced detention in the relocation centers.

His concurring opinion angered Frankfurter and Black immensely. On June 4, 1943, Frankfurter asked Stone to "send for Brother Douglas and talk him out of his opinion by making him see the dangers that he is inviting." Frankfurter was incensed at Douglas's opinion, which in Black's words was an "invitation to bring 'a thousand *habeas corpus* suits in the federal district courts.' " Frankfurter maintained that Douglas, who "ought to act like a collaborator" in the business before the Courts, was instead behaving as though he was engaged "in a rival grocery business."[10]

Douglas was suggesting that Japanese Americans submit to the orders and then request, and legally demand, loyalty hearings. The machinery for such a loyalty examination, argued Douglas in his concurring opinion, "must be made available."[11]

For Frankfurter, the Douglas suggestion went contrary to Stone's "conviction that it is unwise to indicate by direct language that there may be modes of relief for those now in the internment camps. . . . An explicit reservation of opportunities for raising in judicial proceedings questions of individual loyalty or other issues of that sort, inevitably will encourage the institution of many such suits." Both he and Black were trying to convince Douglas to change his mind and kill the concurring opinion, but Frankfurter felt that Douglas would be "obdurate, largely because he will want to make the spread-eagle speech." Frankfurter's ultimate concern was that the Douglas opinion would encourage Japanese Americans to seek release through loyalty hearings: "From the point of view of judicial administration as well as from that of civil liberties, it would be for me deplorable beyond words to hold out hopes by any language that we use. [We ought not] encourage hopes, which, to put it very mildly, are not likely to be fulfilled."[12]

Douglas, troubled by the possible effects of his concurring opinion, sought advice from Justice Wiley Rutledge: "I wish you would turn over in your mind this weekend the question whether I should stick with my concurring opinion in the Jap case if the C.J. takes out all the stuff in his opinion on assimilation and mistreatment."[13] Furthermore, Douglas tried to get the chief justice to modify the majority opinion "to eliminate any suggestion of racial discrimination."

> The first paragraph [of Stone's opinion] implies or is susceptible of the inference that the Japs who are citizens cannot be trusted because we have treated them so badly they will seize on this way to get even. . . . '[R]acial solidarity' and 'lack of assimilation' do not show lack of loyalty as I see it. They may of course give rise to conditions that may breed disloyalty. But that is quite a different matter. Is not the justification for dealing with the Jap citizens as a group the fact that the exigencies of war and the necessities of quick action . . . do not necessarily permit enough time to sort out the sheep from the goats? Is it not necessary to provide an opportunity at some stage . . . for an individual member of the group to show that he has been improperly classified? Otherwise if the military commander knows there are only 10% of the group who are disloyal he can nevertheless hold the entire group in confinement for the duration without any opportunity on the part of the 90% to prove they are as loyal to the United States as the members of this Court.[14]

This suggestion, which prompted great criticism from Frankfurter and Black, goes to the heart of the Douglas position in *Hirabayashi*: there must be some method developed quickly to enable loyal citizens to leave the detention centers and the relocation camps. For Douglas, the military order was "justified only as a temporary expedient. And I would like to have it stated in substantially that way," wrote Douglas in a June 7, 1943 letter to Stone. Douglas understood that these suggestions called "for a departure from one or more of your basic premises." But, he concluded, "the nub of the matter is that I could not go along in an affirmance of the judgment below except on the assumptions (a) that the group treatment was temporary; (b) that the individual must have an opportunity to be reclassified as a loyal citizen. That may be too great a gap for us to bridge."[15]

On June 9, 1943, twelve days before the opinion was announced by the Court, Stone wrote Douglas a letter in which he rejected the suggestions of the junior justice. "It seems to me that if I accepted your suggestions, very little of the structure of my opinion would be left, and that I should lose most of my adherents. It seems to me, therefore, that it would be wiser for me to stand by the substance of my opinion and for you to express your views in your concurring opinion as you have done."[16]

Douglas, in *Hirabayashi*, did publish a separate concurring opinion. Stone, encouraged by Black and Frankfurter, would not yield on the questions of racial discrimination, the temporary nature of the military restriction on Japanese Americans, and on the issue of loyalty hearings.

Mr. Justice Frank Murphy "was perhaps the most sensitive [of the sitting Justices] to racial issues and the most likely to dissent in the *Hirabayashi* case."[17] As a progressive mayor of Detroit, governor of Michigan, and the U.S. attorney general who initiated the Civil Rights Unit in the Department of Justice, Murphy had always been concerned about discrimination and, in *Hirabayashi*, he was especially concerned about the racial discrimination inherent in the military's curfew order.

On June 5, 1943, he informed his colleagues that he was going to write a dissenting opinion because of his belief that the action was primarily a racially discriminatory one. Frankfurter, the field general for the court in these cases, tried to dissuade Murphy from damaging "the *corporate* reputation of the Court" by asking him whether "it is conducive to the things you care about, including the great reputation of this Court, to suggest that everybody is out of step but Johnny."[18]

Nevertheless, Murphy wrote and circulated a dissent that condemned the curfew order and the Supreme Court judgment in upholding it. However, he had second thoughts about his lonely dissent and, after discussions with his friend Justice Reed, turned his dissent into a sharply worded concurring opinion. Frankfurter congratulated him "on the wisdom of having been able to reach a concurrence."[19]

Although no justice dissented in *Hirabayashi*, the Court was clearly split. A six-person majority strongly reaffirmed the power and the responsibility of the military authorities to carry out their task. Stone concluded that there was no unconstitutional deprivation of rights: "In time of war, residents having ethnic affiliations with an invading enemy may be a greater source of danger than those of a different ancestry."[20]

Three justices concurred. Justice Murphy reluctantly concluded that the army actions were taken in good faith but that the actions went "to the very brink of constitutional power."[21] Rutledge voiced the same concern and urged the federal courts to review carefully those actions that come into conflict with a person's rights. Douglas's concerns have already been noted. He concurred because he accepted the military actions as a "temporary treatment on a group basis" and because Hirabayashi had indeed violated the curfew. In a June 22, 1941 letter to Justice Black, Douglas wrote the Alabaman that "we had dinner with some admirers of yours—General and Mrs. DeWitt. They really are grand people. We enjoyed them immensely." One has to speculate as to the impact on these two justices of this friendly association with General DeWitt.[22]

Fred T. Korematsu was charged with violating a Military Exclusion Order which directed that all persons of Japanese ancestry be excluded from a certain part of California. According to the Douglas conference brief prepared by his law clerk, Korematsu had changed his name, undergone an operation to conceal his facial characteristics, and was planning on moving to the Midwest with his Caucasian girlfriend.[23] He was charged with failing to comply with the order's requirement that he report to a civil control station for evacuation from the military zone. Found guilty, he was placed on five years' probation. He appealed to the Ninth Circuit Court of Appeals, arguing that the civilian exclusion order was unconstitutional because:

1. Congress could not authorize the military to incarcerate civilians and citizens of the United States without a trial,
2. the racial discrimination violated the Fifth Amendment,
3. the mass exodus of a racial class of persons constituted cruel and unusual punishment, and
4. imprisonment deprived him of his Fifth Amendment property right to work as a welder.

The Ninth Circuit Court of Appeals, meeting *en banc*, affirmed Korematsu's conviction. In a majority opinion, five of the seven judges (the other two wrote concurring opinions) quickly concluded that "the government of the United States, in prosecuting a war, has power to do all that is necessary to the successful prosecution of a war although the exercise of those powers temporarily infringe some of the inherent rights and liberties of individual citizens which are recognized and guaranteed by the Constitution."[24] Using as authority the *Hirabayashi* case, which involved only the question of a curfew and in which the Supreme Court

majority clearly did not address the issue of the evacuation of a class of people, the circuit court left it for the Supreme Court to decide whether the exclusion, detention, and relocation phases of the military's "Japanese" strategy were valid exercises of presidential and congressional war powers.

In the *Korematsu* conferences there was an even shriller cry for judicial deference to military authority. The justices, meeting on October 16, 1944, four days after the oral arguments concluded in the companion cases of *Korematsu* and *Endo*, were confronted with litigation that challenged the essential core of the military order's weakness: the forced exclusion, the detention and, finally, the relocation of citizens of the United States who had not been formally charged with any crime. The initial vote on the merits in *Korematsu* was 5–4 to affirm the Ninth Circuit Court of Appeals. (The final vote was 6–3; Justice Douglas was the sole jurist to switch his vote in the two months the issue was debated in the Court.)

According to Douglas's notes taken during the conference session of October 16, 1944, four days after the justices heard the oral argument, "the CJ [Stone] would find the authority—in a case of a citizen whose loyalty was not established and who was so ordered to report—[by] treating this as merely an exclusion order." The vote to grant certiorari was 7 to 1, with only Black voting not to bring the case up to the Court. (Stone did not participate in the certiorari vote.) On the merits, five justices voted to affirm the conviction: Chief Justice Stone, Justices Rutledge, Frankfurter, Reed, and Black, who was to write the majority opinion. The four dissenting justices, at the initial conference sessions, were Jackson, Murphy, Roberts, and Douglas.[25]

Reviewing the intracourt memos and letters, two themes emerge: First, the willingness of the six justices who joined in the majority (with one concurring) to drop military reality for political reality in their effort to validate constitutionally questionable military orders. The Black opinion, with the strong encouragement of Stone and Frankfurter (Frankfurter, however, ultimately wrote a separate concurring opinion), had to divorce the exclusion phase of the military orders from the detention and relocation stages of the military plans for the Japanese in order to avoid the constitutional issue. In a December 9, 1944 criticism of the Black opinion, Stone wrote: "But [Korematsu's] principal contention before us was that his presence at the Assembly Center necessarily involved his being subject to a relocation order, and your opinion does not show why this is not true."[26] Black's final opinion, announced on December 18, 1944, cleared up this concern. Second, the struggles Justice Douglas had with the issue of Japanese exclusion in this case reflected the deeper issue of due process in wartime. As *Hirabayashi* indicated, Douglas was distraught by his vision of thousands of citizens incarcerated without benefit of loyalty hearings. In *Korematsu*, Douglas's response in the initial conference sessions was to vote to overturn Korematsu's conviction. Indeed, Douglas circulated a four-page dissent on December 1, 1944; but within a week of the circulation of his dissenting opinion, Douglas sadly joined the majority and cast his vote in favor of the Black opinion—a decision which seemed to haunt him for the rest of his days.

Reviewing Douglas's conference notes, it is clear that Chief Justice Stone dominated the conference and took the lead in developing the factual case and in presenting the points of law upon which the Court had to focus in *Korematsu*. Two basic points the chief justice made were that the Military Exclusion Order "was valid when made" and that its requirement that Korematsu report to an assembly center did not "as a matter of law" mean that he "certainly would" be sent to a relocation center. The chief justice proposed to follow the Ninth Circuit Court of Appeals' approach and "treat this merely as an exclusion order."

The quandary for Douglas was whether the court was "confined to [the] exclusion order" or was the exclusion order, "so tied in with [the] relocation order that it must be considered with others?" Once that question was raised, noted Douglas, "you come to the larger question"—the authority of the military to develop plans for the relocation of tens of thousands of American citizens of Japanese ancestry without trial or hearings processes. "Was confinement included in the authorization—[there is] no suggestion of enforcement in [the] materials before Congress," he jotted down during the course of the discussion among the justices. He was to grapple with this factual and constitutional issue over the next two months.

The other dissenters in the initial conference, Murphy, Jackson, and Roberts, were obviously disturbed by the military action. The process, Roberts believed, was "so violative of constitutional rights of citizens that Roberts thinks he was wrongfully arrested."[27]

The lines were clearly drawn in that first conference session: the majority of five were committed to separating exclusion from relocation, much like the Stone distinction between curfew and exclusion in the *Hirabayashi* case. The dissenters were opposed to this artificial separation of what was to them an integrated, inseparable, and hostile racially discriminatory policy directed toward citizens with Japanese ancestry. In the weeks between the oral arguments and announcement of the decision, the majority coalition had to develop its argument carefully and, at the same time, deflect the hostility of the dissenting opinions.[28]

Under the surveillance and with the assistance of Chief Justice Stone, Hugo Black wrote the majority opinion for the Court. The strategy for holding the majority together and for drawing Douglas to the majority was as follows:

1. To link the curfew validation (an order Douglas felt was constitutional) with the exclusion order by showing that both were designed to protect against espionage and sabotage.
2. To employ *Hirabayashi* as precedent for validating Korematsu's conviction for failing to obey the exclusion order. Even though exclusion poses a greater deprivation than curfew, it has a close and definite relationship to the prevention of sabotage and espionage.
3. The military judgment cannot be rejected by the justices of the Supreme Court. The military leaders have maintained that they cannot bring about an immediate separation of the disloyal from the loyal persons of Japanese ancestry. The exclusion of a class of persons is a *military imperative*, not a group punishment based on racial prejudice and antagonism.
4. The Court should focus on the legal issues surrounding the factual situation: Korematsu was arrested for being illegally in an exclusion zone. "It is sufficient here for us to pass upon the order which petitioner violated, to do more would be to go beyond the issues raised, and to decide momentous questions not contained within the framework of the pleadings or the evidence in this case. It will be time enough to decide the serious constitutional issues which petitioner seeks to raise when an assembly or relocation order is applied or is certain to be applied to him, and we have its terms before us."[29]

Stone's written communications to Black repeatedly emphasized the limited nature of the order in question and the critical importance of accepting the military judgments in this sensitive area of wartime security. The majority opinion, Stone wrote, must take pains to show

> that it is not our apprehension or our judgment of the gravity or the imminence of the danger which governs, but that of the military authorities charged with the responsibilities. . . . [I]t is important for us to make it plain that we do not impose our judgment on the military unless we can say that they have no ground on which to go in formulating their orders.

Stone also admitted that the Court was dealing with a

three-step procedure: exclusion, detention in an assembly center, and possible detention in a relocation center.... [I]t seems plain that we have no constitutional question presented to us with reference to the third or relocation step, but we do have to determine whether the temporary segregation in an assembly center... is an unconstitutional detention.

Stone's attitude on assembly centers was unequivocal:

What is done at an Assembly Center is a mere incident to the authority to control these people given by the Presidential Order and the subsidiary military order; and that insofar as it is but a step to exclusion or other control..., detention at the assembly centers is within the authority of the orders, and has the same constitutional sanction as the curfew order in *Hirabayashi*.[30]

Interestingly, Stone's note refers to Roosevelt's Executive Order 9066 as the "Presidential *Sabotage* Order." In this Freudian slip, Stone expressed his grave fears about the Japanese presence on the West Coast.

By the beginning of December, Stone's concern about the Black opinion that was circulating led the chief justice to send him a brief statement in the form of a concurring opinion which he hoped Black would adopt "and save me the necessity of circulating it." It focused on Korematsu's contention that going to an assembly center would lead him inexorably to one of the relocation centers scattered throughout the United States. Stone emphasized that "this court does not decide moot cases or give advisory opinions. It will be time enough to decide the serious constitutional issue which petitioner seeks to raise here when a relocation order is in fact applied or is certain to be applied to him, and we are advised of its terms."[31] Justice Black heeded the admonition of his chief; the final opinion for the majority included these concerns of Stone in the text.

Although Justice Frankfurter initially endorsed the Black opinion, by December he had decided to write a separate opinion emphasizing, for him, a major theme: judicial self-restraint/noninvolvement in such a serious political issue. "To find that the Constitution does not forbid the military measures now complained of does not carry with it approval of that which Congress and the President did. That is their business, not mine."[32]

In his 1980 autobiography, Justice Douglas, after confessing that the military authority's argument for detention "was not much of an argument, but it swayed a majority of the Court, including myself," alluded to his personal struggles in *Korematsu*:

The severe bite of the military evacuation order was... in the requirement to move out of the West Coast and move into concentration camps in the interior. Locking up the evacuees after they had been moved had no military justification. I wrote a concurring opinion, which I never published, agreeing to the evacuation but not to evacuation *via* the concentration camps. My Brethren, especially Black and Frankfurter, urged me strongly not to publish [because of standards of judicial restraint]... Technically the question of detention was not presented to us. Yet evacuation *via* detention camps was before us, and I have always regretted that I bowed to my elders and withdrew my opinion.[33]

Reviewing his conference notes and the letters sent to other justices, it is clear that in *Korematsu*, as in *Hirabayashi*, Douglas was very troubled by the obvious governmental intrusions—without due process of law—into the constitutional freedoms of U.S. citizens.

The question of the separability of exclusion from relocation had been raised by his law clerk in a memo prior to the oral argument. The clerk pointed out that

1. In view of the fact that the exclusion question was reserved in Hirabayashi, it is difficult to see how that case can be regarded as controlling authority for this.
2. Petitioner contends that this case involves more than exclusion, since the same orders under which the Japanese were excluded provided a complete method of evacuation, detention, and confinement. And if the detention features can be raised here, it is clear that serious constitutional questions are presented.
3. I find it difficult to separate the exclusion and detention features of the order. Compliance with the order not only means evacuation, but evacuation to specified Relocation Centers, and under the direction of the relocation authorities.[34]

At the initial conference session, Douglas was one of four dissenters in *Korematsu*. His dissenting opinion, circulated on December 1, 1944, was an ambiguous, rambling essay that condemned the unauthorized, hence unconstitutional, actions of the military; yet he called the relocation centers fine places that "served a great humanitarian purpose."

Reflecting his law clerk's observations, Douglas argued that evacuation and forced detention were inseparable. As in his *Hirabayashi* concurrence, Douglas was willing to accept a temporary expedient to ensure the safety of the West Coast military zones from possible espionage and sabotage. But, "by May, 1942, evacuation, detention in an Assembly Center and detention in a Relocation center, were but steps in a program which had acquired a unitary character." Korematsu's choice by May 1942, "was to go to jail or submit to indefinite detention in a Relocation Center. That detention was plainly more than temporary detention as an incident to exclusion. I therefore find no authority for it."

Douglas's opinion evidently caused a firestorm in the Court. His remedy, an intolerable one for Stone, Black, and Frankfurter, would have (after two years!) enabled citizens of Japanese ancestry to determine for themselves whether they would go to the relocation center "haven" or whether they would "stand on [their] own." After heavy pressure from the other justices, Douglas caved in on December 6, 1944 and joined the majority opinion. In five days he had gone from a due-process dissenter to a supporter of Black's majority opinion. However, he did ask Black to accommodate his concern by adding a paragraph to his opinion:

> A minority are of the view that evacuation and detention in an Assembly Center were inseparable. After May 3, 1942, the date of the Exclusion Order which is involved in this case, Korematsu was under compulsion to leave the area not as he would choose but via an Assembly Center. The power to exclude includes the power to do it by force if necessary. And any forcible measure *must* necessarily entail some degree of detention or restraint whatever method of removal is selected.[35]

On December 8 Black wrote a note to the members of the Court indicating that he was adding a paragraph to the majority opinion: word for word, it was the Douglas paragraph.[36] After ignominiously retreating from his strong stand on behalf of the rights of U.S. citizens, Douglas, quite understandably, found that "the evacuation case . . . was ever on my conscience."[37]

After stating that "all legal restrictions which curtail the civil rights of a single racial group are immediately suspect," Black—writing for the Court majority—concluded that "pressing public necessity may sometimes justify the existence of some restrictions." Confronted with nothing but an exclusion and accepting the presumption that there were present in the society an "unascertained number of disloyal" Japanese Americans, the military had no option but to act as it did. In modern warfare, Black asserted, "the power to protect must be commensurate with the threatened danger."[38] Justice Frankfurter concurred in the Court's judgment.

There were three dissenters. Justice Jackson argued that military judgments "are not susceptible of intelligent appraisal."[39] To have the judges rationalize a military order in wartime is to validate "for all time the principle of racial discrimination in criminal procedure and of transplanting American citizens."[40] Justice Roberts saw the action as a clear violation of constitutional rights. Korematsu's conviction was "punish-ment for not submitting to imprisonment in a concentration camp."[41] Justice Murphy dissented from "this legalization of racism."[42] Such racial discrimination "in any form and in any degree has no justifiable part whatsoever in our democratic way of life."[43]

THE LOYALTY CASE: *EX PARTE ENDO*, 323 US 283 (1944)

Mitsuye Endo, an American citizen of Japanese ancestry interned at Tule Lake, California, was subsequently moved to the relocation center at Topaz, Utah. She applied to WRA officials for a permit to leave the detention camp in Utah. It was granted on February 16, 1943, by the WRA in accordance with its Administrative Instruction No. 22, dated July 20, 1942. The civilian administrative policy called for FBI assistance in determining whether the applicants—citizens of Japanese ancestry "who [have] never at any time resided or been educated in Japan"[44]—would receive the permit to leave the camp. If granted, the person usually received $25 and a train or bus ticket. However,

> every applicant issued a permit pursuant to this Instruction, and his accompanying dependents, will remain in the *constructive custody* of the military commander in whose jurisdiction lies the relocation center in which the applicant resides at the time the permit is issued. Any such permit may be revoked at any time . . . if the Director shall find such revocation to be necessary in the public interest.[45]

In Endo's case, she was not released from the camp because of "resettlement problems," i.e., out-migration difficulties encountered by loyal Japanese American citizens—"unwanted people"—who tried to relocate in "unprepared communities."[46] However, her "application for a leave clearance was granted, and the Director has admitted that this in effect is a determination that petitioner has been found not to be disloyal."[47] Endo thereupon petitioned the federal district court for a writ of habeas corpus. One problem her attorney immediately encountered was the government argument that the California federal court did not have jurisdiction because Endo was no longer in detention in that state.

The federal district court denied her petition for a writ for want of jurisdiction; it then went to the Ninth Circuit Court of Appeals which then certified a number of questions to the U.S. Supreme Court: First, does the WRA have the authority to detain people without any right to seek release from such custody in a hearing with substantial elements of due process because the people are of Japanese ancestry? Second, after loyalty is determined, can the person be held in the RC until such time as the Director is satisfied that the person will fit into a community? Third, can these judgments be made by the Director without a hearing? And fourth, if a leave is granted, can there be conditions attached?[48]

The government argued that habeas corpus was inappropriate since procedures developed by the WRA had to be exhausted prior to any legal action. Privately, Edward J. Ennis, director of the Alien Enemy Control Unit in the Justice Department, in a memorandum to the U.S. solicitor general, January 21, 1944, argued that in order to help the many thousands of interned Japanese Americans such as Endo, it would be both wise and necessary for the Department of Justice not to waive regulations and let her go free. For Ennis, it was critical that the litigation go to the U.S. Supreme Court, even though Endo was being denied her liberties and should have been able to leave the internment camp much earlier than 1944. "As a matter of constitutional government and proper race relations, a decision that this detention was unlawful would be the first step on the road back to legal, if not economic, equality for this minority. This case should be used realistically as a vehicle to aid in that arduous journey." Ennis's frustration with the War Department's treatment of Japanese Americans was apparent.[49] A week later, Ennis wrote to the U.S. attorney general that

a decision of unconstitutionality of detention of evacuees . . . would not only repair the damage that has been done to their loyalty by detention for so long a time, but would also have a powerful propaganda effect on racial minorities generally, to know that their constitutional rights were not a dead letter, which is presently the case. . . . The Supreme Court decision that detention was not authorized would be very useful. Such a decision in my opinion would be accepted by the public generally and would not result in violent reaction against the Japanese Americans.[50]

Endo was not aware of Ennis's strategy. In the legal brief filed with the U.S. Supreme Court, her attorney argued that

she was entitled to an unconditional release because the whole procedure set up constitutes a denial of due process and hence its requirements may be ignored; because once she has been found to be loyal the remaining requirements for release can be ignored; because the remaining requirements (in the WRA Order No. 22) are invalid for lack of Due Process; because a conditional, revokable indefinite leave as contemplated by the regulations is invalid."[51]

The Supreme Court heard oral arguments and discussed Endo's case at the same time it heard and discussed Korematsu's petition. From the Douglas conference notes, it is clear that there was instant una-

nimity in the Endo case. All nine justices were of the opinion that she was being illegally detained in the relocation center in Topaz, Utah, *after* the WRA director ascertained her loyalty. As Douglas jotted down during the discussion on October 16, 1944, the whole basis of these orders was the presence of disloyal people among the mass of Jap citizens—once loyalty is shown, the basis for the military decision disappears— this woman is entitled to a *summary release*."[52]

The justices, agreed that the federal district court did have jurisdiction to issue a writ of habeas corpus. Furthermore, Abe Fortas, Acting Secretary of the Interior, had indicated that, should a writ be issued, "the court's order will be complied with in all respects."[53]

The strategy Douglas employed in drafting the opinion—from a review of his notes to law clerks and other justices—was to show that the WRA's legitimate functions were fairly narrow and that the Act of Congress, March 21, 1942, did not envision a civilian authority developing and implementing relocation policies and procedures for loyal citizens. In his examination of the legislative history of the act, Douglas concluded that legislators had spent little time discussing relocation. "Most of the persons appearing before the Committee [on Military Affairs]," wrote Douglas's law clerk, "contemplated little or no control over the Japanese once they had left the prohibited area and much of the discussion concerned the problem of directing the Japanese to work areas."[54]

As to the question of loyalty, Justice Reed's letter to Douglas, dated November 9, 1944 (a day after the Douglas opinion was circulated), reflected the Court's view: "I am quite satisfied with the opinion as a whole. . . . So far as I am concerned . . . even where we have espionage and sabotage, since such things are not done by a loyal citizen, it is not permissible to restrain the loyal citizen for the purpose of avoiding espionage and sabotage for a longer time than is necessary to determine loyalty."[55] This was Douglas's view since *Hirabayashi*; in *Endo*, he wrote an opinion summarizing his views on the loyalty question.

Although the opinion was written and approved by a majority (Murphy and Roberts wrote brief concurring opinions) in early November, the chief justice did not release the opinion for over a month. In exasperation, Douglas complained:

The matter is at a standstill because officers of the government have indicated that some changes in detention plans are under consideration. Their motives are beyond criticism and their request is doubtless based on important administrative considerations. Mitsuye Endo, however, has not asked that action of this Court be stayed. She is a citizen, insisting on her right to be released—a right which we all agree she has. I feel strongly that we should act promptly and not lend our aid in compounding the wrong by keeping her in unlawful .confinement through our action any longer than necessary to reach a decision.[56]

Stone, however, held up the announcement in *Endo* until Monday, December 18, 1944, two days after he received final word from the War and Justice departments about the major policy change in a letter from the U.S. solicitor general. The letter contained a copy of the memorandum from Secretary of War Stimson to President Roosevelt, dated December 13, 1944, explaining the rescission of the mass exclusion of persons of Japanese ancestry from the West Coast, and copies of various statements from the War Department, scheduled for release Sunday, December 17, 1944, that announced the change in government policy with respect to loyal citizens of Japanese ancestry.

The *Endo* decision was announced on Monday, December 18, 1944, eighteen hours after the War Department's messages had been released nationally, stating that the West Coast was no longer in danger of sabotage, espionage, and hostile attack and that the loyal Japanese Americans were to be released from the relocation centers. The announcement that the gates would be opened up for all loyal citizens of Japanese ancestry came "just a few hours before the Court interpreted the Constitution in such a way that solely because of race, a loyal, law-abiding citizen of the United States could be dispossessed and publicly humiliated but could not be indefinitely locked up."[57]

It seems clear that the delay to which Douglas alluded in his November 28, 1944 letter to the chief justice was caused by those informal and secret discussions between Stone and officials at the War Department. "What Douglas never learned was that Stone had enlisted in the high-level campaign, directed by John McCloy, to protect President Roosevelt from the political consequences of the decision to end the internment program."[58] In delaying its order releasing Endo, the Court had, as Douglas had stated earlier in his letter, "lent [its] aid in compounding the wrong by keeping her in unlawful confinement."[59]

CONCLUSION

"The job of the Court is to resolve doubts, not create them," wrote Chief Justice Stone, sharply, to Justice Murphy during the Japanese-exclusion arguments.[60] This effectively summarizes the U.S. Supreme Court's response to the issues raised by Japanese American citizens confined in the ten relocation centers scattered across the U.S. The justices, with few exceptions, refused to interfere in the matter. For Stone, the Court's views were "irrelevant."[61] For

Black, military orders called for the "exercise of military, not judicial judgment," and it was "unnecessary . . . to appraise the possible reasons which might have prompted the order to be used in the form it was."[62] Furthermore, at least four of the justices had some contact with government officials involved in the development and implementation of the Japanese exclusion policy and should have recused themselves. Frankfurter had frequent contacts with John J. McCloy of Secretary of War Henry Stimson's staff. Stone acted in concert with War Department officials. Justices Douglas and Black evidently were acquaintances of General DeWitt.[63]

Most of the justices of the Court followed guidelines of military imperative and military necessity. Any justice who created doubts in the matter of Japanese exclusion was not seen as participating in the judicial effort to buttress the military judgment.

Douglas's argument that the WRA should quickly develop machinery to determine the loyalty of Japanese Americans unless they be held indefinitely without due process of law fell on hostile ears. The Court majorities did not want to hear these points and would not support such a development unless the military and the civilian authorities instituted them. The fact that "preventive detention . . . is inconsistent with the Fourth and Fifth Amendments of our Constitution"[64] evidently did not concern most of the justices in 1942 and 1944.

The Court placed its imprimatur on what have been judged to be "grave injustices done to American citizens and resident aliens of Japanese ancestry."[65] Not only did the Court act passively with regard to the legal questions associated with the relocation program, in *Endo* the chief justice, with Court acquiescence, actively participated in a successful effort to prevent the Court from prematurely releasing loyal citizens from the relocation centers. By not releasing the Court opinion for over a month, the chief justice, simply put, obstructed justice. Passivity and judicial deference are more easily understood than the obstructing of justice.

The Supreme Court's actions in the Japanese exclusion diminish the luster of the tribunal. In wartime, the Court's Japanese exclusion decisions demonstrate that some groups' constitutional rights are a dead letter, and individuals may be deprived of due process even if they are loyal, law-abiding citizens. In its 467-page report, *Personal Justice Denied*, released on February 24, 1983, the congressionally appointed Commission on Wartime Relocation and Internment of Civilians stated, regarding delays in the release of loyal citizens of Japanese ancestry until after November 1944, that "the inescapable conclusion from this factual pattern is that the delay was motivated by political considerations."[66]

NOTES

1. Murphy dissent, *Korematsu v. United States*, 323 US 214 (1944), 233.

2. *Hirabayashi v. U.S.*, 320 US 81 (1943), 82.

3. See Wallace Mendelson, *Justices Black and Frankfurter: Conflict in the Court* (Chicago: University of Chicago Press, 1961).

4. Memo, n.d., Harlan F. Stone Papers, Hirabayashi File, Library of Congress.

5. Ibid.

6. See *Ashwander v. TVA*, 297 US 288 (1936).

7. Stone Papers, Hirabayashi File.

8. Ibid.

9. *Hirabayashi v. US*, 320 US 81 (1943), 107, Douglas Concurring Opinion.

10. Stone Papers, Hirabayashi File.

11. *Hirabayashi*, 108.

12. Stone Papers, Hirabayashi File, June 4, 1943.

13. Memo, n.d., Wiley Rutledge Papers, Hirabayashi File, Library of Congress.

14. Stone Papers, Hirabayashi File.

15. Ibid.

16. Stone to Douglas, William O. Douglas Papers, Hirabayashi File, Library of Congress.

17. Peter Irons, *Justice At War* (New York: Oxford University Press, 1983), 242. See also J. Woodford Howard, Jr., *Mr. Justice Murphy: A Political Biography* (Princeton, N.J.: Princeton University Press, 1968) and Sidney Fine, "Mr. Justice Murphy and the Hirabayashi Case," *Pacific Historical Review* (May 1964).

18. Irons, 246.

19. Ibid., 247.

20. *Hirabayashi v. U.S.*, 320 US 81 (1943).

21. Ibid., 11.

22. Ibid., 107, 109. The quotation is from the Hugo L. Black Papers, Box 59, Library of Congress.

23. Douglas Papers, Korematsu File.

24. *Korematsu v. U.S.*, 140 *Federal Supp* 2d 289 (1943).

25. Douglas Papers, Korematsu File.

26. Black Papers, Korematsu File.

27. "Conference Notes," Douglas Papers, Korematsu File.

28. See Howard Ball, *Courts and Politics* (Englewood Cliffs, N.J.: Prentice-Hall, 1980). Chapter seven has an overview of the Supreme Court decision-making process.

29. Draft Opinion, Black Papers, Korematsu File.

30. Letter, Stone to Black, November 9, 1944, Black Papers, Korematsu File.

31. Stone Draft Concurring Opinion, December 1, 1944, Black Papers, Korematsu File.

32. Letter, Frankfurter to Black, November 9, 1944.

33. William O. Douglas, *The Court Years* (New York: Random House, 1980), 280.

34. Memo, Eugene A. Beyer, Jr., to Douglas, Douglas Papers,

Korematsu File. It was actually a *dissenting* opinion, circulated on December 1, 1944. In less than one week, Douglas abandoned his dissent and joined the Black majority.

35. Letter, Douglas to Black, December 6, 1944, Black Papers, Korematsu File.

36. Black, December 8, 1944, Black Papers, Korematsu File, 62. *Korematsu v. U.S.*, 323 US 214 (1944).

37. Douglas, *Court Years*, 281.

38. *Korematsu v. U.S.*, 323 US 214 (1944), 216, 218, 220.

39. Ibid., 245.

40. Ibid., 246.

41. Ibid., 226.

42. Ibid., 242.

43. Ibid.

44. Document, War Relocation Authority, Washington, D.C., D.S. Myer, Director, July 20, 1942, 3 pp., in Douglas Papers, Endo File.

45. Ibid., 1.

46. *Ex Parte Endo*, 323 US 283 (1944), 297.

47. Ibid., 294.

48. Ninth Circuit Certification Questions, in Douglas Papers, Endo File.

49. Memo, Ennis to Fahy, 21 January 1944, Department of Justice Files, Endo Case.

50. Memo, Ennis to Biddle, January 28, 1944, ibid.

51. Memo, Eugene A. Beyer, Jr., to Douglas, n.d., Douglas Papers, Endo File.

52. Douglas, Conference Notes, ibid.

53. Letter, Fortas to Solicitor General Fahy, October 13, 1944, Department of Justice Files, Endo Case.

54. Memo, Eugene A. Beyer, Jr., to Justice Douglas, November 1944, Douglas Papers, Endo File.

55. Letter, Reed to Douglas, November 9, 1944, ibid.

56. Letter, Douglas to Stone, November 28, 1944, ibid.

57. John D. Weaver, *Warren: The Man, the Court, the Era* (Boston: Little, Brown, 1967), 111–12.

58. Irons, 344.

59. Letter, Douglas to Stone, November 28, 1944, Douglas Papers, Endo File.

60. A. T. Mason, *Harlan Fiske Stone: Pillar of the Law* (New York: Viking Press, 1956), 793.

61. Memo for the Court, June 4, 1943, Stone Papers, Hirabayashi File.

62. Black's notes, n.d., Black Papers, Korematsu File.

63. Black Papers, Box 59.

64. William O. Douglas, *The Anatomy of Liberty* (New York: Trident Press, 1963), 69.

65. See Report of the Commission on Wartime Relocation and Internment of Civilians, *Personal Justice Denied* (Washington, D.C.: Government Printing Office, 1982), 15, 227–32, and passim.

66. Ibid.

PART VII

The Redress Movement

188

It is difficult to date with any kind of precision the start of the movement for redress described in the following essays. It can be argued that the handful of Japanese Americans who in 1942 protested, either verbally or by civil disobedience, were the real initiators of the movement. Perhaps a somewhat better case can be made for the very limited Japanese American Claims Act of 1948. But apart from these precursor activities of the 1940s, a more persuasive argument can be made that the proximate causes should be traced to the late 1960s when small groups of Japanese Americans in Southern California, San Francisco, and Seattle began agitating for some kind of compensation for the wrongs done to them and their people during World War II. Sometimes they used the word "reparations," but the softer term, "redress," eventually prevailed.

Soon thereafter some members of the Japanese American community began to organize "pilgrimages" to Manzanar and other relocation centers, and, as early as 1970 the JACL passed the first of three resolutions calling for legislation to make amends for the "worst mistakes of World War II." Little came of the earlier resolutions, initiated by dissident activists from within and without the national organization, as the JACL leadership neither opposed nor acted upon them. Edison Uno, perhaps the most influential of the early proponents of redress, thought in the fall of 1977 that it would take "at least ten years" to get any meaningful action from the national group. After Uno's untimely death at the end of 1977, Dr. Clifford I. Uyeda, who had led the national campaign resulting in a presidential pardon for Iva Toguri, the so-called "Tokyo Rose," took over the struggle for redress within the JACL. The turning point in that struggle came at the organization's 1978 convention in Salt Lake City.

Shortly before the convention, Uyeda's committee published an important rationale for redress. Referring directly to the parallel experience of German Jews—something that would have been unthinkable for the organization a few years earlier—the JACL Redress Committee statement pointed out that:

> German Jews experienced the horrors of the Nazi death camps. Japanese Americans experienced the agonies of being incarcerated for an indeterminate period. Both were imprisoned in barbed wire compounds with armed guards. Both were prisoners of their own country. Both were there without criminal charges, and were completely innocent of any wrong-doing. Both were there for only one reason—ancestry. German Jews were systematically murdered en masse—that did not happen to Japanese Americans, but the point is that both Germany and the United States persecuted their own citizens based on ancestry.

The pamphlet described the billions that the West German government had paid or promised to pay, and, while mentioning no dollar amount, closed by arguing that redress for the injustices of 1942–1946 is not just an isolated Japanese American issue: it is an issue of concern for all Americans. Restitution does not put a price tag on freedom or justice. The issue is not to recover what cannot be recovered. The issue is to acknowledge the mistake by providing proper redress to victims of injustice, and thereby make such injustices less likely to recur.

At the convention itself, Uyeda and his committee unveiled a specific proposal asking for $25,000 for each individual or heir who suffered from the mass incarceration. The proposal was unanimously adopted by the national council. Uyeda, in addition, was elected national president, the first person so elected who had not previously either headed a chapter or been in the JACL administrative hierarchy.

There were those within the organization, the community, and the nation who were shocked that a "model minority" should make such strident demands. Perhaps the chief opponent, and certainly the chief Japanese American opponent, was S. I. Hayakawa, who had been elected as a Republican to the U.S. Senate from California in 1976. A speaker at the 1978 convention, Hayakawa gave an interview that was carried nationally by the wire services in which he argued that the demand for reparations was "ridiculous." The next year Hayakawa went so far as to suggest that the wartime incarceration was good for Japanese Americans:

> As one talks with Nisei today—they are now in their fifties and sixties—one gets the impression that the wartime relocation, despite the injustices and economic losses suffered, was perhaps the best thing that could have happened to the Japanese-Americans of the West Coast. As many say, the relocation forced them out of their segregated existence to discover the rest of America. It opened up possibilities for them that they never would have known had they remained on farms in Livingston or fishing boats in San Pedro.

This infuriated many, if not most of the Japanese American community, who delighted in pointing out that the Canadian-born Hayakawa had spent the war in Chicago and had not suffered incarceration either by his native or his adopted country. But there were many others in the Japanese American community who initially rejected redress for a variety of reasons. Some insisted that no amount of money could compensate them for their suffering; others saw it as a kind of welfare, while still others thought that it was best not to reopen the wounds of the past. My own quite unscientific notion is that, in the early stages of the redress campaign, the ethnic community was divided on the issue in much the same way as John Adams had imagined that colonial Americans were divided about the American Revolution—about a third favored it, another third opposed it, and the final third was not too much concerned one way or another. For Japanese Americans in the late 1970s much of the "unconcern" and even opposition stemmed from a healthy skepticism that anything would come of it.

But the creation by Congress of the Commission on the Wartime Relocation and Internment of Civilians (CWRIC) in 1980, the nationwide hearings held by that body, and its splendid report, *Personal Justice Denied* (1983), have helped dispel much of that skepticism and have created a communal climate of opinion highly favorable to redress. In 1984 and 1985, bills, with powerful sponsors from both parties, have been introduced into Congress to carry out the commission's recommendations, which set the amount to be paid to individuals at $20,000 and would compensate survivors only.

Many of the dimensions of the movement for redress are surveyed in the essays that follow. John Tateishi, a Sansei (b. 1939), whose earliest memories are of Manzanar, has served as chairperson of the JACL Redress Committee. William Hohri, Nisei chair of the Chicago-based National Council for Japanese American Redress (NCJAR), heads a group that opposes the JACL-sponsored efforts as "too little and too late" and has attempted, so far without positive results, to pursue a multibillion-dollar class action suit against the government. Dale Minami, a San Francisco attorney and a leading spirit in the Asian American Law Caucus, describes the fruitful *pro bono* legal efforts as a kind of redress that has been achieved in the federal courts in regard to the wartime convictions of a few Japanese Americans. Shirley Castelnuovo, a political scientist concerned with legal and constitutional issues, contributes a unique essay which analyzes the West German statute providing compensation for Jews and discusses, imaginatively, how such principles might be applied to Japanese Americans. And, finally, to provide a kind of balance, the editors have solicited statements from the two chief surviving architects of the relocation program, former Assistant Secretary of War John J. McCloy and the former head of General DeWitt's Wartime Civil Control Administration, Colonel Karl R. Bendetsen.

In addition to the essays in this section, the following provide a preliminary view of the redress movement. The National Committee for Redress, Japanese American Citizens League, *The Case for Redress* (San Francisco: JACL, 1978); for the campaign for Toguri's pardon, see Clifford I. Uyeda, *A Final Report and Review: The Japanese American Citizens League National Committee for Iva Toguri* (Seattle: Asian American Studies Program, University of Washington, 1980); S. I. Hayakawa, "Giri to One's Name: Notes on the Wartime Relocation and the Japanese American Character" in his *Through the Communication Barrier* (New York: Harper and Row, 1979); the rationale for creating the CWRIC is spelled out in U.S. Congress, Senate, *Commission on Wartime Relocation and Internment of Civilians Act, Hearing before the Committee on Governmental Affairs*, 96th Cong., 2d sess. (Washington, D.C.: Government Printing Office, 1980); CWRIC, *Personal Justice Denied: Report of the Commission on Wartime Relocation and Internment of Civilians* (Washington, D.C.: Government Printing Office, 1982). Although dated December 1982, the report was not released until February 24, 1983. The CWRIC's June 1983 recommendations may be most conveniently consulted in a pamphlet, *Personal Justice Denied: Summary and Recommendations of the Commission on Wartime Relocation and Internment of Civilians* (San Francisco: JACL, 1983). Bill Hosokawa, *JACL: In Quest of Justice* (New York: William Morrow, 1982) is a useful if uncritical "company history." The activities of William Hohri's NCJAR can best be followed through the group's newsletters, 923 West Diversey Parkway, Chicago, Illinois 60614. An early attempt to place the redress movement into a larger historical perspective will be found in Roger Daniels, *Asian America: Chinese and Japanese in the United States since 1850*, soon to be published by the University of Washington Press.

Roger Daniels

The Japanese American Citizens League and the Struggle for Redress

John Tateishi

It is not my intention in this essay to defend or to criticize the Japanese American Citizens League for its actions in the historical event that we in the community refer to as the "Evacuation." Instead, I will focus upon the role that the JACL has played in the current redress movement. The redress movement, as we know it, took shape in Salt Lake City in the summer of 1978 when the JACL held its biennial convention there, and it was at that convention that the issue first caught the attention of the national media. But the redress movement had its birth much earlier.

In 1970, the late Edison Uno of San Francisco introduced a resolution at the JACL convention in Chicago, the first of a series of resolutions calling for redress as an issue of the JACL. It was, in a sense, a quiet birth of what would become the single most burning issue in the Japanese American community.

In 1972, a redress resolution was again introduced at the JACL convention and, in 1974 at the Portland convention, redress became the priority issue of our organization. Because of the many differing views—between those who advocated individual compensation and those who opposed it, to those who felt the past should be left alone—there was a quagmire from which, at the time, we could not extricate ourselves and present a single, coherent position. Consequently, little progress was made during the next two years, even though the JACL had established a National Committee for Redress. In 1976, at the Sacramento convention, this issue was again adopted as the priority issue.

The Sacramento convention witnessed a significant movement as the JACL adopted, as part of its priority resolution, monetary compensation as an essential and necessary part of any effort to rectify the injustices of the internment. There was at that time

little doubt that compensation would become the focus of the issue.

Prior to the 1978 convention, Dr. Clifford Uyeda, who had been appointed as an interim chair of the JACL National Committee for Redress, convened a meeting of representatives from each of the eight JACL districts nationwide. In April 1978, we met in San Francisco to hammer out guidelines to be presented to the delegates of the convention. We recommended the adoption of a $25,000 compensation figure plus the creation of a Japanese American Foundation to serve as a trust for funds to be used for the benefit of Japanese American communities throughout the country.

In the summer of 1978, at the JACL convention held in Salt Lake City, the organization unanimously adopted redress as its priority issue once again. At the same time, the convention delegates also adopted the recommended redress guidelines. It should be noted here that the JACL was the first organization to come out with the $25,000 figure, and that we stood alone at that time in dealing with the issue of redress.

At the 1978 convention Clifford Uyeda, who had been elected as the new JACL national president, appointed me to chair the National Committee for Redress. Immediately following his election, we determined the goals of the JACL's redress program over the next two years, the term of his presidency: first, to take the redress issue from the intra-organization discussions to the public arena by launching a public media campaign as part of the need to educate the American public and, second, to seek the drafting of legislation and to see its introduction in the United States Congress.

We initiated the first objective immediately. Unknown to us, Senator S. I. Hayakawa, who had been invited to speak at the convention, gave a private interview to the local Salt Lake City papers on the final evening of the convention and commented that the JACL's demand for $25,000 was "absurd and ridiculous." We were not invited to respond and were unaware of the statement until the next day. Upon returning to our homes the following day, we learned the story was on the wires and that it appeared in a number of newspapers across the country, but it did give us an opportunity to begin to air the issue nationally.

For the first six months of my chairmanship, Dr. Uyeda and I spent a good part of our time working the media around the country, responding to editorials and letters in an attempt to clarify the issue and to keep it in the public light. Although I found it difficult to get both television and radio to respond to the issue in those early days in areas outside the West Coast, we began to achieve some degree of success in placing the issue on the public forum. It was the first opportunity Japanese Americans had been given to talk publicly about what they experienced during World War II.

The second objective—to seek legislation—was perhaps quixotic considering we had yet to gain even a sense of unity within the Japanese American community, and also because this was still an issue that had been discussed only within the JACL. To achieve this goal, I consulted with Clifford Uyeda to select six members for the JACL's National Committee for Redress whom we knew to be active or committed on the issue.

After meeting with the committee in September 1978, and again a couple of months later, it became evident that we could not make any determinations without some feedback from the Japanese American members of Congress whom we knew to be sympathetic to this issue, namely, Senators Daniel Inouye and Spark Matsunaga, both from Hawaii, and Congressmen Norman Mineta and Bob Matsui from California.

In late January 1979, in what I personally view as a historic meeting, a small delegation from the JACL met with the four Japanese American legislators in Washington to convey our concerns about the issue and to present our proposals for legislation. They suggested to us that before Congress would begin to consider any legislation to seek compensation, we needed first to establish an official determination of wrong in the government's records because the Congress, and indeed the American public, was not convinced that an injustice had occurred. Coincidentally, some of us had previously conferred with a number of professional lobbyists and civil rights advocates, all of whom had suggested that we should seek the creation of a congressional commission to establish an official determina-

tion of the injustice. The Japanese American members of Congress made a similar recommendation, a message we carried back with us.

One month later, on March 3–4, 1979, I convened the National Committee for Redress in San Francisco with specific instructions to the committee that they were being brought together to determine what approach we would pursue. We unanimously rejected a court suit and after two days of discussion, we finally came to a vote. The majority of the committee members expressed the view that if the circumstances allowed, they would vote in favor of legislation directly aimed at compensation. But given the political realities and the mood of the Congress and the public, and given that the responsibility of the JACL was to achieve success in the redress campaign as best possible, we voted in favor of legislation seeking the creation of a federal commission. I later described the atmosphere of that meeting as one in which I felt I could cut the air with a knife.

The final vote was four to two in favor of legislation to seek the creation of a commission. As a committee, we knew that our decision would be unpopular in the Japanese American community and that we, as an organization, would be harshly criticized. And as expected, such was the response. The JACL was accused of "selling out" and of acquiescing to political timidity. Critics admonished us for using the rationale of "political reality" for what many viewed as a lack of courage.

But we knew that the realities of Washington politics and the public attitude did not bode well for us in seeking passage of a $3 billion appropriations bill in Congress. It made sense to us that an official investigation in the form of a report to the president and the Congress would serve to eliminate the myth of military necessity, which had plagued us for so long. To those who criticized us by stating that we *know* that an injustice had occurred, we responded that an official and objective recording of the facts would show the gravity of the injustice committed against Japanese Americans and that it was others who had to be convinced of the truth. We placed our faith in the truth and in the facts, and we were convinced that those facts would generate tremendous media attention and public awareness about the issue.

Despite the harsh criticism from within our own community, we sought the introduction of a bill to create a federal commission. The Japanese American members of Congress, including Senator Hayakawa, agreed to sponsor legislation that would establish an investigatory commission to examine the facts and circumstances surrounding the internment. In addi-

Commission on Wartime Relocation and Internment of Civilians, Washington, D.C. l–r: Joan Z. Bernstein, *Chair*, Hon. Arthur J. Goldberg, Dr. Arthur S. Flemming, and Hon. Hugh B. Mitchell. (Commissioners not shown: Hon. Edward W. Brooke, Hon. William M. Marutani, Hon. Daniel E. Lungren, Father Robert Drinan, and Father Ishmael V. Gromoff.) Courtesy Japanese American Citizens League.

tion, the legislation would mandate the commission to issue recommendations for remedies based on their findings.

On August 7, 1979, Senator Daniel Inouye, along with the principal cosponsorship of Senators Matsunaga, Hayakawa, and Ted Stevens of Alaska, introduced S. 1647 in the Senate. And on September 28, House Majority Leader James Wright of Texas, with the principal cosponsorship of Congressmen Mineta, Matsui, and others as part of 114 cosponsors, introduced H.R. 5499. The Senate bill was referred to the Governmental Affairs Committee and the House bill to the Judiciary Subcommittee on Administrative Law and Governmental Relations.

Both bills lay dormant for approximately six months. Then on March 18, 1980, the Governmental Affairs Committee held a hearing on S. 1647. In early May 1980, the committee approved S. 1647 by a vote of 11–0, and on May 22, 1980, S. 1647 was approved in the Senate by unanimous consent.

Two weeks later, on June 2, the House Subcommittee on Administrative Law and Governmental Relations conducted a hearing on H.R. 5499, and one week later the bill was reported out by a 7–0 vote. Within two weeks, the full subcommittee voted 16–0 to report H.R. 5499 to the House, and on July 21,

1980, the House of Representatives approved the legislation by a vote of 279–109. A JACL representative had testified at both the Senate and House hearings as an advocate of the commission legislation.

On July 31, 1980, President Jimmy Carter held a signing ceremony at the White House. The JACL, as a proponent of the legislation, was invited to send a delegation to the White House signing of Public Law 96-317, which created the Commission on Wartime Relocation and Internment of Civilians.

Significantly, the signing took place on the last day of Dr. Uyeda's term as the JACL national president. In the two years of his presidency, Dr. Uyeda had provided the leadership that had helped bring the redress issue to national status. As we stood in the White House on that July day, I thought about the objectives we had set for the JACL in Salt Lake City two years previously and how we had far exceeded our goals. Redress had become a viable issue of national interest.

The Commission on Wartime Relocation and Internment of Civilians was constituted with nine distinguished members: Joan Bernstein, former general counsel of the Department of Health and Human Services (HHS) and chair of the commission; Congressman Daniel Lungren, vice-chair; former Senator Ed-

John Tateishi, Redress Director, Japanese American Citizens League, testifying before the Commission on Wartime Relocation and Internment of Civilians. Photo by George Wakiji. Courtesy Japanese American Citizens League.

Minoru Yasui testifying in Washington, D.C., before the Commission on Wartime Relocation and Internment of Civilians. Photo by George Wakiji. Courtesy Japanese American Citizens League.

ward Brooke; former Congressman Father Robert Drinan; Dr. Arthur Flemming, chair of the U.S. Commission on Civil Rights; the Honorable Arthur Goldberg, former Justice of the Supreme Court and a former ambassador to the United Nations; Father Ishmael Gromoff of the Pribilof Islands in Alaska; Judge William Marutani, Court of Common Pleas of the state of Pennsylvania and the only Japanese American on the commission; and former Senator Hugh Mitchell.

In July 1981, the commission held a hearing in Washington, D.C., the first of a series of public hearings conducted throughout the country. In August, the commission held hearings in Los Angeles and San Francisco; in September, hearings in Seattle, Alaska, and Chicago; in November, a second hearing in Washington, D.C., and a hearing in New York City; and in December, a final hearing in Cambridge, Massachusetts, at Harvard University.

After hearing from over 750 witnesses, the majority of whom were Japanese Americans who had experi-

enced internment, and after eighteen months of exhaustive research and investigation, the commission completed its work and issued its findings.

In a report titled *Personal Justice Denied* issued to the administration and the Congress on February 22, 1983, the commission was unequivocal in its conclusion: the exclusion and detention of Japanese Americans were not determined by military conditions but were the result of "race prejudice, war hysteria and a failure of political leadership." The commission's findings reiterated for the first time in an official voice of the U.S. government what Japanese Americans had stated all along: that there was no justifiable cause to warrant the suspension of constitutional rights during World War II, and that exclusion and detention were the direct result of racism and economic greed. What we had argued for years in virtual isolation was now substantiated as part of the government's records. The facts were incontrovertible.

On June 16, 1983, the Commission on Wartime Relocation and Internment of Civilians completed its final legislative mandate when it issued its recommendations to the Reagan administration and Congress. Based on the findings of their report and a supplemental report of economic losses estimated as high as $6.2 billion, the commission presented a five-point recommendation as appropriate remedies. Included among the five recommendations was a proposal that each surviving victim of the exclusion and internment be compensated $20,000 as redress for the injustice.

Although the commission's recommended compensation figure did not match the JACL's, our national board nevertheless endorsed the five-point recommendation and mandated that we request legislation to implement all five recommendations. On October 6, 1983, H.R. 4110 was introduced in the House of Representatives by Majority Leader Jim Wright with seventy-two cosponsors, including Representatives Mineta and Matsui, and on November 17, 1983, S. 2116 was introduced by Senator Spark Matsunaga in the Senate, with thirteen cosponsors, among them Senators Inouye and Stevens. Both bills seek the full implementation of the commission's recommendations.

Our belief in the value of a federal commission was well founded in the final analysis. Each of the commission hearings throughout the country received extensive media coverage in both cities where hearings were held and across the United States. And on February 22 and June 16, 1983, when the commission issued its report and its recommendations at Washington, D.C., press conferences, it received national coverage on the three television networks and in every major newspaper in the country. As a result, we could see from press clippings that editorial comments had shifted dramatically. Many newspapers that had previously argued the old myths about the internment were now arguing for compensation to right a major wrong. Because of the commission's work, this nation began to understand for the first time in forty years the nature and extent of the injustice of the internment.

From a personal point of view in the Japanese American community, I think the commission served an even greater value. For the first time, Japanese Americans were given the opportunity to tell their stories of hardship and heartbreak before an official body of the government. There was a release of tears, but there was also a release of anger. And in so doing, there was a catharsis in dealing with all the pain that had been bottled up for forty years. It is my belief that as difficult as it was for our people to face the commission and to face a deeply rooted pain, we found a means to expiate at least a part of the hurt that has plagued us for four decades.

We in the JACL who have stood at the center of the redress program since 1978 have been confident but have not always known with absolute certainty that our decisions were the right ones. But those decisions were always made with a conviction about the issue and a commitment to rectify the injustices of World War II. The major decisions were never easily made, but they were made with the confidence that they would bring us close to a final reckoning on the issue. And they have been with the full knowledge that whether we wish it or not, the major responsibility to bring the issue to its final resolution rests with the JACL.

Redress as a Movement Towards Enfranchisement

William Hohri

The mass, indiscriminate exclusion and detention of all men, women, and children, including elderly, infirm, and disabled persons for the single reason of their Japanese ancestry was a World War II atrocity committed by the United States of America that demands nothing less than the maximum restitution permitted under the law. It has taken over a decade to formulate and to formalize these demands. On March 16, 1983, in the U.S. District Court of the District of Columbia, a class action suit was filed to provide restitution to all 120,000 victims. It delineates twenty-one causes of action and is supported by dozens of allegations of fact. It seeks about $10,000 per cause of action, the maximum permitted by most of the causes of action, or about $210,000 per victim.[1]

The movement to redress this injury is as old as the events themselves. Its sources are found in the acts of angry resistance by a courageous few, whose exploits are only now coming to light and are only slowly being accepted by the Japanese American community. Joseph Y. Kurihara was one of these courageous few, a Nisei, born in Hawaii, who came to the mainland, volunteered for the army in World War I, went to college, became an accountant, a navigator, and an American who believed passionately in democratic ideals. When World War II broke out, he attempted to enter the merchant marine but was rebuffed for racial reasons. He witnessed the harsh forty-eight-hour evacuation of fishing families from Terminal Island. When word of the mass evacuation came, he expected to join in the protest but was sickened to find that, instead of protest, self-anointed community leaders urged cooperation. As he has said, "The goose was already cooked."[2]

Kurihara was sent to Manzanar and there discovered cooperation took on a far more sinister character: informant activity on fellow internees without the benefit of any legal safeguards. As one informant recounted in a letter recorded in Michi Weglyn's *Years of Infamy*, "I didn't meant for you to arrest them."[3] Other informants more proficient in English were not so naive.

As might be expected, this activity triggered a physical attack; and the attack, an arrest. The arrest of Harry Ueno, on the word of an informant-victim, precipitated a massive demonstration. The government's response was negotiation, tear gas, and bullets.

Ten unarmed inmates were shot and two of them died.[4]

Again on the word of an informant, sixteen male inmates were arrested, jailed, and then shipped to a special high-security camp of the War Relocation Authority. Kurihara was among the sixteen. The first special camp was at Moab, Utah. Those who were enemy aliens were sent to internment camps run by the Department of Justice. The Japanese American citizens remained in Moab and were subsequently moved to Leupp, Arizona. From Leupp, on June 1, 1943, Kurihara wrote a letter to Yoshiko Hosoi at Manzanar in which he said:

> The only successful measure left to encourage the industrious Japanese to a permanent resettlement is to compensate them fully for the loss they were made to suffer through evacuation. No definite amount of loss can be determined readily at present, therefore the government should set an approximate damage of $5,000.00 for each and every evacuee of voting age.[5]

Other forms of protest sought relief through the courts. Kiyoshi Okamoto, another Hawaiian Nisei, founded the Fair Play Committee (FPC) in the Heart Mountain, Wyoming, camp. The committee sought to bring themselves and the issue of unjust imprisonment into the courts by violating the law through passive resistance. Dozens of young men refused induction. In a March 26, 1944, press release, Okamoto wrote:

> If we are Americans and Citizens of this Nation by right of birth and Constitutional grant, then, let it be reiterated and decided once and for all, and without equivocation our position as members of this Nation in such ways that future un-constitutional measures need not be visited upon us or any other Minority group to satisfy the lusts of unbridled ambition, bigotry, discrimination or Race hatred. This may be done by placing in the Scale of Justice, the claims and rights of our past, our unhappiness in the present, and guarantees for our future and then, propose and accord us a just and equitable settlement.[6]

He was demanding clarification of his status as a citizen. He added, significantly, the requirement for restitution as a measure of his constitutional birthright.

In all the camps there were 315 draft resisters. The number is substantial when compared to the 815 young men who volunteered for the army.[7] Seven leaders of the Fair Play Committee were convicted of conspiracy to evade the draft and were sent to Leavenworth Prison. On Christmas Eve of 1947, the draft resisters received a presidential pardon. The FPC leaders won a reversal of their decision on appeal. Later, the committee was incorporated as the Fair Rights Committee in the state of California for the purpose of seeking redress, but it failed to coalesce after the 1948 Evacuation Claims Act was passed.

James Omura, English editor of the *Rocky Shimpo* published in Denver, was also arrested and tried as part of the draft-resistance conspiracy. He was arrested because of articles he had written in support of one of the principles of the Fair Play Committee: free us before you draft us. He was acquitted on the basis of the First Amendment rights of a free press. But that he was arrested at all was shocking. Omura, in fact, may be the first person involved in the redress movement. In April 1942, he tried to start a movement to redress the injustices of the camps among the internees but received no support.[8]

The first occasion on which I personally recall hearing about reparations was during the 1970 national convention of the Japanese American Citizens League (JACL) held in Chicago. The Northern California/Western Nevada District Council of the JACL had passed a resolution asking the national body to seek congressional legislation to compensate all evacuees for wrongful incarceration. Edison Uno presented the argument supporting the resolution.

Uno lit a spark. The idea took hold within the Seattle chapter of the JACL. A group known as the Seattle Evacuation Redress Committee was formed in the early seventies and did much of the research into the issue; it also conducted polls among Japanese Americans to solicit their opinions. It was this committee that sought and realized the issuance of "An American Promise," the presidential proclamation by Gerald Ford terminating Executive Order 9066 on February 19, 1976. Two years later, the group launched a series of imaginative consciousness-raising events called the Days of Remembrance, in which communities reenacted the mass exclusion and detention experience. By placing an ad on May 9, 1979, in the *Washington Post* and by holding a series of press conferences, which were televised in Seattle, Los Angeles, San Francisco, and Chicago, they also staged an effective campaign to rebut the antiredress statements of Senator S. I. Hayakawa. What is perhaps most significant, they succeeded in getting the JACL, at its 1978 national convention, to resolve to work towards initiating congressional legislation for redress. The spark had started a fire.

The JACL formed the National Committee for Redress and on March 3, 1979, made a fateful decision to support legislation for a federal fact-finding commission. The commission was to gather the facts and to determine whether any wrong had been committed.

Meanwhile, in Chicago, a small group of us in a tiny United Methodist Church called the Parish of the Holy Covenant had already decided to support the redress initiative of the JACL. We saw our role as limited to the northern Illinois area and confined mainly to the United Methodist Church. In February 1979, we had even started legislation on its way to the regional annual conference of the northern Illinois United Methodist churches, scheduled to convene in June. Our strategy was to gain the support of the annual conference and then do grassroots lobbying in the local churches to support whatever legislation the JACL devised. But the JACL's decision to support a fact-finding commission stopped us in our tracks.

We saw this move as a sign of weakness and confusion, contravening the action of the national JACL convention. We could not agree to continue our support, but we acknowledged that we had committed ourselves to work for Japanese American redress. We realized that we would have to fight separately and to build our own organization. So with forty strong, instead of twenty-four thousand, we resolved to continue and began to search for help.

We found kindred spirits in Seattle. The Seattle Redress Committee felt betrayed. They had written the JACL's resolution. They had had an insider's view of the March 3 decision, since three of their number had been there. They had tapes of the deliberations. They had documents. They had the desire. And they felt they needed a leader.

In May 1979, I traveled to Seattle. There, the National Council for Japanese American Redress (NCJAR) was born, and I was asked to be its leader. While in Seattle, I learned that Shosuke Sasaki, an Issei, had written a proposal for legislation. The Seattle Redress Committee had already received a promise from freshman Representative Mike Lowry, during his campaign, to support redress legislation. Mr. Lowry fulfilled his promise.

NCJAR began by organizing support for the redress bill in Congress. We went to Washington, D.C., and visited the two Illinois senators and several Illinois representatives. We also solicited support from various civil rights groups, such as the American Friends Service Committee (AFSC), the American Civil Liberties Union (ACLU), the National Association for the Advancement of Colored People (NAACP), the Urban League, as well as from the Protestant church leadership, such as the National Council of Churches, and from Jewish organizations. Our success was limited to the AFSC. We engaged in an extensive dialogue with the ACLU but gained nothing more than support for the concept of redress.

In July 1979, NCJAR began meeting each month in Chicago. We emerged into public consciousness through the newsletter we started that summer. We also challenged the decision of the JACL in the Japanese American press and in the *Pacific Citizen*. Congressman Mike Lowry and his staff wrote their bill, making major changes in the original proposal, especially in the controversial area of funding—the original called for a fairly tricky IRS check-off approach, which was dropped in favor of a simple appropriation—although keeping the concept of individual monetary compensation. Lowry introduced the redress bill in November 1979. The JACL had its own commission bill, which was introduced earlier that session in both the Senate and the House. The two bills were reviewed in the House subcommittee hearings in June 1980. Giving Congress a choice between a $1.5 million commission and a $3 billion redress appropriation is no choice at all. The study commission bill prevailed.

A curious and not insignificant occurrence in the House hearings was the vicious attack on the Lowry bill made by Washington lobbyist, Mike Masaoka.[9] The attack was totally unnecessary; only two of us spoke for the Lowry bill, Mike Lowry and myself. All of the Japanese American members of Congress supported the commission. There was a sense of deja vu to 1942 when the same Masaoka felt it necessary to attack Minoru Yasui's legal initiative when a movement was begun to raise a legal defense fund for him.

Some of the themes of the forties still echo forty years later. A substantial group of Japanese American community leaders still oppose redress.[10] But the cycle of life continues: Leadership matures, ages, and fades; new leaders emerge from new episodes involving new lessons. The civil rights movement of the sixties and the peace movement of the late sixties and early seventies gave us, as a nation, a more vocal and firsthand experience in the democratic process.

About two years ago, the Commission on War-time Relocation and Internment of Civilians travelled around the country and conducted hearings so that the victims of the government's atrocity could testify. Most perceived it as a commendable exercise of the democratic franchise. But did we really understand the reality supporting the perception? I can still see chairperson Joan Z. Bernstein urging us to summarize our verbal presentations because, as she explained, all our statements would go into the record. Few realized that there would be no publication of either the spoken or written testimonies. While hundreds attended hearings at which the victims spoke in Los Angeles, San Francisco, Seattle, Chicago, and New York, only a handful were present at the hearings at which the persons active in the government testified, the same persons who were personally responsible for the actions that took place. And in this way they got away with outrageous fabrications. Colonel Karl R. Bendetsen, the architect of the exclusion-detention program, claimed that the camps were built for our protection, that the guns and barbed wire were there to protect us from the violent acts of free citizens. John J. McCloy, "The Most Influential Private Citizen" in America, according to the February 1983 issue of *Harper's*, was the chief decision maker of the program as assistant secretary of war and was completely unrepentant. He opposed both redress and apology, suggesting that members of the 442nd Regimental Combat Team might have switched sides had Japan won the Battle of Midway. McCloy even implied we might consider a comparable program of racial exclusion and detention if Cuba were to invade Florida.[11]

Ultimately, the commission process cannot be considered a proper exercise of the democratic franchise, for the constituents lack control. How many of us who went through the serious effort of gathering our thoughts, committing them to writing, and presenting them under great stress would accept the possibility that they would go unpublished? Were we speaking to Congress and the American people or were we speaking to the shelves of the National Archives? To be fair, the commission did do a creditable job of research among primary and secondary documents. At least its staff did. But I wonder how many of those documents were read by many of the commissioners.

The proper exercise of the democratic franchise requires the exercise of intelligence by the people, the formulation of their will, and the presentation of that informed will through the mechanisms available for self-government. After our experience with the legislative branch of government, we began to look to the judicial branch, to the courts. Even while the commission was conducting its hearings, NCJAR had begun the long, laborious process of research. We located a law firm and began raising funds. The research, perhaps the most extensive ever, has been conducted among the primary documents stored in the National Archives and elsewhere.

We have also conducted extensive legal research to devise strategies for overcoming the serious obstacles that bar our access to the courts. Statutes of limitation and of sovereign immunity are formidable but not insurmountable, and we believe they can be breached by the extraordinary issues in this case. Many documents have only recently been declassified. The three attempts at *coram nobis* in San Francisco, Portland, and Seattle bear witness to this. We cite twenty-one causes of action that define massive violations of constitutional and civil rights; these command attention, even if they do not demand a hearing.

We fully recognize and publicly acknowledge the high-risk nature of this venture. It is therefore noteworthy that we have succeeded in raising over $80,000 to underwrite its cost from about 700 persons, mainly victims, from around the nation. We don't have the problem James Omura had in 1942: we are actively challenging our government. We are placing the issues of exclusion and detention squarely before the bar of justice and the bar of history.

NOTES

1. *William Hohri et al. v. United States*, U.S. District Court for the District of Columbia, March 16, 1983, CA-0750.

2. Michi Weglyn, *Years of Infamy: The Untold Story of America's Concentration Camps* (New York: William Morrow, 1976).

3. Ibid.

4. Ibid.

5. Letter, Joseph Y. Kurihara to Yoshiko Hosoi, June 1, 1943. In possession of the author.

6. Press Release, Fair Play Committee of Heart Mountain Concentration Camp, March 26, 1944.

7. U.S. Department of Interior, *The Evacuated People—A Quantitative Description* (Washington, D.C.: Government Printing Office, 1946).

8. Letter, James Omura to Colladay, Colladay, and Wallace, May 1, 1942. In possession of the author.

9. Hearing before the Subcommittee on Administrative Law and Governmental Relations of the Committee on the Judiciary, House of Representatives, 96th Cong., 2d sess., on H.R. 5499, June 6, 1980.

10. Ibid.

11. Unpublished transcripts of CWRIC hearings, 1980.

Coram Nobis and Redress

Dale Minami

When Fred Korematsu filed his petition for Writ of Error *Coram Nobis* on January 19, 1983, challenging his forty-year-old conviction, he had little idea of how his case would affect the redress movement for Japanese Americans imprisoned during World War II. In fact, neither Korematsu nor anyone on his legal team could have predicted the powerful decision rendered by Judge Marilyn Hall Patel on this extraordinary case ten months later. This was because no case with the unique features of Korematsu's had ever been brought before.

First, there was the nature of the petition—Writ of Error *Coram Nobis*—a device which allows a person convicted of a crime to challenge his conviction on certain grounds after his sentence has been served. This pleading was so unusual that the clerk of the court had to call his superior when the defense team filed the petition to decide how to classify this writ.[1]

Second, there was the issue of time: Korematsu's conviction had been imposed some forty years before the filing of his petition.

Third, his petition sought to set aside a conviction already affirmed by the Supreme Court. Fourth, was the startling and serious allegation based on evidence recently discovered by Professor Peter Irons that officials of the War Department and the Justice Department knowingly altered, suppressed, and destroyed relevant evidence.

Fifth, Korematsu's petition was only one of three filed within the month. Gordon Hirabayashi in Seattle and Minoru Yasui in Portland filed identical petitions seeking to set aside their respective convictions, which the Supreme Court had affirmed as well in similar decisions in 1943.

The filing of the petitions coincided with the redress efforts by Japanese Americans seeking restitution for the unjust exclusion and imprisonment. Thus, by challenging the convictions, the petitioners were actually attacking the underlying legality of the exclusion and imprisonment. Korematsu's petition enhanced the educational potential of the redress movement while strengthening both legal and factual arguments for redress.

Finally, the underlying convictions of Korematsu and Hirabayashi had become landmark Supreme Court decisions in which the Supreme Court validated Executive Order 9066, Public Law 503, and certain military orders. Collectively, the orders and Public Law 503 resulted in the mass incarceration of 120,000 Japanese Americans during World War II with few of the constitutional protections provided for those arrested for ordinary crimes.

The evidence included with the petition and presented before Judge Patel revealed a government determined to win the three cases without regard to legal ethics or the rights of the defendants. Evidence was produced, for example, that officials suppressed documents and reports refuting the government's justification of military necessity for the exclusion and imprisonment. Other documents established conclusively that the government lawyers recognized the falsity of claims by Lieutenant General John DeWitt that Japanese Americans were dangerous and disloyal, yet permitted those claims to go uncorrected to the Supreme Court. In short, the evidence Professor Irons discovered revealed a sordid pattern of ethical violations, manipulation of the judicial process, and violations of petitioners' rights to fair and impartial trials of their cases.

There was, perhaps, no better time to file these petitions, for in the preceding year, 1982, this country had been given an opportunity to hear about the exclusion and imprisonment experiences from testimony by the internees themselves. Through the Commission on Wartime Relocation and Internment of Civilians, established through an act of Congress, hearings were held in selected cities to examine the causes of the evacuation and make appropriate recommendations to Congress.

The activism of organizations in the community such as the Japanese American Citizens League and the National Coalition for Redress and Reparations also contributed to the more sympathetic environment in which we filed the petitions. Their efforts continued and expanded the educational focus to expose the unfairness of the exclusion and imprisonment and explain the enormous toll in human suffering and other losses. Thus, the disclosure of evidence attacking the underlying legal bases which upheld the exclusion and detention coincided perfectly with the redress efforts seeking to persuade the public and Congress that no legal, moral, or factual basis existed for the mass imprisonment. The direct relationship between the *coram nobis* petitions and redress became clear as the attorneys began to appreciate the strength of their cases. By challenging these convictions, the petitioners were actually attacking the underlying legality of the exclusion and imprisonment.

Congress, by establishing the CWRIC, had questioned the evacuation. Earlier, President Gerald R. Ford's Proclamation 4417 in 1976 had admitted the mistake made in incarcerating Japanese Americans. Only the judicial branch of government had failed to reconsider the relocation.

On November 10, 1983, Fred Korematsu had his second day in court. At that time, Judge Patel granted his petition over the objections of the government and vacated the forty-year-old conviction. In so doing, Judge Patel went further than anyone had ever expected. In her oral ruling, for example, she stated:

> Those records show the facts upon which the military necessity justification for the executive order, namely Executive Order 9066, the legislative act that was enacted thereafter attaching criminal penalties to a violation of an exclusion order, and the exclusion orders that were promulgated thereafter were based upon and relied upon by the government in its arguments to the court and to the Supreme Court on unsubstantiated facts, distortions and representations of at least one military commander, whose views were seriously infected by racism.

She went on to say that

> the overwhelming number of Japanese were citizens, were residents of the United States, were loyal to the United States; that the various acts that suggested either the potential for espionage or sabotage that had occurred or could occur in the future, were essentially non-existent or were controverted by evidence that was in the possession of the Navy, the Justice Department, the Federal Communications Commission and the Federal Bureau of Investigation.

Finally, in a written opinion issued on April 19, 1984, Judge Patel also found that

> the substance of the statements contained in the documents and the fact that the statements were made demonstrate that the government knowingly withheld information from the courts when they were considering the critical question of military necessity in this case.

Minoru Yasui's conviction was likewise vacated in Portland on motion of the government. The evidence Peggy Nagae and the other lawyers of the Asian American Law Coalition submitted along with the official report of the CWRIC undoubtedly were major factors in the government's decision to concede the case. Gordon Hirabayashi's case is scheduled for retrial in Seattle.

The decision by the court in *Korematsu v. the United States* and the granting of vacation of conviction to both Fred Korematsu and Minoru Yasui put to rest any argument that the exclusion and detention was legally supportable. By demonstrating to the courts and the public at large that these convictions and thus the underlying orders for exclusion and detention were affirmed by the Supreme Court only through fraud and misconduct, the legal basis for the exclusion and detention has become totally discredited. There is, then, no longer any legal defense to the proposition that Japanese Americans are not entitled to redress for the horrible injustice committed against them during World War II.

NOTES

1. The Korematsu Legal Defense Team was formed from core members of the Bay Area Attorneys for Redress, a committee which submitted a legal brief and arguments to the Commission on Wartime Relocation and Internment of Civilians that the exclusion and imprisonment was illegal and unconstitutional. Members of the Bay Area group and defense team included myself, Peter Irons, and Lorraine Bannai of Minami & Lew in San Francisco; Dennis W. Hayashi of the Asian Law Caucus; Donald K. Tamaki, a private practitioner; Robert L. Rusky, partner in Hanson, Bridgett, Marcus, Vlahos & Stromberg; Karen N. Kai, in private practice; Ed Chen of Coblentz, Cahen, McCabe & Breyer; and Eric Yamamoto and Leigh-Ann Miyasato, both in private practice.

Document

ORAL RULING OF JUDGE MARILYN HALL PATEL

UNITED STATES DISTRICT COURT
NORTHERN DISTRICT OF CALIFORNIA

FRED KOREMATSU,   NO. CR-27635

               Plaintiff,

    vs.

UNITED STATES OF

    AMERICA,   **OPINION**

            Defendant.

Fred Korematsu is a native born citizen of the United States. He is of Japanese ancestry. On September 8, 1942 he was convicted in this court of being in a place from which all persons of Japanese ancestry were excluded pursuant to Civilian Exclusion Order No. 34 issued by Commanding General J. L. DeWitt. His conviction was affirmed. *Korematsu v. United States*, 323 U.S. 214 (1944).

Mr. Korematsu now brings this petition for a writ of *coram nobis* to vacate his conviction on the grounds of governmental misconduct. His allegations of misconduct are best understood against the background of events leading up to his conviction.

On December 8, 1941 the United States declared war on Japan.

Executive Order No. 9066 was issued on February 19, 1942 authorizing the Secretary of War and certain military commanders "to prescribe military areas from which any persons may be excluded as protection against espionage and sabotage."

Congress enacted 97a of Title 18 of the United States Code,

There is thus no barrier to granting petitioner's motion for *coram nobis* relief.

CONCLUSION

The Supreme Court has cautioned that *coram nobis* should be used "only under certain circumstances compelling such action to achieve justice" and to correct "errors of the most fundamental character." *United States v. Morgan*, 346 U.S. 502, 511–12 (1954). It is available to correct errors that result in a complete miscarriage of justice and where there are exceptional circumstances. *See United States v. Hedman*, 655 F. 2d 813, 815 (7th Cir. 1981).

Coram nobis also lies for a claim of prosecutorial impropriety. This Circuit noted in *United States v. Taylor*, 648 F. 2d at 573, that the writ "strikes at the veracity *vel non* of the government's representations to the court" and is appropriate where the procedure by which guilt is ascertained is under attack. The *Taylor* court observed that due process principles, raised by *coram nobis* charging prosecutorial misconduct, are not "strictly limited to those situations in which the defendant has suffered arguable prejudice; . . . [but also designed] to maintain public confidence in the administration of justice." *Id.* at 571.

At oral argument the government acknowledged the exceptional circumstances involved and the injustice suffered by petitioner and other Japanese-Americans. *See also* Response at 2–3. Moreover, there is substantial support in the record that the government deliberately omitted relevant information and provided misleading information in papers before the court. The information was critical to the court's determination, although it cannot now be said what result would have obtained had the information been disclosed. Because the information was of the kind peculiarly within the government's knowledge, the court was dependent upon the government to provide a full and accurate account. Failure to do so presents the "compelling circumstance" contemplated by *Morgan*.

The judicial process is seriously impaired when the government's law enforcement officers violate their ethical obligations to the court.[10]

This court's decision today does not reach any errors of law suggested by petitioner. At common law, the writ of *coram nobis* was used to correct errors of fact. *United States v. Morgan*, 346 U.S. 502, 507–13 (1954). It was not used to correct legal errors and this court has no power, nor does it attempt, to correct any such errors.

Thus, the Supreme Court's decision stands as the law of this case and for whatever precedential value it may still have. Justices of that Court and legal scholars have commented that the decision is an anachronism in upholding overt racial discrimination as "compellingly justified." "Only two of this Court's modern cases have held the use of racial classifications to be constitutional." *Fullilove v. Klutznick*, 448 U.S. 448, 507 (1980) (Powell, J., concurring and referring to *Korematsu* and *Hirabayashi v. United States*, 320 U.S. 81 (1943)). *See also* L. H. Tribe, *American Constitutional Law* 16–6, 16–14 (1978). The government acknowledged its concurrence with the Commission's observation that "today the decision in *Korematsu* lies overruled in the court of history."

Korematsu remains on the pages of our legal and political history. As a legal precedent it is now recognized as having very limited application. As historical precedent it stands as a constant caution that in times of war or declared military necessity our institutions must be vigilant in protecting constitutional guarantees. It stands as a caution that in times of distress the shield of military necessity and national security must not be used to protect governmental actions from close scrutiny and accountability. It stands as a caution that in times of international hostility and antagonisms our institutions, legislative, executive and judicial, must be prepared to exercise their authority to protect all citizens from the petty fears and prejudices that are so easily aroused.

ORDER

In accordance with the foregoing, the petition for a writ of *coram nobis* is granted and the counter-motion of the respondent is denied.

IT IS SO ORDERED.

DATED: April 19, 1984

MARILYN HALL PATEL
United States District Judge

With Liberty and Justice for Some:
The Case for Compensation to Japanese Americans
Imprisoned During World War II

Shirley Castelnuovo

Much has been written and emotions run high over the numerous groups in history's long list of oppressed who have sought reparations. Japanese Americans evacuated from their homes and placed in internment camps because of their ancestry deserve special consideration. American notions of social justice and American views of the obligation of their government to treat citizens and aliens in a fair manner require that Americans as a people carefully examine the arguments for Japanese American reparations.

Initially, some of the constitutional-legal and moral issues relating to monetary compensation will be discussed. For the purposes of examining these issues, it is stipulated that a strong moral case (arguments that could be developed from the social contract model of a political community) and a strong legal case (arguments that could be developed from the illegal suspension of due process rights) have been made for monetary compensation. (Some would argue that the case has already been made in CWRIC's *Personal Justice Denied.*)[1] Japanese Americans who would be eligible for monetary compensation but believe that the damages have been so extensive that a monetary price cannot be attached to them do not have to accept monetary compensation. The major questions to be answered, therefore, involve working out a monetary compensation proposal that is viewed as just by the injured and by the larger political community and their governmental representatives, many of whom were not born when relocation and detention occurred.

My analysis of a number of actual and theoretical examples of past compensation, particularly various American Indian claims acts passed by Congress and the Compensation Law of the Federal Republic of Germany[2] (used to pay reparations to Jewish victims of the Holocaust) has provided the basis for the construction of two compensation models, one based on a group, the other on an individual model. These models will facilitate the examination of a number of the social justice issues which each raises.

The individual compensation model involves establishing a government trust fund, a claims commission, or a foundation. Individuals of Japanese ancestry who were excluded, relocated, and interned as a result of Executive Order 9066 could file claims against the fund, or, if the principals are deceased, the burden could be placed on the government to locate the survivors or their direct heirs. Payment could involve a fixed per capita compensatory payment or a fixed per capita payment plus an amount for each day of detention. The claims commission or foundation could establish categories of damage, with individual claimants filing for compensation in terms of the categories of damage relevant to their individual losses.[3]

The group compensation model also involves setting up a government trust fund or foundation. Organizations and community projects could apply for funding to benefit persons of Japanese ancestry, particularly focusing on the needs of the community: scholarships, aid to the aged, aid to young people, financing business research and publication, supporting religious and community structures, and publicity and education directed toward eliminating racism.

Assuming that the foundation fund to be used in a group compensation program was computed in terms of a justifying rationale, e.g., compensation based on a fixed amount per individual plus a fixed amount for each day of detention, an individual compensation model would have consequences profoundly different from a group compensation model.[4] If sums are paid to individuals, each individual could use his or her sum for individual purposes. The same total fixed sum, if used for group activities, would require a centralized management staff of directors and others who would determine the choice of projects and organizations to be funded.

COMPENSATION TO GROUPS

First, let us consider the broader moral and constitutional-legal issues related to compensation to groups, and then examine some specific examples.

A compensation program focusing on a particular racial group involves using racial classification to make amends. The recent and controversial *Bakke* decision recalls the constitutional problems of "reverse discrimination."[5] The notion of "moral debt" has been raised by members of the Japanese American legal community. This concept raises the issue of whether an obligation that involves singling out a group by virtue of ancestry can be remedied by using the same sort of categorizing. The issue is less significant to the Japanese Americans who were damaged by the use of a racial classification. It might seem appropriate to them to use that classification for the purposes of creating a remedy,[6] however, the current American generation, who will pay for these past damages, might be more troubled by these questions.

The other moral question that needs to be raised relates to the payment by the current generation for wrongs committed by a previous one. At a recent Senate colloquy deploring the internment of Japanese Americans during World War II, Senator Slade Gorton of Washington said:

> I am unsure whether the present generation should be forced to pay so directly for the misdeeds of their predecessors. . . . Federal lands of significant value abound in the West in the former areas of exclusion. Making this kind of transfer would have lasting value for former internees and their families, but would not force an undue hardship on today's taxpayer.[7]

This concern for the current generation suggests that all members of that previous generation are no longer alive, a notion only partially accurate. Many members of that previous generation, indeed a number of the architects of those wrongs, are still alive.

Several themes seem to accompany this issue, which obfuscate rather than clarify the process of analysis. It has been argued that some compensation has been made, if not fully in terms of property and personal losses, at least, the removal of racial barriers. This has enabled Japanese Americans to advance economically and professionally, particularly in comparison with other minority groups who have suffered damages, namely, black Americans and American Indians. This seems to be the basis for a recent *New York Times* editorial opposing monetary compensation for Japanese Americans.[8] The government cannot, it appears, compensate for all the wrongs done to groups in this country; therefore, the most disadvantaged at this time have the strongest claims. The underlying assumption of the *New York Times* position is that the most disadvantaged group, calculated in economic terms, has suffered the greatest wrongs. This conclusion minimizes the harm that may not be reflected by the current economic status. Individuals can be damaged by being deprived of self-respect, the badge of inferiority imposed by mass relocation and detention on the basis of ancestry. The psychological and psychic health effects may be more lasting and damaging than the economic losses. Moreover, the Issei have never been fully restored to their preinternment economic position.[9]

The appropriate moral response to these statements and underlying assumptions is that the current economic status of the victims cannot be the basis for determining the validity of claims. It is patently irrelevant and unjust to the victim of a robbery or illegal imprisonment to inquire about his or her economic condition now as the crucial piece of information required by a judge or jury to decide on the guilt of the robber or the amount of compensation due to the person illegally imprisoned.

It would appear that the more crucial issue regarding the moral and legal claim on a "guiltless" generation relates to clearly identifying the victims to ensure that those who have been actually damaged will be compensated. Unlike damages to black Americans and American Indians, which have been characterized as ancient wrongs, the wrongs done to Japanese Americans are relatively recent. For example, those individuals who were interned can obtain official documentation from the National Archives establishing the exact dates and location of internment. This simple identification process makes it possible to formulate an individual compensation program that would be available only to the victims of internment, even though all the victims are members of one racial group.

Returning to the constitutional barriers to group compensation, e.g., the use of a racial classification, a constitutional amendment is possible, but the process is long and uncertain. The barriers to a group compensation program are more likely moral and political, such as the economic climate and the competition of other wronged and disadvantaged groups and individuals for the tax dollar. But the important point is that Congress has the power to enact a group compensation program. Therefore, CWRIC's focus on the moral and constitutional issues instead of the political climate seems appropriate.

The resolution of American Indian claims through the Indian Claims Commission has often been cited as an example for dealing with group claims. It is useful to keep in mind the jurisdiction of the Indian Claims Commission established in 1946: "The Commission shall hear and determine the following claims against the United States on behalf of any Indian tribe, band, or other identifiable group of American Indians residing within the territorial limits of the United States or Alaska."[10] Recognized tribal organizations take precedence over less-defined groups. Indeed, the commission not only refuses to make payments to individual Indians, it refuses to recognize diverse tribal loyalties and insists on treating Indians as a single unified group.[11]

Can this approach be transferred to the Japanese American community? While the current redress issue has created a greater sense of Japanese American solidarity, the differences over group compensation versus individual compensation within the Japanese American community indicate that this solidarity is fragile. To speak of the Japanese American "nation" as one speaks of the Sioux Nation seems patently false. As a descriptive term, it flies in the face of differences developed among Japanese Americans in terms of education, economic status, religious affiliation, and geographical location. In short, group compensation, using the American Indian Claims Commission approach, involves the creation of one big Japanese American "tribe." For the purposes of dealing with claims, one would have to define a San Francisco group, a Los Angeles group, and so on; perhaps a California group or a Washington group might be considered more relevant. The analogy and the concept is inaccurate at best and at worst could defeat the social justice aims involved in seeking monetary compensation. It would also undermine one of the key claims for compensation, that individuals on the basis of ancestry were deprived of individual constitutional rights.

One scholar has also pointed out that the Indian Claims Commission Act does not cover "claims for injuries to individuals, even if presented by their tribes for the 'general harm—psychological, social, cultural, economic—done the Indians' " by the federal government.[12]

However, for the purpose of examining the group model, let us set aside the previous questions raised about the homogeneity of the Japanese American population and focus on the centralized management and selection of projects. If it is a government foundation, the foundation will choose the institutions, organizations, and projects to be funded. One can expect some version of the Indian Affairs Commission. If the mechanism is a representative group of Japanese American leaders, how will they be selected? Will it be a self-nominating process by organizations? This would raise the question of determining which organizations are more or less representative. If one argues for a plebiscite to determine which organizations are to be the vehicle for funds, will the voters include: (1) only those who were involuntarily evacuated and interned; (2) all those who were relocated, evacuated, and interned, involuntarily or voluntarily; (3) all Japanese Americans, 18 years of age and over, irrespective of exclusion, relocation, and detention? Should a majority Japanese American government foundation, all members appointed by the president, be the mechan-

ism for the distribution of group funds? How does one guarantee fair representation of selected board members as opposed to political partisanship; should this approach be utilized?

Finally, let me turn to the impact of group compensation. The establishment of scholarships, research centers, housing, funds for business, preferential schemes in civil service or the private sector might result in compensating most those who were least injured by exclusion, relocation, and detention. The general understanding is that the Issei were damaged the most severely and might benefit least from such a group compensation approach. However, one significant contribution of educational projects, especially relating to the racist nature of the internment, would be its continuous impact by way of preventing a second such incident.

Such questions need not discourage use of a group model but rather indicate the complexities that need to be worked out, especially given the "Recommendations" of CWRIC. One part of its recommendations involves establishing a "board, the majority of whose members are Americans of Japanese descent, appointed by the President and confirmed by the Senate." This board will administer a fund for public educational activities and projects related to the "general welfare of the Japanese American community."[13]

COMPENSATION TO INDIVIDUALS

If compensation is to be paid to the individuals evacuated and interned, should each individual receive the same benefits or should benefits be assessed individually in terms of hardship? Payment for each day interned would only partially take account of the differences. Testimony before the CWRIC, archival records, and scholarly accounts reveal that some individuals were imprisoned in prisons within the camps without due process for attempting to assert their political and civil rights.[14] Are their due-process damages to be considered equal to those whose due-process rights were violated only by the initial exclusion, relocation, and detention? Are the varying conditions in the camps which affected the internee's experience to be assessed differently? Are the experiences of the segregants, the Japanese Peruvians (forcibly deported from Peru and interned in the United States), and the renunciants to be considered equal with respect to damages?

The twenty-one categories of damage listed in the class action suit (the court via a jury trial being asked to enter individual judgments) are clearly efforts to take account of individual damages. Should the government's opposition to such a class action be overcome, however, the lengthy court proceedings might mean that many of the actual camp survivors will not live to collect damages.[15]

CWRIC has recommended to Congress that "a one-time per capita compensatory payment of $20,000 be made to each of the approximately 60,000 surviving persons excluded from their places of residence pursuant to Executive Order 9066."[16] This recommendation has been accepted by the Japanese American Citizens League and incorporated in H.R. 4110, introduced by House Majority Leader James Wright.[17] The states of California and Washington, the Los Angeles County Board of Supervisors, and the city of San Francisco have used the lump-sum, equalized-payment approach. Legislation permitted several thousand Japanese Americans employed by these governments to collect a one-time payment of $5,000 as reparations.[18] The equalized individual payments approach is based on the notion that some form of monetary compensation is appropriate, but that no monetary compensatory scheme "can fully compensate or, indeed, make the group whole again."[19]

While full compensation may not be possible, given the nature of the damages, it can be argued that the more adequate and the more individualized the compensation plan, the more fully will individuals and, as a consequence, the group of which they are members become whole again. This assumption is the basis for using the German law as a model for individual compensation. The experience of Jews in Nazi Germany and Japanese Americans in the United States was obviously different; however, some crucial similarities should be explored. Both groups were selected because of ancestry, a selection rooted in racism. Selection and detention took place with little or no protest from their fellow countrymen. Citizenship and legal residency provided no protective rights. In short, both peoples experienced betrayal and abandonment by their government and fellow citizens. That the human damage suffered by Japanese Americans was not as catastrophic as the Jews must be attributed to differences between Germany and the U.S. and to some remnants of our constitutional system holding. Yet that democratic constitutional system was also damaged. Then and now, it is a system in which legitimacy of policy is determined not only by the democratic process, e.g., a presidential executive order and congressional legislation, but also by the content of the policy. To be valid, a policy cannot infringe on certain values and rights that are "the very essence of a scheme of ordered liberty" and dignity.[20]

Perhaps each category of damage, each sum paid, and the attendant media coverage can serve as a moral and legal reminder to the political community and its government that certain values and rights are basic to this type of political system and have to be protected against hostile citizens as well as public servants. By the same token, each category of damage paid to each victim may serve as a concrete means of making whole these damages. If part of the rationale in awarding individual monetary compensation is to make amends for injuries, the other part is that paying for these damages and giving media attention to the individuals who suffered them might be educational, as it has been in the German case, and might deter similar actions in the future.

The *Bivens* case has also been suggested as a model for individual compensation.[21] However, a *Bivens* action requires a separate assessment of the damages sustained by each claimant. The application of this approach might seem to be the most just; that is, making a separate calculation of damages and compensation for each victim. However, the mammoth nature of this approach is evident. It would require examining each internment experience, with all the possible variations, as well as weighing the impact of internment, for example, on earning power related to occupation, the impact on physical and mental health, and the impact on educational level as it relates to professional attainment. The individual legal costs in time and money would be enormous. Even more problematic would be the variation in settlements, which is likely to produce among the victims a sense of additional injustice and suffering.

A class action might appear to solve some of the problems inherent in individual *Bivens* actions. A class action, with the class divided into subcategories, i.e., length of incarceration, physical damages, economic damages, might provide the possibility of obtaining individual damages and eliminating the variations in settlements as well as lessening the costs in money, time, and energy.[22] The Hohri class action suit incorporates this approach to compensatory damages. However, the court becomes the vehicle for social justice, with all the attendant problems which were raised in conjunction with the early litigation involving the Sioux Nation, particularly the possibility of the court accepting the government's motion for dismissal.

Congress, in accordance with the CWRIC's "Recommendations," could enact enabling legislation for such a class action; this would remove Congress as the focus for compensatory remedies, but might be viewed as an abdication of responsibility. Congressional action seems particularly appropriate since Congress represents the people and can make good a wrong done to a group within the political community; it can also construct a compensation program incorporating new rights and remedies, if necessary. Indeed, the establishment and funding of CWRIC, which was charged with making recommendations to Congress, further enforces this view.

Congressional responsibility also stems from its previous legislative efforts to compensate Japanese American losses. The Evacuation Claims Act of 1948 gave persons of Japanese ancestry the right to claim from the government real and personal property losses that occurred as a consequence of the exclusion and evacuation. Elaborate proof was required and the processing of claims was costly. The subsequent amendment, which allowed the attorney general to make lump-sum payments not exceeding $2,500, was accepted by many who were frustrated with the complex procedures. As the commission stated, "incentives for settling claims below their full value were built into the Act."[23] A continuing sense of an unpaid moral and economic debt indicates the shortcomings of the claims act. CWRIC's recommendation that Congress enact a simplified administrative approach to per capita compensation to the surviving victims, with the burden on the government to locate survivors without requiring any application for payment, would provide a simplified administrative mechanism for processing claims.[24]

Written and oral testimony presented to CWRIC, the CWRIC report *Personal Justice Denied*, archival material, and other creditable materials could help establish a record on which criteria for eligibility could be established and provisions made to allow institutions, associations, and religious bodies that were significant to the life of individuals in the communities in which they lived to claim damages to property and possessions. Filing for compensation would involve a simplified application to be processed by compensation offices. If a final settlement could not be reached in these offices, claims could be submitted to the Federal Court of Claims with final appeal to the Supreme Court. Legal aid could be made available to those who wanted to file an appeal.

Some of the criteria for eligibility, paraphrasing the German law, might be the following: A victim of Executive Order 9066 is defined as one who was excluded; excluded and relocated; excluded, relocated, and interned; and who suffered loss of life; damage to physical or mental health; loss of liberty; loss of property or possessions; harm to educational and vocational pursuits (with account to be taken of payment made under previous legislation). A claim for compensation could be made by those living in the United States, citizens and permanent resident aliens. Latin American Japanese, permanent resident aliens who left the United States, and individuals who renounced their American citizenship might file a claim. The direct heir of a potential claimant, in the case of the death of the victim, might also file.

An example of one of the German categories of damage is "Loss of Life."[25] This category, in light of the exclusion, relocation, and internment experience might be adapted in the following way. A claim for loss of life could include manslaughter and death as a result of damage to health inflicted on the victim stemming from the exclusion or relocation experience or to living conditions in the internment camps. Suicide, if it related to exclusion, relocation, internment camp experiences, or economic difficulties after release could be the basis for a claim.

The German category of "Damage to Vocational and Economic Pursuits" might be adapted in the following way. A claim can be made if the claimant has suffered significant damage to vocational or economic pursuits. Such damage exists if the victims lost the use of earning power. Self-employed victims are entitled to assistance in resuming former occupations. They have a claim for interest-free loans and may recover for the period in which they were excluded from, or restricted in, exercising their occupations. Compensation in this case takes the form of a capital indemnity or annuity. If an annuity is chosen, a maximum monthly amount of the annuity could be established, e.g. $600; a minimum amount of the annuity could be established, e.g. $100.[26] Minimum and maximum amounts within certain categories of damage can allow for adjusting compensation for particular damages.

CWRIC'S "RECOMMENDATIONS"

CWRIC has recommended what would appear to be a mixed model, combining individual and group payments. It has recommended that Congress legislate a single, equal, per capita, one-time payment to approximately 60,000 surviving victims of Executive Order 9066 and establish a board to fund educational and community projects.

CWRIC's report to Congress, *Personal Justice Denied*, and the personal testimony it collected documents that the damages sustained by the victims of Executive Order 9066 were varied. Nevertheless, CWRIC has recommended "a one-time per capita compensatory payment of $20,000 to each of the approximately 60,000 surviving persons excluded from their places of residence pursuant to Executive Order 9066."[27] Heirs cannot make claims. No individual payments for loss or damage are to be made. However, the commission does recommend that "Congress direct the Executive agencies to which Japanese Americans may apply for restitution of positions, status or entitlements lost in whole or in part because of facts or events between December 1941 and 1945 to review such applications with liberality."[28]

The strength of this part of CWRIC's "Recommendations" is its simplicity in establishing per capita payments and disbursement. Claimants do not have to file claims; the burden will be placed on the government to locate the survivors and make payment without requiring application. The limitations of CWRIC's individual payment approach are the absence of a justification for the designated $20,000 per survivor and the insufficient account of differences in damage. It is also puzzling why the commission states that no individual payment for losses or damage shall be made and then recommends to executive agencies that they take account of positions and entitlements that were lost. (One rationale for the simplified claim procedure was to prevent time-consuming and expensive litigation. The CWRIC's suggested procedure leaves almost no role for lawyers.) Those survivors who lost positions that do not fall into this category may perceive this as an unjust inclusion, a view that could be shared by the larger political community. The commission, if it felt that fully individualized compensation was impossible, should not have made any exceptions, especially in the absence of an accompanying rationale. The individualized approach to compensation would seem to be a more just solution for the victims and would serve as a much more powerful "admonition for the future."[29] The "grave injustice" that was done to Japanese Americans, which the commission recommends be incorporated in a joint congressional resolution to be signed by the president, offering the apologies of the nation "for the acts of exclusion, removal and detention," deserves a fuller, more individualized compensatory program than what the commission has recommended.

The group payments proposal of CWRIC's "Recommendations" also presents problems. While the funds to be disbursed by the board of presidential appointees will not be as large as the fund for individual payments, it will still be substantial. Questions about the selection of board members are not adequately answered by the recommendation that board members be appointed by the president, approved by the Senate, and that a majority of those appointed be Japanese American. Little guidance has been provided as to what projects should be funded. Phrases such as community projects relating to the "general welfare" of the Japanese American community, "aid to the elderly," and "scholarships for education" can be interpreted in a variety of ways. The fund's public educational activi-

ties appear more focused: Comparative studies "of similar civil liberties abuses or of the effect upon particular groups of racial prejudice embodied by government action in times of national stress . . . the distribution of the Commission's findings" are specific projects.[30] A board, constituted in the manner recommended by the commission with the suggested minimal guidelines, would have substantial discretion as to which projects and which groups would be funded.

The outcome of such a group payment proposal also raises a significant social justice issue: Those who benefit, particularly from the "community" funding, are likely to be those who were least injured by the exclusion, relocation, and internment experiences.

CWRIC's recommended mixed compensation proposal might, however, be more acceptable to Congress and to the broader political community because the costs involved are likely to be smaller than an individual compensation program and might be perceived as less accusatory of the government than the German model of individual compensation categories.

Some would argue that the gravity of the injustice and the need to make compensation as full and as fair as possible require that Congress consider the German law as a model to be adapted for individualized compensation. A simplified claims procedure is essential and should be made available to allow individuals as well as institutions, associations, and religious bodies, which were significant to the life of individuals in the communities in which they lived, to claim damages to property and possessions.

Congress should also more fully explore the legal and moral culpability of those officials who formulated and implemented the policy decisions of exclusion, relocation, and internment. The commission particularly recommended that the causes and circumstances of 1942 be illuminated, understood, and remembered. In that spirit Congress should examine the role of the three branches of government vis-a-vis the military and determine why the constitutional principles of checks and balances and the Bill of Rights were nonexistent for Japanese Americans.

NOTES

1. Commission on Wartime Relocation and Internment of Civilians, *Personal Justice Denied* (Washington, D.C.: Government Printing Office, 1982). I thank the Committee on Organized Research, Northeastern Illinois University, for funding the research for the paper.

2. Nehemiah Robinson, trans., *The (West German) Federal Compensation Law (BEG) and Its Implementing Regulations* (New York: Institute of Jewish Affairs, World Jewish Congress, 1957).

3. 'Commission on Wartime Relocation and Internment of Civilians, "Recommendations," presented to Congress (June 16, 1983), 12–13.

4. "Recommendations," 8–12.

5. Ibid., 12–13.

6. Ronald Dworkin, *Taking Rights Seriously* (Cambridge: Harvard University Press, 1977), chapter 9, "Reverse Discrimination."

7. Senator Slade Gorton, as cited in *Internment of Japanese Americans During World War II* (March 22, 1983): 98th Cong., 1st sess., S. Rept. 3562–3563.

8. *New York Times*, August 4, 1981.

9. *Personal Justice Denied*, "Economic Loss," 117–33.

10. Indian Claims Commission Act of 1946, par. 70a "jurisdiction."

11. Boris I. Bitker, *The Case for Black Reparations* (New York: Random House, 1973), 73.

12. Bitker, 78.

13. "Recommendations," 11–13.

14. Michi Weglyn, *Years of Infamy: The Untold Story of America's Concentration Camps* (New York: William Morrow, 1976), chapter 7.

15. Ellen Godbey Carson, one of the three counsels for plaintiffs *William Hohri, et al. v. United States of America*. Telephone conversation with author, November 4, 1983.

16. "Recommendations," 12.

17. U.S. Congress, House Judiciary Committee, H.R. 4110, 98th Cong., 1st sess. (1983).

18. "Recommendations," 9. See also *Pacific Citizen*, February 18, 1983, 1.

19. "Recommendations," 9–10.

20. *Palko v. Connecticut*, 302 US 319 (1937). See also Walter Murphy, "An Ordering of Constitutional Values," *Southern California Law Review* 53 (January 1980): 703–60.

21. *Bivens v. Six Unknown Named Agents of the Federal Bureau of Narcotics*, 403 US 388 (1971).

22. Sheldon H. Nahmod, *Civil Rights and Civil Liberties Litigation: A Guide to 1983* (Colorado Springs: Shepard's McGraw-Hill, 1979), 105–8.

23. "Recommendations," 9.

24. Ibid., 12.

25. *The (West German) Federal Compensation Law*, Part 2, *Categories of Damage*, chapter 1, "Loss of Life," 13–16.

26. Ibid., chapter 7, "Damage to Vocational and Economic Pursuits," 26–46.

27. "Recommendations," 12.

28. Ibid., 10–11.

29. Ibid., 8.

30. Ibid.. 12.

Gordon K. Hirabayashi, author, scholar, and prominent figure in Japanese American history. His case, *Hirabayashi v. United States* (1943), tested the legality of the curfew order on Japanese Americans durign World War II.

PART VIII

Negative Reactions to Redress

Letters from John J. McCloy and Karl R. Bendetsen

LETTER FROM McCLOY TO KAIHATSU

John J. McCloy is the ranking surviving individual who participated in the decision to relocate the Japanese Americans in the winter of 1941–42. Then assistant secretary of war, McCloy has had a distinguished career as a member of the New York bar and as an appointee of Democratic and Republican presidents from Franklin Roosevelt to Jimmy Carter. In this letter,[1] as in testimony before CWRIC, on the "op-ed" page of the *New York Times*, and on television programs such as the "McNeil-Lehrer Report" and "Sunday Morning," McCloy expresses his dissatisfaction with both the substance of the commission's report and the form that the hearings took.

---

1. Letter, McCloy to Jane B. Kaihatsu, April 12, 1984, enclosed in letter, McCloy to Sandra C. Taylor, May 22, 1984.

LETTER FROM JOHN J. McCLOY TO JANE B. KAIHATSU

April 12, 1984

As you are perhaps aware, I have testified already at some length in response to the attempt to further recompense those who were temporarily relocated under the direct orders of President Roosevelt, (who was the only official of the government who could order the step), as a defense to the surprise attack by the Japanese Navy and Air Force on Pearl Harbor, an event which plunged us into the Pacific War and shortly thereafter into the war with Germany. I hope to be given further opportunity to defend the country against what I feel would be a great injustice to the American taxpayer.

The President's action in ordering the relocation of Japanese/Americans from the sensitive military areas of the West Coast was entirely just and reasonable. He did not have the benefit of hindsight to see how we might recover from this devastating attack. It was a calculated attempt on his part to offset the great menace to our security caused by the sinking of our main Pacific Fleet. The President had ample and, indeed, striking evidence of the existence of subversive Japanese and Japanese/American agencies on the West Coast, poised to frustrate any defense against Japanese acts of aggression.

It is always difficult, if not impossible, to attempt to recreate the conditions as they existed long after the event and the Pearl Harbor attack and its consequences are no exception to this rule. The demand for the removal of the Japanese elements along our military installations on the West Coast after Pearl Harbor was very great. And there was good reason for alarm. A large part of our Pacific Fleet had been sunk and the installations on Pearl Harbor had been largely destroyed. The attacking forces had disappeared to the North practically unscathed. There was a constant danger of a recurring attack on what remained of our sensitive Western defenses. These mainly consisted of military installations on our West Coast particularly our bomber plants and it was in these areas that our Japanese/American population was largely congested and distributed. With our Pacific Fleet maimed, one of the chief elements of our national security was threatened at a critical time. If the "Miracle" at the Battle of Midway had not occurred, the loss of our second line of defense would certainly have put us in real jeopardy.

As a defense against this threat, the President saw fit to order the relocation of certain elements of our Japanese/American population. They were permitted to go anywhere else in the country they saw fit to go at the expense of the government. They were not "interned." The President insisted that the move be undertaken by the Army as he felt confident in the fact that the Army was best equipped to manage the operation efficiently and the Army's inspection system could be called on to insure that the operation was carried out humanely.

It is never possible to equate fully the inconveniences, sacrifices, dislocations or sufferings which all segments of a population endure in the time of war. I believe it would be most unjust to all Americans, indeed, to all nationalities who suffered as a result of the Japanese sneak attack on Pearl Harbor, to have those who were affected by the President's order be further compensated for their removal from the sensitive military areas of the West Coast in order to protect the interests of the entire country. Generally speaking, I would say that our Japanese/American population benefited from the relocation rather than suffered, as did so many others of our population as a result of the war.

The so-called investigation which sought to obtain unconscionably large unproven lump sums for added compensation for the relocation which had been given when evidence was fresh and witnesses were alive and in a position to testify was really outrageous. No serious attempt was made to recreate the conditions that the Japanese attack created on the West Coast, nor, the reasonableness of the steps that the President ordered to meet the devastating attack. Instead, a persistent Lobby sought only to support heavy additional unproven payments to the relocatees and this was done at government expense. The Lobby was able to obtain from U.S. taxpayers funds actually to bring a case against the U.S. for what was a perfectly reasonable precaution taken by the President, who did not have the benefit of hindsight, in time of war to protect the security of the whole country. The manner and the atmosphere in which the hearings were held was, as I say, outrageous and a disgrace to our Congressional Investigating Legislative System. It is the manner in which the "investigation" was conducted which should itself be investigated. It is much better for all concerned that Congress refuse these further attempts to compensate for the relocation which President Roosevelt ordered and which provided for our security after the Pearl Harbor attack.

As for myself, I could not and did not originate the order for the relocation of the Japanese/American population following this attack. I could not move a soldier, much less a civilian. I was simply asked to do what I could to assist the Army in carrying out the Commander in Chief's order. I urged that a civilian agency be put in charge of the relocation process as promptly as possible so that the Army could concentrate on the conduct of the war itself.

Our Japanese/American population was generally loyal. This was proven by a number of facts including the splendid record of the 442nd Combat Team, a unit I urged the Army to form. But, reasonable precautions had to be taken against those who might not be. What was needed on the West Coast after the Pearl Harbor attack was to protect against the consequences of the disaster and to deter any further acts such as the Japanese government was guilty of. I cannot prove it but I firmly believe that with the knowledge we now have and which, at the time, was available to the President of the U.S. of the existence of subversive agencies along the West Coast, (I refer particularly to information revealed by MAGIC), that the relocation method against the Japanese was a good reason why serious acts of sabotage did not occur on the West Coast after the President's order was given. In short, I believe it was the effectiveness of the relocation order which added to the security of the West Coast and indirectly to the security of the country as a whole.

It is, of course, true that many of our citizens were never adequately compensated for the sacrifices they had to make as a result of the Pearl Harbor attack. Certainly not those whose bodies are still entombed in the sunken ships at Pearl Harbor or those American citizens who were killed in Italy with the 442nd Combat Team.

If there are any further hearings to be held on this subject, I hope in all fairness and in good conscious [sic]

that a free and objective opportunity be given to those who would wish to support this entirely just order which President Roosevelt issued for the relocation of certain segments of our Japanese/American population on the West Coast after the disasterous [sic] bombing of Pearl Harbor by the then Japanese Government.

Sincerely,
John J. McCloy
(signed)

/tr

Ms. Jane B. Kaihatsu

While some of those involved in the decision to relocate Japanese Americans, such as Supreme Court Justice Tom C. Clark, later publicly stated that they regretted what they had done, others continue to believe that what they did was proper and something that, were the circumstances repeated, they would do again. Among these is former U.S. Army Colonel Karl R. Bendetsen, who, as he himself put it, "conceived method, formulated details and directed evacuation of 120,000 persons of Japanese ancestry from military areas."[1] Colonel Bendetsen's testimony before the CWRIC on November 2, 1981 took up some 150 pages of transcript. A recent succinct statement of his current views follows:[2]

---

1. A. N. Marquis Company, *Who's Who in America, 1946–1947* (Chicago, 1946), 173. See also his oral history at the Truman Library, Independence, Missouri.

2. Letter, Bendetsen to Jane B. Kaihatsu, April 9, 1984 enclosed in letter, Bendetsen to Sandra C. Taylor, May 22, 1984.

LETTER FROM KARL R. BENDETSEN TO JANE B. KAIHATSU

April 9, 1984

I testified for several hours before the Commission with which you are certainly familiar. My official testimony as reproduced by the Commission was not filed in the archives as I had given it and did not accurately record what I had said. It had been deliberately changed after I had reviewed and corrected it.

Toward the close of my three-hour testimony, two hours of which was direct, and one hour in answering questions, one of the Commission members made this statement: Is it not your present opinion that the Executive Order of the President 9066 ordering relocation from the Western Sea Frontier was a mistake on the part of The President and those senior officials who recommended it? My answer was this:

If The President who signed the Order and the senior officials who recommended it, including the Secretary of

War Mr. Stimson, the Chief of Staff General Marshall, the Assistant Secretary of War Mr. McCloy and the Commanding General of the 4th Army and Western Defense Command General DeWitt, had known then what we know today, the Order would never have been issued at all. There would have been no evacuation. The unprovoked sneak attack of Japan had destroyed substantially all of the United States Pacific Fleet. The West Coast of the U.S. was literally defenseless. The Japanese forces invaded the Aleutian Islands and there was no way whatsoever that these officials could have known what we know today, that the Japanese forces would not ultimately attack.

If a major attack had come and if there had been no evacuation *most Japanese* residents along the Western Sea Frontier, whether U.S. or Japanese born, would have supported the invading forces, *even* though some would not have welcomed them. Under the circumstances of war, servicemen, families of servicemen, mothers and fathers, husbands, brothers and sisters, children, friends suffered a great deal. Those who were evacuated were not interned. It is a totally false claim. Everyone was completely free to leave the Western Sea Frontier. Many thousands did. Everyone was free to leave the assembly centers and the evacuation centers so long as they did not return to the Sea Frontier. Families were not separated.

The testimony before you has been false that evacuees' property was seized. It was not. Their household effects were stored with warehouse receipts issued to each. Their crops were harvested and sold. The proceeds of those sales were faithfully deposited to their bank accounts. Those who chose to stay in evacuation centers had many benefits. Their children were educated, they had free medical care and food. They administered their own centers. They had excellent food because the residents of the centers chose it. Those of that age were sent to college and university free, at Federal expense. No one was detained in a relocation center.

Everyone could have left at will, but many of them chose not to do so. They worked near by and had free room and board. They had protection. They did not suffer nearly as much as many citizens whose loved ones were killed, wounded and who never have been compensated.

No person of Japanese ancestry who lived east of the Western Sea Frontier was asked to move.

The hearings of this Commission on the West Coast were held without any protection of favorable, truthful Japanese witnesses who wished to speak the truth. They were violently treated by the many 'anti-American' Japanese citizens who attended these hearings.

The Supreme Court of the U.S. ruled that the evacuation was constitutional. Notwithstanding, there were payments made to those who were relocated. They fared better than millions of non-Japanese, whether citizens or not. Under these circumstances, if you objectively consider what I have said, you would not make any additional redress but would objectively take into account the facts rather than the false allegations.

This then is my statement.

Sincerely,
Col. Karl R. Bendetsen,
U.S.A. (ret.)
(signed)

LETTER FROM KARL R. BENDETSEN TO SANDRA C. TAYLOR

May 22, 1984

I note your statement that my "role in relocation itself is well documented elsewhere." This statement depends on the specific "elsewhere" documents to which your comment refers.

I testified before the Commission. My testimony as filed by the Commission in the Archives and elsewhere is falsely inaccurate. My actual testimony was never officially used as an authentic part of the record of its hearings. I enclose a copy of my actual testimony. . . .

Toward the close of the unbroken three hours of my testimony, Commissioner Goldberg asked me whether I would now say that the 1942 decision of President Roosevelt was a mistake. My answer which is not reported in the Commission's official filing of my "alleged" testimony was this:

> Justice Goldberg, if the Commanding General of the Western Defense Command and Fourth Army General DeWitt, the Chief of Staff of the Army General Marshall, the Secretary of War Mr. Stimson, the Attorney General of the United States and the President had known then what you know now, no such decision would have been made. Under the then circumstances, entailing the destruction of most of our Pacific Fleet and of our defenses, the Japanese Naval, Air and Ground Forces were certainly in a position to invade the West Coast of the United States. They remained so for at least a year and a half to two years after December 7, 1941. They did invade the Aleutian Islands. Both the Nisei and the Kibei would have been in a very different position and their attitudes might well have been very different than you are now assuming they would have been. The situation could well have been disastrous.

The word "internment" was inserted in the name of the Commission by its proponents. Newspaper stories of recent years have adopted the word even though the same newspapers never employed the word at the time of the evacuation nor in the immediate weeks and months before, and years after, Executive Order 9066. All principal newspaper morgues in the United States and certainly the Western states would reflect this. The term is falsely used.

Executive Order 9066 of President Roosevelt interned no one. Persons of Japanese ancestry were excluded from remaining in the military frontier of the

Pacific Coast. All such people were free to relocate any place they chose in the United States (other than in the frontier). Thousands did so relocate themselves. The Army helped them to do so. Any and all persons of Japanese ancestry in relocation centers were free to move anywhere in the United States they chose other than the war frontier. Many of them remained in the relocation centers wholly by choice. They could leave during the day to work for compensation in private employment. Thousands did so. They had free board and room. They had free medical care. Their children were educated, many through to college degrees. They were not interned. The wives and children of military draftees were not given such advantages.

Sincerely,
Col. Karl R. Bendetsen,
U.S.A. (ret)
(signed)

Enclosures (2)